SHELLEY
HIS THOUGHT AND WORK

SHELLEY

HIS THOUGHT
AND WORK

BY

DESMOND KING-HELE

SECOND EDITION

MACMILLAN

First edition 1960
Reprinted 1962
Second edition 1971

Published by
THE MACMILLAN PRESS LTD
London and Basingstoke
Associated companies in New York Toronto
Dublin Melbourne Johannesburg and Madras

SBN 333 12268 2 (hard cover)

Printed in Great Britain by
FLETCHER AND SON LTD
Norwich

PREFACE TO THE FIRST EDITION

IN this book I have tried to make a new appreciation of Shelley's poetry, both lyrics and longer poems, for readers who have no special knowledge of the subject. In the past seventy years there have been many biographies of Shelley, and many books on particular aspects of his work, but no balanced survey of his poems. The nearest approach to such a survey, Carlos Baker's study of *Shelley's Major Poetry*, excludes the lyrics by which he is best known to most readers.

I have consciously disturbed the balance of the book in only one respect, by laying extra emphasis on Shelley's scientific interests, which, it seems to me, previous commentators have unduly neglected, with the result that some of his richest poetry has not been fully appreciated.

Shelley's poetry cannot properly be divorced from his life. So I have taken the poems chronologically, and have included a thin linking thread of biography. Shelley's last four years, in Italy, when he did his best work, take up nearly three-quarters of the book, his first twenty-six years being covered in Chapters I-IV. These early chapters, especially the first, therefore carry the heaviest load of biography, and can be regarded as introductory.

The text is intended to be read without the numbered notes, most of which merely record the sources of quotations or give references for further reading.

I am grateful to Laurence Kitchin for valuable advice over a period of several years; to John Buxton, Fellow of New College, Oxford, for many comments on points of detail; and most of all to my wife, Marie, who has read and criticized the successive drafts of the book and has helped so much to improve it.

D. K.

FARNHAM,
October 1958

PREFACE TO THE SECOND EDITION

FOR this second edition the book has been thoroughly revised to take account of new material that has become available in the past ten years. In particular I have largely rewritten Chapter 1, so as to include discussion of the poems in the Esdaile notebook, first published in 1964; and I have altered the form and content of the book list, with the aim of providing a guide to the literature rather than a mere list of books. I have also reconsidered and sometimes amended my interpretations of Shelley's poems, particularly the *Ode to the West Wind* and *To a Skylark*. I have added two maps; given essential references to recent critical studies; and corrected the texts of all quotations from Shelley's poems and letters in the light of new editions, particularly F. L. Jones's definitive edition of Shelley's letters (1964). I am grateful to Neville Rogers and Herbert Dingle for many cogent comments which have helped me in revising the book.

D. K.

FARNHAM,
    May 1970

CONTENTS

vii

MAP OF BRITAIN
Showing places associated with Shelley

I

DISJOINTED VISIONS

Full of great aims and bent on bold emprise.

THOMSON, *Castle of Indolence*

1

IN 1792 the old Sussex family of Shelley had known re-spectability and occasional distinction for over 400 years, and another name seemed likely to be added to the roll of worthy country gentlemen when in the junior branch of the family a son and heir, Percy Bysshe Shelley, was born on the fourth of August. His birthplace, where he lived for nineteen of his thirty years, was a country house two miles north-west of Horsham, Field Place in the parish of Warnham. There his father, Timothy Shelley, had settled in 1791 after marrying Elizabeth Pilfold. Field Place still stands much as it was then, a solid homely mansion built and roofed with the rough grey Horsham stone, which after brief weathering begins to look like the lichen-coated natural outcrop. To the south and west of the house, beyond a ha-ha, lies the landscaped park, with two lakes cut in the clay and a variety of trees — cedar, cypress, pine, oak and chestnut — planted singly, or arranged in clumps and avenues. A splash of brighter colour is pro-vided by the flower gardens, for which Field Place is now most famous.[1] Hidden glades, soft turf, flowers, pleasing vistas across the park, vivid reflexions of house, trees and clouds in the sheltered lakes — all combine to make Field Place a rare delight on a summer's day.

1792 was a year of upheaval and shifting loyalties. Before the baby Shelley was a week old the French monarchy was virtually ended when the mob stormed the palace of

the Tuileries, and the September massacres which followed
were 'a most heart-breaking event'[2] for Englishmen like
Fox who had looked kindly on the Revolution. In England,
too, revolutionary fever was spreading, and Pitt was soon
to begin his repression of the radicals, which culminated in
the trial of the twelve reformers in 1794.

In Parliament this was the period when the Whigs were
hopelessly split. Between 1784 and 1830 they were in
office for only fourteen months —

> Nought's permanent among the human race,
> Except the Whigs *not* getting into place.[3]

To the Shelleys, this situation was of more than academic
interest, for the poet's father, Timothy Shelley (1753–1844),
and grandfather, Bysshe Shelley (1731–1815), were both
dabbling in politics as Whigs, under the wing of the Duke
of Norfolk, a close ally of Fox and a notorious boroughmonger. In the 1790 election the Duke decided to try his
luck in the borough of Horsham, with Timothy Shelley as
his candidate. His method was to buy property, for some
of which he had to pay ten times the usual price, and to
install as chief poll-clerk his steward, Timothy's cousin
Mr. Medwin. Timothy was duly elected, because the poll-
clerk disqualified enough of the opposing voters. But the
trickery was too obvious, and Timothy was unseated in
1792 when a charge of corrupt practices was proved.[4] After
a decent interval he reappeared in the House of Commons
as member for New Shoreham, which he represented from
1802 till 1818. While the short-lived 'Ministry of all the
Talents' was in power in 1806 his family's services to the
party were rewarded: Bysshe received a baronetcy to
which Timothy succeeded in 1815.[5]

As Timothy's son grew up he no doubt heard much
talk of politics, but the stories of his childhood give no hint
either of this or of the later quarrels with his father. As
far as we can tell, his early years were serene and happy.
He enjoyed leading his four younger sisters in imaginative
games or telling them of strange monsters like the Great

Tortoise of Warnham Pond. His sister Hellen remembered him as gentle, considerate and 'full of cheerful fun'.[6] Until he was 10 he had daily lessons from the Vicar of Warnham, for his father wanted him to be 'a good and Gentlemanly Scholar'.[7] Soon, to the credit of his tutor, he was the proud author of some poems and a play. Their printing was paid for by his grandfather, then living in a humble cottage at Horsham, after having built, near Worthing, the grandiose Castle Goring, a strange hybrid of Gothic and Palladian architecture. Old Bysshe took a fancy to his grandson, perhaps because he saw gleams of his own eccentricity emerging. Timothy was more concerned with grooming his son as Squire of Field Place: the boy liked making the round of the tenants, but hunting and shooting were less to his taste.

Then in 1802 he was sent away to school. So far, life had been sheltered and unexacting: the rough-and-tumble and the new code of behaviour baffled him, and he retired into his shell. The school, Syon House Academy, Brentford, was perhaps not the most suitable for a young sprig of the aristocracy, for many of the boys were tradesmen's sons, and a touch of class warfare may have been added to the usual brutality. But the very idea of physical tyranny, no matter whether exercised by masters or boys, was enough to harden his innate anti-social traits. He was a confirmed rebel by the time he left Syon House for Eton, in 1804, and he showed it by staging a demonstration against Eton's fagging system. The boys, quick to recognize such oddity, made him a butt for 'baiting'. The Eton cloisters would ring with his name as his schoolmates closed in on him, knocking books from under his arm and indulging in the petty cruelties characteristic of schoolboys *en masse*. Eton taught him what to expect in the wider world, showing in miniature how a group treats a member who tries to discredit its accepted values, even if for the group's ultimate benefit. At Eton, as later, his reply was to withdraw from the fray and wander alone reading.

Though small-scale conflicts like these meant more to

Shelley than wars between nations, it is well to remember that the threat of invasion hung over England during his schooldays. His father's constituency on the Sussex coast, the port of New Shoreham, was an attractive landing point, and Field Place was only seventeen miles inland. So the Shelleys had as much reason as anyone to worry about Napoleon's plans. The battle of Trafalgar put an end to fears of invasion, and Shelley, then 13, no doubt gained some reflected glory at school : for H.M.S. *Ajax*, of seventy-four guns, seventh ship in the battle-line led by the *Victory*, was under the command of his uncle, John Pilfold. Trafalgar came in Shelley's second year at Eton and it was in his fifth year there that Wellington assumed command in the Peninsula.

What Shelley learnt at Eton was not entirely what his teachers intended. He did acquire a thorough grounding in classics, being particularly facile in Latin verse, but he was attracted most by subjects on the fringe of the curriculum. At both Syon House and Eton regular lectures on science were given by Adam Walker, a self-taught encyclopaedist, who knew how to rouse the boys' imagination by concentrating on the 'marvels of science' and speculating boldly when facts failed. No one was keener than Shelley in privately extending Walker's experiments to dangerous extremes. He gave his tutor a severe shock with an electrical machine. He flew fire-balloons. He made a steam engine, which blew up. Gunpowder was his familiar, and he poisoned himself with chemicals. At home, too, his 'hands and clothes were constantly stained and corroded with acid'.[8] He passed easily from bizarre scientific experiment to the raising of ghosts at midnight and vigils in deserted graveyards. These Faustian goings-on hardly deserve to be called psychical research ; they were inspired more by the 'Gothic' mystery stories, which Shelley began reading at Syon House. All this would hardly have been approved by his headmasters, Dr. Goodall, a genial scholar who lived up to his name, and his successor Dr. Keate, the most famous of Eton headmasters, whose mass floggings have now a legendary air.

The spark that fired Shelley's imagination came not from Eton but from outside: first, as we have seen, from Adam Walker, and later from Dr. James Lind (1736–1812), who lived only a mile away, in Windsor. Lind, who should not be confused with his more famous namesake (1716–94), the conqueror of scurvy, was a scientist and a traveller: after studying medicine at Edinburgh he visited China as a naval surgeon in the 1760s, and in 1772 went on a scientific expedition to Iceland with Sir Joseph Banks. In 1777 Lind became a Fellow of the Royal Society and physician to the Royal Household at Windsor. He was also skilled in astronomy, and was friendly with Sir William Herschel, the greatest of observational astronomers, whose observatory was nearby at Slough. Until he left Scotland in 1765, Lind had been a close friend of James Watt and had eagerly followed Watt's progress with his improved steam engine. Lind kept up his interest in technology, and his cousin James Keir was one of the pioneers of the chemical industry.

Shelley was influenced more deeply by Lind than by anyone else he met, because Lind shaped his mind in its most impressionable years.[9] How did Lind gain this hold over Shelley? He was in touch with the leading men of science in the country and made Shelley himself feel almost one of that magic circle. Lind was over seventy, white-haired, tall and extremely thin — the very model of a sage, to a schoolboy nurtured on Gothic stories. And, even more important for Shelley, he was a sage who encouraged rebellious attitudes; for Lind himself was regarded as 'eccentric' — a polite way of saying that he was a radical in the Royal Household. He had his own printing press, and was suspected of issuing subversive pamphlets. On top of all this, Lind was kind and patient with Shelley: 'he was exactly what an old man ought to be, free, calm-spirited, full of benevolence, and even of youthful ardour. . . . I shall never forget our long talks. . . .'[10] In those long talks during his last year at Eton, the writings of Godwin and Erasmus Darwin were no doubt discussed, and Shelley's mind was being primed with the explosive ideas which were to propel him vigorously though erratically through the twelve remaining years of his life.

2

Shelley's fame springs from the poems he wrote in Italy during his last four years, 1818–22. Before that, from 1812 to 1818, came the years of trial and, more often than not, error, with only a few short poems which succeed completely. Before 1812 his writings are worth little artistically: but they are worth mentioning, because they reveal nakedly the enthusiasms animating Shelley's meteoric career.

Shelley's first solid literary works were two novels in the Gothic style, *Zastrozzi* and *St. Irvyne; or, The Rosicrucian*, both written before he left Eton, when he was 16 or 17. In a Gothic novel it was customary for inscrutable characters in the grip of strong passions to play out a melodrama amid background scenery designed to heighten the mystery and horror. Shelley mastered the Gothic technique only too well, and his novels are very horrid indeed. *Zastrozzi* is much the better of the two. The stock situations of the plot are neatly strung together, and there are few pauses in the action because the characters feel so intensely —

Her passions were now wound up to the highest pitch of despera-tion. In indescribable agony of mind, she dashed her head against the floor — she imprecated a thousand curses upon Julia, and swore eternal revenge.

The scenery is worthy of such passions:

On the right, the thick umbrage of the forest trees rendered un-distinguishable anyone who might lurk *there*; on the left, a frightful precipice yawned, at whose base a deafening cataract dashed with tumultuous violence. . . .

Matilda, the headstrong heroine, is desperately in love with Verezzi, who, though quite inoffensive, persists in loving someone else, Julia. So Matilda, aided by her mysterious henchman Zastrozzi, plans a gory end for Julia. The climax comes when Matilda and Julia meet face to face:

'Die! detested wretch,' exclaimed Matilda, in a paroxysm of rage, as she violently attempted to bathe the stiletto in the life-blood of her rival; but Julia starting aside, the weapon slightly wounded her neck, and the ensanguined stream stained her alabaster bosom.[11]

Financially *Zastrozzi* was Shelley's most successful work: he is said to have been paid £40 for it. Nor were the reviews entirely damning. The *Gentleman's Magazine* thought it 'a short but well-told tale of horror, and, if we do not mistake, not from an ordinary pen'.[12] If *Zastrozzi* is almost readable, *St. Irvyne* is quite unreadable. Its preposterous unfinished plot is an insult no reader would tolerate.

Shelley's novels must be judged among other products of the Gothic convention, not by any high external standards. In his day the leading Gothic novelists were M. G. Lewis, whose most spectacular success was *The Monk* (1795), and Mrs. Anne Radcliffe, now best remembered for her *Mysteries of Udolpho* (1794). Lewis was expert at cloaking sadism and sexual titillation in polite phrases, whereas Mrs. Radcliffe did not usually go beyond the more respectable horrors like highway robbery, dank dungeons, spectres and secret passages. Shelley's style is half-way between Lewis and Mrs. Radcliffe, and he borrows freely from *Zofloya, or the Moor* (1806), by 'Rosa Matilda'. It would be easy to write off Shelley's novels as trash. Yet *Zastrozzi* is no worse than many of the Gothic tales. And Shelley knew the style was absurd: that is why he left *St. Irvyne* unfinished.[13]

Gothic themes dominated much of his verse too at this time. His sister Elizabeth collaborated with him in *Original Poetry by Victor and Cazire*, printed at Worthing in 1810. The adjective *Original* was probably a boyish prank, for one poem was stolen from Lewis's *Tales of Terror*, and another, *Ghasta, or the Avenging Demon!!!*, has a verse lifted from Chatterton's *Aella* and a line from *The Monk* to help it towards this grisly climax:

> Thunder shakes th' expansive sky,
> Shakes the bosom of the heath,
> 'Mortal! Mortal! thou must die' —
> The warrior sank convulsed in death.
>
> 856. 197-200*

Shelley was fascinated by the legend of the Wandering Jew who, because he taunted Christ on the way to Calvary, was doomed to roam the earth until the second coming, with a branded cross on his forehead. *The Wandering Jew* is the title of Shelley's first long poem, written in 1810, possibly with help from his cousin Tom Medwin. The young author (or authors), impressed by Scott's success with *The Lay of the Last Minstrel* (1805) and *Marmion* (1808), chose a narrative form and made free with Scott's techniques. Though no doubt pleased by the Gothic touches in Scott's poems, Shelley disapproved of his aristocratic tone, and Scott's influence is evident only in this early poem. *The Wandering Jew* is occasionally quite professional, as in the lines

> yon abbey's tower,
> Which lifts its ivy-mantled mass so high;
> Rears its dark head to meet the storms that lour,
> And braves the trackless tempests of the sky,[14]

though echoes of Gray and Marlowe can be heard. But most of the poem is cheap Gothic frippery, with plenty of thick rheumy gore, hideous screams, strong convulsions and loud-yelling demons. Shelley never again attempted an ambitious poem in the Gothic style: *The Wandering Jew* convinced him of its futility. Having supp'd full with horrors he was ready for more wholesome food.

The cult of the Gothic which so enthralled the young Shelley was a decadent end-product of a revolution in sensibility which began early in the eighteenth century when the landscape garden began to oust the formal garden. With the landscape garden came a taste for the 'picturesque'; the tame-

---

* Numbers after verse quotations indicate page and line numbers in the demy-octavo Oxford edition of *Shelley's Poetical Works*, edited by T. Hutchinson, first published (crown octavo) in 1905.

Nature scenery of a Claude landscape. The complement of the picturesque was the sublime, scenery able to inspire terror. The Gothic style exaggerated the sublime and expressed a violent reaction against the eighteenth-century ideal of the rational civilized man, at the expense of an absurd exaggeration of feeling. Though Shelley soon escaped from the Gothic groove, it left a permanent mark. 'Ghastly' remained one of his favourite words, used forty-eight times in his poems; *The Cenci* and *The Mask of Anarchy* both have a Gothic air; and situations from *Zastrozzi* — e.g. a cave being split open by lightning — recur in *The Revolt of Islam*. The style is always ready to pop out and add a piquancy to his verse.

In these early years, however, the Gothic flavour was more than piquant: it was overpowering, and often obscured the subject matter. This is a pity, because the poems of the Esdaile Notebook, first published in 1964, show that even in 1809 Shelley was treating serious themes, ill-suited to Gothic extravaganza. The most important of these early poems is *Henry and Louisa*, a violent attack on war and militarism, which begins well:

> Where are the heroes? Sunk in death they lie.
> What toiled they for? Titles and wealth and fame.
> But the wide heaven is now their canopy,
> And 'legal murderers' their loftiest name. . . .[15]

The next 100 lines record a conversation between two lovers, Henry and Louisa; then Henry, a soldier, leaves England for service in Egypt. The second half of the poem is set in Egypt, where we find Louisa scouring a battlefield in search of Henry and coming upon him mortally wounded. She dies with him. The point of this rather absurd story is that Henry and Louisa begin as supporters of a patriotic war, sanctified by religion, but come to realize their folly. The source of the ideas in the poem is Godwin's *Political Justice*, which Shelley had probably read and discussed with Dr. Lind; and the poem's language betrays the influence of Southey and Erasmus Darwin.[16] *Henry and Louisa* offers a preview of *Queen Mab*, and Shelley's fling against religion in this 1809 poem nicely prepares us for the events of his life in 1810–11:

> Religion, hated cause of all the woe
> That makes the world this wilderness! Thou spring
> Whence terror, pride, revenge and perfidy flow! . . .[17]

3

During 1809 Shelley met his cousin Harriet Grove and began a regular correspondence. He did not see her often because she lived nearly 100 miles away, at Fern in Wiltshire, but by the early summer of 1810 they seem to have been genuinely in love with each other. A few months later Harriet's father and mother (who was Mrs. Shelley's sister) became alarmed at Shelley's atheistic opinions, and Harriet was forbidden to meet him again. Shelley was very upset: that is one of the reasons why he acted so unwisely in the next twelve months.

After leaving Eton in July, just before his eighteenth birthday, Shelley went into residence at University College, Oxford, his father's college, in the Michaelmas Term of 1810. University College is at the very heart of Oxford, on the High Street half-way between Carfax and Magdalen Bridge. Among the illustrious sons of the College whose portraits hang in the Hall are Charles Jenkinson, father of the Lord Liverpool who was Prime Minister for the whole of Shelley's adult life, and Lord Eldon, Lord Chancellor of England for twenty years (1807–27), whom Shelley came to think of as his bitterest foe. Shelley's portrait is conspicuous by its absence, but the College has its Shelley memorial, a sentimental piece of sculpture, which reposes in a square vault under a green dome. Passers-by in the High Street a few feet away often think this is the University College observatory. They are wrong, but the site does have scientific associations: in the house which used to stand there Robert Boyle the great chemist lived from 1654 to 1668, and there he discovered Boyle's Law, relating air pressure and volume. Shelley, an impetuous chemist who relished all aerial phenomena, could have chosen no better site for his memorial. Though the site is apt, the memorial itself is incongruous, and all the more so for the massive iron grille around it. A casual visitor might think the grille was to stop him carving his initials on the monument; and this estimate of his habits might seem to be confirmed by a revealing notice seen in the Hall: 'Visitors please do not walk on the tables'.

As Shelley was sitting at one of these tables during his first dinner in Hall, a fellow-undergraduate two terms his senior, Thomas Jefferson Hogg, spoke to him, and began a lifelong friendship. Hogg was clever, sarcastic, witty and prepared to argue interminably on almost any subject. The pattern of their friendship was set by their first conversation that evening in Hall, when they hotly disputed the relative merits of German and Italian literature, though each afterwards admitted he knew nothing of either. Academically, Oxford was still in its eighteenth-century torpor in 1810, with dons who cared more for port and gossip than learning, and the mental exercise provided by Hogg was most valuable for Shelley.

Hogg, ever paradoxical, described his new friend as follows:

His figure was slight and fragile, and yet his bones and joints were large and strong. He was tall, but he stooped so much that he seemed of a low stature. His clothes were expensive, and made according to the most approved mode of the day; but they were tumbled, rumpled, unbrushed. His gestures were abrupt, and sometimes violent, occasionally even awkward, yet more frequently gentle and graceful. . . . His features, his whole face, and particularly his head, were, in fact, unusually small; yet the last *appeared* of a remarkable bulk, for his hair was long and bushy.[18]

Descriptions of Shelley by others who knew him tally well on the whole with Hogg's, if we allow for his habitual exaggeration, and since no satisfactory portrait of Shelley exists it is worth adding to Hogg's some of the other descriptions:

a fair, freckled, blue-eyed, light-haired, delicate-looking person, whose countenance was serious and thoughtful [Horace Smith[19]]. . . . His complexion, fair, golden, freckled, seemed transparent with an inward light [Hazlitt[20]]. . . . His eyes were large and animated, with a dash of wildness in them [Leigh Hunt[21]].

There are conflicting reports about his voice, which seems to have been clear, soft and pleasing when he spoke quietly or read, but high-pitched and discordant when he became excited.[22]

At Oxford Shelley was a voracious reader, to be found book in hand at all hours of the day, even while walking along busy streets. When Hogg first met him Shelley was using his rooms as a chemical laboratory, and continually making experiments which promised nothing but disaster. Hogg did not care for science, and since the two often spent most of the day together the experiments dwindled. The two friends would go for long walks, arguing intensely about literature, philosophy, religion and all the other topics dear to the undergraduate.

The grave gave way to the gay, however, in Shelley's volume of poems published during November, *The Posthumous Fragments of Margaret Nicholson*. The poems are advertised as the literary remains of the 'noted Female' who had tried to assassinate King George III in 1786 with a dessert knife. In fact Margaret Nicholson was still alive in 1810: indeed she outlived Shelley and might have read his *Posthumous Poems* in 1824 if 38 years in Bethlem had left her with any appetite for reading.[23] Shelley, the 'editor' of the *Fragments*, poses as her nephew John Fitzvictor. The hoax had method in it, for the *Fragments* include inflammatory verses against kings and oppressors, with remarks like 'thy work, Monarch, is the work of Hell', which might otherwise have provoked a prosecution.

Shelley and Hogg had centred their serious reading on Plato, Locke and Hume. The two latter, though they held no lasting sway over Shelley, did give him a comfortable feeling that his religious scepticism was philosophically justifiable. Once he thought he had cleared his mind of cant he inclined towards positive system-building philosophers, including, after a gap of some years, Plato once again. When Shelley returned home for Christmas he found little profit in discussing religion with his father. Timothy could only bluster and recommend reading Paley, or 'Palley' as he insisted on pronouncing the name. Shelley was not impressed either by his father or by Paley and he decided to try out his views on others, a technique learnt from Dr. Lind. We do not know how many astonished country gentlemen received broadsides from Shelley during that Christmas vacation. The one who replied was named by Shelley as 'Wedgewood'. This was probably Josiah Wedgwood II, son of the great potter, who had until about 1806 been a near neighbour of Harriet Grove's family: Wedgwood lived at Tarrant Gunville in Dorset, six miles south of Fern; his house was sold to relatives of Harriet and was the home of her brother Thomas until 1810.

Wedgwood's reply spurred Shelley to further correspondence, and soon, in consultation with Hogg, he had put together a little pamphlet called *The Necessity of Atheism*, which was printed at Worthing before Shelley returned to Oxford towards the end of January 1811. Probably only one out of a hundred who know the strident title of the tract has read it, and most of the other ninety-nine would be surprised at its temperance. The following preamble introduces its seven tiny pages:

As a love of truth is the only motive which actuates the Author of this little tract, he earnestly entreats that those of his readers who may discover any deficiency in his reasoning, or may be in possession of proofs which his mind could never obtain, would offer them, together with their objections to the Public, as briefly, as methodically, as plainly as he has taken the liberty of doing. *Thro' deficiency of proof*

AN ATHEIST[25]

The argument, mostly borrowed from Hume, is as follows. There are three sources for belief in a Deity: the direct evidence of the senses, the decision formed after applying reason to one's experience, and the testimony of others, provided this is not contrary to reason. From these premisses, and the axiom that 'belief is not an act of volition', it is deduced that 'there is no proof of the existence of a Deity', and that 'no degree of criminality is attachable to disbelief'.

Shelley knew he ought to be circumspect in publicizing his religious views[26] and he evidently thought the pamphlet's anonymity was protection enough. Since he genuinely wished to hear counter-arguments from those best able to give them, he sent the pamphlet, often with a polite letter signed 'Jeremiah Stukeley', to all the Bishops and to various bigwigs of the University, including the heads of Colleges. This naïve action proved his undoing, for one of the recipients, Rev. Edward Copleston, Professor of Poetry, was a militant and energetic Churchman. He forced the Master of University to take action, and on 25 March Shelley was called before a meeting of the Fellows. He refused to deny he was the author, and was summarily expelled: the Professor of Poetry had succeeded in ridding Oxford of its greatest poet. Hogg then declared he was equally implicated, and he too was expelled.

Shelley's expulsion was an irretrievable disaster. Discipline was easy at Oxford and at the expense of a few timely gestures of prudence, such as attending compulsory chapel, he could have studied there in peace. Instead he spent the next three years in continual upheavals, making himself responsible for too many dependants.

Why was Shelley so determined a rebel at Oxford? His family cannot be blamed, for though sometimes at odds with his father he was free to do as he liked at home. The contrast with the tyranny of physical discipline at school thus struck him all the more forcibly. English public schools make a fetish of tradition, and nothing is more infuriating to a boy like Shelley than blind adherence to outworn ceremonial. At Eton the strong-armed majority supinely accepted convention and refused to be 'illuminated'. Oxford was even more hidebound: 'The scheme of Revelation, we think, is closed, and we expect no new light on earth to break in upon us. Oxford must guard that sacred citadel.'[27] So wrote, in 1810, the vicar of St. Mary's, the same Edward

Copleston who so ably defended the citadel against illumination by Shelley.

4

Shelley and Hogg left Oxford for London on 26 March 1811, and found lodgings in Poland Street, off Oxford Street. Shelley had first to make peace with his father, no easy task. The Shelley baronetcy was only five years old, and Sir Bysshe, with his eccentric habits, did it little credit. Timothy would not tolerate any further blots on the scutcheon, and at once ordered his son to return home, where he would be placed under supervisors chosen by his father and forbidden to communicate with Hogg. Shelley couldn't desert Hogg, who had so generously shared his expulsion, and he rejected his father's conditions, which, after some wrangling, were relaxed. In April, however, Hogg left London to begin legal training at York, and Shelley, a trifle homesick, set out for Field Place in mid-May. He broke his journey ten miles off at Cuckfield, where he stayed with his uncle, Captain Pilfold. The veteran of Trafalgar was not dismayed by the bogy of atheism. His scapegrace nephew was duly grateful: 'He is a very hearty fellow, and has behaved very nobly to me, in return for which I have illuminated him.'[28] Shelley did not enjoy himself at Field Place, however, for his father was now distinctly frosty, and in July he left to visit his cousin Thomas Grove at Cwm Elan in central Wales, a visit that was to end abruptly.

Some six months previously Shelley had met Harriet Westbrook, a school friend of his sisters, and as the Westbrooks lived in London he had often seen her after his expulsion. She returned to school for the summer term minus her religious beliefs, and for this lapse she was sent to Coventry by all her schoolmates except Shelley's sister Hellen, that 'divine little scion of infidelity' as he called her.[29] Harriet didn't like the idea of going back to school in September, and asked Shelley to help her. 'Her father has persecuted her in a most horrible way, and endeavours to compel her to go to school,' he wrote to Hogg, '*she* has thrown herself

upon *my* protection. . . . How flattering a distinction: —
I am thinking of ten million things at once.'[30] Shelley
promptly returned from the wilds of Wales to London, took
her to Scotland, and married her at Edinburgh on 28 August.
The bride was just 16 years old, the bridegroom just 19.

Three separate factors contributed to Shelley's hasty and
foolish marriage: Harriet's appeal, his own impulsiveness
and his father's coldness. If he had been welcomed to
Field Place after his expulsion from Oxford, his acquaintance with the Westbrooks would probably never have
ripened. Shelley knew his father would not approve of the
marriage: the English obsession with social distinctions was
at its most outrageous at this time, and Harriet's father had
made his living from a coffee-house near Grosvenor Square.
Timothy was so deeply shocked by his son's *mésalliance* that
he converted what might have been a temporary coolness
into a permanent breach. Timothy usually stood on his
dignity at the wrong moments and he was unwise to communicate with his son only through his attorney, the die-hard
Whitton. Shelley was willing to negotiate, but he would not
make hypocritical apologies and renunciations. His sense
of filial duty had been shaken by Godwin's maxim that men
should be valued for their talents, not because of blood-
relationship. And duty was not replaced by respect, for
Shelley had a low opinion of 'the honourable member's
headpiece'. Yet by a few blandishments and half-meant
promises he could have been reconciled with his family —
as he very much wished — and freed from the money
troubles which plagued him. On hearing that his son had
'set off for Scotland with a young female',[31] Timothy had
stopped his allowance, and it was only through the generosity
of Captain Pilfold that Shelley and Harriet were able to
subsist in Edinburgh.

Hogg lost no time in visiting his newly-wed friend at
Edinburgh, and he was favourably impressed by Harriet:

She was fond of reading aloud; and she read remarkably well.
. . . Morality was her favourite theme; she found most pleasure

in works of a high ethical tone. . . . She was always pretty, always bright, always blooming.[32]

She had one peculiar trait:

She often discoursed of her purpose of killing herself some day or other, and at great length, in a calm, resolute manner.[33]

When Hogg returned to the conveyancer's office in York where he was working, Shelley and Harriet were with him. Shelley was in need of money and he immediately went to see his father. When he came back, empty-handed, he found to his dismay that Hogg had 'attempted to *seduce my wife*'.[34] Hogg was now in deep disgrace and Harriet's sister Eliza, thirteen years her senior, was given a good excuse for installing herself as a chaperone. She soon became general manager of Shelley's household: 'Eliza keeps our common stock of money . . . [and] gives it out as we want it'.[35] Shelley found her pleasant enough at first, and he hoped to 'illuminate' her: but she proved immovable, in every sense, and in the end he came to hate her. If she was half as repellent as Hogg's biased pen suggests, the wonder is that he endured her so long.

At the beginning of November the *ménage à trois* — Shelley, Harriet and Eliza — left York for Keswick without telling Hogg. For three months they stayed at the cottage on Chestnut Hill which still stands beside the Keswick–Ambleside road, overlooking Derwentwater and Bassenthwaite Lake. Shelley was impressed by the scenery round Keswick. He had never seen a mountain till his holiday in Wales earlier in the year, and now his appetite for sublime scenery, first roused by Gothic novels, was growing.

Another reason for staying at Keswick was its links with the Lake Poets. Shelley was disappointed not to meet Wordsworth and Coleridge, but he had long talks with Southey at Greta Hall. Southey, seeing in Shelley a replica of 'himself when young', was well placed to judge him, and did so perceptively: 'He will get rid of his eccentricity, and he will retain his morals, his integrity and his genius, and unless I am greatly deceived there is every reason to believe he will become an honour to his name and his country'.[36]

Southey, who was to be made Poet Laureate within two years, had long outgrown the radical hopes of his own youth. Shelley found his advice unpalatably tame, but, like all Southey's guests, he was charmed at the cordial welcome he received, being particularly fond of Mrs. Southey's home-made tea-cakes.

Shelley had a further reason for remaining at Keswick: Greystoke Castle, only eleven miles away, was a seat of the Duke of Norfolk, the one man who might be able to mend the quarrel with his father. The eleventh Duke of Norfolk, then 65 years old, was an uncouth and powerful nobleman very much on the left wing of the Whig party. To further his political career he had renounced his Catholic faith in 1780, though malicious rumour spoke of a priest as well as a mistress concealed in the depths of his ancestral castle. The Duke looked on Shelley as a promising Whig recruit: he would be a more active M.P. than his estimable father, who spoke only once during his eighteen years in the House. In the past the Duke had been kind to Shelley and now he extended his generosity to Harriet and Eliza, inviting all three to Greystoke for a week in December. Shelley wrote a conciliatory letter to his father under the Duke's auspices, and, after suitable delay, his father restored his allowance of £200 a year. Harriet's father began to pay her a similar allowance. And so, by the end of January 1812, their worst financial straits were past.

5

In his last year at Eton Shelley had read Godwin's *Political Justice*, and had been much impressed by its exposure of social evils and its utopian recipes. At Keswick he was astonished to learn from Southey that 'the immortal Godwin' was still alive. Shelley promptly wrote to Godwin:

The dearest interests of mankind imperiously demand that a certain etiquette of fashion should no longer keep 'man at a distance from man', and impose its flimsy barriers between the free communication of intellect. . . . I had enrolled your name on the list of the honourable dead. I had felt regret that the glory

of your being had passed from this earth of ours. It is not so —
you still live, and I firmly believe are still planning the welfare
of human-kind.[37]

Godwin's book had been hailed as a wonder of the age when
it appeared in 1793. Yet by 1810 he had sunk into such
utter obscurity that Shelley assumed he was dead. Calmly
enjoying his posthumous fame proved a poor substitute for
worldly prosperity, and Godwin welcomed this promising
new disciple from a wealthy family, who could write such
a flattering yet apparently sincere letter. Godwin was soon
urging Shelley not to risk inflaming discontent by efforts at
practical reform, and in the end his advice was heeded.

But at Keswick in January 1812 Shelley, impatient of
the millennium, and with £400 a year to spend, was planning
immediate action. With all the confidence of his Age in
the sovereign power of argument, he first embarked on the
conversion of the Irish. This was to be the beginning of
his campaign to illuminate the nations of the world. Shelley,
Harriet and Eliza reached Dublin in mid-February after a
long and stormy crossing. Shelley at once had 1500 copies
printed of his latest pamphlet, *An Address, to the Irish People*.
These were promptly distributed: sixty went to public-
houses, and Shelley threw many more from a balcony to
'likely-looking' passers-by, much to Harriet's amusement.
In the *Address*, Shelley deprecates mob violence and warns
the Irish not to rely on the Whigs or the Prince Regent.
He argues in favour of Catholic emancipation on the ground
that religious intolerance is wrong, and looks forward to a
'happy state of society', with men loving and living in peace
with their fellows. The change would be slow — 'We can
expect little amendment in our own time'[38] — and the
sooner everyone prepared for it the better:

I wish you O Irishmen to be as careful and thoughtful of your
interests as are your real friends. Do not drink, do not play,
do not spend any idle time. . . . Do your work regularly and
quickly; when you have done think read and talk. . . . O
Irishmen, REFORM YOURSELVES.[38]

The few Irishmen who paused to read his address must have had a good laugh at this high-minded plea for virtue. Shelley's lay sermon is acute, ridiculous and naïvely charming in turn; but it is nowhere inflammatory. This last point is worth stressing, for Shelley's behaviour in 1811–12 often seems wild. Yet even in the first of his political pamphlets he holds out the bait of an ideally happy society, and then calmly says, 'We can expect little amendment in our own time'. Those are not the words of a demagogue rousing the rabble.

The *Address*, 'wilfully vulgarized' in style, was for the common people; a second pamphlet, *Proposals for an Association*, more abstract and with politer phrases, was for the 'upper classes'. Shelley proposed a philanthropic association, with the aims of promoting Catholic Emancipation and repealing the Union Act of 1800. He asked interested readers to communicate with him. The response was almost nil.

While in Dublin Shelley also addressed a meeting called by the Catholic Committee, but he was hissed when he spoke of religion.

Shelley's expedition stirred hardly a ripple in the angry sea of Irish discontent. Though recognizing his good motives, the Irish looked askance at a non-Catholic who supported their religious claims and an Englishman who analysed their national vices. They obviously did not intend to heed him. And Godwin kept telling him he was wasting his energy. The upshot was that he left, disillusioned yet unrepentant:

I have seen and heard enough to make me doubt the omnipotence of truth in a society so constituted as that wherein we live. . . . Good principles are scarce here. . . . I am dissatisfied with my success, but not with the attempt.[39]

After seeing Dublin's slums he was all the keener to devote himself to reform, and with this abortive expedition behind him he had a securer practical basis for political theorizing.

Shelley returned from Dublin a sadder and a wiser man early in April 1812. Two months of city life had sharpened his appetite for natural beauty, and he spent a week looking for a house in Wales. He thought he had found one, called

Nantgwillt, in the mountainous region near Cwm Elan where he had stayed the previous summer. But he was unable to clinch the lease, and in June he moved off to North Devon. Here he took a cottage at Lynmouth, chosen because it was finely placed where the gorges of the East and West Lyn rivers meet. At Lynmouth, or Lymouth as it was then called, Shelley continued his propaganda campaign, sometimes resorting to methods more showy than effective: he would tie pamphlets to balloons, or set them afloat in bottles and waxed boxes, trusting to the strong tidal currents of the North Devon coast.

The cargo afloat off Lynmouth included a prose pamphlet, the *Declaration of Rights*, and a ballad, *The Devil's Walk*. The material of the *Declaration of Rights* is borrowed from *Political Justice*, Tom Paine's *Rights of Man* and two French Declarations of Rights (1789 and 1793); the style is admirably terse —

Man has no right to kill his brother. It is no excuse that he does so in uniform: he only adds the infamy of servitude to the crime of murder. . . .[40]

The doggerel ballad *The Devil's Walk*, modelled on *The Devil's Thoughts* of Coleridge and Southey (1799), must have puzzled the Devon beachcombers and might have earned Shelley prosecution for libel on the Prince Regent:

For he is fat, — his waistcoat gay,
When strained upon a levee day,
   Scarce meets across his princely paunch;
And pantaloons are like half-moons
   Upon each brawny haunch.   879. 71-5

Another product of his Lynmouth days was the *Letter to Lord Ellenborough*, printed circumspectly at Barnstaple. In May Lord Ellenborough, the Lord Chief Justice, had sentenced Daniel Eaton to be imprisoned for eighteen months, and pilloried, for publishing 'a blasphemous and profane libel on the Holy Scriptures', the third part of Paine's *Age of Reason*. Eaton's defence was a statement explaining why he rejected Christianity. Ellenborough called it 'shocking

to every Christian present', and without more ado pronounced his harsh sentence. Shelley's open letter is a
spirited piece of polemic, remarkable for a boy of 19. He
argues that morality need not derive from supernatural
dogma: a deist need not be a scoundrel, as the Attorney-
General had implied at the trial. Moreover, errors in opinion
should be corrected by reasoning, not force:

The unprejudiced mind looks with suspicion on a doctrine that
needs the sustaining hand of power. . . . To torture and
imprison the asserter of a dogma, however ridiculous and false, is
highly barbarous and impolitic. How, then, does not the
cruelty of persecution become aggravated when it is directed
against the opposer of an opinion *yet under dispute*, and which
men of unrivalled acquirements, penetrating genius, and stain-
less virtue, have spent, and at last sacrificed, their lives in
combating.[41]

Shelley could not expect to continue issuing subversive
pamphlets unhindered, for 1812 was a troubled year and
punishments were severe, as Eaton had found. In Europe
1812 saw Wellington's victory at Salamanca and Napoleon's
retreat from Moscow. In England corn was scarce and
there was dangerous unrest in the industrial north, where
machine-breaking was rife: seventeen men were hanged at
York after Luddite riots. Home Office spies were everywhere, and the army holding down the manufacturing
districts was larger than Wellington's original expeditionary
force to Portugal. 'It was widely believed that the first few
days of May would see a general, rational outbreak verging
upon revolution',[42] and there was one act in the best tradition
of bloody revolutions, the assassination of the Prime Minister,
Spencer Perceval, by a desperado. In parallel with the outbursts of violence went an increase in the organized agitation
for Parliamentary reform. In the years since Grey's reform
motion of 1797 this agitation had been feeble, and 1812 marks
the beginning of the campaign which culminated in the 1832
Reform Bill. Shelley was adding his mite to the agitation,
and he was taken seriously. The Home Secretary himself,
Lord Sidmouth, advised that spies should watch him. This

advice came too late, for Shelley had hastily decamped from Lynmouth at the end of August after his servant had been arrested for distributing the *Declaration of Rights* in Barnstaple.

By the time he left Lynmouth Shelley had another Elizabeth in his household, namely Elizabeth Hitchener, a school-teacher from Hurstpierpoint, near Brighton. Hogg, wickedly sarcastic, called Miss Hitchener 'tall and thin, bony and masculine, of a dark complexion; and the symbol of male wisdom, a beard, was not entirely wanting'.[43] Shelley had met her in Sussex a year before, through Captain Pilfold, and, delighted to find someone with the same opinions as himself, he wrote her dozens of uninhibited letters full of his plans, hopes and enthusiasms. It is easy to laugh at Miss Hitchener now; yet her friendship was then a great solace to Shelley, who called her 'the sister of my soul'. Unfortunately she did not live up to the exalted image created by her letters, and soon acquired the nickname of 'brown demon'. She remained with the Shelleys four months, then left unregretted.

After the hasty departure from Lynmouth Shelley's party of four travelled through Wales, finally coming to rest at Tremadoc, Caernarvonshire, in September 1812. Tremadoc was a new town, the creation of William Madocks, M.P., one of Sir Francis Burdett's group of reformers. Madocks was also responsible for building a mile-long embankment across the nearby estuary, thus reclaiming 7000 acres from the sea. The embankment, completed in 1811, was breached by the sea in February 1812 and remained in urgent need of repair. Could a young and energetic philanthropist look complacently upon such a scene? No. Shelley at once began to give all the help he could. He spoke at a meeting called at Beaumaris to raise funds, and a few days later, on a visit to London, he was giving his moneyed friends in Sussex the privilege of subscribing towards this noble project. Their replies convinced him they were 'cold, selfish and calculating animals'.[44]

Disappointment in his old friends was compensated by meeting several new ones. It was to see his chosen mentor William Godwin that he had made the journey to London.

In the course of his visit he also met the learned vegetarian
J. F. Newton, and T. L. Peacock, then known only for his
poem *The Genius of the Thames*. Peacock, who was to be the
most reliable of friends, at once rekindled Shelley's interest
in Greek and Latin, which had lapsed since his Oxford days.
Another close friendship, with Leigh Hunt, can also be said
to have begun about this time, though Shelley had briefly
met Hunt before. In December 1812 Hunt and his brother
John, joint editors of *The Examiner*, were brought to trial for
libel on the Prince Regent. Lord Ellenborough sent them
both to prison for two years and fined them £1000. Shelley,
'boiling with indignation at the horrible injustice and
tyranny of the sentence',[45] wanted to organize a subscription
list. Though he had been arrested for a debt a few months
before, he sent £20 as a token contribution, only to find that
the Hunts were refusing financial aid.

At Tremadoc Shelley was living comfortably in Madocks's
own house, the elegant Tan-Yr-Allt, which still stands, white
against the black rock, looking out over the estuary towards
Penrhyndeudraeth. But, as spring approached, Shelley
found that his self-chosen post as Chief Executive Embankment Repair was involving him in much tedious and unre-
warded office-work. Few of the local people appreciated his
efforts; and he was beginning to wonder whether Madocks
was a benefactor or a megalomaniac, for the embankment
had merely turned a beautiful bay into an ugly, barren,
sandy marsh. The time was ripe for another of Shelley's
hurried exits, and this took place at the end of February 1813,
after what he thought was a murderous attack upon him one
stormy night. This incident has aroused much controversy.
Probably an intruder did attack Shelley, perhaps at the
instigation of a local landowner, Robert Leeson, who wanted
to drive him away.[46] But a second 'attack', at 4 a.m. in
the morning, could have been created by Shelley firing at a
figment of his imagination. Whatever the truth may be,
Shelley was given a fine excuse for abandoning Tremadoc and
its embankment. Abandon it he certainly did, and he never
again played the rôle of the man of action. Renouncing action

went against the grain, for Shelley was by temperament a practical reformer, as Flecker's picture of his 'old fighting days' recalls —

O shining servant of the evening star
Whom no soft footfall of Lethean song
Delighted, but a strong celestial war
To batter down the gates of earthly wrong.[47]

But now he was forced to admit, tacitly if not openly, that one young man could not hope to batter down so solid a barrier, or persuade men ruled by self-interest to co-operate in schemes for improving the lot of mankind in general. His mentor Godwin was a theorist and frowned on his practical schemes; his hopes of financial independence on his twenty-first birthday were fading; and Tremadoc was even more disillusioning than Ireland. There was no escape: in future he would confine his missionary zeal to literary work.

After fleeing from Tremadoc the Shelleys visited Ireland again, being particularly impressed by the beauty of Killarney's lakes. They returned to England in April 1813 and stayed in or near London for three months. In May or June the long poem Shelley had been working on since the spring of 1812, Queen Mab, was printed by Hookham.

NOTES TO I: DISJOINTED VISIONS

Abbreviations in the notes:
Jul = The complete works of Shelley, Julian edition, edited by R. Ingpen and W. E. Peck, 10 vols. (London and New York, 1926–9).
Letters = The Letters of Percy Bysshe Shelley, edited by F. L. Jones, 2 vols. (Oxford, 1964).
Hogg = T. J. Hogg, The Life of Percy Bysshe Shelley, 2 vols. (London, 1933).
Peacock = T. L. Peacock, Memoirs of Shelley (London, 1933).
White = N. I. White, Shelley, 2 vols. (London, 1947).
Cameron = K. N. Cameron, The Young Shelley (London, 1951).
The title of a book may be shortened if it appears in the book list on p. 374.
    1. See A. G. L. Hellyer, English Gardens open to the public (Country Life, 1956), pp. 60–1, and G Nares, Country Life, Vol. 118, pp. 724–7 and 788–91 (1955).
    2. Fox's phrase. See E. Lascelles, Life of Charles James Fox (1936), p. 241.
    3. Byron, Don Juan, xi. 82.
    4. See Albery, Parliamentary History of Horsham, pp. 123–91, for a full account of this unsavoury election.
    5. The Shelley baronetcies are confusing. For two complementary family trees see Ingpen, Shelley in England (after p. 711) and Diary of Frances Lady Shelley, vol. 2, p. 1.

6. Hogg, i. 25.
7. Ingpen, *Shelley in England*, p. 242.
8. *Shelley Memorials*, third edition, p. 10.
9. See D. King-Hele, *Keats–Shelley Memorial Bulletin*, XVIII (1967), p. 1; and Hughes, *Nascent Mind of Shelley*, pp. 26–9.
10. Hogg, 1. 35.
11. For these three quotations see *Jul* v. 53, 59, 89.
12. See N. I. Wh te, *The Unextinguished Hearth*, p. 33.
13. For more details of Shelley's novels, see Hughes, *Nascent Mind of Shelley*, pp. 29–38; Cameron, pp. 30–3; Blackstone, *Lost Travellers*, pp. 220–5; Chesser, *Shelley and Zastrozzi;* Halliburton, *Keats–Shelley Journal*, vol. 16, (1967) p. 39.
14. *Jul* iv. 368. For details of *The Wandering Jew*, see Cameron, pp. 306–13.
15. *Esdaile Poems* (ed. N. Rogers), p. 79.
16. See *Esdaile Notebook* (ed. K. N. Cameron), p. 269, and D. King-Hele, *Keats–Shelley Memorial Bulletin*, XVI (1965), p. 26.
17. *Esdaile Poems*, p. 85.
18. Hogg, i. 47.
19. Beavan, *James and Horace Smith*, p. 137.
20. *Edinburgh Review*, July 1824.
21. Hunt, *Autobiography*, p. 329.
22. See Peacock, p. 315, and Thornton Hunt, *Shelley—by one who knew him* (1863).
23. See Cameron, *Shelley and his Circle*, vol. I, p. 38.
24. See *Letters* i. 85; Medwin, *Revised Life of Shelley*, p. 13; and Cameron, p. 71.
25. *Jul* v. 205. Most of *The Necessity of Atheism* is reprinted in a Note to *Queen Mab*, Oxford edition, pp. 812–15.
26. See e.g. Letter to Hunt, 2 Mar. 1811. *Letters* i. 54.
27. E. Copleston, *A Reply to the Calumnies of the Edinburgh Review against Oxford* (1810).
28. *Letters* i. 82.
29. *Letters* i. 76.
30. *Letters* i. 131.
31. T. Shelley, letter to Hogg's father, 8 Sept. 1811, quoted in Ingpen, *Shelley in England*, p. 316.
32. Hogg, i. 264–5.
33. Hogg, i. 280.
34. *Letters* i. 168.
35. *Letters* i. 257.
36. Southey, letter to John Rickman, 6 Jan. 1812 (Cameron, pp. 112–13).
37. *Letters* i. 220.
38. *Jul* v. 229–36.
39. *Letters* i. 277; i. 264; i. 282.
40. *Jul* v. 273.
41. *Jul* v. 289–94.
42. Darvall, *Popular Disturbances and Public Order in Regency England*, p. 6.
43. Hogg, ii. 55.
44. *Letters* i. 330. For the story of Tremadoc and the embankment, see E. Beazley, *Madocks and the Wonder of Wales* (Faber, 1967).
45. *Letters* i. 353.
46. See H. M. Dowling, *Keats–Shelley Memorial Bulletin*, XII (1961), p. 28. For other theories, see Cameron, pp. 205–14; White, i. 281–5; and Grabo, *Shelley's Eccentricities*, pp. 39–42.
47. Flecker, 'Ode to Shelley'. *Collected Poems*, third edition, p. 13.

II

QUEEN MAB

That monster, custom, who all sense doth eat.

Hamlet

1

IN *Queen Mab*, a poem of some 2300 lines, we have a frank
record of Shelley's beliefs at the age of 20. He tells us
clearly what he thinks the evils of society are, and how
much better we should be without them. His opinions were
still changing. and he hesitated to expose them too openly
to the public eye. *Queen Mab* was privately printed, only
about seventy copies being circulated. Though these
qualms are worth remembering, there is no need for a
great show of apology over the poem, provided we do not
let its emphatic tone mislead us into thinking that Shelley
is expounding a rigid dogma. Unfortunately, since he
never again spoke out quite so loud and clear, the widespread
delusion persists that *Queen Mab* fairly represents his later
opinions. Shelley's ideas are regularly undervalued because
too many critics are quick to judge, and condemn, the
stripling author of *Queen Mab* and conveniently ignore the
subsequent changes in his views.

Many of the ideas in the poem derive from Godwin's
Political Justice. When Shelley read this book at Eton in 1809
its findings were a revelation to him. With reason as his
probe Godwin had examined the brazen façade of existing
institutions and, in Shelley's view, had made some devastat-
ing incisions. The riot of iconoclastic rationalism in *Queen
Mab* was the first effect of Godwin's ideas, as presented in
Political Justice and modified in letters to Shelley during
1812. Godwin's humaner doctrine of universal benevolence

27

did not make its full impression on Shelley until later, notably in *The Revolt of Islam* in 1817. After that, his devotion to Godwin waned, though *Political Justice* remained the basis for most of his opinions on politics and morals.

Political Justice was published in 1793 when active young radicals, greatly excited by the French Revolution, needed a firm theory to anchor their inflated hopes. *Political Justice*, lucid, acute and elegant in style, and free from the rancour which marred political writing in the 1790s, met their need, and they seized on it eagerly, as Hazlitt remembered:

No work in our time gave such a blow to the philosophical mind of the country as the celebrated *Enquiry Concerning Political Justice*. Tom Paine was considered for the time as a Tom Fool to him; Paley an old woman; Edmund Burke a flashy sophist.[1]

And this report is amply confirmed: by Wordsworth;[1] De Quincey;[2] Southey, who 'almost worshipped Godwin';[3] Coleridge, who in a sonnet was ready to 'bless' Godwin's 'holy guidance';[4] and even the staid Crabb Robinson, who admitted in old age that the book 'directed the whole course of my life'.[5]

Godwin believed that man is perfectible, *i.e.* capable of continual moral improvement, and that character and intelligence are moulded more by environment than heredity. He predicted that, after suitable reforms of existing institutions, benevolence could be universal and men could live together happily, rationally and peacefully, without government or class distinctions. Though it may now seem that Godwin expected too much of human nature, many of his arguments remain valid.

The keystone of Godwin's 'philosophical anarchism' is his stern ideal of Justice. The just man always acts so as to promote the greatest general good, while taking care that his immediate motives are never unworthy. The just man gives his surplus wealth to the needy, and neither expects nor deserves gratitude: for to be grateful is to be surprised at generosity, and this is a slander on the benefactor when all are benevolent. The just man rarely makes a promise, for he must be free to act with reasoned benevolence and not be crippled by prior commitments. The just man is completely sincere. Polite lies, flattery and empty ceremonies are out of place in a society of free, frank and fearless men.

Godwin sees much injustice in the world about him, and he condemns most existing institutions because they tend to perpetuate injustice either actively, or passively, by their very inertia. The worship of wealth is at the root of many injustices, and one of the reformers' hardest tasks will be to deprive wealth of its universal attraction; to persuade the pauper 'that an embroidered garment' may 'cover an aching heart'. Luxurious chattels, says Godwin, exist only for display, and will vanish as soon as those who lack them cease to covet them. Government, which was usually in the hands of the wealthy, caused many human ills, being particularly objectionable because it opposed personal freedom. Godwin also condemns religious tyranny, no doubt reacting against the ultra-Calvinistic dogma he was taught as a boy. But he admits that many religious leaders were fine moral teachers who cloaked their doctrines with the superstitions of their place and time. Godwin is very scathing about the law, 'an institution of the most pernicious tendency', which is framed to benefit the rich, and inflicts revenge instead of trying to reform the criminal. And he deplores the marriage laws and customs of his day:

The method is for a thoughtless and romantic youth of each sex, to come together, to see each other, for a few times, and under circumstances full of delusion, and then to vow eternal attachment. What is the consequence of this? In almost every instance they find themselves deceived. They are reduced to make the best of an irretrievable mistake. They are led to conceive it their wisest policy, to shut their eyes upon realities, happy, if, by any perversion of intellect, they can persuade themselves that they were right in their first crude opinion of each other. Thus the institution of marriage is made a system of fraud; and men who carefully mislead their judgments in the daily affair of their life, must be expected to have a crippled judgment in every other concern.[6]

Free love, even at the risk of lust, is preferable, he concludes.

In his 'genuine society' none of these evils would survive. After dispensing with government and restrictive laws in a series of gradual reforms, men would be free, happy, sincere and peaceful. Mechanical aids would reduce labour to two hours daily,[7] and no one would slack because all would 'be animated by the example of all'. Godwin borrows many ideas from earlier theories, as he acknowledges in footnotes. Giving one's goods to the poor is among Christ's doctrines, though most Christians can find good reasons for not following it, and Godwin is also indebted in varying degrees to Plato, Rousseau and Helvétius.

Godwin knew he had neglected 'the empire of feeling', a flaw which he thought would not affect his conclusions. Shelley spent some years trying to mend the flaw, and emerged with a philosophy hardly recognizable as Godwinism. Godwin did not realize how difficult it would be to convert man from the slave of his emotions to an apostle of reason. That is why he favoured free love, which at first seems an oddity in his Puritan theory. He believed that once the taboos were removed, the violent passions which mar relations between the sexes would decay, and he hoped the sexual drive would subside into a vague wish to propagate the species. To-day this hope seems vain, for, with Freud behind us, we are more conscious of the unconscious than Godwin was, and so much the less confident. Yet Godwin did appreciate that the unconscious could spoil his plans:

Sleep is one of the most conspicuous infirmities of the human frame. . . . Our tired attention resigns the helm, ideas swim before us in wild confusion . . . we contemplate sights of horror with little pain, and commit the most atrocious crimes with little sense of their true nature.[8]

Sleep then must be abolished, and if sleep, why not the long sleep, death itself? Certainly Godwin looks forward to steady improvements in health, and longer life-spans. The idea that men may become immortal he calls 'conjecture'. This is typical of the bold speculation which impressed his contemporaries : he seemed forearmed against every objection.

Godwin would no doubt be a little hurt to learn how low his reputation stands to-day, yet pleased to see how many of his ideas we have accepted. Indeed his book, with two other near-contemporaries which Shelley also admired, Tom Paine's *Rights of Man* (1791–2) and Mary Wollstone-craft's *Rights of Woman* (1792), contain between them most of the ideas behind the modern Welfare State. Godwin would approve the levelling of distinctions in 'rank', the decay of flattery, the redistribution of property, free school-ing, longer life, the reform of the criminal code and freer relations between the sexes. The sum of gratitude at large has, as he wished, diminished, because the Welfare State displaces private benefactors and no one can be grateful to an abstraction ; and modern State propaganda, flirting with the techniques of *Brave New World* and *1984*, vindicates his faith in the power of education, however much it may pervert his aims.

2

Queen Mab is a most ambitious poem. In a letter to his prospective publisher Shelley claimed that 'the Past, the Present and the Future' were its 'grand and comprehensive topics'. As the basis for his plot he uses the well-worn eighteenth-century artifice of the conducted tour, probably with Volney's once-famous book *The Ruins* as his immediate model. Shelley's tour covers the whole universe. The fairy Mab, who acts as guide, comes down to earth and steals a mortal victim (Ianthe, a sleeping girl), who has to watch passively while Mab unfolds Shelley's chosen world-picture. Cantos 1 and 2 of the poem are devoted to Ianthe's abduc-tion and a hasty survey of the past. In cantos 3-7 Shelley attacks present ills, notably tyrants, war, commerce, wealth and religion, and in cantos 8-9 he describes a utopian future. Ianthe is then brought back to Earth thoroughly indoctrinated.

In 1811 Shelley's favourite poems were that trio of oriental epics, Southey's *Thalaba* and *Curse of Kehama* and Landor's *Gebir*, and the versified science of Erasmus Darwin's *Botanic Garden*. When, unsure in verse technique, Shelley began *Queen Mab*, it was to Southey that he turned, and in particular to the irregular metre of *Thalaba*, which had been thought a bold innovation when it first appeared, in 1800. This 'free verse' of Southey's, despite its defects, helped to lead Shelley towards the unusual verse-forms which proved to be his forte. *Queen Mab* begins with a play upon the first line of *Thalaba*, 'How beautiful is night':

> How wonderful is Death,
> Death and his brother Sleep!
> One, pale as yonder waning moon
> With lips of lurid blue;
> The other, rosy as the morn
> When throned on ocean's wave
> It blushes o'er the world.
>
> 763. 1-7

The first canto of *Queen Mab* is a charming fairy story in verse: the note of wonder in the opening lines is sustained throughout. We are told how Mab visits the earth in a chariot drawn by 'celestial coursers' which, like dying earth-satellites,[9] strike sparks with their hoofs from the palpable air. Mab beckons the soul of the sleeping Ianthe, which promptly rises from her body and enters Mab's car. They drive off to the 'black concave' of interplanetary, and eventually interstellar, space.

In the second canto Ianthe reaches Mab's palace and sees the universe evolving under the inexorable rule of Newton's law:

> The circling systems formed
> A wilderness of harmony;
> Each with undeviating aim,
> In eloquent silence, through the depths of space
> Pursued its wondrous way.
>
> 767. 78-82

Ianthe, duly impressed, is told she will next see visions of the past, present and future of the earth. The review of the past is cursory, showing man as a transitory and irrelevant parasite, his seeming-solid monuments doomed to be ignobly razed.

Shelley really gets into his stride with the review of the present, which begins in the third canto with an attack on tyrannical kings. He shows us a king, with fawning courtiers, sitting secure behind the palace sentinels and enjoying every luxury. The starving masses outside endure the king's misrule only because of the 'unconquered powers of precedent and custom'. Once Reason has 'waked the Nations' absolute monarchy is doomed. On the evils of authority Shelley follows Godwin closely:

> Power, like a desolating pestilence,
> Pollutes whate'er it touches; and obedience,
> Bane of all genius, virtue, freedom, truth,
> Makes slaves of men, and, of the human frame,
> A mechanized automaton.

773. 176-80

The submissive labourer has to do what the king orders: he even 'fabricates the sword which stabs his peace', a curious phrase borrowed from Thomson,[10] whose influence on *Queen Mab* almost equals that of Southey and Darwin.

The next evil, war, comes under the lash in canto 4. First, there is an edifying preamble, with a picture of a quiet winter night; then this is shattered abruptly with war's alarums, which at first sound most like an air raid —

> . . . the jar
> Frequent and frightful of the bursting bomb;
> The falling beam, the shriek, the groan, the shout,
> The ceaseless clangour, and the rush of men
> Inebriate with rage.

774. 41-5

War, we are told, results not from the evil of men in general, but from the intrigues of kings and others who have a vested interest in war:

> War is the statesman's game, the priest's delight,
> The lawyer's jest, the hired assassin's trade.

777. 168-9

The self-preserving mechanisms of the present system enrage Shelley :

> grave and hoary-headed hypocrites . . .
> Who, through a life of luxury and lies,
> Have crept by flattery to the seats of power,
> Support the system whence their honours flow.

777. 203, 205-7

The wretches who are in the tyrant's pay can hardly be blamed. They are deluded by 'specious names learned in soft childhood's unsuspecting hour'. Shelley picks on three names, God, Heaven and Hell, which are favourites with the tyrant and his yes-men : they spread the fiction that God is an all-seeing policeman who lets into Heaven those submissive to the régime and consigns the rebels to the torture-chambers of Hell. Dictators always make emotive use of catchwords like these to discipline the people, and Shelley did well to analyse the malpractice.

Next on the blacklist is commerce, that

> venal interchange
> Of all that human art or nature yield ;
> Which wealth should purchase not, but want demand,
> And natural kindness hasten to supply.

779. 38-41

This particular Godwinian principle was a dangerous one to apply prematurely, as Shelley found in the next five years, when he used up much of his own 'natural kindness' trying to satisfy Godwin's own insatiable demands.

One of commerce's foulest products is money, whose power enables tyrants to keep men in perpetual drudgery at subsistence-level and persuades them to ignore their consciences. Shelley devotes a whole canto to commerce and its ramifications, thus letting himself be side-tracked into mauling what is merely a limb on the tree of Injustice, not its trunk.

He next turns to religion. He reserves his fiercest fire for two targets, power-seeking priests and the concept of a revengeful anthropomorphic God. The power-seeking Churchmen pay lip-service to Christian ideals, while perverting the Church into a machine for grinding down the

poor and preserving the established order. Again religion
is used emotively as a catchword to justify un-Christian
policy, war for example. Shelley asserts indignantly in a
note that 'the blood shed by the votaries of the God of
mercy and peace, since the establishment of His religion,
would probably suffice to drown all other sectaries now on
the habitable globe'. Shelley could not forgive the Christian
Church for religious wars, for the tortures inflicted by the
over-zealous in its name, and for its continued censorship of
thought. In Shelley's day this censorship was felt most. A
word against the Church was a word against the law: [11]
that was why Timothy had been so perturbed by *The
Necessity of Atheism*. Shelley's other quarrel is with 'God',
whom he chooses to depict as a revengeful tyrant, 'the
prototype of human misrule', sitting on a throne in heaven
like an earthly king, a picture inspired by primitive Deities
like the Old Testament Jehovah. Just as the paid agents
of the king keep men's bodies in bondage, so the priests of
this God enslave men's souls: the earthly and heavenly
tyrants are in league. The heavenly tyrant is the worse
offender because, having planted in men the urge to sin,
he takes a malicious pleasure in torturing them in Hell
when they succumb to temptation. To prove this point
Shelley drags in a 'wondrous phantom', who turns out to
be Ahasuerus, the Wandering Jew. He rails against the
cruelty of the God who persecutes him. Ianthe conveniently
provides another shot in Shelley's fusillade by remembering
that her mother once took her to see an atheist burnt. It
was a touching scene: the atheist faced his doom 'with
dauntless mien', while dark-robed priests looked on, gloat-
ing. Shelley had little to learn from the priests about the
propaganda-value of martyrs. The attacks on religion in
Queen Mab would have been much milder if the poem had
been written a year or two later, for in the *Essay on Christianity* (1816?) his tone is almost friendly.

In canto 8 the dark deeds of past and present give way
to rosy dreams of the future. Secure in the beliefs that
'every heart contains perfection's germ' and that the germ

would flourish under the light of a liberal education, Shelley merely describes the happy society he foresees, and does not bother to explain the processes of change. His new world is not nostalgia for the past, like *News from Nowhere* or the Golden Age described by the Greek poets and widely accepted in the eighteenth century. But he does borrow from two of the most famous accounts of Golden Ages, Thomson's in *Spring* and Milton's Eden, since his world, like theirs, is pastoral. Shelley looks forward to controlling Man's environment by every means which the advance of science may offer. Deserts are converted into pasture, the polar regions are thawed (apparently without a rise in sea level), 'bright garden-isles' begem the oceans, and 'fragrant zephyrs' replace the storms which once deformed 'the beaming brow of heaven'. Best of all, man has fulfilled himself: he is kindly, peaceable, free and healthy. He conquered disease by turning vegetarian:

> no longer now
> He slays the lamb that looks him in the face,
> And horribly devours his mangled flesh.
>
> 795. 211-13

The wild beasts too are tamed, and Man stands among the animals as an equal, instead of trying to slaughter them. The aged are active and unwrinkled, being free from disfiguring passions and crippling diseases. Love needs no fetters and 'prostitution's venomed bane' no longer 'poisons the springs of happiness and life'. Cathedrals and palaces, silent reminders of the past, stand derelict.

The show is over, and it is time for Ianthe to go home. After being urged to fight tyranny, falsehood and 'heart-withering custom', and being warned that reform will be slow, she drives in the enchanted car through 'Heaven's untrodden way' until she sees

> Such tiny twinklers as the planet orbs
> That there attendant on the solar power
> With borrowed light pursued their narrower way.
>
> 800. 223-5

One important feature of *Queen Mab* has not yet been mentioned. In the first six cantos Shelley continually invokes the 'Spirit of Nature'.

> Spirit of Nature! here!
> In this interminable wilderness
> Of worlds, at whose immensity
> Even soaring fancy staggers,
> Here is thy fitting temple.
> Yet not the lightest leaf
> That quivers to the passing breeze
> Is less instinct with thee:
> Yet not the meanest worm
> That lurks in graves and fattens on the dead
> Less shares thy eternal breath.
>
> 766. 264-74

In short, the Spirit, Shelley's substitute for God and one that needs 'no prayers or praises', pervades every link in the Great Chain of Being. The Spirit is akin to the 'Universal Soul' or 'Sovereign Spirit of the World' to be found in poems like Thomson's *Seasons*, Akenside's *Pleasures of the Imagination* or Young's *Night Thoughts*. Shelley has also made use of Wordsworth's 'something far more deeply interfused', and of the popular eighteenth-century concept of a physical 'subtle fluid' filling up the interstices of matter, though his Spirit is more active than any of these. Shelley never decides whether the Spirit has free-will or not. This confusion is apparent when he deals with the microscopic:

> I tell thee that those viewless beings,
> Whose mansion is the smallest particle
> Of the impassive atmosphere,
> Think, feel and live like man;
> That their affections and antipathies,
> Like his, produce the laws
> Ruling their moral state;
> And the minutest throb
> That through their frame diffuses
> The slightest, faintest motion,
> Is fixed and indispensable

As the majestic laws
That rule yon rolling orbs.

769. 231-43

Shelley's picture is intriguing : each of the ultimate particles
enjoys a ration of free-will while still conforming to the laws
of Nature. The modern view is curiously like his : each
particle is allowed a small range of uncertainty, its behaviour
being governed by probability laws which degenerate into
the macroscopic laws of Nature when the numbers of
particles are large. Though Shelley may have had the
idea of sentient atoms straight from Lucretius, his interest
was probably roused by the eighteenth-century vogue for
microbes, which he would have met in Thomson's *Seasons*.[12]
The very small had come into the limelight again late in
the seventeenth century, after the invention of the microscope, the infinitesimal calculus of Newton and Leibniz,
and the actual observation of animalcules by Leeuwenhoek.
The craze for microbes followed early in the eighteenth
century, and is summed up in Swift's couplet :

> Great fleas have little fleas upon their backs to bite 'em,
> The little fleas have lesser fleas, and so ad infinitum.

3

In the so-called 'Notes' on *Queen Mab*, which are nearly as
long as the poem, Shelley tries to justify in closely reasoned
essays the views he baldly asserts in the poem. Few of his
arguments are original. He picks threads from a tangled
heap of ideas and weaves them into a somewhat garish
fabric of his own. The authors he most relies on are Holbach,
the French materialist, Godwin and J. F. Newton the
vegetarian. His supporting cast of authorities, bewildering in
its variety, is headed by Lucretius, Pliny, Bacon, Milton and
Spinoza. We need not pause to examine their credentials :
some of them were very superficial acquaintances of Shelley's,
included to add lustre to the show of erudition.

Shelley begins with some detailed astronomical notes.
He marshals his facts nonchalantly, and manages to present

them without serious error, apart from two arithmetical lapses. With one figure he gives, the distance of Sirius, he is by chance ahead of the professional astronomers. Until Bessel first measured stellar parallax in 1838, only a lower limit, much less than the real distance of a star, could reliably be assigned. The distance Shelley quotes for Sirius, with totally unjustified five-figure accuracy, is 54,224,000,000,000 miles — quite near the correct value of about 51 billion miles. Shelley's chief speculation must, however, be judged wrong. He thought the obliquity of the ecliptic would gradually decrease, instead of oscillating about the mean value near 23½ degrees. Under Shelley's mistaken hypothesis the seasons would become identical. Seasonal lusts would then, he hoped, be replaced by universal mildness.

Having proved by his appetite for detail that he is no sciolist, Shelley points to the insignificance of the Earth in the Universe, a fact which has since been over-exploited for atheistic purposes. Shelley's atheism, if it can be called that, is based on Newtonian science, as expounded with a philosophical bias towards Necessity in Holbach's *Système de la Nature*, 'the Bible of all Materialism'.[13] In *Queen Mab* Shelley makes great play with Necessity, a concept which has now lost its urgency and is frequently written off as a mere quillet in terminology. Necessity, he believed, implies either no God at all, or a God indifferent to man's welfare, responsible for earthquakes and tyrants as well as sunshine and liberty. Soon after finishing *Queen Mab* Shelley seemed to realize that Necessity was a barren concept, and we hear very little more about it.

As another of the religious notes Shelley reprints *The Necessity of Atheism* with minor alterations, and in a third note he attacks Biblical history. This note reminds us that such attacks were being made long before the heated controversies in the 1860s. It was the growing prestige of science, plus Charles Darwin's book, which provoked the Victorian quarrels. In Shelley's day the geologists were at loggerheads : were the rocks laid down gradually or formed in a single cataclysm ? The uniformitarian theory had not yet displaced the catastrophic theory, which vindicated the Mosaic cosmogony and was stoutly defended by Cuvier, the 'dictator of biology'. Most laymen were of Cowper's persuasion :

> Some drill and bore
> The solid earth, and from the strata there
> Extract a register, by which we learn
> That he who made it, and reveal'd its date
> To Moses, was mistaken in its age.[14]

The religious notes to *Queen Mab* are carried a stage further in a separate pamphlet of over 10,000 words, *A Refutation of Deism*. This is in the form of a Socratic dialogue in which Theosophus, a Deist, argues with Eusebes, a Christian. The outcome of the argument is left vague, because Shelley did not want to be prosecuted for blasphemy. But he hoped to persuade the discerning reader that both Christianity and Deism were untenable. Theosophus asks why, if God is omniscient and benevolent, He tempted man and then punished him for succumbing. Why does not God reveal himself openly and so save from perpetual torment the many good and wise men who err in their belief? Theosophus deplored the 'loathsome and minute obscenities' of the Old Testament writers and the savagery of their God. Could 'a weak and wicked king of an obscure and barbarous nation', who tortured his neighbours 'because they bowed before a different and less bloody idol than his own', be the 'man after God's own heart'? These are typical of the arguments, most of which are taken from current anti-religious books, especially Part I of Paine's *Age of Reason*.

Two of the notes on *Queen Mab* are inspired by Godwin. In the first, Shelley states a dogma which, if not strictly true, was a helpful corrective to the commercial spirit of the Age : 'there is no real wealth but the labour of man'. In the second, an attack on the marriage laws, Shelley dovetails the somewhat diverse arguments of Godwin, Gibbon, Mary Wollstonecraft and James Lawrence, author of *The Empire of the Nairs* and *Love, an Allegory*. Shelley holds that the object of morality should be happiness, which in Christian morality is only subsidiary. Asceticism, he thinks, is wrong, chastity a 'monkish and evangelical superstition'. Love withers under constraint. Law cannot govern the undisciplinable wanderings of passion. Rigid marriage laws provoke domestic tyranny and prostitution. A husband and wife ought to part if they no longer love each other. If love were free, promiscuity would be the exception, not the rule. Shelley never recanted his early opinion of the marriage laws. In real life he submitted to the ceremony because the woman suffered most when it was neglected.

The longest note, of some 5000 words, had been published separately a month or so earlier as *A Vindication of Natural Diet*. At the end of the eighteenth century, when steady advances were being made in the war against disease, it was to be expected that many panaceas would be suggested. The vegetable diet, a specific of great antiquity, was resuscitated, and its merits were argued anew in various pseudo-scientific treatises. Of these Shelley was most indebted to J. F. Newton's *Return to Nature*, or *A Defence of the Vegetable Regimen* (1811). Shelley also restates Plutarch's arguments and makes use of the popular eighteenth-century theory of the primitive herbivorous man, to be found in *The Seasons*, the *Essay on Man* and Rousseau. Shelley himself had become a vegetarian at Dublin in March 1812, so he could confirm the benefits of the diet. He begins his essay by twisting two allegories, Adam and Eve eating of the tree of evil and Prometheus stealing fire, to point the obvious vegetarian morals — don't eat meat and don't cook. Comparative anatomy teaches us that man is naturally herbivorous :

It is only by softening and disguising dead flesh by culinary preparation that it is rendered susceptible of mastication or digestion ; and that the sight of its bloody juices and raw horror does not excite intolerable loathing and disgust.

Once begun, flesh-eating, like alcohol-drinking, soon becomes a habit ; thus our natural appetites are forcibly perverted in childhood. Instead, Shelley advises dining on vegetables and drinking pure water. That is the way to sharpen the

D

bodily sensations and cure physical and mental disease. To-day, knowing more about diet and hygiene, we can see the places where Shelley lets his zeal run away with him. We shouldn't laugh too loud, however. For, though rabid meat-eaters may scoff at vegetarians, Shelley's advice has not always gone unheeded. Bernard Shaw, perhaps the most famous vegetarian of our time, was converted to the vegetable diet (and to socialism) by Shelley's example.[15] 'I was a cannibal for twenty-five years. For the rest I have been a vegetarian. It was Shelley who first opened my eyes to the savagery of my diet.' [16]

4

Shelley aimed too high in *Queen Mab*, and he threw together independent theories without realizing they were irreconcilable. Two forces were warring within him: on the one hand, anti-clerical radical materialism; on the other, a vague humanism, with pantheistic trappings such as the Spirit of Nature. Sometimes Shelley contradicts himself completely. After telling us that man is a trivial parasite in a determinate universe, he continues as if it were most important that the more down-trodden parasites should, presumably in defiance of determinism, dispose of their oppressors and develop Godwinian virtues.

Bernard Shaw called *Queen Mab* 'a perfectly original poem',[17] and in one sense he was right. It is the greatest revolutionary poem of the Age, a remarkable blend of diverse strands in radical thought. In another sense it is entirely unoriginal. All the ideas in it can be traced to one or more of the sources which scholars have dug out. The chief of these we have already glanced at. The rest we may leave to languish in the obscurity most of them deserve. In the long list of authors quoted by Shelley there are, however, three interesting absentees: Wordsworth, Coleridge and Bentham. Shelley ignored Wordsworth's innovations in poetic technique, seduced instead by the sparkle of Southey, Darwin and Thomson; he knew nothing of

Coleridge's favourite German philosophers; and Bentham's moderation was alien to the uncompromising spirit of *Queen Mab*.

Shelley was indebted to Southey for more than the free-verse form. He took over Southey's poetic vocabulary and 'theatrical props', and he never discarded them. His poems are crowded with chariots or 'cars' floating through the aether, and boats unshakably buoyant adrift on river or ocean. And roughly half his longer poems have oriental settings. In *Queen Mab* he faithfully copies, too, the mannerisms of *Thalaba* and *Kehama*, their rhetorical questions, the exclamations like *And lo! . . .*, and the Southey–Coleridge trick of repetition, used so effectively in the *Ancient Mariner*.

Sometimes the verse of *Queen Mab* is stumbling or barely competent, and Shelley fails to communicate his intention. At other times the writing is pithy and conclusive, especially when someone else has already prepared the ground. For example, Erasmus Darwin in his long poem *The Temple of Nature* explained how ambition leads to war:

> While mad with foolish fame, or drunk with power,
> Ambition slays his thousands in an hour.[18]

Shelley takes over Darwin's idea and some of his words, but he improves on Darwin by emphasizing earthy realities instead of letting abstractions dominate:

> When merciless ambition, or mad zeal,
> Has led two hosts of dupes to battlefield,
> That, blind, they there may dig each other's graves,
> And call the sad work glory.
>
> 786. 178-81

The strength and weakness of Shelley's technique are fairly displayed in the following lines:

> The habitable earth is full of bliss;
> Those wastes of frozen billows that were hurled
> By everlasting snowstorms round the poles,
> Where matter dared not vegetate or live,
> But ceaseless frost round the vast solitude
> Bound its broad zone of stillness, are unloosed;

And fragrant zephyrs there from spicy isles
Ruffle the placid ocean-deep, that rolls
Its broad, bright surges to the sloping sand
Whose roar is wakened into echoings sweet
To murmur through the Heaven-breathing groves
And melodize with man's blest nature there.

                                        793. 58-69

The first six lines are rather clumsy. *The habitable earth is full of bliss* means *the whole earth is habitable and full of bliss*, and in the second sentence four lines of digression separate the subject and verb. In contrast the last six lines foreshadow his mature style, though the syntax is still a trifle strained, and the adjectives too many and too trite.

Queen Mab is a poem for the young, and it usually provokes an all-or-nothing response. To a suitably irreverent reader young enough to be impressed, the verses twinkle along, pausing only to release barbs shrewdly aimed at the weaker joints in the armour of conventional society. To a 'little Conservative' the poem is a distasteful rigmarole of error. This latter reaction may be shared by many readers old enough to have come to terms with life. For Shelley does not spare his seniors. Nearly all of them, he thinks, have either won power and a place in the world by sacrificing their youthful ideals, or have striven obscurely in vain. He uses *hoary-headed* almost as a term of abuse, to qualify *selfishness* or *hypocrites*. The hoary-headed, for their part, can hardly be expected to approve of an insolent youth who makes free with the conventions evolved by society for its own protection after centuries of trial and error. Shelley, never himself a slave of habit, could not see that the apparently useless social customs he was attacking might help to preserve a veneer of civilization in a community whose members are too lazy to think for themselves, and to foster the stability and security which must precede the reforms he hoped for. He was sure it was right to hate shams, and he easily deluded himself that every custom was a sham. Like many undergraduates — and Shelley would still have been an undergraduate had he remained at Oxford — he

preferred his own private rules of behaviour, and, being
Shelley, he had to divulge the good news before he knew
it was authentic.

Shelley soon outgrew *Queen Mab*; but it lived on to
embarrass him. He amended about half of it in 1815, diluting
the propaganda, and renaming the poem *The Daemon of the
World*.[19] Then in 1821 *Queen Mab* was published piratically
by the radical London bookseller William Clarke. When
Southey tried to stop the piracy of his *Wat Tyler* he was
thwarted by the judicial ruling that seditious works were
not entitled to legal protection. Shelley was in a similar
quandary: he was ashamed of *Queen Mab* yet unable to
suppress it. He was more ashamed than he need have been,
for he was unable to find a copy and his memory deceived
him. He said the poem was 'villainous trash'[20] with 'long
notes against Jesus Christ, and God the Father and the
King and the Bishops and marriage and the Devil knows
what'.[21] The Society for the Suppression of Vice shared
Shelley's wish to suppress *Queen Mab*: so suppressed it was,
and Clarke went to gaol. Despite its faults *Queen Mab*
remained by far the most popular of his poems for many
years. It rose to the dignity of a bowdlerized edition as
early as 1830, and by 1840 at least fourteen separate editions,
most of them piratical, had appeared.[22] The poem occupies
a small but permanent niche in the history of radical thought.
Robert Owen, whom Shelley may have met at Godwin's
house, admired it, and the Owenites' publisher twice reprinted it.[23] Bernard Shaw heard that it had been known
as 'the Chartists' bible', and gave Karl Marx as his authority
for the statement that 'Shelley had inspired a good deal of
. . . the Chartist movement'.[24]

The reviewers thought *Queen Mab* very subversive, and
the guardians of public morals denounced its author as a
monster of depravity. One reviewer half expected that 'a
cloven foot, or horn, or flames from the mouth, must have
marked the external appearance of so bitter an enemy to
mankind'.[25] Reviews of this type did Shelley lasting harm,
and even in 1865 we find a Sussex historian apologizing

when he mentions Shelley, whose very name, he says, 'is generally regarded' with 'abhorrence'.[26]

How should we sum up *Queen Mab*? Shelley's 'passion for reforming the world' was at its fiercest when he wrote the poem, and because he died so young it has won an unduly prominent place as a statement of his political and social aims. No one judges Coleridge and Southey by their project for a Godwinian Pantisocracy on the banks of the Susquehanna. Coleridge was 22 at the time of that escapade; Shelley was 20 when *Queen Mab* appeared, and he too deserves a generous discount for youth and high spirits. Partial success is all that can be expected from a poem so ambitious by an author so young, and *Queen Mab* succeeds often enough to make it one of the best poems ever written by a 20-year-old. And the notes, as Sir Herbert Read remarked, 'show a mastery of exposition and dialectic which would be hard to match among the intellectual prodigies of the world'.[27] *Queen Mab* should not be printed in small type or cheerfully omitted as a first sacrifice by editors pressed for space. Its plain words are the best base from which to sally forth towards the prickly redoubt of Shelley's later opinion.

NOTES TO II: *QUEEN MAB*

1. Hazlitt, *Spirit of the Age*, Everyman edition, p. 183.
2. De Quincey, *Collected Writings*, xi, 327.
3. Quoted in R. Glynn Grylls, *Godwin*, p. 36.
4. Coleridge, *Poetical Works*, Oxford edition, p. 86.
5. H. Crabb Robinson, *On Books and their Writers*, p. 3.
6. *Political Justice*, ii. 507 (wording of third edition). F. E. L. Priestley's edition of *Political Justice* (University of Toronto Press, 1946, 3 vols.) is used here for giving references. In this edition, the two volumes of Godwin's third edition of 1798 are reprinted photographically, and in a third volume variant readings in the first and second editions are listed. There is no other complete modern reprint of *Political Justice*, only H. S. Salt's edition of Book VIII (1890), R. A. Preston's abridgement (1926) and A. Rodway's excerpts (1952).
7. Half an hour in *Political Justice* (ii. 484), later amended to two hours in *The Enquirer*.
8. *Political Justice*, iii. 226 (wording of first edition).
9. See *Nature*, Vol. 182, p. 426 (1958), and Vol. 221, p. 130 (1969).
10. *The Seasons, Summer*, l. 756.
11. So Lord Ellenborough ruled in the trial of Eaton in 1812. See Hughes, *Nascent Mind of Shelley*, p. 148.

12. *The Seasons, Summer*, ll. 289–311.
13. F. A. Lange, *History of Materialism* (London, 1925), p. 93.
14. Cowper, *The Task*, iii. 150–4.
15. See S. Winsten, *Days with Bernard Shaw*, p. 127.
16. Bernard Shaw, *Sixteen Self-Sketches*, p. 53.
17. *Notebook of the Shelley Society*, Part I, p. 31.
18. E. Darwin, *Temple of Nature* iv. 103–4. For Darwin's influence, see *Keats–Shelley Memorial Bulletin*, XIII, p. 30 and XVI, p. 26.
19. See Oxford edition, pp. 1–14.
20. *Letters* ii. 298.
21. *Letters* ii. 300.
22. See J. P. Anderson's bibliography in W. Sharp's *Life of Shelley*; and H. Buxton Forman, *Notebook of the Shelley Society*, Part I, pp. 25–30.
23. See Hughes, *Nascent Mind of Shelley*, p. 189.
24. Bernard Shaw, *Pen Portraits and Reviews*, p. 244.
25. Dowden, *Life of Shelley*, ii. 414 (*London Literary Gazette*, 19 May 1821).
26. M. A. Lower, *The Worthies of Sussex*, p. 64.
27. H. Read, *The True Voice of Feeling*, p. 268.

III

UNREST (1813–16)

By nature's gradual processes be taught.

WORDSWORTH, *Excursion*

1

ON his twenty-first birthday in August 1813 Shelley could
have looked back on his early career without seeing much
to be ashamed of. While still in his teens he had thrashed
out for himself a philosophy of life, and had tried hard to
convince the world that his views were right, only to meet
invincible apathy or stiff opposition. So, turning to literature, he had propounded his philosophy, not without skill,
in a long poem and half a dozen pamphlets.

Ahead, the prospect was not so bright. For he now
realized, or was about to realize, that he was in a blind
alley, intellectually, financially and emotionally. He knew
that if he publicized his opinions he would suffer an obscure
and futile imprisonment; thus England's severe laws at
least saved him from turning into a busy, thwarted agitator.
Coming of age did not fulfil his expectations of gaining
access to part of the Shelleys' riches; instead he was forced
to retrench. Inaction threw a greater strain on his marriage.
It broke, and in the ensuing upheaval poetry was mislaid.
The poet was almost silent for two years until at last he
found his *métier* late in 1815.

During the early summer of 1813 Shelley and Harriet
remained in London. Their first child, Ianthe, was born
in June. Shelley was now seeing more of his friends, old
and new. Hogg was quite restored to favour; Godwin's
advice was still sought, and sometimes heeded; the Newtons'
house was like a second home for Shelley; and the teasing

48

Peacock corrected his wilder whims and fancies. Peacock no doubt often exercised his wit on the Newtons, for they were nudists as well as vegetarians, and when Hogg first visited them he was startled to see five naked children scuttle up the stairs, like the angels on Jacob's ladder. Mrs. Newton introduced Shelley to her sister Madame de Boinville (or Mrs. Boinville), a French *émigrée* whose husband had died in February during the retreat from Moscow. Mrs. Boinville, a woman of refined manners and liberal views, impressed Shelley so favourably that he referred to her years after as 'the most admirable specimen of a human being I had ever seen'.[1] She and her married daughter Cornelia were living in London when Shelley first met them. They soon moved to Bracknell, Berkshire, however, and the Shelleys followed them there in July. Apart from an autumn tour to the Lakes and Edinburgh with Peacock and Eliza, Shelley and Harriet spent most of the time between July 1813 and June 1814 at Bracknell, or at near-by Windsor.

It was at Windsor that they endured the rigours of the 1813-14 winter, which was the coldest in that series of cold winters which, by impressing Dickens as a child, gave us the myth of White Christmas. In only one of the ten years from 1807 to 1816 was the average temperature for the months December to March above the long-period average (for the 250 years 1701-1950). The last of the Thames frost-fairs began at the end of January 1814, the coldest month in England since before 1800, a degree or two chillier than January 1963. Since Shelley was abnormally sensitive to cold, these severe winters probably helped to drive him to Italy. If so, it is ironical that the first 'winter' month after he left, November 1818, was the warmest November ever recorded in England.[2]

Eliza was still with the Shelleys at Bracknell in the spring of 1814, exercising almost parental control over Harriet. Shelley could never be master in his own house while she remained, and he was now at the end of his patience. 'I certainly hate her with all my heart and soul.'[3] He was beginning to 'pick flaws' too in the once 'close-woven happiness' of his marriage. Harriet's had been a mind unformed when she married, but Shelley's hopes of moulding it to his own design had proved vain. Harriet had lost all her intellectual leanings without finding humaner interests. She began to indulge in finery and refused to nurse her child. It was all very natural : why should she be expected to transcend convention ? To regain his father's goodwill Shelley had only to renounce his heretical opinions. Would he not make this small sacrifice so that his wife could assume the social status she deserved ?

Friction at home drove Shelley more into the company of Mrs. Boinville and her circle of friends. He dramatized his sensations on returning home from the Boinvilles' one April evening, in the poem sometimes called *Remorse* :

Away ! the moor is dark beneath the moon,
    Rapid clouds have drank the last pale beam of even :
Away ! the gathering winds will call the darkness soon,
    And profoundest midnight shroud the serene lights of heaven.

Pause not ! The time is past ! Every voice cries, Away !
    Tempt not with one last tear thy friend's ungentle mood :
Thy lover's eye, so glazed and cold, dares not entreat thy stay :
    Duty and dereliction guide thee back to solitude. . . .

Thou in the grave shalt rest — yet till the phantoms flee
    Which that house and heath and garden made dear to thee
      erewhile,
Thy remembrance, and repentance, and deep musings are not
      free
From the music of two voices and the light of one sweet smile.
        521. 1-8, 21-4

The owner of the sweet smile was Cornelia Turner, Mrs. Boinville's attractive and accomplished daughter, who was teaching Shelley Italian. Mrs. Boinville scented danger — that is why her mood is *ungentle* in the poem — and she put a stop to Shelley's visits soon after. Harriet's faults stood out more sharply when he had Cornelia Turner to remind him of the sympathy which might be his —

Thou hast disturbed the only rest
That was the portion of despair!
Subdued to Duty's hard control,
I could have borne my wayward lot.

521. 3-6

In March 1814 Shelley told Hogg he had 'sunk into a premature old age of exhaustion'.[3] He already knew he had failed in what he thought was his vocation, reform, and in his private life, where the mistake was of his own making. The mature Harriet was not the Harriet he had married. The poems already quoted show that, in the darkest recesses of his mind, he must have been prepared for a complete break, though he had then no idea how overwhelming the crisis would be when it came.

In June 1814 Harriet moved from Bracknell to Bath. Shelley was to join her there as soon as he had finished arranging a loan of £3000 for Godwin. Meanwhile, that needy philosopher made Shelley welcome at his house in Skinner Street, off Holborn.

There Shelley met Godwin's large and confusing family. Godwin's first wife, Mary Wollstonecraft, had died in 1797 after giving birth to a daughter Mary, now nearly 17. Mary Wollstonecraft's illegitimate daughter Fanny Imlay (born 1794) had also been left in Godwin's care and was always known as Fanny Godwin. The two children had needed a foster-mother, but none of the ladies Godwin had asked would oblige him with her hand, until a next-door neighbour, Mrs. Clairmont, seeing him at a window, introduced herself, so the story goes, with the flattering gambit, 'Is it possible that I behold the immortal Godwin?' She married Godwin in 1801 and tried to boost his finances by publishing children's books.[4] Mrs. Clairmont brought under Godwin's wing her two children Charles (born 1795) and Jane (born 1798); and in 1803 she bore a son William.

Godwin's daughter Mary had been away in Scotland when Shelley first met the family. Now she was at home, and Shelley proceeded to fall desperately in love with her. Peacock, a cool and impartial witness, wrote:

Nothing that I ever read in tale or history could present a more striking image of a sudden, violent, irresistible, uncontrollable passion, than that under which I found him labouring when, at his request, I went up from the country to call on him in London.[5]

He was indeed hardly sane. One day he rushed into the Godwins' house wanting to 'unite' himself to Mary with the aid of a small pistol he was carrying. Later he took a dangerous overdose of laudanum, which left him ill for a week.

The month of June 1814 saw the Allied leaders, including the Czar Alexander, the King of Prussia, Metternich and Blücher, parading through London in triumphal procession to celebrate the victory over Napoleon. Soon English tourists were flocking to Paris, so long forbidden ground. Among them were Shelley and Mary, who eloped at dawn on 28 July. Jane Clairmont, ever craving for excitement, went with them, apparently deciding to do so on the spur of the moment, because she could speak French: evidently Eliza Westbrook had not cured Shelley of the *ménage à trois*. Since Jane's mother was in hot pursuit, the three truants crossed the Channel in the first boat they could engage. To this Gothic-novel situation the elements added a fitting *décor*: as night fell a storm sprang up, lightning played around, and waves broke over their small boat. Before dawn, however, the wind dropped and the boat limped into Calais. There Jane rejected the overtures of Mrs. Godwin, who had crossed on the packet. The three then pushed on to Paris. The city had fallen to the Allies four months earlier, and the land to the south-east had been ravaged during the last desperate campaign of Napoleon's remnant of an army. Napoleon himself was now at Elba, but his disbanded troops were still at large, a menace to travellers. Shelley, Mary and Jane were more worried by shortage of funds and disgustingly dirty inns than by hypothetical marauders. They walked from Paris to Troyes, where Shelley wrote a curious but characteristic letter inviting Harriet to join them. From Troyes they went on to Lucerne, where they took lodgings for six months. But after three days they left, sailing down the Rhine almost to its mouth and reaching

London penniless on 13 September, the day Castlereagh arrived in Vienna for the Congress to settle Europe's future.

Godwin, as became a respectable citizen, shut his doors on the sinful pair, and a most unhealthy situation developed during the autumn of 1814 and the following winter. Shelley spent much of his time hiding from bailiffs and wrangling with usurers, who advanced him cash on his expectations, at ruinous rates of interest. He and Mary drifted from one set of lodgings to another. The lively Jane Clairmont, who now assumed the more romantic Christian name of Clare,[6] was frequently with them, chafing at Mary's prior claim on Shelley and staging tantrums to gain notice. Mary had her trials, too, for she was often too ill to go out with Shelley and she had to watch Clare go instead. Mary retaliated by encouraging *tête-à-tête* visits from Hogg, one of the few friends still loyal to Shelley.

In January 1815 Shelley's grandfather Sir Bysshe died, leaving about £200,000. Shelley renounced benefits he could have obtained if he had agreed to prolong the entail, and instead, after bargaining with his father, secured himself an income of £1000 a year. These money matters took time, and his hectic makeshift way of life did not end until August, when he and Mary settled down alone at Bishopsgate, near Virginia Water.

2

Shelley's rooted habit of omnivorous reading continued throughout the emotional disturbances of 1814-15; his poetry, a more fragile growth, did not. When he arrived at Virginia Water in August 1815 he could look back on two years almost barren of poetry. The Bracknell poem, 'Away! the moor is dark . . .', is the best of the poor bunch, for it does strike a new note, surer and more sombre than any sounded before.

Poetry's resurrection came in September 1815, when Shelley, Mary, Peacock and Charles Clairmont rowed up the Thames from Windsor towards its source. Shelley

thoroughly enjoyed the trip, and the scene which coaxed
poetry into the open again was Lechlade churchyard at
sunset :

> The wind has swept from the wide atmosphere
> Each vapour that obscured the sunset's ray ;
> And pallid Evening twines its beaming hair
> In duskier braids around the languid eyes of Day :
> Silence and Twilight, unbeloved of men,
> Creep hand in hand from yon obscurest glen. . . .

524. 1-6

The language of the poem and its title, *A Summer Evening
Churchyard*, remind us of Gray's *Elegy written in a Country
Churchyard* and the ode *To Evening* of William Collins, who,
like Shelley, was a native of West Sussex. When reading
Nature-poems like the *Summer Evening Churchyard*, it is well
to remember Shelley was Sussex born and bred. As Edmund
Blunden has remarked,

It has constantly puzzled me, who am the descendant of many
Sussex men, that the biographers of Shelley pay so little regard
to the fact that Shelley was a Sussex man, and, so turning aside,
do not apply in his instance amid their critical conjectures the
rule that poets live most on their youngest and least premeditated
discoveries in the world about them.[7]

It is these early ties that matter, not the fact that, after 1811,
Shelley only twice darkened his father's door — once when
he came in disguise, and again at the reading of Sir Bysshe's
will, when he sat on the doorstep reading *Comus* because his
father would not let him in.

A Nature-poem written in 1815 might be expected to
show signs of Wordsworth's influence, but the *Summer Evening
Churchyard* certainly owes more to Gray and Collins. Shelley's
Nature-poetry was a plant, slow to mature, which only came
to its splendid flower in Italy after 1818. At first, in *Queen
Mab*, Thomson had been his model, and it was not until
late in 1815 that Wordsworth's influence became important.
Shelley regretted Wordsworth's decline since 1805, and he
was speaking for his generation when he mildly rebuked the
master in a sonnet :

Poet of Nature, thou hast wept to know
That things depart which never may return :
Childhood and youth, friendship and love's first glow,
Have fled like sweet dreams, leaving thee to mourn.
These common woes I feel. One loss is mine
Which thou too feel'st, yet I alone deplore.
Thou wert as a lone star, whose light did shine
On some frail bark in winter's midnight roar :
Thou hast like to a rock-built refuge stood
Above the blind and battling multitude :
In honoured poverty thy voice did weave
Songs consecrate to truth and liberty, —
Deserting these, thou leavest me to grieve,
Thus having been, that thou shouldst cease to be.

526. 1-14

Shelley gained much from Wordsworth's pioneer work in
writing about Nature simply. Though Nature was rarely
all in all for Shelley, he was ready to follow Wordsworth's
gospel of communion with Nature when it suited him.

3

Shelley's second long poem, *Alastor*, was written at Virginia
Water in the autumn of 1815. A fundamental change had
come since 1813. In *Queen Mab* he had tried to solve the
world's political and social problems ; the tone had been
impersonal and doctrinaire, the background often urban.
Alastor, on the other hand, deals only with one rather odd
young man ; there are plenty of questions but few answers,
and the background is wholly rural. Mary had done much
to rouse the humaner streak in Shelley, for he believed he
had found in her the ideal blend of intellect and love.[8]
Since he had to be more than a rationalist before he could
succeed as a poet, the change was for the better. The
rationalist in him remained, however, as a watchdog to curb
the wilder excesses of sensibility. This conflict has been
analysed rather differently by F. Stovall,[9] who contrasted
the egoistic and altruistic impulses which swayed him.

Thus *Queen Mab*, with its concern for the public weal, is altruistic, while *Alastor*, with its emphasis on private happiness, is egoistic. Yet another way of defining these warring elements was most popular in the 1880s when it was usual to divide Shelley's poems into (admirable) lyrics and (objectionable) programmes for reform. In each of these contrasts — humanist *versus* rationalist, egoist *versus* altruist, and singer *versus* reformer — the same basic conflict is being interpreted. The conflict is worth remembering, though we are free to choose the interpretation most to our taste.

The hero of *Alastor* is an innocent youth whose education has been designed to shelter him from every worldly taint. He has read widely and eagerly among the best books, and when he ventures into the world of men, he is fortified with the precepts of his chosen authors. At first he devotes himself to the glories of Nature. The crisis of the poem comes when he rejects ideal beauty in Nature and seeks it in woman. He searches for a companion with a mind as uncorrupted as his own, but in vain. So he promptly 'descends to an untimely grave'. Shelley claims in his preface that *Alastor* is 'allegorical of one of the most interesting situations of the human mind', and so it might be if we saw the poet-hero colliding with, instead of succumbing to, the world. As it is, the high talents he is said to have are never used and his inaction is irritating: he goes into a decline more readily than the most drooping heroine of Victorian fiction. Shelley never gives his hero a name, referring to him merely as 'the Poet'. In the rarefied atmosphere of *Alastor*, as on the imaginative heights of the *Ancient Mariner*, anything so mundane as a name would have brought an unwanted touch of bathos.

Alastor begins with a Miltonic invocation which soon develops into Nature-worship as fervent as Wordsworth's:

> Mother of this unfathomable world!
> Favour my solemn song, for I have loved
> Thee ever, and thee only. . . .
>
> 15. 18-20

Praise of Nature leads easily to the Poet, who is now privileged
to sleep with Nature. Because of this introduction from the
graveside the story opens on too necrotic a note :

> There was a Poet whose untimely tomb
> No human hands with pious reverence reared,
> But the charmed eddies of autumnal winds
> Built o'er his mouldering bones a pyramid
> Of mouldering leaves in the waste wilderness : —
> A lovely youth, — no mourning maiden decked
> With weeping flowers, or votive cypress wreath,
> The lone couch of his everlasting sleep.
>
> 16. 50-7

The phrases have a precise, mincing competence ; but the
technique is somewhat mechanical, for there are two nouns
in each line, and fourteen of the sixteen nouns are preceded
by adjectives a little too apt. Technically, Shelley was still
an amateur, and over-elaboration, 'the vice of amateurs',
shows itself in a surfeit of adjectives, which gives the poem
a luxurious air.

The Poet, Nature's votary, samples all her products. He
explores volcanoes, ice-fields, underground rivers, barren
islets and also the ruins of antiquity, since time has lent
them an almost 'natural' dignity. He wanders far during
this tour of inspection, and it is in Kashmir that he

> dreamed a veilèd maid
> Sate near him, talking in low solemn tones.
> Her voice was like the voice of his own soul
> Heard in the calm of thought.
>
> 18. 151-4

Here Shelley first states one of his firmest beliefs, the Platonic
view that a man's ideal mate is his 'other half', having a
mind in tune with his own. He may spend many years
seeking this ideal in vain, for souls are not worn openly like
badges : as a rule, the soul's shining core is, as Shelley puts
it, veiled. The Poet in his dream, however, can see through
the veil, and the spectacle proves too much for him : 'His
strong heart sunk and sickened with excess of love'. When
he wakes, Nature's delights are tame. He is obsessed by the

E

apparition in his dream, and he spends the rest of the poem vainly roaming about the Middle East in search of her. He is soon reduced to a haggard, almost spectral figure, and in portraying him Shelley again harks back to his favourite Wandering Jew. Shelley's devotion to this second Ulysses may now seem excessive, but he was not the only author to exploit the legend. The Wandering Jew figured prominently in Lewis's famous novel *The Monk*, appeared in the finale of Wordsworth's *Borderers*, and won himself a further lease of life in the person of the Ancient Mariner.[10]

In the course of his travels the Poet reaches 'the lone Chorasmian shore', where he sees a little shallop floating near by:

> It had been long abandoned, for its sides
> Gaped wide with many a rift, and its frail joints
> Swayed with the undulations of the tide.
> A restless impulse urged him to embark
> And meet lone Death on the drear ocean's waste;
> For well he knew that mighty Shadow loves
> The slimy caverns of the populous deep.
>
> 21. 301-7

This theme of the frail boat adrift on stormy seas appears again and again in Shelley's poems. Boating was one of his favourite pastimes. He relished first the spice of danger, then the sense of domination, as the boat rises bravely to the crest of the wave which seems about to overwhelm it. Since he couldn't swim, this was for him an exhilarating challenge to Nature, on the same level as that of the test pilot or the racing motor-cyclist, and one which Nature accepted in the end. A small boat also aptly summed up a part of his own personality. Often he seemed to glide like a coracle across the ocean of life, sometimes battling against the current, sometimes drifting apathetically with it, but always with his principles locked away in a watertight box beyond reach of the contaminating flood. With this analogy in mind, we can see why he came to use a boat's progress, across the ocean or down a river, as a symbol for a soul's journey through life, representing emotional crises by rough waters.

A new fluency pervades the verse as the Poet sets sail in the shallop. A storm begins to brew at once, but the boat survives and, as the moon rises at midnight, drifts into a cavern under gaunt Caucasian cliffs. From here an underground stream runs into the bowels of the earth via an enormous whirlpool. The boat is swept to the outer edge of this vortex and through a narrow spillway into a rivulet which flows quietly through a thick forest: the Poet is safe again.

His subterranean voyage would not have seemed so far-fetched then as it does now, for underground streams helped to assuage the mania for sublime scenery, and Shelley was merely following the fashion. Southey's epics, for example, are riddled with submarine caverns and subterranean rivers; a shallop which drifts into a cavern figures in Beckford's *Vathek*, which Shelley read in 1815; and, of course, there is the sacred river Alph in *Kubla Khan*, then still unpublished and probably unknown to Shelley.

In describing the Poet's progress down-river through the forest Shelley makes good use of his own recent river-voyages, down the Rhine in 1814 and up the Thames in 1815. Though not yet free of Thomson's influence Shelley's technique is much improved. He is seeing more in Nature than meets the common eye, and in his word-pictures of the riverside trees and shrubs he is learning to communicate this special insight. When he looks at the trees, for example, he picks out the creepers for special mention:

> Like restless serpents, clothed
> In rainbow and in fire, the parasites,
> Starred with ten thousand blossoms, flow around
> The grey trunks, and, as gamesome infants' eyes,
> With gentle meanings, and most innocent wiles,
> Fold their beams round the hearts of those that love,
> These twine their tendrils with the wedded boughs
> Uniting their close union.

24. 438-45

Though the syntax could be improved, the sentiment better concealed, and the adjectives pruned, this is no conventional exercise in Nature-poetry but a distinctive interpretation of a closely-observed scene, a foretaste of the genre in which Shelley was to reign supreme — minute analysis of Nature conducted with vividly human metaphor. This process at its best can expose fresh levels of appreciation. At its worst, in the hands of poets who have the trick without the insight, it degenerates into shallow pictorial verse.

Another habitual technique of Shelley's first becomes prominent here, when we find him lingering over images in still water :

> . . . yellow flowers
> For ever gaze on their own drooping eyes,
> Reflected in the crystal calm. The wave
> Of the boat's motion marred their pensive task,
> Which nought but vagrant bird, or wanton wind,
> Or falling spear-grass, or their own decay
> Had e'er disturbed before.
>
> 23. 406-12

In later poems Shelley continually exploited the emotional appeal of water-images. His persistence would best be explained by some strong childhood memory, and to find one we need look no further than the lakes at Field Place, which produce remarkably clear reflexions of overhanging trees and the house behind. Living near Virginia Water after a year in London had probably revived his interest in water images, and he had a touch of narcissism, which may also have contributed.[11]

The Poet at last leaves his boat and tramps through the forest. He still follows the stream, for he sees in it an epitome of his own life, now placid, now turbid. The river leads him into more barren country, until finally it plunges over a precipice. This is plainly his death sentence. He stumbles into a nook among the rocks, sheltered from wind and rain, and gives up the ghost just as the horns of the young moon vanish behind the western mountains. (The astronomy is a little irregular, for this was the moon which rose the previous midnight, being then about three weeks old.)

. It only remains to lament the innocent genius of the dead Poet. Here Shelley tries a technique he later perfected, a contrast between the earthy and the ethereal. The touch of bathos in

> Heartless things
> Are done and said i' the world, and many worms
> And beasts and men live on. . . .
>
> 29. 690-2

serves as an apology for the well-sustained apostrophe which ends the poem

> Let not high verse, mourning the memory
> Of that which is no more, or painting's woe
> Or sculpture, speak in feeble imagery
> Their own cold powers. Art and eloquence,
> And all the shows o' the world are frail and vain
> To weep a loss that turns their lights to shade.
> It is a woe too 'deep for tears', when all
> Is reft at once, when some surpassing Spirit,
> Whose light adorned the world around it, leaves
> Those who remain behind, not sobs or groans,
> The passionate tumult of a clinging hope;
> But pale despair and cold tranquillity,
> Nature's vast frame, the web of human things,
> Birth and the grave, that are not as they were.
>
> 30. 707-20

4

In *Alastor* Shelley improves his verse technique, and extends his sphere of operations with fine imaginative *brio*. But he fails to make his intention clear because the main thread of the story is often lost in the rich detail surrounding it. Some years were to pass before he set about clearing these lush growths choking his channel of communication; it was a problem he was hardly aware of in 1815.

The poem's title and the explanation of it have caused much needless confusion. The first possible error is to assume that 'Alastor' is the poet's name. This mistake is avoided easily, though not easily enough for some of Shelley's hastier critics, such as F. R. Leavis.[12] But beyond that

error lurks another false scent, laid by Peacock, who wrote:
'Shelley was at a loss for a title, and I proposed that which
he adopted: *Alastor, or, the Spirit of Solitude.* The Greek
word Ἀλάστωρ is an evil genius.'[13] The innuendo is misleading. Shelley finished the poem without knowing this
interpretation would be foisted into it, and he is unconvin-
cing when he belatedly tries to justify it in the preface by
referring to 'the furies of an irresistible passion pursuing
[the Poet] to speedy ruin'. The furies are not mentioned in
the poem and are best ignored.

This is not the last of the inconsistencies in *Alastor*. No
one would guess from the tone that the Poet is at all to be
blamed for his decline. Rather he seems to be glorified, as
if it were a natural and admirable thing to drift along in a
boat until one dies of hunger, especially if one is a talented
young poet. Yet Shelley's aim was, apparently, to emphasize the dangers of either shutting oneself off from society
or conjuring up unattainable ideals of female perfection.
He himself was not immune from either temptation, and
the poem may have been written to exorcize his hero's
errors from himself and offer thanks for having avoided
them by analysing them. The Poet's history is what Shelley's
might have been if he had surrendered to every transitory
bout of melancholy. In her note on *Alastor* Mary tells us
that earlier in 1815 'an eminent physician pronounced that
he was dying rapidly of a consumption', and in *Alastor* he
was burying that afflicted former self. The various Eminent
Physicians who wrongly diagnosed Shelley's complaint,
whatever it may have been, must certainly bear the blame
for some part of his preoccupation with death in the poems
he wrote in England. 'Romantic death-wishes' are only
too probable if doctors pronounce death sentences whenever
diagnosis baffles them.

Shelley plays havoc with the laws of Nature during the
Poet's voyage via cavern and whirlpool. The boat drifts,
without motive power, along an underground Caucasian
stream tapping the waters of the Caspian Sea and into a
river flowing down to, presumably, the Black Sea, which is,

however, some eighty feet above the Caspian. And when the Poet follows the river's course after disembarking he finds himself at the top of a cliff which 'seems to overhang the world'. Since Shelley concocts a plausible mechanism to let the shallop escape from the whirlpool, we should not lightly assume that his defying of gravity is due to negligence. The whole tenor of the poem would have been altered if the Poet had exerted himself to the extent of rowing or mountaineering. Yet he must *aspire* in his quest. Shelley therefore overturns the laws of Nature and makes the river, paralleling the Poet's life, flow upwards; so much so that when the Poet reaches the end of his journey we feel he is within a stone's throw of the dome of heaven.[14]

In *Alastor* Shelley's technique, though much improved, is not yet assured, and the rather unsophisticated phrases plainly reveal his literary debts. The deepest, to Wordsworth, is proclaimed in the third line with *natural piety*, a phrase alien to Shelley's normal usage, and confirmed in two direct quotations from the *Immortality* ode, *obstinate questionings* and *too deep for tears*.[15] From Wordsworth, too, he probably learnt the trick of ending lines with a rambling Latin adjective followed by a curt Saxon noun: 75 of the 720 lines in *Alastor* end with a monosyllabic noun immediately preceded by an adjective of three syllables or more. Southey's influence is almost as strong as Wordsworth's. The central motif of uncorrupted youth may well have been suggested by Thalaba's 'heart, pure and uncontaminate', and many examples of heroes afloat in fragile boats can be found in *Thalaba* and Southey's other epics.

5

A number of Shelley's essays probably belong to the year 1816. The longest of these, the unfinished *Essay on Christianity*, expresses the views he continued to hold, almost unchanged, for the rest of his life. Few would suspect that the author of *Queen Mab* is speaking in the *Essay on Christianity*, so different are the tone and the approach. Shelley begins with a tribute to the 'extraordinary genius' of Jesus Christ, 'the wide and rapid effect of his unexampled doctrines, his invincible gentleness and benignity',[16] and proceeds to interpret Christ in his own way. The two teachings which he stresses most are: 'Love your enemies, bless those who curse you', and 'all men are equal in the sight of God'. A mild and benevolent man like Christ, he says, could never have regarded the 'execrable doctrine' of eternal torture after death with anything but distaste. When Christ claims supernatural power and uses the concept of God familiar to his audience, he is, in Shelley's view, adopting a benevolent artifice to make men heed his moral teaching. Shelley thought Socratic and Christian ethics had much in common, and he approved, in the main, of both, while regretting that Christ's teaching had been perverted by Churchmen and theologians. Judging Christ as a man and as a moralist, not as a divinity, Shelley finds him a shining example of Godwinian virtue, so much so that the New Testament soon became his favourite reading. Indeed he even had a whim to become a clergyman, telling Peacock: 'Assent to the supernatural part of Christianity is merely technical. Of the moral doctrines of Christianity I am a more decided disciple than many of its more ostentatious professors.' [17] The *Essay on Christianity* is Shelley's last open pronouncement on the subject. As the years wore on, he grew more reluctant to expose his private feelings to public censure, at any rate in the stark clarity of prose.

In his short essay *On the Punishment of Death*, Shelley treats with cool logic a subject often submerged in seething floods of emotion. Recent disputes on the subject have been severely practical. Shelley's three reasons for wishing to see the death penalty abolished are, by comparison, abstract. First, he says, reform, not revenge, should be the chief motive of the penal code. Second, the punishment is equivocal: for who can tell whether death is a good or an evil? Third, public executions arouse in the spectators the basest passions.

In the disconnected *Speculations on Metaphysics*, Shelley

intended to probe into the 'intricate . . . caverns' of the human mind. His proposed method is astonishingly like Freud's: 'Let us reflect on our infancy, and give as faithfully as possible a relation of the events of sleep'.[18] The catalogue of his dreams which follows might have been fascinating if he had persevered with it; but it ends in the middle of the second dream with the note, 'Here I was obliged to leave off, overcome by thrilling horror'.

6

Shelley and Mary were happy in their cottage at Bishopsgate, near Virginia Water, on the edge of Windsor Great Park. They lived there from August 1815 until May 1816, and their son William was born there in January 1816. Peacock and Hogg were the most frequent of their few visitors, and with two such classical enthusiasts to stimulate Shelley's new liking for Greek, the winter was 'a mere Atticism'. The strain of defying convention went on, however, and would go on as long as Godwin persisted in reminding them they were unmarried. By 'dishonouring' Godwin's daughter, Shelley had, via a process which might almost be called blackmail, become the chief financial prop of the Skinner-Street household. He had given Godwin over £1000 during 1815. Yet Godwin was continually writing to ask for more, while at the same time maintaining his moral superiority by refusing to speak to Shelley. It was a curious game: Shelley had applied one Godwinian principle, free love, for his own convenience; so Godwin retaliated by invoking another, though *Political Justice* does not sanction surliness towards benefactors. Godwin's reputation would stand higher to-day if he had suffered as a martyr in the repression of the 1790s instead of living on, a mere husk of his former self, to figure ignobly in Shelley's biography.

Godwin's behaviour was not the only cloud marring the scene: Shelley awaited the fate of *Alastor*, his first serious published poem, with all the unfledged author's over-intense hopes and fears. Since Wordsworth was still not respectable as a poet in 1816, it is easy to guess how *Alastor* was treated. The few reviewers who did not condemn it outright complained that it was incomprehensible. A holiday abroad, far from Godwin and the reviewers, seemed an attractive prospect to Shelley that spring. But he was not bitter against England, 'that most excellent of nations' [19] as he called it :

So long as the name of *country* and the selfish conceptions which it includes shall subsist, England, I am persuaded, is the most free and the most refined.[20]

During their nine months at Bishopsgate Shelley and Mary had seen little of Clare Clairmont, much to their relief. Clare's interest had been centred elsewhere. She had been one of the many to fall in love at a distance with Lord Byron, who for three years past had been enjoying a glittering fame such as few poets have ever known. Clare was persistent enough to establish herself as his mistress before 'the British public in one of its periodical fits of morality' drove him abroad in April 1816. Shelley and Mary planned to visit Italy during the summer, but before they set off, in May, Clare persuaded them to head for Geneva, where Byron was expected to stay. Before Byron tired of her (the process took about a month) Clare figured in one of his best-known lyrics,

> There be none of Beauty's daughters
>   With a magic like thee ;
> And like music on the waters
>   Is thy sweet voice to me. . . .

Otherwise her liaison brought her only misery, and she suffered more than enough to atone for her indiscretion. Byron often pretended, as part of his cynical pose, to be bored with his current mistress, but his protests about Clare ring true :

as to all these 'mistresses' — Lord help me — I have had but one. Now don't scold — but what could I do ? A foolish girl in spite of all I could say or do, would come after me, or rather went before, for I found her here. . . . I could not exactly play the Stoic with a woman who had scrambled eight hundred miles to unphilosophize me.[21]

When Byron and Shelley first met at Geneva, in May 1816, Byron was 28, Shelley 23. Both had just left England with unpleasant memories of the penalties of broken marriages. Both were poets born into the ruling class, and nursing a grievance against it. Both were ripe for new and disturbing acquaintance: Byron had just cut adrift from his social group; Shelley had made no new friends since eloping two years before, and he was delighted to meet the most famous poet of his Age, whose *Corsair* had sold 13,000 copies on the day of publication. Byron, still smarting at the aftermath of his disastrous marriage, was firmly attached to the philosophy of ' "man delights not me", and only one woman — at a time'. The grandeur of the Alps conspired with Shelley's eager, unworldly talk to correct Byron's cynicism. Shelley himself was entranced by the Swiss scenery: 'I never knew, I never imagined what mountains were before. The immensity of these aerial summits excited, when they suddenly burst upon the sight, a sentiment of ecstatic wonder, not unallied to madness.' [22] Not every English visitor to Switzerland that summer was so impressed, as Brougham's letter to Creevey shows: 'There is *no resource whatever* for passing the time, except looking at lakes and hills, which is over immediately'.[23] Shelley and Byron found much to interest them among those mountains and especially round the shores of the Lake of Geneva, the sacred ground of Rousseau's *Nouvelle Héloïse*. During an eight-day tour of the Lake by boat they visited Lausanne and the Castle of Chillon, and, like Rousseau's hero and heroine, very nearly foundered when caught in a sudden squall.[24] In the evenings Shelley, Byron and the others would talk together, and on one occasion when they discussed the supernatural, Byron suggested that everyone should write a ghost story. This was the origin of Mary's *Frankenstein*, which stands to-day in a unique position half-way between the Gothic novel and the Wellsian scientific romance. Though Mary could not foresee its historical status, she did have the melancholy satisfaction of knowing it was far more popular than anything of Shelley's : during 1823 stage versions were presented at three different theatres.[25]

7

In the two poems he wrote in Switzerland Shelley was groping for the right way of treating themes which were new to him. He tried hard, and there is much to admire in the products, despite their flaws. The first of the two poems, the *Hymn to Intellectual Beauty*, is a rather inflexible ode in an eighteenth-century vein. Shelley's Italian poems have supple verse-forms and words which seem to shuffle themselves spontaneously into suitable patterns. In contrast the *Hymn to Intellectual Beauty* has the bones of its structure protruding :

> The awful shadow of some unseen Power
>   Floats though unseen among us, — visiting
>   This various world with as inconstant wing
> As summer winds that creep from flower to flower, —
> Like moonbeams that behind some piny mountain shower,
>   It visits with inconstant glance
>   Each human heart and countenance. . . .
>
> 529. 1-7

The awkward repetition of *unseen* and *inconstant*, the ambiguous *shower*, and the daunting set of vague presences — awful shadow, unseen Power, various world and inconstant glance — all suggest that Shelley is composing painfully, as if entangled at the outset in the intricacies of the rhyming, and weighed down by the solemnity of his theme. He was in effect trying to define a private theology, with the Spirit of Intellectual Beauty as a substitute for God. In the average man's life this Spirit is felt, if at all, only in the rare moments when self-interest is forgotten and all the faculties co-operate to let him perform some altruistic act beyond his normal powers. The Spirit is seen and recognized from time to time by artists and thinkers in their deepest flashes of insight. Shelley came late, in 1815 or 1816, to that sense

of being at one with Nature which imbues the mystic in his
communion with what he may call God. Shelley had
first to exhaust the gamut of rational revolutionary hopes.
But once he had shared the revelation — and the mood of
Tintern Abbey could well be relived among the Swiss Alps —
he was quick to define Intellectual Beauty and relate it to
his own experiences.

The vagaries of English usage since 1816 have given
Shelley's phrase *intellectual beauty* an unkind twist, for to-day
it could be misread as a glamorous girl-graduate. In
Shelley's day it would have been read as 'beauty of the
mind and of the soul', or incorporeal beauty as opposed to
physical beauty. Lingering over the literal meaning of the
phrase is not very helpful, since it must in the last resort,
like 'God', be interpreted subjectively. The idea of intellectual beauty arises from looking at the world through
Platonic spectacles, which encourage the mind to 'fill up
the interstices of the imperfect images' [26] seen on earth and
to imagine the flawless archetype. Though Shelley's version
of intellectual beauty is of his own making, he may have
taken his cue from the conversation of Socrates and Diotima
in the *Symposium*, and he drew on the parable of the cave in
the *Republic* for the shadow phraseology.

Looking back to his school-days, Shelley fancies he can
isolate in his memory the moment when the shadow first
fell on him:

While yet a boy I sought for ghosts, and sped
  Through many a listening chamber, cave and ruin,
  And starlight wood, with fearful steps pursuing
Hopes of high talk with the departed dead.
I called on poisonous names with which our youth is fed;
  I was not heard — I saw them not —
  When musing deeply on the lot
Of life, at that sweet time when winds are wooing
  All vital things that wake to bring
  News of birds and blossoming, —
  Sudden, thy shadow fell on me;
I shrieked, and clasped my hands in ecstasy!

531. 49-60

Then and there he vowed to 'dedicate his powers' to the Spirit's service. By this over-dramatization of what was probably a gradual process Shelley risks offending the modern reader. We may admit that he kept his vow, but we feel it is hardly decent of him to tell us about it so bluntly. This is another way of saying that the language is too stiff and formal for modern ears. Shelley was returning to the eighteenth century for his technique — and also for one of his lines, 'Hopes of high talk with the departed dead' being taken almost verbatim from *The Seasons*.[27] There are over sixty abstract nouns in the eighty-four lines of the *Hymn*. When a poet carries abstraction so far he risks creating the impression that he is broadcasting a statement of principles to the lowly reader, instead of sending a special personal message. The *Hymn* is, however, vigorous enough to survive the fiercest storms of such technical criticisms, and despite its unfashionable tone it still finds favour with anthologists.

In the second poem, *Mont Blanc*, the mood is again awed contemplation of Nature, but the theme is wider, an analogy between the workings of the mind and of Nature. Shelley sees the mind retaining, or profiting from, a tiny proportion of the stream of ideas which pass through it, these being but part of a larger flow.

> The everlasting universe of things
> Flows through the mind, and rolls its rapid waves,
> Now dark — now glittering — now reflecting gloom —
> Now lending splendour, where from secret springs
> The source of human thought its tribute brings
> Of waters, — with a sound but half its own. . . .
>
> 532. 1-6

This is to be compared with the deep, dark ravine of the river Arve, through which Power flows with muffled thunder from its 'remote, serene and inaccessible' source among the snows of Mont Blanc, whose apex, far off, 'pierces the infinite sky'. Mont Blanc,

> A city of death, distinct with many a tower
> And wall impregnable of beaming ice,

is the god-like creator of the glaciers, ice-cliffs and avalanches.
For the moment Shelley was sufficiently impressed to outdo
Wordsworth in mountain-worship :

> Thou hast a voice, great Mountain, to repeal
> Large codes of fraud and woe ; not understood
> By all, but which the wise, and great, and good
> Interpret, or make felt, or deeply feel. . . .

533. 80-3

There are two curious borrowings from Coleridge in
Mont Blanc. Shelley undoubtedly modelled his poem on
Coleridge's *Hymn before Sunrise in the Vale of Chamouni.* He
has the same reverent tone, a few of the same phrases, a
similar sub-title, *Lines written in the Vale of Chamouni* and
similar topography. This last similarity is surprising, for
Shelley was on the spot, whereas Coleridge had never seen
the Alps, and based his *Hymn* on a German poem.[28] The
other echo of Coleridge is a fascinating rehash of lines from
Kubla Khan. Coleridge wrote :

> *from this chasm with ceaseless turmoil seething* (1). . . .
> Through wood and *dale* (2) the sacred *river* (3) ran
> Then reached the *caverns measureless to man* (4)
> And sank *in tumult* (5) to a lifeless *ocean* (6).

Shelley followed with :

> *vast caves* (4)
> Shine in the rushing torrents' restless gleam,
> Which *from those secret chasms in tumult welling* (1) (5)
> Meet in the *vale* (2), and one majestic *River* (3). . . .
> Rolls its loud waters to the *ocean* (6) waves.

Kubla Khan was published that summer at Byron's request,
but Shelley did not receive a copy until about a month after
finishing *Mont Blanc.* Byron had memorized part of *Christabel*
and recited it to the Shelleys on 18 June. He was familiar
with *Kubla Khan* and may have recited that too. If so,
Shelley would have had a confused memory of *Kubla Khan*'s
imagery, which he might unwittingly have utilized.[29]

Shelley was right to call *Mont Blanc* an 'undisciplined
overflowing of the soul'. There are fine things in it, but
they are not properly organized. He never fully brings out

the analogy between thoughts running through the mind
and the Arve flowing down its ravine, an analogy which is
the more confusing because it is inexact. In *Mont Blanc*, as
in *Alastor*, Shelley was struggling to interpret Nature, and
from both struggles he learnt much.

8

Shelley and Mary came back from Switzerland in September
1816, both the better in health for their holiday. They
settled quietly at Bath for the winter, little guessing what
troubles were in store.

One of the friends they were most glad to see again was
Fanny Godwin, a charming girl who did not allow the fits
of depression she suffered to embitter her. Fanny's position
in the Godwin household was difficult, for Mrs. Godwin
had not been pleased to lose Clare and keep Fanny, who
was no relation of hers and carried the stigma of illegitimacy.
Fanny often wrote to Shelley and Mary, but they were
quite unprepared for the 'very alarming letter' they received
from her on 9 October. Shelley hurried to Bristol in search
of her. He was too late. Fanny had taken an overdose of
laudanum at an hotel in Swansea. Unselfish to the last, she
hoped, by dying anonymously there, to shield the Godwins
from scandal. Shelley had seen her only a fortnight before,
and blamed himself for not sensing her despair :

> Her voice did quiver as we parted,
>   Yet knew I not that heart was broken
> From which it came, and I departed
>   Heeding not the words then spoken.
>   Misery — O Misery,
> This world is all too wide for thee.
>
> 546. 1-6

The sorry tale continues with the death of Shelley's
legal wife Harriet, who had been missing for a month when
she was found drowned in the Serpentine on 10 December.
After vain efforts to reclaim Shelley, she had for the past two
years been living chiefly with her parents, and looking after

her two children, Ianthe and Charles. She had been receiving £200 per annum from both Shelley and her father.[30] Though Shelley felt her death as a reproach all his life, he was hardly to blame for it; he could not have known that his desertion would lead, however indirectly, to her suicide. Even to mention suicide is to beg a question, for the manner of her death is still disputed.[31] The verdict of the coroner's jury, admittedly only negative evidence, was 'found dead'.

The circumstances of Harriet's death were painful enough to have preyed on a mind far less sensitive than Shelley's. He worked off some of his remorse in a strong and gloomy lyric.[32] The first of its four stanzas sets the scene in taut, clipped verse, with a minimum of fuss:

> The cold earth slept below,
>   Above the cold sky shone ;
> And all around, with a chilling sound,
>   From caves of ice and fields of snow,
>   The breath of night like death did flow
>   Beneath the sinking moon. . . .
>
> 527. 1-6

Harriet's death left Shelley and Mary free to marry, and, after consulting Sir Lumley Skeffington, an authority on etiquette, they decided there should be no delay. 'On the 30th December 1816,' Mary wrote in her journal, 'a marriage takes place.' Shelley contented himself with a reference to 'the ceremony so magical in its effects'. Godwin, the erstwhile champion of free love, was not so reticent:

I went to church with this tall girl some little time ago to be married. Her husband is the eldest son of Sir·Timothy Shelley, of Field Place, in the county of Sussex, Baronet. . . . You will wonder, I daresay, how a girl without a penny of fortune should meet with so good a match. But such are the ups and downs of this world.[33]

Early in January Harriet's relatives filed a bill in Chancery to restrain Shelley from taking charge of his children, Ianthe and Charles. The Westbrooks engaged as counsel Sir Samuel Romilly, who had already earned Byron's hatred

F

by his professional services to Lady Byron. Romilly was widely expected to become Whig leader in the Commons before his suicide in 1818, but he had little need of his great talents in building up the case against Shelley. By quoting *Queen Mab* he was able to misrepresent Shelley's character very damagingly, and the Lord Chancellor, Eldon, gave judgement against Shelley. The verdict shook him more than recent biographers have been prepared to admit. He had long felt himself a social outcast, but never before had society thwarted him so directly. Though Eldon, with his usual procrastination, did not deliver his final judgement until Shelley had left England, the damage had been done, as Peacock's aside indicates :

Shelley often spoke to me of Eton, and of the persecutions he had endured from the elder boys, with feelings of abhorrence which I never heard him express in an equal degree in relation to any other subject, except when he spoke of Lord Chancellor Eldon.[34]

He never forgave Eldon, though he could only reply with the bitterest and most vitriolic of all his poems, *To the Lord Chancellor*. The verdict inflamed all his old animosity against the established order, which had slowly been cooling, and spurred him on with *The Revolt of Islam*, the last poem in which he tried to influence the standards of contemporary society.

The last of the domestic tribulations, scarcely less tragic than the others in its consequences, came on 12 January 1817, when Clare gave birth to a daughter, for whom Byron chose the name Allegra.

The woes of that winter were not entirely unrelieved, for Shelley found a true friend just when he needed one. Leigh Hunt's prescient article on three 'Young Poets' appeared in the *Examiner* on 1 December 1816 :

Of the first . . . we have, it is true, yet seen only one or two specimens . . . but . . . if the rest answer to what we have seen, we shall have no hesitation in announcing him for a very striking and original thinker. His name is Percy Bysshe Shelley. . . .

The second poet was J. H. Reynolds, who hardly fulfilled his early promise. The third was 'just of age':

His name is John Keats . . . a set of his manuscripts was handed us the other day, and fairly surprised us with the truth of their ambition, and ardent grappling with Nature.

Though Hunt's literary taste was often faulty, nothing can deprive him of the credit for discovering such a pair of unknowns. No literary editor is likely to make so famous a catch again, however wide he casts his nets, for two such fish rarely swim together.

Before Christmas Shelley had visited Hunt at his cottage in the Vale of Health, Hampstead, and there within a few weeks he met Keats, Hazlitt and Horace Smith. Though textbooks bracket Shelley and Keats together, they were never close friends. They are so firmly linked in tradition partly because their most popular poems are odes to a skylark and a nightingale, partly because of *Adonais* and partly because the patterns of their lives in space-time were so similar: they both left England for Italy at the age of 25, and they died there within seventeen months of each other, to be buried together at Rome. Hazlitt seems to have disliked Shelley, but Horace Smith became the most useful of his friends. While Shelley was in Italy, Smith, who was a stockbroker as well as a poet, acted as his banker and saved him endless worry.

In January and February 1817, when he was meeting these friends of Hunt, Shelley was kept in London by the Chancery business. With his departure to the country in March a new chapter of his life begins.

NOTES TO III: UNREST (1813-16)

1. *Letters* ii. 92.
2. Statements in this paragraph are based on tables given by G. Manley in *Quarterly Journal of the Royal Meteorological Society*, Apr. 1953, pp. 255-61.
3. *Letters* i. 383-4.
4. Including the Lambs' *Tales from Shakespear.*
5. Peacock, p. 336.

6. Also often spelt *Claire*. Shelley usually wrote *Clare* in his letters, and Professor F. L. Jones tells me that Mary did the same until 1819, when she changed to *Claire*. Miss Clairmont herself in later years favoured *Claire*. Her baptismal names were Clara Mary Jane — which only makes the confusion worse.

7. E. Blunden, *Cricket Country* (1944), p. 64.

8. See Muriel Spark, *Child of Light*, p. 32.

9. F. Stovall, *Desire and Restraint in Shelley*, Ch. 7.

10. See J. L. Lowes, *The Road to Xanadu* (1930), Ch. 14.

11. See W. H. McCulloch, *Keats–Shelley Memorial Bulletin*, VIII, pp. 20–31.

12. F. R. Leavis, *Revaluation*, p. 221.

13. Peacock, p. 341.

14. See G. Wilson Knight, *The Starlit Dome*, pp. 186–7.

15. For Wordsworth's influence, see Blackstone, *Lost Travellers*, pp. 236–51.

16. *Jul* vi. 227.

17. Peacock, p. 327.

18. *Jul* vii. 66.

19. *Letters* i. 489.

20. *Letters* i. 474–5. See also *Jul* vi. 78.

21. Byron, letter to Augusta Leigh, 8 Sept. 1816.

22. *Letters* i. 497.

23. Brougham to Creevey, 15 Aug. 1816. *Creevey Papers*, i. 258.

24. Rousseau, *Nouvelle Héloïse*, Letter 136.

25. The English Opera House, the Royalty Theatre and the Royal Coburg Theatre. See Nicoll, *Early Nineteenth-century Drama*, i. 96.

26. *Jul* vii. 228.

27. *The Seasons, Winter*, l. 432.

28. See De Quincey, *Recollections of the Lake Poets*, p. 24.

29. *Mont Blanc*, dated 23 July 1816, was probably finished by the end of July. Shelley received a copy of the *Christabel* volume on 26 Aug., according to Mary's journal. The poem 'I read the Christabel . . .' (Maurois, *Byron*, p. 276) shows that Byron was familiar with *Kubla Khan*.

30. Shelley's contributions did not begin until he had money, in 1815, but he made up the back-payments.

31. See E. Blunden, *Shelley*, pp. 141–4, for a sceptical view. The episode is surrounded by a morass of false testimony, forged letters and documents withheld from publication. See *The Shelley Legend*, Parts III and IV, and T. G. Ehrsam, *Major Byron*, pp. 116–28. The fullest and most convincing account of Harriet's last days is that by K. N. Cameron, *Shelley and his Circle*, Vol. IV, pp. 769–810.

32. See S. Reiter, *Shelley's Poetry*, pp. 8–10, for an appreciation of the poem.

33. Godwin, letter to his brother Hull, 21 Feb. 1817. C. Kegan Paul, *William Godwin*, ii. 246.

34. Peacock, p. 312.

IV

THE LAST OF ENGLAND

Sweete Themmes runne softly, till I end my Song.

SPENSER, *Prothalamion*

1

IN March 1817 Shelley and Mary moved into Albion House at Marlow, and remained there for a year. Marlow was only twelve miles from their previous home at Virginia Water, and even nearer Bracknell and Eton, scenes of remoter and more disturbing memories for Shelley. He was glad to live by the Thames again, and on one of its loveliest stretches, for the Thames was among the few fixed points in his restless life : from 1802 until he left England in 1818 he spent more than half of every year, except the years of travel, 1811–12, within ten miles of the river.

Albion House was often full in the summer of 1817. Hunt and his family, and Godwin, came to stay ; and there were visits from Peacock, who lived at Marlow, from Horace Smith and from Hogg. Among the permanent residents were Clare, her baby daughter Allegra and the one-year-old William Shelley. And in September the Shelleys' daughter Clara was born.

Soon after arriving Shelley was hard at work on his 'summer task', an epic poem, most of it written beside the river, either in his boat or in Bisham Wood. The poem was published in 1818 under the title *The Revolt of Islam*. At first it had been called *Laon and Cythna*, but the publishers, Charles and James Ollier, took fright after issuing a few copies, one of which unfortunately went to the *Quarterly Review*. The Olliers insisted Shelley should disguise the outspoken attacks on the established order, and he complied by altering 61 of the 4819 lines in *Laon and Cythna* and

77

renaming the poem *The Revolt of Islam*. This expurgated version is now the accepted text.

A clue to Shelley's aim in the poem is supplied by his original sub-title, *The Revolution of the Golden City*, which echoes the then usual rendering of Tasso's *Gerusalemme liberata*, *The Recovery of Jerusalem*.[1] Tasso, by glorifying the First Crusade, hoped to induce his patron to take up the Cross again and liberate the Holy City from the infidel. Shelley, by glorifying his hero and heroine, Laon and Cythna, whose struggle against a tyrannic king ends in martyrdom, hopes to make us declare war not on infidels, but on oppressive rulers. There the link with Tasso ends, for Shelley avoids protracted single combats, the stock-in-trade of the classical epics, and leaves his geography vague so that the moral may seem applicable to any tyrant. The *Islam* of the title is part of the bowdlerization, aimed to dispel any suspicions that the poem might be anti-Christian, and, though the *Golden City* of the sub-title is at one point treated as Constantinople, its exact location is of no importance.

The Revolt of Islam is written in Spenserian stanzas and divided into twelve cantos, like the books of the *Faerie Queene*. In the dedication *To Mary* prefacing the first canto, Shelley mentions again the revelation so prominent in the *Hymn to Intellectual Beauty* :

> I do remember well the hour which burst
> My spirit's sleep : a fresh May-dawn it was,
> When I walked forth upon the glittering grass,
> And wept, I knew not why ; until there rose
> From the near schoolroom, voices, that, alas !
> Were but one echo from a world of woes —
> The harsh and grating strife of tyrants and of foes. . . .
>
> And from that hour did I with earnest thought
> Heap knowledge from forbidden mines of lore,
> Yet nothing that my tyrants knew or taught
> I cared to learn, but from that secret store
> Wrought linkèd armour for my soul, before
> It might walk forth to war among mankind.

37. 21-7 ; 38. 37-42

Time and again Shelley had rejected curricula drawn up by authorities whose motives he distrusted, and delved into 'forbidden mines of lore': the child's urge to undo the locked cupboard remained long after serving its useful purpose. He would learn only from teachers selected by himself. Some of these oracles, Southey for example, disappointed him and toppled from their pedestals. Others endured through thick and thin, notably Godwin, who remained to the end the revered sage of Skinner Street.

2

The first canto of *The Revolt of Islam* is a detached introduction to the main body of the poem. Shelley utilizes a puppet narrator, who climbs to

> The peak of an aëreal promontory,
> Whose caverned base with the vexed surge was hoary,

and watches 'an Eagle and a Serpent wreathed in fight'. After a day-long air battle the eagle emerges victorious, and the narrator climbs down to the sea-shore where he finds a woman nursing the serpent. He sails away with them, and the woman explains that the serpent is the Spirit of Good, the eagle Evil. The narrator falls asleep as the boat is nearing icy mountains, and he wakes to see an improved version of Pope's 'Temple of Fame' and Erasmus Darwin's 'Temple of Nature':

> a Temple such as mortal hand
> Has never built, nor ecstasy, nor dream
> Reared in the cities of enchanted land.

> 51. 559-61

Here in a domed hall, seated on sapphire thrones, are the great departed. Two spirits fresh from 'the world's raging sea' come to join this 'mighty Senate'. They are Laon and Cythna, and the symbolism of the first canto becomes clearer when Laon has told their story, which fills the next eleven cantos.

As a boy, Laon sees his country, Greece, suffering under harsh misrule, which his countrymen bear supinely because they know nothing better. The only rebels are Laon and his constant companion Cythna, a girl of his own age who shares his ideals. One morning she is carried off to slavery by the tyrant's hirelings. Laon tries to rescue her, but is captured and imprisoned on top of a tall tower. There, like Prometheus, he is chained and left to the mercy of the elements. He soon becomes delirious. Then he is miraculously released and carried away in a boat, by an aged hermit, a god-like figure, modelled on Dr. Lind, who had once hurried to Shelley's bedside when he was ill.[2] After seven years of convalescence in the hermit's cave, Laon recovers his sanity. In the interim the resistance movement has prospered, and one of its chief glories is a nameless maiden priestess who preaches liberty and equality. As soon as he is fit, Laon hurries to join the rebel forces, now well organized. He has no difficulty in passing the sentry: he merely says 'A friend' in a tone which shows he is a true lover of liberty. But while he is still chatting with the sentry the camp is overrun by 'those false murderers', the tyrant's troops. Disaster threatens the rebels, until someone utters the war-cry 'Laon', whereupon the enemy flee in panic. The rebels then enter the Golden City, and Laon restrains the mob from lynching Othman, the fallen tyrant. The next morning Laon goes to meet the maiden priestess, who, needless to say, is Cythna. She greets him with an elaborate hymn to mark the beginning of heaven on earth :

> My brethren, we are free ! the plains and mountains,
> The gray sea-shore, the forests and the fountains,
> Are haunts of happiest dwellers ; — man and woman,
>   Their common bondage burst, may freely borrow
>   From lawless love a solace for their sorrow ;
> For oft we still must weep, since we are human. . . .
>
> 92. 2227-32

Then, as suddenly as before, we find the 'despot's bloodhounds . . . gorging deep their gluttony of death': in short, the city is lost. In the *mêlée* the hermit is felled as he stands at Laon's side. When all seems lost, the enemy ranks part in terror as Cythna appears on a huge black steed.

She rescues Laon and carries him off to a rocky ruin far
among the mountains. There Laon and Cythna first console themselves with lawless love. Then Cythna tells Laon
how she has fared in the past seven years. She too had
been miraculously released, and she was able to exploit the
miracle by preaching the liberal gospel as if divinely inspired.
She soon became so popular that the tyrant dared not silence
her by force.

Every night Laon leaves their mountain retreat to go
foraging on the outsize horse, and he soon finds that the
tyrant is punishing his rebellious subjects by massacring
them in millions. Seeing war's aftermath in France in
August 1814 no doubt helped Shelley to visualize the
ensuing desolation :

> Day after day the burning sun rolled on
>   Over the death-polluted land — it came
> Out of the east like fire, and fiercely shone
>   A lamp of Autumn, ripening with its flame
> The few lone ears of corn ; — the sky became
>   Stagnate with heat, so that each cloud and blast
> Languished and died, — the thirsting air did claim
>   All moisture, and a rotting vapour passed
> From the unburied dead, invisible and fast.
>
> 133. 3901-9

To sum it all up we have the ominous lines

>   The deeps were foodless, and the winds no more
>   Creaked with the weight of birds.
>
> 134. 3949-50

As winter advances, famine and plague attack the city-
dwellers, and the public square is soon piled with corpses.
To appease God's anger, an Iberian priest suggests that
Laon and Cythna be burnt. Their pyre is soon prepared,

>   for Fear is never slow
> To build the thrones of Hate, her mate and foe.
>
> 139. 4165-66

Laon leaves Cythna in the mountain retreat, and, with a
hermit's vest as disguise, goes into the city to address the
tyrant's senate. In his speech he refers to America :

There is a People mighty in its youth,
A land beyond the Oceans of the West,
Where, though with rudest rites, Freedom and Truth
Are worshipped. . . .

146. 4414-17

Laon asks that Cythna be sent there, and when the senate
agree he reveals himself. Amid jubilation he is taken to the
pyre; but just as the slaves are about to light it, Cythna
arrives on her steed and joins him. They endure their fiery
martyrdom and are translated to a dream-world with persistent echoes of *Kubla Khan*:

And round about sloped many a lawny mountain
    With incense-bearing forests, and vast caves
Of marble radiance, to that mighty fountain;
And where the flood its own bright margin laves,
Their echoes talk with its eternal waves. . . .

151. 4612-16

The inevitable frail boat, 'one curved shell of hollow pearl',
soon appears, and they sail in it down a calm swift-flowing
river. Their journey's end is the Valhalla of the first canto.

3

Shelley asked Godwin to look on *The Revolt of Islam* as akin
to 'the communication of a dying man'.[3]   To accept this
suggestion is the most charitable course open to us, for the
poem is a caricature of his soberer intentions, fanatical in
tone, undisciplined, and breathlessly urgent: a stage direction 'Poet collapses and expires' at the end would not come
amiss. The plot, dictated by subconscious fantasy, needs
a strong thread to connect its nightmare episodes. Instead
the story jerks from one incident to the next, the incidents
are often obscured in a welter of imagery or symbolism, and
the flashback technique is overworked. The spotlight shifts
uneasily over a stage devoid of solid background, picking
out one surrealist figure after another. Laon, for example, is
a passionate portrait of what Shelley in his wildest excesses
as a propagandist wanted to be. It is no accident that the

names he chose for himself in other poems, Lionel and Julian, are so very like Laon.

The battles in the poem are particularly dream-like. Powerful armies appear out of the blue and vanish as mysteriously as they came. When battle is joined, it is more like a war between men and Martians than between men and men, for the two sides have no common norm of behaviour. Shelley's eye for propaganda is here at its sharpest. He uses the age-old warmongering device of painting enemies blacker than they are, and he twice allows the rebels to be attacked unexpectedly, thus implying that they are amateurs in warfare whose chief weapon against the tyrant's 'hired assassins' is the justice of their cause. When the tyrant recaptures the city the insurgents are unarmed, and only by chance do they find some pikes,

> the instrument
> Of those who war but on their native ground
> For natural rights.
>
> 97. 2444-6

Laon never confers with his lieutenants : he has none. He is the unquestioned rebel leader not because of his military prowess but because the flame of liberty burns brightest in him. He is a religious leader, fit hero for a poem which is more of a divine text than a weighing of rights and wrongs. *The Revolt of Islam* is, as it were, Shelley's Old Testament. It chronicles the struggle of his chosen people, and, just as Jehovah's wishes are invoked to justify the wars in the Old Testament, so the war against the tyrant is justified by its being fought under the aegis of his god Liberty.

Though the poem is full of propagandist tricks, Shelley's bias is so obvious that there is little risk of his making converts. He persistently exploits the emotive possibilities of such words as *tyrant* and *slave*. He never defines the tyrant's régime, which cannot be entirely autocratic since it includes a senate. And he never tells us how the arrival of liberty alters people's daily lives. He is most at his ease when Laon and Cythna are in their mountain retreat far from the hurly-burly of city life, and he can dream of crusades for liberty unhampered by the nagging detail of actuality. His prose pamphlets show that he did not think this detail unimportant; but it was out of place in the dream-world of *The Revolt of Islam*. His error was to make the Golden City too like a real one. He corrected both this error and his too-biased tone in *Prometheus Unbound*, where he resisted the temptation to play the advocate and chose his *dramatis personae* from among the immortals and daemons.

Shelley's lapses into propaganda are not wholly wilful; he was merely failing to discard an obsolete epic convention. In many of the great epic poems, including Shelley's models, the *Gerusalemme liberata* and the *Faerie Queene*, the author observes the action in the distorting mirror of a rigid ideology, and this usually makes his poem much less readable to-day. Where Spenser and Tasso condemn anyone outside their (respective) Christian sects, Shelley denounces anyone who won't set liberty above all other gods. If Shelley's poem was never as popular as theirs, it was partly because they were reflecting the climate of thought in their day, as successful epics usually do, while Shelley was flying in the face of respectable opinion and so had to protest too much.

If we wish to see the best in *The Revolt of Islam*, we must ignore the public issues — the offhand treatment of the community's problems and the blatant propaganda — and look instead at the private ones. For, in Shelley's eyes, the crucial experiences occur when Laon and Cythna endure solitary confinement far from the tainting herd. By these Promethean purifying agonies they are fitted to lead the revolt, and it is only when they are ready that the struggle begins in earnest. In the epic convention accepted by Tasso and Spenser the ebb and flow of the battle is all-important: single combat between Knight A and Knight B decides whether Good or Evil shall prevail. Shelley adopts this convention only half-heartedly, for he seems quite unperturbed when the forces of Good are defeated. Laon and Cythna do not scour the country raising new armies. On the contrary, they retire to their rocky retreat, thus implying that private joys come before their mission to free the oppressed. Because they were friends in childhood it is taken for granted that they love each other : for Shelley accepts Godwin's doctrine of universal love —

> And such is Nature's law divine, that those
> Who grow together cannot choose but love,
> If faith or custom do not interpose,
> Or common slavery mar what else might move
> All gentlest thoughts.

103. 2686-90

Once Laon and Cythna are in their mountain hideout it would be decent to draw a veil over their actions ; or so the furtive English approach to sex, the product of strict sexual laws long enforced, would seem to dictate. Instead Shelley gives a good deal of matter-of-fact unforced detail, a new achievement in English poetry, as Edmund Blunden has remarked.[4]

In no other poem does Shelley lay such emphasis on the principle of sexual equality. It is the most successful piece of propaganda in the poem, and it is neatly linked to the main theme by the catch-phrase, 'Can man be free if woman be a slave?' To guide him he had a bible at hand in the *Rights of Woman*, which he had first read in 1812. Its author, Mary Wollstonecraft (who would, of course, had she lived, have been his mother-in-law), is recognized as the chief pioneer of women's emancipation, and Cythna deserves to be recognized as the first 'new woman' in English poetry. The pre-Romantic ideal, as expressed in *Émile*,[5] for example, had been the spaniel-wife, who stood on the sidelines making vague encouraging noises to her spouse as he engaged in the battle of life. The ideal wife *à la* Cythna feels the equal of her mate ; she shares his interests and is as bold as he in promoting them, within her powers. Thus Cythna is active in spreading propaganda, but, unlike the stout dames of Tasso and Spenser, she takes no part in the fighting. Tasso and Spenser constantly bring in female warriors as an easy way of gaining their readers' sympathy, and Shelley deserves credit for not following in their footsteps.

In the original version of the poem, *Laon and Cythna*,

Shelley had carried the theory of romantic love a little too far for his publishers to stomach, by making Laon and Cythna brother and sister. We need not start searching for sinister psychological explanations. Incest was a popular motif in Shelley's day,[6] for the theory of romantic love required the interests of the two lovers to coincide, and this would be most certain if they were brought up together from childhood. Making them brother and sister is one possible logical conclusion to this process. Shelley said he wished to 'startle the reader from the trance of ordinary life'. But when he realized that reviewers would seize the chance to link liberty with incest, and that friendly readers might be alienated, he was willing to throw out this glaring red herring.

The truth is, that the seclusion of my habits has confined me so much within the circle of my own thoughts, that I have formed to myself a very different measure of approbation or disapprobation for actions than that which is in use among mankind; and the result of that peculiarity, contrary to my intention, revolts and shocks many who might be inclined to sympathise with me in my general views.[7]

In *The Revolt of Islam* Cythna is no longer Laon's sister but 'an orphan'. Typical examples of the other changes, chiefly euphemistic, are *Power* or *Heaven* instead of *God*, *infidel* instead of *atheist* and, most confusing of all, *Iberian priest* in place of the *Christian priest* who recommended that Laon be burnt.

In addition to all these overt examples of sex in *The Revolt of Islam*, the poem depends heavily on subconscious sexual fantasy. Alex Comfort has remarked that the cremation of Laon and Cythna is 'to complete their mutual ecstasy'; afterwards they wake in a fantasy of 'alarming intensity, where sexual excitement, masochism, lyrical poetry and revolutionary politics are inextricable and interchangeable.'[8] Burning is not a substitute for normal sexual pleasure, which they have already enjoyed, but a bonus: the martyr's crown is a final honour welcomed by the true revolutionary.

The struggle for freedom and the strong thread of romantic love in *The Revolt of Islam* both have their place in

the myth of the first canto, which frames the poem's action.
The lifelong fight of Laon and Cythna against tyranny corresponds to the day-long aerial battle between eagle and
serpent. The theme of romantic love comes in when the
serpent, defeated, falls into the sea : for, in myth, serpents
and water often have sexual implications. And the name
'Cythna', with its hissing sound and its hint of a swan,
serpent-necked, afloat on a still lake, again links serpents
and water. Byron called Shelley 'the Snake' because of the
way he walked, but the nickname really went deeper, for
Shelley was always fascinated by snakes, perhaps because as a
child he had heard the legends of dragons and serpents ter-
rorizing the fastnesses of St. Leonard's Forest, near Horsham.[9] He was equally fascinated by eagles, but since he
usually stressed their nobility and liked to make them
personify young nations throwing off the yoke of tyranny,
it is odd that he should choose the eagle to symbolize evil.
Presumably he wished on this occasion to emphasize its
cruelty, strength and apparent arrogance, which contrast
with the serpent's unassuming air. Thus in the myth the
arrogant tyrant is seen crushing the uprising of the meek
grown desperate. Eagle-serpent battles are frequent in
literature, ancient and modern, and there is no need to
invent a psychic conflict in Shelley to account for this one.
At least five such battles, in the *Iliad*, in Aeschylus's *Choephori*,
Virgil's *Aeneid*, Ovid's *Metamorphoses*, and the *Faerie Queene*,[10]
would probably have been familiar to Shelley. The subject
was also painted by Northcote, and figures in the national
flag of Mexico. Shelley's myth, which is Zoroastrian, and is
borrowed from Peacock's unfinished epic poem *Ahrimanes*, is
bewildering at the first reading; it adds little to the main
story when understood ; and it relies on the topography and
many of the phrases of *Kubla Khan* and the *Ancient Mariner*.
The only thing to be said in its favour is that it does let him
round off the poem neatly.[11]

The conscious symbolism of the myth is supplemented by
a further growth in Shelley's stock of unconscious symbols,
which G. Wilson Knight has studied in *The Starlit Dome*. As

in *Alastor*, a man's voyage in a boat symbolizes the progress of his soul through life. In *Alastor* the Poet's mental crises correspond to the storms rocking his boat. In *The Revolt of Islam* epic convention demands that the clash of opposing principles be resolved in battle, and so the boat trips usually occur in the intervals of quiet between crises in the action. Thus for Shelley calm water became firmly established as a paradise-symbol. With these symbols, and others, Shelley was following in the track of Coleridge, probably not deliberately but because his unconscious and Coleridge's were, so to speak, running along the same lines. Coleridge, for example, liked to represent the human journey through life by a voyage in a boat, a device used on the grand scale in the *Ancient Mariner*; and the dome, cave, river and fountains of *Kubla Khan* appear continually in *The Revolt of Islam*. Their common store of imagery suggests that Shelley and Coleridge, had they met, would have found much in common. Coleridge sensed this, and, referring to Shelley's stay at Keswick in 1811, he wrote:

Now — the very reverse of what would have been the case in ninety-nine instances out of a hundred — I *might* have been of use to him, and Southey could not. . . . Shelley would have felt that I understood him.[12]

Another of Shelley's contemporaries, Sir James Lawrence, had some influence on *The Revolt of Islam*. Shelley never bothers to give his poem a proper background, but the little he does provide seems to be based on Lawrence's *Empire of the Nairs*, a propagandist novel about an Oriental land where free love is practised with great benefit to all, chastity is regarded as 'the most absurd of all prejudices', incest is no crime, and the way of Nature, equated with the way of God, receives fulsome praise. Shelley read the book in 1812 and again in 1814.

The chief of Shelley's other literary debts, those to Tasso and Spenser, affect the general outline of the poem more than its details. The only incident obviously filched from Tasso is the martyrdom of Laon and Cythna, which is almost a carbon copy of the burning of Olindo and Sophronia in the

Gerusalemme liberata.[13]   From Spenser Shelley took the nine-line stanza, which he was later to master so thoroughly.   Here the chief oddity in his technique is that he rarely pauses for breath at the end of the fourth line ; and the chief virtue is his resounding final line, which galvanizes the lines before it and dominates the stanza.   Shelley seems to have specially liked the Spenserian stanza : he often read Spenser aloud and he wrote no fewer than 525 of the stanzas in *The Revolt of Islam*.   There may have been another reason for the poem's excessive length, however : at times the matter is spread so thin that we begin to wonder whether he was deliberately spinning it out.   Medwin may have been right with his report [14] that Shelley and Keats agreed early in 1817 each to write a long poem within six months.   If *The Revolt of Islam* and *Endymion* did originate in this way, it would explain why both are so diffuse.

A poem like *The Revolt of Islam*, which presents us with an unusual code of conduct in the hope that we shall admire and copy, prompts the question, 'How does the average reader react ?', and raises the wider issue of the man-in-the-street's attitude towards Shelley's reformist poems in general. A convenient spokesman for this mythical man-in-the-street is Charles Lamb, who was interested more in humdrum incident than in world-shaking ideas, and preferred crowded streets to country solitude : 'I am not romance-bit about Nature'.[15]   The gregarious Lamb hesitated to venture on the snowy summits of Shelley and complained of his 'theories and nostrums . . . ringing with their own emptiness'.[16] Lamb is indeed a good litmus-paper for clarifying a contrast in temperament as fundamental as that between acid and alkali.   We have only to think of Keats delighting in a loaded banquet-table, and Shelley nibbling at dry bread and raisins, to guess how the convivial Lamb reacted to each.   Lamb registers too the contrast between Shelley, who prescribes remedies for every social ill, and Shakespeare, who accepts life as he finds it so completely that men of all creeds have caught him reflecting traces of their own dogmas. This contrast is worth pursuing, since it exposes Shelley's

G

worst defect as a poet. Though he worried far more than
Shakespeare about man in the abstract, he did not have
Shakespeare's humanity, his untiring interest in men as they
are. Shelley 'loved men not because they were men but
because they might be gods'.[17] Yet no one was more alert
to the sufferings of his fellows, and he was always planning
their betterment : he caught ophthalmia through visiting
the poor distributing blankets at Marlow in 1817; he
would go out of his way to give a beggar his last shilling or
his shoes; and still his poetry is wanting in sympathy for
the commonplace man. This is not really paradoxical, for
worry over the good of mankind often overwhelms interest
in men as individuals. Einstein, for example, despite his
sunny nature, always lacked the 'desire for direct association
with men and women'; [18] and Bernard Shaw's work is,
like Shelley's, deeply humanitarian without being humane.
Shelley and Shaw, unlike Shakespeare, Keats or Lamb, are
more often intellectual than intuitive in their approach.
Shelley reacts emotionally, it is true, when he sees the weak
wronged. But he feels for them just as much when they
are out of sight, unlike the man-in-the-street, who conforms
to the adage, 'What the eye sees not the heart rues not'.
The man-in-the-street is kind to pets, but he ignores the
torturing of distant wild animals to satisfy the lust for fur-
coats; while Lamb, his representative, liked to meet boy
chimney-sweeps, and was kind to them, but made no
protest against their employment.

4

'The Hermit of Marlow' was Shelley's *nom de plume* in the
two pamphlets which marked his return in 1817 to the
prickly subject of political reform. In the first, *A Proposal
for putting Reform to the Vote*, he suggests a plebiscite to be
carried out by voluntary house-to-house canvassers; and
he offers one-tenth of his own income, £100, in the hope
that others will follow his example and so build up a fund
to defray expenses. If the people decide against reform, the

champions of reform 'must retire to their homes in silence'.
If reform is favoured, he proposes extending the elective
franchise in carefully controlled steps. To give every male
adult the vote would 'be to place power in the hands of men
who have been rendered brutal and torpid and ferocious
by ages of slavery'.[19] After *The Revolt of Islam* such a mild
programme comes as a salutary shock, to remind us that in
the poem he let his enthusiasm override his better judgement.

Shelley's prose is often a year or two more mature in
opinion than his poetry. It was as if an idea had to circulate in his bloodstream for a time before it dissolved
sufficiently to pass the poetic filter. If we accepted this
theory we should see *Queen Mab* (1813) as the delayed
reaction to his reading of *Political Justice* at Eton in 1809,
embodying ideas expressed in the prose pamphlets of early
1812. And *Alastor*, published in 1816, would be seen as the
outcome of the emotional crisis before his elopement in 1814,
a crisis reflected immediately in a hectic fragmentary prose
romance, *The Assassins*.[20] Most striking of all, *The Revolt of
Islam* is, in its religious and political attitudes, at least two
years behind the *Essay on Christianity* and the *Proposal for
Reform*. This time-lag theory must not be pressed too far,
however ; the next prose pamphlet seems to flout it.

This pamphlet is the *Address to the People on the Death of
Princess Charlotte*. Most Englishmen had been eagerly awaiting the day when the Prince Regent's lively daughter
Charlotte would succeed her unpopular father, and there
was widespread grief when she died in childbed in November
1817. Shelley was one of the many authors who took
advantage of this wave of sentiment. In his pamphlet he
admits it is right to grieve over a young and amiable princess.
But, he contends, the execution for high treason of three
Derbyshire labourers, Brandreth, Ludlam and Turner,
leaders of the futile Pentrich Revolution, is a greater calamity.
For they were egged on by a government agent, Oliver the
Spy, who then exposed them.[21] They were slaughtered by
their fellow-men, not by Nature. Shelley concludes by
linking Princess Charlotte with the Spirit of Liberty for

joint mourning : 'Let us follow the corpse of British Liberty slowly and reverentially to its tomb'. It was hardly in the best of taste so to exploit popular feeling, though as a piece of journalism the pamphlet was well timed and well argued.

5

In the poems he wrote at Marlow, Shelley was not, except in *The Revolt of Islam*, preoccupied with any one theme. There are poems of swooning delight, like *To Constantia Singing*, a very flattering tribute to Clare's singing voice. There are poems of hate, some touched off by the Chancery proceedings, and others apparently motiveless, like the curious *Hate-Song* :

> A Hater he came and sat by a ditch,
>   And he took an old cracked lute ;
> And he sang a song which was more of a screech
>   'Gainst a woman that was a brute.
>
> 550. 1-4

There are poems of brooding sorrow, too, for ghosts from the past were still trying to drag Shelley back into the half-light to relive the previous winter, and sometimes he propitiated them with lines like these addressed to Harriet's shade :

> That time is dead for ever, child!
> Drowned, frozen, dead for ever!
>   We look on the past
>   And stare aghast
> At the spectres wailing, pale and wild,
> Of hopes which thou and I beguiled
> To death on life's dark river. . . .
>
> 546. 1-7

In contrast there are a few poems of complete detachment, and among these is one of his best, *Ozymandias*.

Few of Shelley's sonnets can bear comparison with Shakespeare's, but in *Ozymandias* he successfully challenges the master on his favourite ground, the ravages of time. Shelley seems here to wriggle out of the fetters of the sonnet form, flouting the rules with narrative, doubly reported speech, and a curious rhyme-scheme. He is justified by the result, one of those rare poems which can, on occasion, please even a poetry-hater :

> I met a traveller from an antique land
> Who said : Two vast and trunkless legs of stone
> Stand in the desert. . . . Near them, on the sand,
> Half sunk, a shattered visage lies, whose frown,
> And wrinkled lip, and sneer of cold command,
> Tell that its sculptor well those passions read
> Which yet survive, stamped on these lifeless things,
> The hand that mocked them, and the heart that fed :
> And on the pedestal these words appear :
> 'My name is Ozymandias, king of kings :
> Look on my works, ye Mighty, and despair !'
> Nothing beside remains. Round the decay
> Of that colossal wreck, boundless and bare
> The lone and level sands stretch far away.
>
> 550. 1-14

In *The Revolt of Islam* we were bludgeoned ; here the detached tone lulls our suspicions and the irony appeals to our vanity. The first ten words of the poem, though standing apart, contribute to the effect, for in them Shelley exploits the age-old lure of travellers' tales and at the same time implies he himself will merely report, not interpret, what the traveller has to say. The tale begins well, with a series of arresting visual images. Then we have the deliberate diminuendo of the lines about the sculptor, with the involved grammar, the gentle speculation and the archaic *mocked* (for *mimicked*) creating an olde-worlde air. We are by now persuaded that the traveller is a reliable fellow, quick to observe relevant detail and not too wild in interpreting it. The quiet interval also lets us recover from the poem's first impact and focus our attention on the simple *fortissimo* statements to follow. The crux of the poem is the inscription on the pedestal, and this is far removed from any hint of bias, because it is the veracious traveller's report of what someone else wrote. The last three lines of the poem, flat and direct, seem innocent enough, yet they have a compelling finality. How is this achieved ? There is the music of the verse, the satisfying sequence of vowels and the deft alliteration.

There is *nothing beside remains*, a sentence which is the richer for seeming to include, as an undercurrent, 'no other remains exist near by'. Finally, there is the orator's trick of repetition, artfully disguised : 'sand, bare, level and boundless, surrounds that colossal wreck' conveys the meaning in nine words instead of eighteen, but the air of finality, as well as the music, has been lost.

The poem subtly flatters our vanity. We feel after reading it that we are wiser than Ozymandias, who never knew the irony of his inscription, and wiser too than the traveller, who seems unaware of any moral to be drawn from his plain tale. A real traveller's tale does lie in the background, for *Ozymandias*, like *Kubla Khan* and the ballad of *The Revenge*, is one of those poems which can clearly be tracked to a prose source. Ozymandias was one of the Greek names for Rameses II, and the first of the two key lines in the poem paraphrases an inscription on an Egyptian temple recorded by Diodorus Siculus, 'I am Ozymandias, king of kings'. The traveller may have been Dr. Pococke, who described such statues in 1743.[22]

No one who was asked to select a typical poem of Shelley's would choose *Ozymandias* : intuitively one feels the poem is completely *un*typical, and it is not difficult to see why. First there is the subject : Shelley usually wrote about things dear to his heart, while Ozymandias is a little remote. Then there is the tone, which, partly because of the subject, is passionless, objective and calm, instead of being passionate, subjective and excited. Last, and perhaps most important, there is the aim. Shelley's habit was to aim high, sometimes impossibly high, and even though he would often turn out that most rewarding type of poem which yields new layers of meaning at each re-reading, his success was rarely complete. In *Ozymandias*, however, he is content with a limited objective, a straightforward piece of irony, and he succeeds completely.

The quotation from Diodorus Siculus in *Ozymandias* is a sign of Shelley's growing interest in things Greek, which emerges more clearly in *Prince Athanase*, a poem begun in December 1817. We do not have to look far to discover why his interest was growing, for Shelley saw Peacock a great deal during 1817, and every reader of his novels will agree that Peacock richly deserved the nickname 'Greeky-Peeky' which Thomas Taylor gave him.[23] The seed Peacock planted vastly enriched his friend's poetry when it flowered in Italy. But *Prince Athanase* was a premature attempt to commit this enthusiasm to paper and it exists only as irreparably disconnected fragments. Prince Athanase, like the hero of *Alastor*, is young, wise, liberal, fearless and frank; and he grows 'weak and grey before his time' because he nurses a secret grief. He has a friend and tutor Zonoras, a twin brother of the hermit in *The Revolt of Islam*:

> An old, old man, with hair of silver white,
> And lips where heavenly smiles would hang and blend
> With his wise words; and eyes whose arrowy light
> Shone like the reflex of a thousand minds.
>
> 162. 126-9

Zonoras includes Plato in his pupil's curriculum, and Athanase so relishes his training as a philosopher-king that he soon outruns his tutor. But he is smitten by a secret yearning, and he wanders far and wide trying to assuage it. Then the poem disintegrates into ever-smaller fragments, without embarking on its main theme. In her note on the poem Mary says that in the first sketch, under the title *Pandemos and Urania*, Athanase was to have met 'a lady who appears to him to embody his ideal', only to find she was Pandemos, the earthbound Aphrodite, 'who, after disappointing his . . . dreams . . . deserts him'. The true Urania was to arrive as he lay dying.

Shelley may have abandoned the poem because it was too like Peacock's *Rhododaphne*. Whatever the reason, the loss is no great one, for the theme was the same as *Alastor*'s. Two hints of things to come in the poem are, however, worth noting: the fresh verse-form, Shelley's first try at the *terza rima* he was to use in his last poem *The Triumph of Life*; and the streak of Platonism. For example, it is Pausanias, in Plato's *Symposium*, who draws the distinction between Uranian and Pandemian love; and Athanase — the name means *deathless* — meets his end seeking the immortal essence behind the veil of the temporal.

Shelley's next poem, *Rosalind and Helen*, he described in the preface as, 'undoubtedly, not an attempt in the highest style of poetry'. It is an innocent gossipy tale in a style which Scott and Wordsworth sank to when least inspired, and with a plot calculated to draw an infallible tear if adapted as a serial for television. Rosalind and Helen, firm friends as children, became estranged. They meet many years after on the shores of Como, and tell their stories. Rosalind's bridegroom had died of shock on the altar-stair when told he was her half-brother. She married another, a hard man who died young in years but aged by his 'quench-less thirst of gold'. In his will he denounced Rosalind, leaving his wealth to her three children, provided she never saw them. Helen's life-story is a little brighter. Her lover Lionel was a young man of rare powers; but 'a spirit of un-resting flame' goaded him to travel. He returned apathetic and disillusioned, and the 'ministers of misrule' imprisoned him. On his release Helen drove with him through the city:

> the blood in our fingers intertwined
> Ran like the thoughts of a single mind,
> As the swift emotions went and came
> Thro' the veins of each united frame.
> So thro' the long long streets we passed
> Of the million-peopled City vast;
> Which is that desert, where each one
> Seeks his mate yet is alone.
>
> 182. 940-7

Soon afterwards Lionel died. Their stories over, Helen, with her child Henry, and Rosalind, with her daughter restored to her, live happily together.

The poem's flat metre, relieved by the ever-varying rhyme-pattern, suits its subject well, and Shelley took more care than usual to make the plot tidy, chiefly because neither metre nor matter interested him. He left the poem un-finished for many months, and but for Mary's pleas, he would never have completed it. She liked it because he had for once provided an element of human interest, and also because she saw it as the story not of Helen and Rosalind but of Mary and Isabel — Isabel Baxter. From 1812 till 1814 Mary had found a second home with a Mr. Baxter of Dundee — that was why she never met Shelley on his earlier visits to Godwin — and Mr. Baxter's daughter Isabel had been her closest friend. But Isabel had married a Scotsman of strict views, who frowned on the bohemian Shelley *ménage*, and saw to it that his wife was not contaminated by their company. This real-life parallel was carried further when Shelley died; for Mary, like Helen, was left a young widow with a son to rear, and in 1823 she probably met Isabel again, to cap the reunion in the poem. To judge from the tone of Mary's note to the poem, this example of life copying art may have helped to console her.

Shelley tells Helen's story more sympathetically than Rosalind's, as if to imply that love without marriage is better than marriage without love. As presented, neither seems very pleasant, because Death stalks as a familiar through *Rosalind and Helen*, laying his hand in turn on all the bridegrooms, legal and illegal. Since *Queen Mab*, Shelley had written four long poems, *Alastor*, *The Revolt of Islam*, *Prince Athanase* and *Rosalind and Helen*, and in every one of them Death claims the hero at an early age. Only Laon shows any spirit; the other three unheroic heroes first succumb to wanderlust and then feebly expire. If Laon is what Shelley sometimes wished to be, Prince Athanase, Lionel and the Poet in *Alastor* are what he dreaded he might become. His fears of an early death are responsible for these morbid self-centred heroes, and Lionel is the last of them: for in the glare of the Italian sun those fears fled like ghosts at dawn.

NOTES TO IV: THE LAST OF ENGLAND

1. See, *e.g.*, the reprint of Fairfax's translation, ed. C. Knight, Windsor, 1817.

2 For other possible prototypes of the hermit, see Baker, *Shelley's Major Poetry*, p. 79, and J. O. Fuller, *Shelley*, p. 199.

3. *Letters* i. 577.

4. E. Blunden, *Shelley*, p. 165.

5. Rousseau, *Émile*, Book V.

6. See pp. 135–7.

7. *Letters* i. 582.

8. A. Comfort, *Darwin and the Naked Lady* (1961), p. 82.

9. See E. V. Lucas, *Highways and Byways in Sussex*, Ch. 13.

10. *Iliad*, XII, 200–7 (quoted in Plato's *Ion*); *Choephori*, 247–9; *Aeneid*, XI, 751–6; *Metamorphoses*, Bk. IV; *Faerie Queene*, I, v, 8. See also B. Taylor, *Animal Painting in England* (1955), p. 47.

11. For further details of the myth, see C. Baker, *Shelley's Major Poetry*, pp. 64–70, and R. G. Woodman, *Apocalyptic Vision*, pp. 88–102.

12. Hogg, i. 300. Coleridge did meet Mary when she was a child.

13. *Gerusalemme liberata*, ii. 14–34. A similar incident occurs in Calderón's *El Mágico Prodigioso*.

14. T. Medwin, *Revised Life of Shelley*, pp. 178–9.

15. C. Lamb, *Letters*, Everyman edition, i. 166.

16. C. Lamb, *Letters*, Everyman edition, ii. 124.

17. F. Stovall, *Desire and Restraint in Shelley*, p. 64.

18. P. Frank, *Einstein, his Life and Times* (1948), p. 66.

19. *Jul* vi. 68.

20. Reprinted in the Nonesuch *Shelley* (1951), p. 947. For the source of *The Assassins*, see J. O. Fuller, *Shelley*, pp. 159–61.

21. For details of the Pentrich Revolution, see R. J. White, *Waterloo to Peterloo*, Ch. XIV.

22. See A. M. D. Hughes, *Shelley, Poetry and Prose*, pp. 189–90, and H. M. Richmond, *Keats–Shelley Journal*, Vol. 11 (1962), p. 65.

23. See C. van Doren, *Life of T. L. Peacock*, p. 130. For the growth of Shelley's Greek interests, see Barrell, *Shelley and the Thought of his Time*, pp. 104–119.

V

ITALY

the promised land
Lies at my feet in all its loveliness.

ROGERS, *Italy*

1

SHELLEY's health fluctuated with the seasons almost as
surely as a plant's, and was generally at its lowest ebb
from December to February. In 1817 he was already ill
by the end of September and showed no signs of improving
as autumn hardened into winter. So he was ready to listen
when the doctors urged him to abandon the river-valley
damps of Marlow and spend the next winter in a warmer
climate. There were three other motives to speed him on
his way. First there was the problem of Clare's daughter
Allegra. Byron had now settled in Venice, which was so
co-operative in hiding his lameness, and Allegra would
obviously be better off under his protection than at Marlow,
where she was exposed to vexing local gossip about her
parentage. Then there were Shelley's own children, William
and Clara, whom he still half expected would be stolen
from him by the Chancery Court, for Eldon had not yet
pronounced his final judgement. The third motive was
financial. Most of Shelley's friends were also his pensioners,
and distance would attenuate their ever-growing demands.
Also in Italy living was cheap. In short, everything pointed
towards Italy. So, in March 1818, after a month in London,
visiting 'the Opera . . . Exhibitions, Concerts, and
Theatres',[1] Shelley left England, never to return. 'No
sooner had we arrived at Italy than the loveliness of the
earth and the serenity of the sky made the greatest difference
in my sensations.'[2] Not only in his sensations, but also in

his poetry: during his last four years, under Italy's smiling skies, all the sketchy promise of the poems written in England was generously fulfilled.

The party that arrived at Milan in April 1818 consisted of Shelley, Mary, Clare, a Swiss nurse and the three children William, Clara and Allegra. Shelley came prepared to admire, and he was soon fascinated by Milan cathedral, thus revealing, incidentally, two attitudes which grew upon him in Italy. First, he was awakening to the visual arts, and second he was overcoming the bias which marred *The Revolt of Islam*: he did not now automatically condemn a finished work of art because he disliked the ideological motives behind it. His new interest in Man's work was not at the expense of Nature's. He was just as enthusiastic about Lake Como, but since no suitable house was to be had near its shores the party moved on in May from Milan to Leghorn. There they met Mr. and Mrs. Gisborne, who were to be the most reliable of their friends in Italy. To Mary, Mrs. Gisborne was no stranger: for, in 1797, when Mary was left motherless as a baby, Mrs. Gisborne, then Mrs. Reveley, kindly acted as her foster-mother. Mr. Reveley died soon after, and his widow received a prompt offer of marriage from Godwin, that 'most marriage-seeking of misogamists'.[3] She rejected him, however, and instead married Mr. Gisborne, a man whose 'prodigious' nose stirred Shelley to one of his rare personal remarks: 'It is a nose once seen never to be forgottèn. . . . I, you know, have a little turn-up nose; Hogg has a large hook one; but add them both together, square them, cube them, you would have but a faint idea of' Mr. Gisborne's.[4]

Early in June, leaving the bustle of Leghorn behind them, the Shelleys retired to the Bagni di Lucca, a summer resort in a quiet, shady mountain valley. They intended to remain there until the summer's heat was past, but their stay was cut short by the first reminder of a problem which was to exercise Shelley's tact for the rest of his life, the problem of Byron and Clare. Byron was now pursuing a life of the deepest dissipation at Venice. His *palazzo* resounded with screams and shouts from the animals of his menagerie and from that 'fine animal' La Fornarina, his quarrelsome, illiterate and violent mistress. Allegra had been handed over to him in April reluctantly because he said he would not let Clare see the child again. In the hope of making him relent, Shelley went with Clare to Venice in August. Though Byron refused to write or speak to Clare, he offered Shelley a house at Este, thirty miles south-west of Venice, where Clare would be able to stay for a month or two with Allegra. Shelley could not but accept, and Mary came to join him, bringing with her the children William and Clara. Little Clara, who was unwell when they set out, was further weakened by the rigours of the journey. She became seriously ill at Este, and died in Venice on 24 September. It was a sad household at Este that autumn, with Shelley and Mary grieving over Clara, and Clare brooding about Byron's coldness and her imminent parting from Allegra.

2

In the first seven months of 1818 Shelley did no creative work; he was busy absorbing new experience. In his last poems in England he had seemed in danger of slipping into a groove, regurgitating the *Alastor* theme with minor variations. The fallow period was most beneficial. When he found his voice again he spoke in a new tone, richer and calmer.

The first whisperings of the new voice were to be heard among the groves of the Bagni di Lucca in July, where Shelley, finding himself incapable of original work, spent ten days translating Plato's *Symposium*. Though he transmits the spirit rather than the letter of the original, the number of Greek scholars who have commended and used his translation vouches for its general fidelity.[5]

The *Symposium* deals with Love, and explains it by imaginative myths which, in their kind, have never been bettered. But, because Plato obviously approves of homosexual love, the circulation of this, perhaps his most perfect dialogue, has been restricted. Even to-day the *Symposium* is not thought ideal as a text for school use; in 1818, the year of Bowdler's *Family Shakespeare*, the translator's problem was far worse. Shelley tries to overcome the difficulty by explaining in a prefatory essay how and why 'the Manners of the Ancients' differed from our own. He first asks the reader 'to cast off the cloak of his self-flattering prejudices' and not to let differences in sexual conventions 'interfere with his delight and his instruction'.[6] The difference arose, he explains, because the Greek women, never having the chance of education, were wanting in sensibility and intellectual vigour. The men of Greece 'had arrived at that epoch of refinement, when sentimental love becomes an imperious want of the heart and of the mind', and 'being deprived of their natural object' they had perforce to seek 'a compensation and a substitute'. 'In this circumstance, and in the abolition of slavery', the modern Europeans have, in Shelley's view, decisively improved 'the regulation of human society'.[6] Those who think better of the Greek women than Shelley did [7] may question his explanation; yet it was in its point and psychological acuteness well ahead of its time, as the history of its publication shows. When Mary edited Shelley's prose in 1840, she knew her allowance from Sir Timothy Shelley would be stopped if anything unpalatable by or about his son were published. Her text of the *Symposium* was consequently so bowdlerized as to be almost insipid, while the prefatory essay became pointless, since all hints of the convention it sought to explain had been censored. Some bowdlerization was no doubt necessary, but by neglecting to mention it Mary became party to a conspiracy which is not yet broken. No widely circulating edition of Shelley gives the full text of both essay and translation.[8]

For a glimpse of Shelley's style in the *Symposium*, which is as poetic and delicate as Plato's own, we may turn to Agathon's speech in praise of the god of Love :

. . . our most excellent pilot, defence, saviour and guardian in labour and in fear, in desire and in reason ; the ornament and

governor of all things human and divine; the best, the loveliest;
in whose footsteps every cne ought to follow, celebrating him
excellently in song, and bearing each his part in that divinest
harmony which Love sings to all things which live and are,
soothing the troubled minds of Gods and men.[9]

3

When Shelley climbed the steps of the Palazzo Mocenigo at
Venice in August 1818, it was just two years since he and
Byron had last met. Byron greeted him cordially and at
once arranged a ride along the Lido:

> I rode one evening with Count Maddalo
> Upon the bank of land which breaks the flow
> Of Adria towards Venice: a bare strand
> Of hillocks, heaped from ever-shifting sand,
> Matted with thistles and amphibious weeds,
> Such as from earth's embrace the salt ooze breeds,
> Is this; an uninhabited sea-side,
> Which the lone fisher, when his nets are dried,
> Abandons. . . .
>   I love all waste
> And solitary places; where we taste
> The pleasure of believing what we see
> Is boundless, as we wish our souls to be.
>   190. 1-9, 14-17

So begins *Julian and Maddalo*, the poem which Shelley
(Julian) left as a memento of his talks with Byron (Count
Maddalo) in Venice that summer. On their way home
from the ride, the poem tells us, the conversation centred
on 'God, freewill and destiny', with Shelley defending his
optimistic philosophy against the fatalism of Byron, who
could never shake off his Calvinist upbringing.

The next morning Julian called before Maddalo was up.
While waiting Julian played with Maddalo's child, Allegra,
who had not quite forgotten him,

> For after her first shyness was worn out
> We sate there, rolling billiard balls about.
>   193. 156-7

As soon as he is alone with Maddalo, Julian returns to the previous night's topic :

'it is our will
That thus enchains us to permitted ill —
We might be otherwise — we might be all
We dream of, happy, high, majestical.
Where is the love, beauty, and truth we seek
But in our mind ? and if we were not weak
Should we be less in deed than in desire ? '
'Ay, if we were not weak — and we aspire
How vainly to be strong ! ' said Maddalo :
'You talk Utopia.'

193. 170-9

To justify his gloomy attitude, Maddalo takes his friend to an island madhouse. There they interview one of the inmates, who tells them, somewhat incoherently, how he has gone mad through being crossed in love. When Julian and Maddalo leave the madhouse on their way home, their argument has been stilled by this bombshell from real life. Soon Julian has to leave Venice, and when he returns Maddalo's daughter is a grown woman. The maniac has died, she tells him, and Maddalo is travelling in the wilds of Armenia. It was bad prophecy : Shelley, Byron and Allegra were all dead within six years.

In *Julian and Maddalo* Shelley effects a fine compromise between the language of conversation and the language of poetry. In his hands the rigid rhyming couplet becomes pliant enough to cope with the fits and starts of discussion. Yet the couplet also retains enough of its old associations to provoke, amidst the free-and-easy flow of the verse, quite a spate of epigrams, such as

men
Are cradled into poetry by wrong,
They learn in suffering what they teach in song.

201. 544-6

Most poets of Shelley's day, reacting against the style of Pope, avoided epigram. To scan the pages of Wordsworth, Coleridge, Keats and Shelley in search of epigram is an unrewarding task. Living poets, however, can all produce a

sheaf of epigrams, for the hotter pace of life has forced
them to be terse. Readers attuned to the modern mode who
are uneasy with the slower tempo of Shelley's day would do
well to sample the urbane dialogue of *Julian and Maddalo*.

This is not to say the poem can be recommended as a
whole, for Shelley fails to decide whether his talk with
Byron or the madman's biography is the main theme. The
madman is brought in merely to illustrate a point in the
argument, but his personality proves so compelling that
the argument is forgotten. This is an outcome likely enough
in real life but hardly satisfying as art. The madman's tale
is unduly mystifying, too, especially in its hints of a real-life
prototype. Three possible prototypes are Byron, in his
darker mood, Shelley himself, distraught after Clara's death,
and the poet Tasso, whose biography Shelley had recently
read.[10] Tasso is the most plausible of the three, for Shelley
had intended to devote the summer of 1818 to writing a
tragedy about Tasso's madness, and the short fragment
which exists has Count Maddalo as one of its characters.
Perhaps Shelley was salvaging the remains of this abandoned
project. If so, it was a sad come-down for a tragic hero to
edge on to the margin of a narrative poem as an anonymous
lunatic. And Shelley may have created the mystery to hide
a debt to Byron, whose *Lament of Tasso* had been published
the previous year. Whether or not Tasso was his model, the
madman was a dangerous re-growth of that half-forgotten
hydra, the *Alastor*-type hero, and also a convenient mouthpiece for expressing his own distress at Clara's death.

Though the sadness in his household inevitably filtered
into his verse, Shelley did his best to argue himself out of its
toils in the *Lines written among the Euganean Hills* by musing
upon the islands of Delight which stud the sea of Misery:

> Many a green isle needs must be
> In the deep wide sea of Misery,
> Or the mariner, worn and wan,
> Never thus could voyage on —
> Day and night, and night and day,
> Drifting on his dreary way. . . .   554. 1-6

H

The islands are random, unexpected, and the voyager can do little to steer himself towards them : happiness foreseen is often illusory.

The Euganean Hills rise just north of Este, a mere hummock amid the vast expanse of the Po Valley. Shelley's metaphor is inspired by their situation, an island among the levels — and almost a real island when the Po floods set in — but he does not fully exploit the comparison. More to his purpose is the view from the hills. For, after working off his fit of depression in the first sixty-five lines, he is ready to accept Nature's bounty as he watches the sunrise from his vantage point :

> Beneath is spread like a green sea
> The waveless plain of Lombardy,
> Bounded by the vaporous air,
> Islanded by cities fair ;
> Underneath Day's azure eyes
> Ocean's nursling, Venice lies,
> A peopled labyrinth of walls,
> Amphitrite's destined halls,
> Which her hoary sire now paves
> With his blue and beaming waves. . . .
> Column, tower, and dome, and spire,
> Shine like obelisks of fire,
> Pointing with inconstant motion
> From the altar of dark ocean
> To the sapphire-tinted skies. . . .
>
> 555. 90-9, 106-10

For Shelley, Venice was primarily a city of fiery reflexions, the product of a torrid sun playing on the water of the canals and the white pinnacled buildings. This same feature attracted Turner, and in his paintings we can best see Venice as Shelley saw it. The theme which stirred Byron and Wordsworth, the city's past glory, was for Shelley secondary.

Shelley stays on the hill-top till late in the morning, when a summery haze fills the air, though in places the leaves are still crisp with October frost. In the haze all Nature seems to coalesce about him, until the 'olive-sandalled

Apennine, in the south dimly islanded', the leaves at his feet, the vines, the very blades of grass, the distant snows of the Alps and his own spirit,

> which so long
> Darkened this swift stream of song,
> Interpenetrated lie
> By the glory of the sky.

557. 311-14

The effort of interpretation, with its fanciful fusion of human, vegetable and mineral, has rescued him from the sea of Agony, and now, letting the impetus of his wishful thinking master him, he ends the poem by transforming his metaphorical isle into a real one:

> Other flowering isles must be
> In the sea of Life and Agony:
> Other spirits float and flee
> O'er that gulf: even now, perhaps,
> On some rock the wild wave wraps,
> With folded wings they waiting sit
> For my bark, to pilot it
> To some calm and blooming cove,
> Where for me, and those I love,
> May a windless bower be built,
> Far from passion, pain, and guilt,
> In a dell mid lawny hills,
> Which the wild sea-murmur fills,
> And soft sunshine, and the sound
> Of old forests echoing round,
> And the light and smell divine
> Of all flowers that breathe and shine. . . .

558. 335-51

Here Shelley communicates the gist of one of those semi-mystical experiences before Nature which, as time wore on, he came to value more and more, both as a solace and as poetic material. His subjective record of what the Italian landscape meant to him is also an early example of the 'stream of consciousness'.

In this poem the words are simple, the meaning is plain and the details fit neatly. So we can savour the form and

texture of the verse, its rhythms and indeed its counterpoint,
for it has enough of music to remind us how closely Shelley
resembled Mozart in his liking for thin and fragile melodies
unrelated to the coarser fabric of everyday life. If we had
to choose similes, a single, sparkling river of melody would
fit Mozart and Shelley, because both rely so much on the
order of their phrases, while for Beethoven and Keats we
might choose a wide valley with a rich patchwork-quilt of
fields. Shelley liked Mozart's operas; yet it would be a
mistake to suppose that he learnt any technical tricks from
Mozart. For, though many of his own songs seem to invite
musical setting, Shelley never learnt an instrument and
remained a complete amateur in his appreciation of music.
In his poems he rarely refers to any musical instruments
except the lute and the harp, which are so hackneyed that
they often kill or at least maim any metaphor unlucky enough
to contain them. If those nights at the Opera in 1817 and
1818 left a mark, it was by plucking some chord deep in his
unconscious, and releasing latent energies he himself hardly
recognized.

In the *Lines written among the Euganean Hills*, a simple
metre, basically seven syllables with four stresses, is made to
express every mood from joy to despair, from calm to
tumult. The changes in stress, which often go with the
changes in mood, prevent the poem from slipping into a
sprightly measure, like *L'Allegro*, or a mechanical sing-song,
like *Hiawatha*. With lines so short and metre so simple, more
strain is thrown on the individual words, and the poem is
sufficiently unspecialized to give a fair picture of Shelley's
vocabulary. We notice at once in the *Euganean Hills* a habit
which was to grow on him, the use of compound adjectives:
olive-sandalled Apennines, *sapphire-tinted* skies, *harvest-shining*
plain, *tempest-cleaving* swan. He was just as fond of long
adjectives with Latin prefixes, like *interpenetrated, unpremeditated, antenatal* and the Miltonic *interlunar*. All this
is plain enough. What is not so easy to decide is whether
Shelley's vocabulary is unduly restricted. This question is
pertinent, because many readers think they can recognize

Shelley at once, merely by the kind of words he uses, and some critics, such as F. R. Leavis and Donald Davie, have accused him of overworking his 'pet' words. Dr. Leavis's list of fifteen such words was rather wide of the mark, since Shelley uses six of them less than twenty times. But even if we chose a better list we should still not know whether the words were really overworked, because there is no proper mathematical theory of literary vocabulary. G. U. Yule, in his pioneer textbook on the subject, *The Statistical Study of Literary Vocabulary* (1944), isolated and analysed the many traps for the unwary, which scholars innocent of mathematics continually fall into. But he found the mathematical theory rather intractable, chiefly because an author's total vocabulary remains unknown. A better mathematical framework may soon emerge, however, as a by-product of work on the use of computers for translation.[11]

4

In the months which Shelley spent near Venice and Este, September and October 1818, he wrote two poems with a strong local flavour, *Julian and Maddalo* and the *Euganean Hills*. He also began work on a poem of wider scope, the lyrical drama *Prometheus Unbound*. Only Act I was written at Este, and fourteen months were to pass before the poem was finished.

At the end of October the time came for handing Allegra back to Byron, and the Shelleys began a slow journey by road to their chosen winter-quarters at Naples. Stopping *en route* at Ferrara, where they inspected the relics of Tasso and Ariosto, and at Bologna, where they found much to admire in the art galleries, they arrived in Rome on 20 November. Shelley, going on alone to look for lodgings in Naples, had an unpleasant preview of local customs. As his coach entered the city a man was murdered in the street a few yards away. This alone was more than enough to upset Shelley; but even worse was the attitude of his fellow-passenger, a priest, who laughed at him for worrying over such a trifle. This incident seems to have cast a shadow over the whole of their three-month stay in Naples. When not kept in by illness they would go on sightseeing tours, but they often came back more disgusted by the squalor than impressed by the sights.

Shelley disliked many of the Italian cities, but the country's scenery, architectural relics and art galleries made their mark on him, as his letters show. For now, cut off from his friends in England, he regaled them by post with detailed travelogues, in which art and scenic beauty share first place. Peacock received a series of letters from Italy which are unsurpassed as descriptive pieces. The most favoured of his other correspondents were Mr. and Mrs. Gisborne, Ollier his publisher, Leigh Hunt, Godwin and that most faithful of friends Horace Smith.

Shelley is not among the great letter-writers, because he lacked their talent for gossip and their desire to broadcast their experiences. Nevertheless, Matthew Arnold once paid him a double-edged compliment by remarking that 'his delightful Essays and Letters' would 'finally come to stand higher than his poetry'.[12] Arnold probably liked his letters for their cool and careful style : Shelley was never slack in his standards, and he kept emotion out. What is missing in his letters is the continuous personal touch. When he does speak of himself, the result is not Byron's sparkling cynicism but a self-conscious introspective analysis, of more interest to a biographer than to readers seeking entertainment. Among the most interesting of his letters are those to his publisher, Ollier, for they show us Shelley the business man, schooled in long years of negotiation with moneylenders. In these lucid and efficient directives he pays scrupulous attention to detail, taking great care to allow for the possibility of packages being lost in the post. It is in these letters, too, that he gives his own opinion of each poem as it goes to Ollier ; and he tantalizes us by offhand references to his lyrics, which he was apt to regard as mere padding for his slender volumes of verse. Those volumes were sent regularly to eight people : Hunt, Peacock, Horace Smith, Godwin,

Keats, Byron, Hogg and Moore.[13]   It is a laughably ill-
assorted group — a good house-party for one of Peacock's
novels — yet all its members, except possibly Hogg, enjoy a
meed of literary renown in their own right.   Though, of
course, Shelley didn't choose them with an eye on posterity,
his choice speaks well for his judgement.   Not many writers to-
day would be able to name, even by accident, eight among
their circle of friends who will be remembered in 2100.

It is in his letters, too, that his new interest in architecture, painting and sculpture chiefly emerges.   Often he
contents himself with graphic descriptions of the works of
art he saw and these are excellent.   When he begins to
interpret and criticize, he at once exposes what can best be
called a Platonic bias.   He expected a painter to represent
ideal beauty incarnate, and, since he equated ideal beauty
with a smooth finish, he was better pleased by Raphael than
by Michelangelo, who let tortured undercurrents interfere
with what Shelley considered his proper task.   After seeing
the 'Day of Judgement' in the Sistine Chapel, he remarked
that Michelangelo had 'no sense of beauty'.   Though
Shelley professed to despise current taste, he inevitably
reflected it because his own theories of art were half-formed,
and apart from his Platonic foible he was conventional in his
judgements.   Thus when we find him giving the seventeenth-
century Bolognese school — Caravaggio, Guido Reni, Dome-
nichino and the Caracci — a place equal to, or higher
than, the masters of Florence and Venice, an appropriate
gloss is the statement in Reynolds's second Discourse that
Ludovico Caracci came the nearest of any artist to perfection
in style.[14]   When viewing sculpture Shelley's bias is Hellenic
rather than Platonic.   His veneration for the fragments of
Greek sculpture is reminiscent of the early Renaissance.   In
his *Notes on Sculptures in Rome and Florence*, a statue of classical
origin evokes a detailed panegyric, and no breath of censure
pollutes the air until he returns to the work of the native
Italians.   Since Shelley is never likely to be acclaimed as an
art critic, there is no need to give further details of his
Notes.   What is important is that as a result of this new

interest and experience he was looking on Nature with
more of an artist's eye. As he said in a letter to Peacock,
'You know not how delicate the imagination becomes by
dieting with antiquity day after day'.[15]

Shelley's art criticism is typical of those fits of conventionality which stand out as isles of calm in the troubled
sea of his rebellion, to use his own metaphor. Poetic technique is another of these isles, for Shelley was not one of the
great innovators, like Wordsworth, nor was he out of the
main stream, like Blake. The pattern made by these islands
of calm is easy to decipher. Shelley was unconventional in
manners and morals because he revolted against dogma
forced down his throat as a child. His antipathies reflect the
interests of the society he grew up in. It was lucky that Sir
Timothy preferred Paley to Wordsworth, and that the
Sussex gentry valued hunting and politics more than art and
poetry.

Shelley was sad and lonely at Naples, if the poems he
wrote there are any guide. When misfortune came, Mary
would withdraw to brood alone. It was in this, if in anything, that she failed Shelley as a wife, for he soon suc-
cumbed to despair when there was no one to rally him.
The best he could do then was to remind himself of Mary's
unique virtue : she was the sole descendant of William
Godwin and Mary Wollstonecraft. Such cold logic may
have given their marriage a latent strength, but it was a
poor substitute for a cheerful Mary. Shelley's fits of sadness are not wholly to be deplored, however, for some of his
most haunting poems sprang from despair observed. In
particular, there are the *Stanzas written in Dejection near Naples*,
with the reluctant theme, 'I am one whom men love not'.
Again he looks to natural beauty to distract him from his
black humours, even if it cannot dispel them :

> I see the Deep's untrampled floor
>   With green and purple seaweeds strown ;
> I see the waves upon the shore,
>   Like light dissolved in star-showers, thrown. . . .

It was natural that the submarine growths he had seen in the pellucid waters of the Bay of Naples should figure in the poem. But underwater vegetation had begun to fascinate him, and soon grew into one of his favourite images. Sea flowers appeared in the *Euganean Hills*, and there is more underwater scenery in the *Ode to the West Wind, Sensitive Plant, Prometheus Unbound, Ode to Liberty, Ode to Naples* and *Recollection*.[16] The present interest in undersea exploration reminds us that this is one of several modern pastimes and sciences which Shelley foresaw in imagination.

As he sits by the shore he contrasts everyone else's happiness with his own despair and regrets he is so restless, envying the tranquil man — like Socrates, whose vigil before Potidaea fascinated him.

> Alas! I have nor hope nor health,
>   Nor peace within nor calm around,
> Nor that content surpassing wealth
>   The sage in meditation found,
>   And walked with inward glory crowned —
> Nor fame, nor power, nor love, nor leisure.
>   Others I see whom these surround —
> Smiling they live, and call life pleasure ; —
> To me that cup has been dealt in another measure.
>
> 561. 19-27

These lines mark the nadir of this winter of his discontent.

A less gloomy poem is *The Woodman and the Nightingale*,[17] a delicate fragment in defence of birds and dryads. First, seeking parallels for the nightingale's song, Shelley unleashes a chaotic pack of sense-images. Then, in a pantheistic tribute to the magic of a leafy wood in summer, he pretends that all lively Nature, whether plant, insect, wave or wind, listens rapt to the nightingale. Only the brutish Woodman is deaf to her music :

> this man returned with axe and saw
> At evening close from killing the tall treen,
> The soul of whom by Nature's gentle law
> Was each a wood-nymph, and kept ever green

> The pavement and the roof of the wild copse,
> Chequering the sunlight of the blue serene
> With jaggèd leaves. . . .
>
> 563. 40-6

Shelley's theme, suggested perhaps by Coleridge's *Raven*, seems at first to be a variation on 'Woodman, spare that tree'. But there is a sting in the tail, where he suddenly widens the scope of his argument. He has unconsciously been projecting his own personality into the nightingale's:

> The world is full of Woodmen who expel
> Love's gentle Dryads from the haunts of life,
> And vex the nightingales in every dell.
>
> 564. 68-70

At the end of February 1819 the Shelleys returned from Naples to Rome, where Shelley at once responded to spring's approach by setting to work again on *Prometheus Unbound*. He tells us in the preface that he wrote Acts II and III at Rome during March and April, in the open air 'upon the mountainous ruins of the Baths of Caracalla, among the flowery glades, and thickets of odoriferous blossoming trees, which are extended in ever winding labyrinths upon its immense platforms and dizzy arches suspended in the air'. Rome's blue sky gave no hint of a noisome cloud already on its way. The successive deaths of Fanny Godwin, Harriet and Clara had shown him how frail was life's tenure within his family circle. Fate's next blow fell early in June, when Mary's only surviving child, the 3-year-old William, died after a few days' illness. Mary was utterly disconsolate for a month or two, and again she seems to have withdrawn into a private world of woe. This time, however, Shelley himself was more resilient. In May he had begun work on his drama *The Cenci*, and he returned to it after a short break, in desperation perhaps, but with unflagging vigour. For he had entered upon his *annus mirabilis* of poetic creation.

It is fruitless to look for a rational explanation of Shelley's prodigious output between March 1819 and August 1820. We may mutter 'thyroid-pituitary personality', but that really tells us nothing, for glandular analysis, like its illegiti-

mate cousin psychoanalysis, shies away before the idea of
quality, reducing genius and nonentity to the same level,
and so obscuring the very thing we want to see explained.

We might just as well attribute Shelley's outburst to a
certain something in the air at the time, for no four-year
period in English literary history bore so splendid a crop
as the years 1818–21. During these four years Shelley and
Keats produced nearly all the poems for which they are remembered, and Byron wrote the best part of his *chef-d'œuvre
Don Juan*, plus many other pot-boilers and best-sellers.
Wordsworth, Blake, Clare, Moore, Landor, Campbell,
Crabbe and the Laureate Southey were foremost among
other active poets; supreme among the silent ones —
silent, that is, on paper — stood Coleridge, though he could
have pointed to the *Christabel* volume of 1816 and the *Biographia Literaria* of 1817 had anyone dared to scold him for
low productivity. The great trio of essayists, Hazlitt, Lamb
and Hunt, were at their best. De Quincey's *Confessions of an
English Opium Eater* were appearing in the short-lived
London Magazine, which also boasted Miss Mitford's sketches
later collected in *Our Village*, and essays from Lamb and
Hazlitt. Scott regaled his huge public with eight novels in
these four years, including some of his most famous — *Kenil-
worth, The Heart of Midlothian, Ivanhoe* and *The Legend of
Montrose*. Peacock continued his lively series of conversation-
pieces with his most pointed satire on the Romantic poets,
and on Shelley in particular, *Nightmare Abbey*. Maturin's
Melmoth, perhaps the finest of Gothic novels, came out in
1820 and Galt's *Annals of the Parish* in 1821, while 1818 was
the great year for women novelists, with the publication of
Jane Austen's *Persuasion* and *Northanger Abbey*, Susan Ferrier's
Marriage and Mary Shelley's *Frankenstein*. Several other
writers outside the usual cliques deserve a mention: Landor,
living at Pisa and deterred from visiting Shelley by malicious
scandal, began his *Imaginary Conversations*; Cobbett made
the first of his *Rural Rides*; Bentham, with whom Peacock
dined weekly for many years,[18] was quietly abetting the
political aims of the 'literary' radicals; his friend James

Mill, whom Peacock was to succeed as Examiner of Correspondence at India House, published his *History of British India* and *Elements of Political Economy*; and the economist among the Utilitarians, Ricardo, was gaining great prestige with his theories.

This 'spirit in the air' seems to have affected other arts too. The greatest of English painters, Turner, visited Italy in 1820, often following in Shelley's footsteps, and there began evolving the technique he perfected in old age, a technique unknowingly summed up by Shelley in *Julian and Maddalo*:

> as if the Earth and Sea had been
> Dissolved into one lake of fire.

191. 80-1

Constable, too, was at the height of his powers,[19] and the list of other artists admired then or now includes Blake, Bonington, Cotman, Cox, Crome, De Wint, Fuseli, Haydon, Lawrence, Linnell, Raeburn, Rowlandson and Wilkie. The most spectacular product of Regency architecture, John Nash's Royal Pavilion, was taking its final shape at Brighton, while the soberer façades of his planned new London were materializing. And in the theatres of the capital, great players trod the boards — Kean, Kemble, Macready and Mrs. Siddons.

It is a time apt to rouse the enthusiasm of historians. 'The men of that day seemed to inhale vigour and genius with the island air', as G. M. Trevelyan put it in his *History of England*.[20] This is the background to bear in mind as we watch Shelley writing a new page in English literary annals.

NOTES TO V: ITALY

1. See *New Shelley Letters*, p. 107.
2. *Letters* ii. 3.
3. G. Saintsbury, *Cambridge History of English Literature*, xi. 294.
4. *Letters* ii. 114.
5. See J. A. Notopoulos, *The Platonism of Shelley*, pp. 399–401.
6. Quotations from Shelley's *Discourse on the Manners of the Ancients. Jul* vii. 223–8.

7. See, e.g., H. D. F. Kitto, *The Greeks* (1951), pp. 219–36; and C. Seltman, *Women in Antiquity* (1956), pp. 93–119.

8. The limited *Julian* edition (1926–9) was the first to give the full text of both. They can also be found (with many notes, and Shelley's other translations from Plato), in J. A. Notopoulos, *The Platonism of Shelley*, pp. 376–603. The Nonesuch edition of 1951 gives the complete *Symposium*, and the bowdlerized version of the essay.

9. *Jul* vii. 192.

10. The case for Tasso is argued by C. Baker, *Shelley's Major Poetry*, pp. 127–135.

11. See G. Herdan, *Language as Choice and Chance* (Noordhof, Groningen, 1956); J. Leed (ed.), *The Computer and Literary Style* (Kent Univ. Press, Ohio, 1966); and C. B. Williams, *Style and Vocabulary* (Griffin, 1970).

12. M. Arnold, *Essays in Criticism*, second series, Byron.

13. *Letters* ii. 118.

14. Sir J. Reynolds, *Discourses* (Seeley, London, 1905), p. 29. See p. 200 for his valuation of the Bolognese and Venetian schools.

15. *Letters* ii. 88.

16. *Euganean Hills*, ll. 129–30; *West Wind*, 38–41; *Sensitive Plant*, 592–8; *Prometheus Unbound*, II, ii. 72–3; *Ode to Liberty*, 54; *Ode to Naples*, 28–31; *Recollection*, 31–2.

17. N. Rogers, *Shelley at Work*, p. 263, suggests that this poem belongs to 1821. See I. Massey, *Posthumous Poems of Shelley*, pp. 98–107, for collation of the manuscripts and texts.

18. C. van Doren, *Life of T. L. Peacock*, p. 147.

19. See C. R. Leslie, *Memoirs of the Life of John Constable* (Phaidon, 1951), p. 72.

20. G. M. Trevelyan, *History of England* (3rd edition), p. 508.

A map of Italy, showing places associated with Shelley, appears on page 373.

VI

THE CENCI

In cancred malice and revengefull spight.

SPENSER, *Faerie Queene*

1

By the summer of 1819 the round of sightseeing was over. In Shelley's three remaining years of life the ferment of continual travel is stilled at last. Apart from a brief visit to Ravenna, he kept within a radius of fifty miles from Pisa, living at Leghorn, Florence, Pisa itself and Lerici. Shelley and Mary had intended to leave Rome in the summer of 1819, because Mary was expecting a baby in the autumn and they knew of only one good doctor, who would then be at Florence. William's death hastened their departure to Tuscany, and in mid-June they moved to Leghorn, where they rented a pleasant house a little way out of the town, the Villa Valsovano. At the top of the house Shelley found an ideal study, very small and more a glass-covered terrace than a room. The confined space became unbearably hot to all but Shelley, who with his 'salamander's temperament'[1] basked happily in the sun. As Browning noted long ago, he was a 'sun-treader', often in his poems equating heat with pleasure, and ice with pain.

Mary's distress at losing William was aggravated by letters from her father, who rebuked her for not meeting misfortune like a philosopher. Godwin also asked her to extort even more money from 'that disgraceful and flagrant person'[2] her husband. These abusive demands may not have seemed quite so ungracious then as they do now, because there was a convention that men acclaimed as leaders in art or thought need not bother about money.

Coleridge and Haydon, for example, relied on friends and providence, though Haydon was artless enough to admit that sponging was 'a fallacious principle and one I deprecate in all other cases but my own'.[3] Godwin himself was eventually given a sinecure by the Whigs in 1833, and ended his days at New Palace Yard, Westminster, as a yeoman usher of the Exchequer.

In October 1819 the Shelleys moved from Leghorn to Florence, 'the most beautiful city I ever saw'[4]. Mary's baby, a boy, was born there on 12 November. He was christened Percy Florence: his parents were not to know that Florence would be popularized as a girl's name by the Miss Nightingale who was born there six months later. Percy Florence managed to escape the Italian graves of his brother and sister, and he inherited the Shelley baronetcy when Sir Timothy died in 1844.

2

As he roasted in his eyrie at the Villa Valsovano during June and July 1819, Shelley wrote the greater part of his only completed play for the stage, *The Cenci*, a five-act tragedy in blank verse. The very existence of *The Cenci* causes a slight shock of surprise, for he had previously been rather hostile to the theatre. He once spoke of 'the withering and perverting spirit of comedy', and he felt an actor's character must suffer through continually repressing his own personality, an attitude probably learnt from Godwin. Robust English fun — laughing at someone else's downfall or loss of dignity — did not much appeal to him, because he saw the cruel before the comic. He would rather, like Aristotle, have emphasized that comedy exposed a deformity, harmless but still ugly, than have admitted that ridiculing 'the absurdity of the imperfect' could help 'to glorify the perfect'.[5] When Peacock took him to see *The School for Scandal* he was not amused :

When, after the scenes which exhibited Charles Surface in his jollity, the scene returned, in the fourth act, to Joseph's library, Shelley said to me : 'I see the purpose of this comedy. It is to associate virtue with bottles and glasses, and villainy with books.' I had great difficulty to make him stay to the end.[6]

As he matured Shelley became more tolerant of the theatre, as of other institutions, but the relics of his early distaste lingered. He cast several of his later poems in dramatic guise ; but they can be performed only in the theatre of the mind.

In language, as in form, *The Cenci* is more of a *tour de force* than a logical step forward. Those digressions on natural beauty, which had adorned all his poems since *Alastor*, are missing. Nor does the play conform to any party line, political or metaphysical. For he was breaking new ground, by presenting a conflict of the human will, played out in an atmosphere thick with the primitive emotions of fear, hate and love, and so concentrated in its action that doctrine was out of place. He gained much from his attempt, for behind the outward display of mere versatility lay a new concern with dramatic values, such as sustaining tension and making the dialogue plausible. He took pains, too, with the narrative and pruned his style, avoiding ornate images and exploiting the technique of understatement so dear to the English. The purging of language was indeed so thorough that Keats, on reading *The Cenci*, offered Shelley some rather dangerous advice: 'load every rift of your subject with ore'.

These unShelleyan qualities of *The Cenci* suggest, rightly, that some unusual stimulus was acting. At Leghorn during the previous summer Shelley came across an Italian manuscript which purported to tell how the noble family of Cenci had fallen into ruin at the end of the sixteenth century, and he thought the tale interesting enough to have it copied. At Rome everyone seemed to know the story, as if, like a Greek myth, it appealed to something in man's collective unconscious. He then saw that it might make a popular play : the very rag-and-bone men with their cries of '*cenci! cenci!*' could advertise it. His interest quickened when he visited the ruins of the Cenci Palace for local colour, and, above all, when he stood in the Barberini Palace before the portrait of Beatrice Cenci attributed to Guido Reni, a portrait which some years later was to appeal just as strongly to Stendhal and to Dickens. Shelley did not stop to ask whether manuscript or portrait was authentic : he was writing a tragedy not a history. In fact, the portrait is not of Beatrice and probably not by Guido, and the manuscript was inaccurate.

The true story is as follows. Beatrice's grandfather, Cristoforo Cenci, was treasurer-general of the Apostolic Chamber and took his chances to embezzle the Pope's moneys. He died in 1562, leaving his illegitimate son Francesco, born 1549, as his wealthy heir. Francesco grew up violent and lustful : he would beat servants almost to death for trivial errors. As a result of these and other peccadilloes, such as sodomy and murder, he was often in prison, and his money gradually returned to the Papal coffers in the form of huge fines. Cenci was married before he was 14, and among his twelve legitimate children were Giacomo (born 1568), Beatrice (1577) and Bernardo (1581). After the death of his first wife he married again, in 1593. In 1595 he took his wife, Lucretia, and his 18-year-old daughter Beatrice to the remote castle of Petrella and locked them up. When Beatrice, chafing at this captivity, wrote asking friends in Rome to help free her, she was flogged by her father. Soon afterwards Olympio Calvetti, seneschal of the castle, became Beatrice's lover. In 1598, at her instigation, and with the assent of Giacomo and Lucretia, Olympio and Marzio Catalano killed her father with a hatchet and flung his body from a balcony to simulate an accident. Suspicion soon grew, however, and after many months of questioning and torture the truth came out. Marzio died in prison, having admitted his guilt ; Olympio was murdered before he could be arrested. At the trial Beatrice's counsel charged her father with incest. Nevertheless the Pope had Beatrice, Lucretia and Giacomo executed in 1599, and confiscated the Cenci estates.[7]

Shelley did not know the true story. In the manuscript

I

version on which he based his play, the incest is accepted
and many details are erroneous. When it suited him he
altered the details, using other versions of the story which he
heard in Rome; but since these versions were just as inaccurate the alterations rarely brought him nearer the truth.

3

The first line of *The Cenci*, prosaic and melodramatic —

> That matter of the murder is hushed up —

warns us at once of the change in Shelley's style. The
murder referred to is one of Count Cenci's, and as the play
opens he is listening to Cardinal Camillo:

> *Camillo.* That matter of the murder is hushed up
> If you consent to yield his Holiness
> Your fief that lies beyond the Pincian gate.
> It needed all my interest in the conclave
> To bend him to this point: he said that you
> Bought perilous impunity with your gold;
> That crimes like yours if once or twice compounded
> Enriched the Church, and respited from hell
> An erring soul which might repent and live: —
> But that the glory and the interest
> Of the high throne he fills, little consist
> With making it a daily mart of guilt. . . .
>
> 279. 1-12

— a fair sample of the play's conversational blank verse.
After this, Shelley points out Cenci's faults, obliquely at first
and then in their full enormity:

> *Cenci.* All men delight in sensual luxury,
> All men enjoy revenge; and most exult
> Over the tortures they can never feel —
> Flattering their secret peace with others' pain.
> But I delight in nothing else. . . .
>
> 280. 77-81.

The scene ends with hints of his designs against his daughter
Beatrice, who is introduced in the second scene as a gentle,
submissive, friendless girl, fiercely loyal to her brothers and

her step-mother Lucretia. We see her rejecting lukewarm
offers of help from Orsino, a worldly prelate who is broad-
minded enough to condone her father :

> Old men are testy and will have their way ;
> A man may stab his enemy, or his vassal,
> And live a free life as to wine or women,
> And with a peevish temper may return
> To a dull home, and rate his wife and children ;
> Daughters and wives call this foul tyranny.
>
> 284. 74-9

In scene iii Count Cenci is the urbane host, welcoming the
noblemen of Rome to a grand banquet. When he jovially
declares that the banquet is to celebrate the accidental deaths
of two of his sons in Spain, the guests are shocked into
protest. But none dares respond when Beatrice pleads to
be rescued from her father's clutches. As a boy Shelley had
revelled in *Macbeth*'s witches and ghosts, and we find him
resurrecting situations in *Macbeth* (though not the words)
when Cenci's feast dissolves in most admired disorder and,
after the feast, when Cenci screws his courage to the sticking-
place to perform his deed without a name — the raping of
Beatrice, which is in fact delayed until Act III.

Act II shows us the Cenci family at home, with Beatrice
and her young brother Bernardo refusing to desert their
timid step-mother Lucretia, Cenci's second wife. Beatrice's
eldest brother Giacomo, who has been robbed by his father,
appeals to the Pope for redress. But the Pope, determined
on 'blameless neutrality', chooses to see both sides of the
quarrel and thinks it dangerous to weaken paternal power,
'being, as 'twere, the shadow of his own'. The long-
suffering Giacomo, stung to action at last, cautiously sounds
Orsino about murdering Cenci. This fits in with Orsino's
own schemes, for he tells us in a soliloquy that he loves
Beatrice, rather against his will, but cannot win her unless
Cenci is removed.

When Act III begins Cenci has had his way with
Beatrice, who enters hysterical. On recovering she thinks
only of revenge. Cenci has planned to go with Beatrice

and Lucretia to the castle of Petrella, some forty miles north-
east of Rome, deep among the mountains.   Beatrice plots
with Orsino to have him killed *en route* and she at once hits
on the spot for the ambush, a point where the road crosses a
deep ravine.   This is the signal for the only digression in the
play, the section beginning

> there is a mighty rock,
> Which has, from unimaginable years,
> Sustained itself with terror and with toil
> Over a gulf, and with the agony
> With which it clings seems slowly coming down. . . .
>
> 302. 247-51

The ambush miscarries; but Cenci will not long be safe
within Petrella, for Beatrice has suborned two ruffians to
murder him.

The scene shifts to Petrella, where Cenci is enjoying his
last moments of power.   Lucretia, knowing his hour is near,
tries, like a good Catholic, to make him repent; but he flies
into a fury, and orders Beatrice to come to him.   When she
refuses he curses her luridly in words recalling Lear's.   Next
we watch the murderers Olympio and Marzio plucking up
courage.   When they go in to do the deed, Beatrice and
Lucretia remain below, listening intently, like Lady Macbeth.
Just as Beatrice is rewarding the murderers with a bag of
gold, a trumpet sounds and the drawbridge is lowered, as if
to parallel the knocking in *Macbeth*.   The visitor is the
Papal legate Savella, with a warrant for Cenci's arrest, and
like Macduff he arrives to stumble on murder.   As she
awaits the hue and cry Beatrice remains unwaveringly
defiant, convinced that the revenge was just.   The echoes
from *Macbeth* continue:

> *Beatrice.*   The deed is done,
> And what may follow now regards not me.
> I am as universal as the light;
> Free as the earth-surrounding air; as firm
> As the world's centre.   Consequence, to me,
> Is as the wind which strikes the solid rock
> But shakes it not.
>
> 316. 46-52

When the assassin Marzio is captured, still clutching his gold, suspicion quickly falls on Beatrice and Lucretia. They are arrested and taken to Rome.

In Act V, which Mary in her Note called 'the finest thing he ever wrote', Shelley first lets Orsino flee the country, and then proceeds to the *pièce de résistance* — Beatrice's trial. She is arraigned with her mother and brothers before a Papal Court presided over by Camillo. Marzio confesses under torture, and the chief judge, remarking 'this sounds as bad as truth', calls in Beatrice. She does not at once deny her guilt. Instead she tries to undermine the Court's authority by exposing the barbarity of its methods :

> Cardinal Camillo,
> You have a good repute for gentleness
> And wisdom : can it be that you sit here
> To countenance a wicked farce like this ?
> When some obscure and trembling slave is dragged
> From sufferings which might shake the sternest heart
> And bade to answer, not as he believes,
> But as those may suspect or do desire
> Whose questions thence suggest their own reply . . .
> . . . Speak now
> The thing you surely know, which is that you,
> If your fine frame were stretched upon that wheel . . .
> . . . would say, 'I confess anything' :
> And beg from your tormentors, like that slave,
> The refuge of dishonourable death.
>
> 323. 35-43, 45-7, 55-7

Camillo is moved, and Marzio recants his confession. But the other judges vote for the procedure then usual in this most Christian of courts —

> Let tortures strain the truth till it be white
> As snow thrice sifted by the frozen wind.
>
> 326. 169-70

Beatrice endures the tortures, having convinced herself that she has nothing to confess ; the others admit their guilt. Camillo intercedes for the prisoners, only to be told by the Pope why the death sentences on Beatrice, Lucretia and Giacomo must be confirmed :

> Parricide grows so rife
> That soon, for some just cause no doubt, the young
> Will strangle us all, dozing in our chairs.
> Authority, and power, and hoary hair
> Are grown crimes capital.
>
> 331. 20-4

Beatrice believed God would recognize her essential innocence and arrange for a last-minute reprieve. When all hope
is gone she has a moment of despair; but she recovers her
poise before the guards come in for the last time, and bids
farewell calmly to her young brother Bernardo and her step-
mother:

> One thing more, my child:
> For thine own sake be constant to the love
> Thou bearest us; and to the faith that I,
> Though wrapped in a strange cloud of crime and shame,
> Lived ever holy and unstained. And though
> Ill tongues shall wound me, and our common name
> Be as a mark stamped on thine innocent brow
> For men to point at as they pass, do thou
> Forbear, and never think a thought unkind
> Of those, who perhaps love thee in their graves. . . .
>
> Here, Mother, tie
> My girdle for me, and bind up this hair
> In any simple knot; ay, that does well.
> And yours I see is coming down. How often
> Have we done this for one another; now
> We shall not do it any more. My Lord,
> We are quite ready. Well, 'tis very well.
>
> 334. 145-54, 159-65

4

The Cenci was one of the very few poems Shelley wrote with
an eye to popularity. Though he cared nothing for popular
success, he could not help being dismayed by the fact that
none of his poems had sold more than a handful of copies,
and he decided in *The Cenci* to accept current conventions.
Unfortunately 'the Spirit of the Age', usually so helpful, let
him down, for the theatrical conventions he accepted were

stultifying. Melodramas and farces were most popular with theatregoers, and the journeymen who concocted these cheapened the dramatist's prestige. So most of the Romantic poets, on turning to drama, saw not a new discipline but a rather unworthy field for their imaginations to run riot in. The result was Coleridge's *Remorse*, Wordsworth's *Borderers*, Byron's *Marino Faliero* and *Sardanapalus*, and Keats's *Otho*, all of which sport simple chivalrous heroes and deep-dyed villains, and pay scant attention to dramatic values. From these we turn with relief to *The Cenci*, for Shelley avoided their grosser errors. He realized, as they did not, that inspiration was not enough, and he imposed on himself a severe discipline, which, though it may not to our eyes seem a wholly valid one, was much better than none at all. He had a genuinely tragic story to tell, and he was ready to submit his poetic talents both to the discipline and to the needs of the story. The result is that *The Cenci* stands head and shoulders above all the other plays of its time. It is perhaps the best serious English play written between 1790 and 1890. But what is its status in the wider world of drama?

Knowing Shelley, we might begin by looking for flaws in the structure. It is true that after introducing the cast deftly in Act I, he dithers in Act II, most of which could well be cut; but after that every scene furthers the plot, and he is obviously taking care to unfold the narrative coherently. The plot includes murder, incest and torture, and, to avoid repugnant scenes like the putting out of Gloucester's eyes in *Lear*, some of the action has to be reported. Shelley recognized this, but he pushed the process too far: everything happens behind the scenes. His ignorance of the theatre is to blame for this and for most of the play's other defects. The scene-changes are too frequent; the speeches are over-long; there are more soliloquies than in *Hamlet*; too much of the talk is between two persons only and not enough is the cut and thrust of real conversation. Shelley was eking out the little he knew of theatrical technique by borrowing from the Elizabethan dramatists, among whom he had read widely, and sometimes from the Greek dramatists. For the frequent scene-changes and the soliloquies we can blame the Elizabethans (though our present aversion to these two techniques may be only a passing phase in sensibility). Long speeches and few characters on-stage are the mark of the Greek tragedians, Aeschylus in particular. *The Cenci* has the primary tragic requirements, the sense of inevitability, tension and characters of tragic stature; but its borrowed technique robs it of subsidiary dramatic qualities and hampers its success as an acting play.

Shelley deliberately soaked himself in the atmosphere of Elizabethan drama, and it is no surprise to find him duplicating several of Shakespeare's situations and occasionally rephrasing his very words. When his own mind was blank, Shelley seems to have filled the vacuum by unconsciously recasting some half-remembered Shakespearean scene. This was unwise of him, for everyone knows Shakespeare: the earliest critics spotted the plagiarisms, though that did not prevent one modern critic, bent on revaluation, from discovering some of them again. Most of the parallel situations have already been mentioned: Cenci's murder and Duncan's; Beatrice's hardness after the murder and Lady Macbeth's before; Cenci's persecution of his children and Lear's *by* his; Cenci's curse on Beatrice and Lear's on Goneril; Beatrice's trial and Vittoria Corombona's in Webster's *White Devil*. In contrast, it is worth noting that Shelley wisely abandons the Elizabethan convention that a tragedy should end leaving the stage strewn with corpses.

The possible verbal echoes of Shakespeare in *The Cenci* number over twenty.[8] Of these some are clear echoes, others vague reverberations. The three examples which follow are intended as a fair selection. The first example, an obvious echo, is Beatrice's reaction to the death-sentence —

> My God! Can it be possible I have
> To die so suddenly? So young to go
> Under the obscure, cold, rotting, wormy ground!
> To be nailed down into a narrow place;
> To see no more sweet sunshine; hear no more

Blithe voice of living thing ; muse not again
Upon familiar thoughts, sad, yet thus lost —
How fearful! to be nothing! Or to be . . .
What? Oh, where am I? Let me not go mad !
Sweet Heaven, forgive weak thoughts! If there should be
No God, no Heaven, no Earth in the void world ;
The wide, gray, lampless, deep, unpeopled world! —

331. 48-59

which resembles Claudio's in *Measure for Measure* :

Ay, but to die, and go we know not where ;
To lie in cold obstruction and to rot ;
This sensible warm motion to become
A kneaded clod ; and the delighted spirit
To bathe in fiery floods, or to reside
In thrilling region of thick-ribbed ice ;
To be imprisoned in the viewless winds,
And blown with restless violence round about
The pendent world ; or to be worse than worst
Of those that lawless and incertain thought
Imagine howling : — 'tis too horrible !

III. i. 119-29

Though there are only three significant words in common, the same tone permeates both. We should not be misled into comparing the two passages, for Shakespeare is at his best and Shelley at his worst because the writing is not spontaneous. The second example, a typical one, is Cenci's threat —

cross not my footsteps. It were safer
To come between the tiger and his prey —

312. 173-4

which is to be compared with Lear's injunction to Kent —

Come not between the dragon and his wrath —

Lear, I. i. 124

a line echoed, strangely enough, by Lear himself a minute or two later —

thou hast sought . . .
To come between our sentence and our power.

I. i. 168, 170

The third example, a dubious one, is Cenci's meditation —
> the charm works well;
> It must be done; it shall be done, I swear —
>
> 288. 177-8

which may echo two lines from *Macbeth*,

> Peace! the charm's wound up. . . .
> I go, and it is done.
>
> I. iii. 37; II. i. 62

Every writer, however independent, uses phrases which have lodged in his memory, and there is no disgrace in doing so, in moderation. Shelley does not go beyond moderation, for less than five per cent of the lines of the play are under suspicion, and even if all the Shakespearean echoes were clearly proven, which they are not, they would be only a minor flaw in a lasting structure, on a level with those in *Venice Preserved*.

It is easy to blame Shelley for writing in the Shakespearean blank verse which hamstrung all the nineteenth-century poet-dramatists. Had he not done so, however, he would have had to invent either a new dramatic idiom, like Ibsen, or a new language, like the poet-dramatists of our day. From start to finish, *The Cenci* kept him busy for less than three months. To create a new language and write a play in it so quickly is a tall order, and if he had tried devoting more time to it his patience would soon have been exhausted. As a result he was unable to practise the principles stated in his preface: 'in order to move men to true sympathy we must use the familiar language of men . . . it must be the real language of men in general and not that of any particular class to whose society the writer happens to belong'. Though thwarted in this aim, he did at least strive to make himself clear: this was a salutary discipline, for in *Alastor* and *The Revolt of Islam* he was concerned to express himself, caring little whether anyone understood; in *The Cenci* he was achieving clarity at the expense of self-expression; in some later poems he combined the two. If we accept the fact that he had to use blank verse, it is only fair to say how excellent that verse is. As well as being clear it is easy and supple, and laced with all his usual melodic tricks. The quality of the verse sets *The Cenci* above a play like Stephen Phillips's *Paolo and Francesca*, which it otherwise resembles both in its anachronistic technique and in its dark Italian theme.

It is a tribute to the power of the writing that Count Cenci, far from being a mere cardboard figure set up to be shied at, like Shelley's previous tyrants, is a man to be feared. His almost incredible cruelties could so easily have made us laugh, not shudder. Cenci is not a tragic figure, because his abnormal behaviour is not the result of normal human impulses warped by circumstance; he is set in his ways when the play begins. He resorts to physical cruelty less than when he was young. Instead he takes an artistic pleasure in torturing the minds of his victims. He wants to break Beatrice's will by forcing her to endure something invincibly repugnant. The incest is thus essentially irrelevant; any form of 'extreme mental cruelty' would do. No one can feel regret at Cenci's murder, but Shelley, like Shakespeare in *Julius Caesar*, has to find a new foil for the murderers, and the Papal judges he brings on are an anticlimax.

Beatrice is Shelley's first interesting piece of characterization. Many actresses have coveted the part, perhaps because it is one of the longest in English drama, the female counterpart of Hamlet, but more probably because the forced growth in her character, from the almost saintly girl of Act I to the determined liar of Act V, gives the actress plenty of scope. While her father lives, and the cloud of fear over the family darkens, Beatrice is coerced into murder. Once Cenci is dead, the stimulus distorting her judgement is removed and she sees she will be judged guilty by the world while remaining innocent in her own eyes. She grows a hard protective shell and represses compunctious visitings of nature. At times we may wish that she didn't forfeit our sympathy in Act V by her brazen lies. But if she had tried to justify her crime, Shelley would have had to weigh the rights and wrongs of it, thereby clouding the action with discussion, and reducing a tragic heroine to a mere disputant. His solution of the difficulty is probably the best. Because he avoids condoning the murder he can make Beatrice a genuine tragic figure instead of a plaster-saint, like Laon.

Shelley was also adding to his repertoire with Cardinal Camillo, the embodiment of merciful justice, who speaks for the 'gentle reader' in the last Act and performs the function of the Greek chorus by doing 'what any decent man would do in the circumstances'. He mediates between the prisoners and the Pope, who is shown as severe yet just. Because Camillo often reports his very words the Pope lives as a character, though he never appears in person. He, like Camillo, is portrayed fairly, even over-generously, for Clement VIII was not the saintliest of Popes and he dismally failed to live up to his name in the Cenci affair. It was widely believed that he got rid of Beatrice, Lucretia and Giacomo so that he could seize the Cenci estates, and it was not to his credit that he made Bernardo sit on the scaffold and watch the proceedings, which included the quartering of his brother Giacomo. In his *Queen Mab* days Shelley would have made religious capital out of this episode. In *The Cenci* he tactfully drops the curtain before the execution, and so shuts out the welter of dubious emotions aroused by such scenes. To set against Camillo and the Pope there is the worldly churchman, Orsino. His motive in plotting against Cenci is gain, not release from persecution. He is unworthy to share even the faint aura of martyrdom which hangs over Beatrice and her family. Shelley was probably wise to remove him, ignominiously and abruptly, at the start of Act V. Had he stayed to bear false witness against Beatrice he would have destroyed the judicial atmosphere which makes Act V so moving.

In throwing the spotlight on Beatrice, Shelley leaves the rest of her family in shadow, to point the contrast between her defiance and their resignation. The pious and con-ventional Lucretia, who seems always wringing her hands, the querulous weak-willed Giacomo and the young Bernardo never spring to life.

The changes Shelley made in adapting the manuscript version of the story show he was alert to dramatic values. He excludes some of the balder horrors, for in the manuscript version (though not in the true story) Beatrice has to watch Cenci's meetings with courtesans, and she kills him herself by driving nails into his head. Shelley also uses irony to give the facts more bite: *e.g.* one of the sons whose deaths are celebrated at Cenci's feast is, in the play, said to be killed by a church collapsing while he was at prayer. Shelley also plays tricks with Cenci's religion. The manuscript, whose author was pious, in a bloody-minded way, makes Cenci outwardly religious and at heart an atheist. Shelley may only be yielding to bias when he makes Cenci a believer, but Cenci's pride is then more plausible. God's ministers on earth merely fine him, so he expects the same treatment from those in the next world. Shelley makes Beatrice deeply religious, and her frequent appeals to God — a word which occurs eighty times in the play — have a flavour more Teutonic than Italian. Religion in Italy, Shelley emphasized in his preface, depended on piety and observing the ritual; it was a convention rather than a passion. Again dramatic effect has come before historical truth. Shelley also exploits the drama latent in the story. The move to the remote castle of Petrella, for example, sharply increases the tension, and, because Cenci wants to carry on his cruelties unseen, the move comes naturally — much more naturally than the miraculous eggs and changing wind in *Saint Joan*, a play by a master of theatrical technique.

Though the chief attraction of the Cenci story was that it might make a best-seller, Shelley may also have liked the way it fitted his favourite pattern of tyrant, slaves and resisting heroine. In *The Revolt of Islam* he seems to divide men into four categories: (1) the oppressor and his jackals; (2) the resistance movement; (3) the supine multitudes, easily swayed by demagogues; and (4) the impartial thinking minority, among whom he presumably included his readers. Though *The Cenci* is far more than an example to fit a theory, the same categories recur: for Cenci would fit in class (1); Beatrice and perhaps Giacomo in (2); the sheep-like Lucretia and Bernardo in (3); and Camillo, with the Pope, in (4).[9] Shelley would have been surprised to learn of this elaborate classification, and quite astonished probably to hear the suggestions that Beatrice is a self-portrait and Cenci a sublimation of his father-hatred. Such glib quarter-truths abound as explanations in Shelley criticism because so much is known of his life. Mary's daily entries in her journal are specially tempting. Her records of his reading, for example, are complete enough to ensure that few 'influences' have been missed; and how easy it is to imagine an influence when none exists. There is little danger of such a mistake with *The Cenci*, for the journal's list of thirty-six Elizabethan plays read by him amply confirms that his models were Shakespeare, Webster and Middleton. The only other influence worth mentioning is Calderón. Shelley had been introduced to the great Spanish dramatist by Mrs. Gisborne and was soon learning Spanish to read him. The description of the chasm in Act III of *The Cenci* is based on a passage in Calderón's *El Purgatorio de San Patricio*, as Shelley admits in his preface.

The reputation of *The Cenci* has had its ups and downs. Most of the reviewers condemned it, because it was by Shelley and about incest. But some of Shelley's closest friends, Hunt for example, and Mary, thought it his finest achievement. It was the first of his longer works to be accepted by the literary world, and most of the Victorian critics upheld Wordsworth's verdict, that it was 'the greatest tragedy of the age'.[10] From Charles Cowden Clarke's dithyrambics in 1836 to H. S. Salt's in 1887 the chorus of praise is almost unbroken.[11] At the end of the century the new outlook on drama promoted by Ibsen and Shaw brought hostile criticism. In 1908 came the excellent study by E. S. Bates, which subsequent outbursts from enthusiasts and debunkers have done nothing to discredit.[12]

The Cenci has not often been staged. Shelley hoped Beatrice would be played by Miss O'Neill, who was in 1819 the reigning queen of tragedy during Mrs. Siddons's semi-retirement; and he would have liked to see Kean as Count Cenci. In fact, the play was refused by the Covent Garden manager, and was not performed until May 1886, when the Shelley Society arranged a splendid private production with Alma Murray as Beatrice and Hermann Vezin as Cenci.[13] The enthusiasm of the invited audience was gratifying. But the newspaper critics did not approve, partly no doubt in reaction against the wild applause, and partly too because the performance lasted four hours. William Archer ended his notice in *The World* by saying: 'No one who reads *The Cenci* intelligently can doubt that there were in Shelley the makings of a dramatist; but after seeing it one has to read it over again to reassure oneself of the fact'. *The Cenci* next appeared on the London stage in 1922, at the New Theatre. Four successful performances were given, and after seeing Sybil Thorndike as Beatrice in the trial scene Bernard Shaw 'said he had found the actress for Joan'.[14] *The Cenci* would seem well suited to radio, since there is little visual action and much talk between two characters only. This was confirmed in 1947 when a neatly cut version was produced by Sir Lewis Casson, with Rosalie Crutchley as a memorable Beatrice. *The Cenci* was again staged in London from April to June 1959, at the Old Vic Theatre, in a production which stressed Beatrice's persecution by the Papal authorities. The play was well received, and was marked by a superb performance from Barbara Jefford as Beatrice.

If Shelley did really want the play to be staged he should have cut out the incest, a theme likely to appeal more to a sixteenth- than a nineteenth-century audience. To-day incest is *démodé* as a subject for discussion and is apt to provoke either boredom or disgust. Its occurrence in *Laon and Cythna*, *Rosalind and Helen* and *The Cenci* seems odd to us; but we should be wrong to assume that it indicates some morbid streak in Shelley. There are other good reasons for its appearance. The great liberating force of the Romantic Movement came from its determination to explore all forms of experience. Among them was incest, though now we can see it as a by-product of the obsession with disease and death which constitutes the seamy side of every Romantic movement,[15] it was not so easy then to distinguish between a fine excess and a ridiculous excess. To trace direct influences on Shelley we have only to consult the lists of his reading. Wieland's romantic novel *Agathon*, Lawrence's *Empire of the Nairs*, Byron's *Bride of Abydos* and *Parisina*, Godwin's *Mandeville*, Lewis's *Monk* and Hunt's *Story of Rimini*, for example, all have incest, or 'Platonic' love between brother and sister, as leading threads in their plots. Rousseau's *Julie*, probably Shelley's favourite novel, has a reference to the 'horrid idea of incest'; [16] Crabb Robinson's diary, that indispensable barometer of the literary climate, shows the idea was much in the air at the time; [17] and Byron was suspected of putting it into practice. So if Shelley had been a true mirror of his Age he would at least have been interested in the subject. As it happened, this interest was heightened because he had given intellectual assent at Oxford to Godwin's theories that love should be free and that friendship should be unaffected by blood-relationships. His first, feeble attempt to put the free-love theory into action, when he tried to arrange an unfettered union between his sister Elizabeth and Hogg, met with the rebuff, 'Is this the honourable advice of a brother?' [18] Shelley himself submitted to the marriage ceremony: free love was a theory he did not insist on practising. Incest was even further in the realms of theory. It arose in *Laon and Cythna*, as we have seen, merely as a logical conclusion to the theory of romantic love. There it happens to occur, as if it were normal; in *Rosalind and Helen*, and especially in *The Cenci*, it is deliberately exploited for the reason which tempted many great dramatists, from Sophocles and Euripides to Shakespeare and Calderón,[19] and which Shelley himself summed up:

Incest is like many other *incorrect* things a very poetical circumstance. It may be the excess of love or of hate. It may be that defiance of everything for the sake of another which clothes itself in the glory of the highest heroism, or it may be that cynical rage which, confounding the good and bad in existing opinions, breaks through them for the purpose of rioting in selfishness and antipathy.[20]

Shelley is restrained in using the theme, unlike Byron or Chateaubriand, who liked to pile on the agony by making the girl take vows of chastity beforehand and die soon after, preferably by violence — a triple defiance of the taboos calculated to rouse the most sluggish reader. The same motives animated those persistent devotees of incest, the Gothic novelists. The mention of 'Gothic' completes the picture by reminding us of the occasional Gothic flavour which is obvious enough in *The Cenci*, and throwing up one not quite irrelevant final footnote, that the name of the ghostly bleeding nun in *The Monk* was Beatrice.

NOTES TO VI: *THE CENCI*

1. See *Letters* ii. 349.
2. *Letters* ii, 109.
3. Haydon, *Autobiography and Journals*, p. 267.
4. *Letters* ii. 33.
5. The phrases are from A. C. Bradley, *Shelley's View of Poetry*.
6. Peacock, p. 330.
7. The Cenci story is told in Corrado Ricci's *Beatrice Cenci*. See also Bates, *A Study of Shelley's Drama The Cenci*, pp. 31–4, F. Prokosch's novel *A Tale for Midnight* (1956), and A. Moravia's play *Beatrice Cenci* (1965).
8. The following may possibly be plagiarisms:

The Cenci	Shakespeare
I. i. 141–4	*Macbeth*, II. i. 56–60
I. iii. 5	*Richard III*, I. i. 7
I. iii. 173–5	*Richard III*, IV. iv. 168–71
I. iii. 177–8	*Macbeth*, I. iii. 37; II. i. 62
III. i. 85–9	*Lear*, II. iv. 279–81
III. ii. 11–18, 51–3	*Othello*, v. ii. 7–14
III. ii. 78–80	*Macbeth*, II. ii. 14–15, 22
IV. i. (128–36), 141–57	*Lear*, I. iv. (299–304), 276–89
IV. i. 173–4	*Lear*, I. i. 121
IV. i. 179–80	*Macbeth*, II. ii. 36, 39
IV. ii. 30	*Macbeth*, II. ii. 6
IV. ii. 36	*Macbeth*, III. i. 138
IV. iii. 1, 5–22	*Macbeth*, II. ii. 4, 10–22
IV. iv. 40–1	*Hamlet*, I. iii. 78–80
IV. iv. 46, 43–51	*Macbeth*, II. ii. 14; III. iii. 21–4
IV. iv. 139	*Macbeth*, v. i. 69–70
v. i. 19–24	*King John*, IV. ii. 220–41
v. iii. 86–9	*Othello*, v. ii. 306–7
v. iii. 123–7	*Twelfth Night*, II. iv. 41–5

The Cenci	Shakespeare
v. iv. 48–59	*Measure for Measure*, III. i. 118–32
v. iv. 56–7	*Lear*, I. v. 43
v. iv. 101–9	*Merchant of Venice*, IV. i. 71–80

Also Orsino is a character in *Twelfth Night*, Bernardo in *Hamlet*, and Iachimo in *Cymbeline*.

9. See Bates, *Study of Shelley's Drama The Cenci*, Ch. VII.

10. H. Crabb Robinson, *On Books and their Writers*, p. 409.

11. See *Keats–Shelley Memorial Bulletin*, III, p. 42, and Bates, *Study of Shelley's Drama The Cenci*, p. 20.

12. J. M. Robertson launched the attack on the play in *New Essays towards a Critical Method*, 1897. A notorious later assault is that by F. R. Leavis, in *Revaluation*.

13. *Notebook of the Shelley Society*, Part I, pp. 50–80, gives a full account.

14. H. Pearson, *Bernard Shaw* (Collins, 1950), p. 377.

15. See M. Praz, *The Romantic Agony*; F. L. Lucas, *The Decline and Fall of the Romantic Ideal*; and G. R. Taylor, *Sex in History* (1954), pp. 189–90.

16. J.-J. Rousseau, *Eloisa*. (London, 1795), i. 55.

17. H. Crabb Robinson, *On Books and their Writers*, pp. 27, 55.

18. See *Jul* viii. 112.

19. *Oedipus, Hippolytus, Hamlet, Cabellos de Absolom.*

20. *Letters* ii. 154.

VII

ENGLAND IN 1819

the death-white shore
Of Albion, free no more.

1

IN the spring and early summer of 1819 Shelley had been occupied with high poetic themes, Acts II and III of *Prometheus Unbound* and *The Cenci*. On finishing the latter his mood changed, and during the autumn he cast a critical eye on the homeland he so often wanted to return to,[1] her system of government, her people's wrongs, and the hardening of the arteries in her leading poet, Wordsworth.

England in 1819, four years after the most exhausting war she had known, was still trying to jog along within the eighteenth-century pattern which events and inventions had rendered obsolete. The Prince Regent's nine years as head of the State had so signally failed to endear him to his people that he hardly ever dared show his face in public. His Prime Minister was the tactful and easy-going Lord Liverpool, who was halfway through his fifteen-year spell as Premier. The chief members of his Tory Cabinet were Castlereagh, Foreign Secretary and leader of the House of Commons, Eldon the Lord Chancellor, Lord Sidmouth the Home Secretary and Wellington, who was Master-General of the Ordnance. The government's home policy was one of studied inaction, punctuated by occasional repressive measures to scotch popular risings. Potentially the most dangerous of the risings had been the Luddite riots provoked by the trade depression in 1812. The inadequate 'police' forces at the disposal of the Lords Lieutenant of the counties chiefly affected — Nottingham, Yorkshire and

Lancashire — had crumbled in face of these spontaneous protests from the industrial proletariat. Though the Luddites had these counties at their mercy, the government was in little danger since there was no revolutionary leader to co-ordinate the rioters and widen their local and limited aims. If a real threat had arisen in 1812 it would probably have been ignored until too late, for Perceval's murder in May had led to a lengthy ministerial crisis, and the government, when it did at last come into being, was too engrossed by the war to worry about home affairs.

When the disturbances broke out again in 1817 the war was over and the government, more alive to the danger, replied by suspending Habeas Corpus, and, later, by passing the six 'Gag' Acts. In 1819 this policy seemed to be leading the nation to the brink of revolution. But by 1821 trade was recovering and, without the spur of hunger, popular discontent slackened. At the same time open agitation for Parliamentary reform was growing, for in peacetime reformers were no longer automatically classed as traitors or Jacobins. The reformers were still a small minority, however, and the government, by ignoring the rights of the industrial population, was able to preserve the *status quo* for ten years more. Only severe pressure from outside would make a comfortable and privileged society like the House of Commons sign its own death-warrant, and in Shelley's lifetime that pressure had not built up. Behind the façade of stability the cogent forces of change were remoulding the face of England. The new factories proclaimed that Britain led the world in mechanization. The jerry-built slums beginning to spring up around them warned the world not to follow her example too eagerly, and set that industrial urban pattern which is one of the most familiar and least admired legacies of the nineteenth century. In contrast to the slums and social injustice are the literary and artistic glories of the period, and these latter will in retrospect seem more important, just as the pyramids of Egypt and the Greek thinkers come to mind before the slaves who toiled around them. Those living at the time could not take this retro-

spective view, and it is no accident that the long line of
English reformers is at its richest during the thirty years of
Shelley's life. The list includes names as diverse as Godwin
and Grey, Cobbett and Bentham, Mary Wollstonecraft and
Elizabeth Fry, Fox and Robert Owen, Tom Paine and
William Wilberforce. Their germinal ideas, which bore
most fruit after 1830, are responsible for a large part of the
better conditions we take for granted to-day. Shelley had
always been an ally of the reformers, and in 1819, having
left the heat and smoke of the conflict, he was ready to
analyse the political situation in England more coolly.

His last and longest sortie into the 'great sandy desert
of Politics' is an unfinished essay of some fifty pages, *A Philosophical View of Reform*. He begins by reviewing notable
systems of government, from the Roman Empire onwards.
He looks at them with a strong liberal bias, assuming that
creative activity will be stifled whenever a tyrannic government is in league with a strong acquiescent Church, and that
the arts begin to flourish whenever political freedom revives.
Though despotism seemed on the wane all over Europe,
Shelley saw most hope for the future in America, a land
with no king, no hereditary aristocracy, and no established
Church.

Shelley devotes much of his essay to reform in England,
then, he believed, at a crisis in her destiny. Parliament, he
argues, no longer represented the English people, because
the unfranchised poor had multiplied and the link which
once united aristocracy and people, distrust of the monarch,
had been broken. As the King's power declined, the landed
aristocracy had grown into a despotic oligarchy, keeping
their position not by force but by the fraudulent device of
credit, public and private. By means of credit notes the
rich can enjoy the advantages of wealth they don't possess.
When they use this privilege they produce, in the political
cant of the day, 'an increase in the national industry':
that is, they condemn the workman to a sixteen-hour day
and foment the evil of child labour — 'the vigorous promise
of the coming generation blighted by premature exertion'.[2]

Shelley's tirade against paper-money and his neglect of other causes of industrial distress serve to remind us that he was an approving reader of the *Political Register*, which he received regularly. Politically, in 1819, he stood halfway between Cobbett and the Whigs.

To remedy the abuses, Shelley proposes to pay off the national debt, to disband the standing army, to abolish sinecures (while respecting the rights of existing holders), to make all religions equal in the eye of the law and abolish tithes, to make justice cheap, certain and speedy, and, of course, to reform Parliament. There need be no insurrection, he says, if Parliament is wise enough to reform itself: the rotten boroughs should be disfranchised and their rights transferred to unrepresented cities, with the ultimate aim of equalizing the population in each constituency at about 40,000; Parliament should be elected every three years; the franchise should be gradually extended, first to include all small property owners, then to adult male suffrage, and finally to universal adult suffrage, the logical end of the process, but an end which England was not yet ready for.

Most of Shelley's proposals are now accepted as commonplaces. Only the most radical one, paying off the national debt by orderly confiscation of lands, calls for any explanation. The national debt was incurred, he contends, in two unjust wars undertaken by the privileged classes to protect their own interests. Their property was already mortgaged : 'let the mortgagee foreclose'. Shelley goes on to distinguish between what we now call earned and unearned income, and restricts his capital levy to those who enjoy the latter. Some, he says, would lose a third, some a quarter of their wealth.

The Marxist picture of a dictatorship decaying spontaneously into free associations would never have seemed practical to Shelley, who, though at times loath to accept human nature as it is, was realistic enough to assume that privileged groups fight hard to preserve their status. He was most anxious, too, that the forces of privilege should be ousted without bloodshed. The outcome of the French Revolution had confirmed him in his conviction that ill-won power corrupts, and that a *coup d'état* leads the insurgents into habits of violence and mistrust, which jeopardize the new régime and stultify the benefits expected of it. To avoid this ruinous national rake's progress Shelley calls for passive resistance and non-co-operation. Some martyrs there would be, at first; but English soldiers would not for long consent to slaughter their unresisting countrymen. The non-co-operation should take such forms as refusing to pay taxes, and showering the House of Commons with petitions.

A Philosophical View of Reform, the last and best of Shelley's political utterances, falls naturally into place beside its predecessors. Having learnt from *Queen Mab* that poetry's heightened language was unsuitable for political dialectic, he was, in subsequent poems, usually content to glorify freedom in the abstract, relying on the incantation of the verse to edge readers towards his own camp. His practical schemes for political and social reform he put into a series of prose essays, which grew in wisdom with the years. Even the 1812 pamphlets seem temperate and responsible, almost over-cautiously so, when compared with say the *Letter to the Bishop of Llandaff* which Wordsworth wrote when he was 23. The ingenuous moments which mar the early pamphlets are eliminated in the more realistic *Proposal for Putting Reform to the Vote* of 1817. The *Philosophical View of Reform*, unfinished though it is, marks the final advance.

The more is the pity, therefore, that it remained unpublished for a hundred years, while the 1812 pamphlets were often reprinted. This is one reason why Shelley was dismissed as a child in politics by most Victorian critics. Even to-day the *Philosophical View of Reform* is hard to come by: of the three existing reprints, two are rare or expensive — the first published edition of 1920, and volume vii of the Julian edition of 1926 — and the third, *Political Tracts of Wordsworth, Coleridge and Shelley* (1953), is a specialized book unlikely to have a wide circulation. The most widely read of the volumes containing Shelley's political essays are possibly the Camelot Classics *Essays and Letters* (1887) and the Nonesuch edition of 1951. These contain six political essays, and only one, the *Princess Charlotte* pamphlet, is post-1812. Most readers of Shelley thus still receive their first-hand impressions of his political writings only from the 1812 pamphlets, and the Victorian valuation tends to linger on, so that a mild protest against it is not out of place even now. That is not to say that Shelley's proposals are strikingly original : most of them were at one time or another to be found in the programmes of some political party or pressure-group. What is important is that his plan has since found its way into the statute-book almost in its entirety. Because we now accept most of his proposals, he can often speak to us in our own language when others seem to be babbling in a strange tongue, bound by a set of values foreign to us.

Insistently in the *Philosophical View of Reform* Shelley advocates a limited step forward if the full reform arouses a frenzy of opposition in the diehards. He thus foreshadows the piecemeal growth of the reforms later in the century. Since 1900 reform has continued in the spirit though not according to the letter of his plan. His proposal to deprive landowners of a part of their property, for example, has come to apply, more stringently than he suggested, in the system of recurrent death-duties. He might not approve of this more drastic system : for when he made his proposal he was excited by the flagrantly unjust division of wealth between the landowners — 'no class had ever enjoyed such riches as the landed gentry of England' [3] in his day — and the needy poor, whom he saw during their worst winters, 1811–12 and 1816–17.[4] Remembering those winters, he looked on England in 1819 as dry tinder wanting only the spark of a financial crisis to flare into insurrection. In fact, as we have seen, economic conditions were on the mend (though there was no reason to foresee it in 1819), and the government staved off the inevitable for over ten years. When the inevitable came, the long years of agitation had left their mark even on the diehards, with the result that the ship of State was able to weather the squalls and reach the reasonably safe anchorage of the first Reform Bill in 1832. Shelley's hopes of avoiding a bloody revolution were thus realized, by the very means he had proposed.

2

On 16 August 1819, while Shelley was putting the finishing touches to *The Cenci*, a meeting in St. Peter's Field, Manchester, was due to be addressed by the radical orator Henry Hunt. Some 50,000 people, many of them carrying banners, had gathered in orderly groups to hear him. The local magistrates became alarmed at the size of the crowd, and ordered the troops under their command to arrest Hunt. In the ensuing *mêlée* 11 of the crowd were killed and about 400 injured. When Shelley heard of the 'Peterloo Massacre' early in September, he confessed to a 'torrent of indignation . . . boiling in my veins',[5] and this frenzied language truly reflected his feelings. By the end of the month he had distilled his indignation into a poem of some 400 lines, *The Mask of Anarchy*. As in *The Cenci*, he avoids elaborate metaphor : there are no glaucous sea-woods or purple chasms to perplex the oppressed poor who, he hoped, would read the poem. Instead the language is simple, unpolished sometimes, direct and vigorous, and the story is easy to follow. The most obscure feature of the poem is its title; *mask* should be read as *masque*, rather than disguise, and *anarchy* as *misrule*, rather than lack of rule.

Though the sting of the topical allusions has faded, the first five stanzas are still compelling :

> As I lay asleep in Italy
> There came a voice from over the Sea,
> And with great power it forth led me
> To walk in the visions of Poesy.
>
> I met Murder on the way —
> He had a mask like Castlereagh —
> Very smooth he looked, yet grim ;
> Seven bloodhounds followed him :

> All were fat; and well they might
> Be in admirable plight,
> For one by one, and two by two,
> He tossed them human hearts to chew
> Which from his wide cloak he drew.
>
> Next came. Fraud, and he had on,
> Like Eldon, an ermined gown;
> His big tears, for he wept well,
> Turned to mill-stones as they fell.
>
> And the little children, who
> Round his feet played to and fro,
> Thinking every tear a gem,
> Had their brains knocked out by them.
>
> 338. 1-21

The seven bloodhounds following Castlereagh are the nations of the 'holy alliance'. In 1819 Castlereagh himself, whose skill in foreign affairs is now generally admired, was detested in England because of policies at home. He was the only one of the Cabinet 'Big Five' in the Commons, and he never shirked responsibility when introducing the government's unpopular repressive measures in the House. The cheers and boos which greeted his funeral procession in 1822 may make us squirm now; but they do show that Shelley was merely accepting the popular view, not being specially vindictive. Against Eldon, on the other hand, Shelley did have a personal grudge. It was only a year since Eldon had finally deprived him of his right to bring up Ianthe and Charles. So Shelley naturally stresses the Chancellor's duties as guardian of wards in Chancery, while making capital too out of Eldon's habit of weeping on the Bench.

Last in the poem's 'ghastly masquerade', symbolizing England's repressive laws, came Anarchy:

> He rode
> On a white horse, splashed with blood;
> He was pale even to the lips,
> Like Death in the Apocalypse.

And he wore a kingly crown ;
And in his grasp a sceptre shone ;
On his brow this mark I saw —
'I AM GOD, AND KING, AND LAW !'

338. 30-7

Accompanied by uniformed 'hired murderers', among them
the butchers of Peterloo, he trampled down the populace
in the provinces and rode with pomp into London 'to meet
his pensioned Parliament'. Then Hope, a 'maniac maid',
lay down in the street before his cavalcade. A misty light
promptly appeared, and, while the bystanders are still
watching it, Anarchy and his crew have been annihilated,
and Hope has begun to speak :

'Men of England, heirs of Glory,
Heroes of unwritten story,
Nurslings of one mighty Mother,
Hopes of her, and one another ;

'Rise like Lions after slumber
In unvanquishable number,
Shake your chains to earth like dew
Which in sleep had fallen on you —
Ye are many — they are few.'

341. 147-55

In Shelley's eyes every man of England who opposed the
existing regime wore a halo, and from the other side of the
Alps those haloes shone brightly enough to blot out venial
faults. These heirs of glory are next reminded of the slavery
they know too well :

'Tis to work and have such pay
As just keeps life from day to day
In your limbs, as in a cell
For the tyrants' use to dwell. . . .

'Tis to hunger for such diet
As the rich man in his riot
Casts to the fat dogs that lie
Surfeiting beneath his eye.

341. 160-3, 172-5

In contrast is what Shelley hopes to see when Freedom
reigns :

> For the labourer . . . bread
> And a comely table spread
> From his daily labour come
> In a neat and happy home.
>
> 342. 217-20

And how is the change to be brought about ? Not by violent
revolt, but, as the parable of Anarchy and Hope has hinted,
by passive resistance. A 'vast assembly' should gather and
make a solemn declaration of rights. If the oppressors inter-
vene, as they did at Manchester, the people's course is
clear :

> With folded arms and steady eyes,
> And little fear, and less surprise,
> Look upon them as they slay
> Till their rage has died away.

> Then they will return with shame
> To the place from which they came,
> And the blood thus shed will speak
> In hot blushes on their cheek.
>
> 344. 344-51

The language is as simple and passionate as that of Blake's
songs, and seems the more sincere for being so artless.
Shelley ends by reiterating the catchy verse

> Rise like Lions after slumber
> In unvanquishable number. . . .
>
> 344. 368-9,

scarcely the best slogan for promoting the stoic virtues of
passive resistance.

The Mask of Anarchy is one of the best polemical poems of
its kind. Though professedly partisan, Shelley never lapses
into hysteria, and he comfortably succeeds in performing the
task he sets himself — to put on record in verse, doggerel
even at times, his faith in gradual reform. Though his own
reaction to social injustice was to fight, he knew that the
passions aroused by fighting were often worse than the evils

the fight aimed to remove. So instead he advocated passive resistance, and he deserves great credit for the wise foresight of this suggestion. In recent years passive resistance has all over the world become a standard technique for crusading minorities confident enough to believe that the majority will recognize the justice of their cause. The nuclear disarmament demonstrations organized in London during 1961 by the Committee of 100 followed Shelley's prescription quite closely, and the guiding hand behind the demonstrations was that of Lord Russell, who was strongly influenced by Shelley for many years.[6]

The *Mask of Anarchy* was not published in Shelley's lifetime, nor in the *Posthumous Poems* of 1824. Soon after finishing it Shelley sent it to Leigh Hunt for his *Examiner*. But Hunt, who had already been imprisoned once for seditious libel, was too wary to invite another prosecution. He kept the poem by him until 1832, when he published it as a pamphlet, in time for it to be quoted by political speakers during the struggle for the Reform Bill.[7] And a hundred years later the poem was chanted by hunger-marchers in Toronto.[8]

When, as in the autumn of 1819, Shelley allowed himself to be lured again into the tangled thicket of politics, his indignation overflowed into shorter poems. The most poignant of the 1819 crop is the ballad about Parson Richards, who turned away a starving woman and her baby.[4] More direct in its challenge to the ruling classes is the *Song to the Men of England* (which George Orwell parodied in the first chapter of *Animal Farm* with the song 'Beasts of England'):

> Men of England, wherefore plough
> For the lords who lay ye low?
> Wherefore weave with toil and care
> The rich robes your tyrants wear? . . .

> 572. 1-4

Another spirited piece of treason is his revised version of the National Anthem:

> God prosper, speed, and save,
> God raise from England's grave
> Her murdered Queen!

> Pave with swift victory
> The steps of Liberty,
> Whom Britons own to be
> Immortal Queen. . . .
>
> 574. 1-7

Returning from hope to reality, Shelley catalogued the country's ills in a powerful and untidy sonnet, *England in 1819.* The sestet comes before the octet, and the punctuation is so bad that I have been driven to alter it. Despite these eccentricities, or because of them, the poem usually pleases those who like to admire the non-Romantic facets of Romantic poets:

> An old, mad, blind, despised, and dying king;
> Princes, the dregs of their dull race, who flow
> Through public scorn — mud from a muddy spring;
> Rulers who neither see, nor feel, nor know,
> But leech-like to their fainting country cling,
> Till they drop, blind in blood, without a blow;
> A people starved and stabbed in the untilled field;
> An army, which liberticide and prey
> Makes as a two-edged sword to all who wield;
> Golden and sanguine laws which tempt and slay;
> Religion Christless, Godless — a book sealed;
> A Senate — Time's worst statute unrepealed; —
> Are graves, from which a glorious Phantom may
> Burst, to illumine our tempestuous day.
>
> 574

The rude vigour of the first twelve lines contrasts well with the abstract, diffident final couplet. It is as if a phalanx of English aristocrats with their well-fed families and retainers — something like the Peers' chorus in *Iolanthe* augmented — were set beside a handful of scraggy reformers anxiously peering into the distant haze, which may hide a 'glorious Phantom'. The ironic stress on *may* makes the contrast the more poignant.

3

Shelley had always found it painful to watch Wordsworth siding with the reactionaries in the political struggle, and to receive year by year his ever more stilted and laborious verses. When he read the latest of these, *Peter Bell, a Tale*, his disappointment broke out into satire.

Peter Bell was given to the world in April 1819 after twenty years of incubation, as Wordsworth recalled in his introductory letter 'To Robert Southey, Esq., P.L., etc., etc.':

The Tale of Peter Bell . . . has, in its Manuscript state, nearly survived its *minority* : — for it first saw the light in the summer of 1798. During this long interval, pains have been taken at different times to make the production less unworthy of a favourable reception; or rather to fit it for filling *permanently* a station, however humble, in the Literature of our Country.

Peter Bell, Wordsworth tells us, was a hawker of earthenware, a savage and lawless man with 'a dozen wedded wives'. Though wont to roam far and wide over the country plying his trade, he was blind to Nature's charms :

> A primrose by a river's brim
> A yellow primrose was to him
> And it was nothing more.

One day he came upon an Ass, whose master had been drowned in the river Swale. True to his reputation, Peter tried to steal the Ass by riding away on it, but the faithful beast refused to budge until he had recovered the body from the river. Then it carried him back to its master's widow. Peter was so impressed by this example of loyalty and sagacity in a dumb animal that he 'forsook his crimes' and 'became a good and honest man'.

When the poets of the younger generation heard of *Peter Bell*'s impending publication a parody was hastily put together by J. H. Reynolds. His poem *Peter Bell, a Lyrical Ballad*, appeared a few days before Wordsworth's and had just as pompous a preface :

It has been my aim and my achievement to deduce moral thunder from buttercups, daisies, celandines, and (as a poet, scarcely inferior to myself, hath it) 'such small deer'. . . .

In the brilliant parody which follows, Reynolds imitates Wordsworth's verbal tricks, and pokes fun at his rustic heroes and his ponderous philosophizing.

Shelley models the Dedication to his *Peter Bell the Third* on Wordsworth's :

Let me observe that I have spent six or seven days in composing this sublime piece; the orb of my moonlike genius has made the fourth part of its revolution round the dull earth . . . and I have been fitting this its last phase 'to occupy a permanent station in the literature of my country'.

Shelley then continues the story of the newly reformed 'polygamic Potter' where Wordsworth left off. In old age Peter becomes troubled about his early crimes, and when his spiritual adviser hints that he may be predestined to damnation he grows so violent that

> The Parson from the casement lept
> Into the lake of Windermere.
>
> 348. 31-2

At once the pangs of death assail Peter, and soon the Devil carries him off to Hell.

> Hell is a city much like London —
> A populous and a smoky city;
> There are all sorts of people undone,
> And there is little or no fun done;
> Small justice shown, and still less pity.
>
> 350. 147-51

Peter, by now a caricature of Wordsworth, becomes a footman in the service of the Devil, who is suspiciously like the Prince Regent. Peter soon shows himself a cut above his fellow-servants, for, though unimaginative, he sees familiar things in a new way. He has his limitations, however :

> from the first 'twas Peter's drift
> To be a kind of moral eunuch,
> He touched the hem of Nature's shift,
> Felt faint — and never dared uplift
> The closest, all-concealing tunic.

> She laughed the while, with an arch smile,
> And kissed him with a sister's kiss,
> And said — 'My best Diogenes,
> I love you well — but, if you please,
> Tempt not again my deepest bliss.'

One of the Devil's guests, 'a mighty poet and a subtle-souled psychologist', is Coleridge, under whose spell Peter begins to write poetry, not unsuccessfully:

> Peter's verse was clear, and came
> Announcing from the frozen hearth
> Of a cold age, that none might tame
> The soul of that diviner flame
> It augured to the Earth. . . .
>
> For language was in Peter's hand
> Like clay while he was yet a potter;
> And he made songs for all the land,
> Sweet both to feel and understand,
> As pipkins late to mountain Cotter.
>
> 356. 433-7, 443-7

Peter resolves to pursue his new calling, and leaves the service of the Devil, who replies by bribing the reviewers to abuse him. Peter gradually changes his views:

> Peter ran to seed in soul. . . .
> Turned to a formal puritan,
> A solemn and unsexual man.
>
> 358. 543, 550-1

At last he is even willing to write odes to the Devil, and is duly rewarded with a sinecure. But soon his verse becomes so deadly dull that no one will read it, and he infects his neighbours for miles around — a dig at Southey, who lived some twelve miles from Rydal Mount.

Shelley had two conflicting aims in *Peter Bell the Third*: to satirize the pretentious trivialities which the ageing Wordsworth had substituted for inspiration; and to pay his tribute to the Wordsworth of 1800. This conflict of intention is enough to ruin the poem as a work of art. A personal satire, if it is to have any sting, must exaggerate the victim's faults and ignore his virtues. Shelley does just the opposite, pausing amid his ridicule to point out those virtues. He did not intend the poem as an insult to Wordsworth, and if by our standards it seems so, we must make allowances for the ingrained Regency custom of using strong language. Wordsworth suffered far fiercer abuse from reviewers.

Shelley had too much respect for Wordsworth's best work to want to vilify him, as Mary's note emphasizes : 'No man ever admired Wordsworth's poetry more; he read it perpetually, and taught others to appreciate its beauties'. He was thus well placed to assess Wordsworth's achievements, and he did so shrewdly. The epigrammatic judgements of *Peter Bell the Third*, made thirty years before *The Prelude* was published, shine brightly and almost alone through the murk of controversy which surrounded Wordsworth in his lifetime, and would in themselves be enough to justify the poem's existence. But there is no denying that *Peter Bell the Third* is primarily a satire, and if the interpolated criticisms were removed it could be read as such.

Does it then succeed as satire? Wordsworth invited parody in *Peter Bell* because he dragged out a pedestrian and trivial tale to an unconscionable length, and told it in an incongruously formal style heavy with naïve moralizing. It is the *reductio ad absurdum* of the theory that the humble and humdrum make good grist for the poetic mill. Shelley's poem, too, is far longer than it need be. Though witty in places, it is often flat-footedly facetious, and is marred by outcrops of the lowest doggerel. Severe cutting would have given it more bite; but it was only a skit, hastily written, and Shelley didn't think it worth revising.

Mary, in her note of 1839, remarked this 'the poem was written as a warning — not as a narration of the reality'. It was better prophecy than she knew, for in 1843 Southey's death left Wordsworth free to qualify for the final phase in Peter's career by accepting the Laureateship.

NOTES TO VII: ENGLAND IN 1819

1. See *Letters* ii. 26; ii. 98; and ii. 114.
2. Page 237 in R. J. White's *Political Tracts of Wordsworth, Coleridge and Shelley*, the most accessible reprint of the *Philosophical View of Reform*.
3. A. Bryant, *The Age of Elegance*, p. 311.
4. See W. J. McTaggart, *England in 1819: Church, State and Poverty*.
5. *Letters* ii. 117. For details of the massacre, see D. Read, *Peterloo*.
6. See *Keats–Shelley Memorial Bulletin*, XVI (1965), p. 39.
7. See G. M. Trevelyan, *Lord Grey of the Reform Bill*, p. 337.
8. See F. E. L. Priestley's edition of *Political Justice*, iii. 108.

VIII

A NEWTON AMONG
CHEMISTS?

Nourishing a youth sublime
With the fairy tales of science, and the long result of time.

TENNYSON, *Locksley Hall*

1

DECEMBER 1819 saw the completion of the fourth and last
Act of *Prometheus Unbound*, which was written in a remarkable
new style, best described, perhaps, as 'lyricized science'.
This was the final fruit of Shelley's early scientific interests.
At Eton and Oxford (1809–11) he was a keen experimenter;
at Tremadoc (1812) he was sure science could better Man's
lot; and in *Queen Mab* (1813) he was sure it justified Necessity. Then from 1814 till 1819, if we judge from poems
alone, science was buried beneath a humanistic landslide:
who can imagine the Poet in *Alastor* doing anything practical,
plugging a leak in his boat even? Shelley's interest in
science, though buried deep, was not extinct, however, and
his scientific reading continued. We saw in a previous
chapter how ideas sometimes had, as it were, to circulate
awhile in his bloodstream before dissolving enough to pass
the poetic filter, and this process certainly applied to
scientific ideas. In *Queen Mab* those ideas were dragged in
to back up a mechanistic philosophy. Six years later, having
passed the filter, they appear in subtler guise, fully integrated into his habitual style. The new scientific slant is
far less obvious and far more profound than the old.

Prometheus Unbound loses half its bite if the scientific
allusions are missed. So I have added this preparatory
chapter, which reviews briefly Shelley's interests in science,
seen against the background of scientific progress.

2

Science advanced somewhat haphazardly during the eighteenth century, because there were few fruitful new theories. 'The Age of Reason', whatever its defects as a label for the age as a whole, applies well to the scientific scene, if *reason* is understood in the narrow sense. Reason allied with imagination, the mark of the supreme genius — the Newton, Darwin or Einstein — was in short supply during the eighteenth century. In the first quarter of the nineteenth century better progress was made, but the new ideas travelled slowly and were resisted stoutly. So, with some exceptions, the system of thought Shelley inherited was that existing in 1800, which was by no means coherent.

Newton's seminal ideas dominated scientific thinking in the eighteenth century, and many of the best minds were kept busy quarrying the vein of ore he had uncovered. Even in France, the home of Descartes, Newton's theories had triumphed by the 1730s, and two French mathematicians, Lagrange and Laplace, did most to carry them to their logical end. Together these two laid bare the mechanism of the known universe. The energetic Laplace explained the discoveries in textbooks like the monumental *Mécanique Céleste* and in popular expositions like the *Système du Monde* (1796), which Shelley cited in *Queen Mab*. Newton's laws affected the climate of thought most by bringing determinism into a realm where unfathomable spiritual forces had been supposed to act, and Laplace was expressing the confidence felt by every user of these laws when he claimed that a supremely competent mathematician, given the present state of all particles in the universe, could predict its future history.[1] Had this superman existed he would have needed as raw material for his study the exact positions and motions of the stars, data which observational astronomy was not yet ready to supply. There were, however, notable improvements in observational methods. Herschel, armed with fine telescopes of his own design, carried out his surveys of the heavens, proved that our stellar system is disc-shaped, and made the first recorded discovery of a new planet when he identified Uranus in 1781. Herschel's telescopes serve as a reminder of the many advances in technology and instrumentation during the century, most of them based on principles accepted in 1700 : the steam engine, accurate chronometers and thermometers, achromatic lenses and the machines which brought about the Industrial Revolution.

But in those branches of physical science which were beyond Newton's scope, 'Nature and Nature's laws' still 'lay hid in night'. The fundamentals of light, heat, electricity and chemistry defied analysis, and too many fallacious ideas were poisoning the air. Both the wave and corpuscular theories of light had their adherents, and it was not until 1801 that Young's experiments on the interference of light showed the wave theory was valid and pointed the way forward. In the theory of heat, a step back was taken when our modern view of heat, as an agitation among the atoms (a view held by Bacon among others), was discarded in favour of the idea that heat was a 'subtle fluid' (one of many then in fashion, which was called 'caloric'. Caloric was elastic, invisible and weightless, and it was alleged to fill the nooks and crannies between the atoms of a substance. Rumford cast doubt on the caloric theory in 1798, but it was not entirely abandoned until about 1850.[2] A sounder basis existed in one branch of electricity, for by 1800 the laws of electrostatics were well known : it is no accident that Shelley's most successful experiment was making his hair stand on end. Current electricity, on the other hand, was not understood because it was not even recognized until the invention of the Voltaic cell in 1800 enabled steady currents to be generated. This new tool, the 'pile of Volta' as it was called, was put to good use by Davy, who succeeded in isolating many chemical elements by passing electric currents through their fused compounds. Thanks to Davy and others, chemistry was advancing quickly after the stagnation of the early eighteenth century. The crucial experiments discrediting the old phlogiston theory, which held that all burning substances gave off 'phlogiston' to the air, were made in the 1770s by Priestley, Scheele and Lavoisier; and Lavoisier's *Traité élémentaire de Chimie* (1789) is recognized as inaugurating the modern era in chemistry. The phlogiston theory was deeply entrenched, however, and lingered on for many years, so persistently indeed that Shelley can almost be said to have lived and died before the modern picture was accepted. Davy's brilliant experiments (1807–1812) and Dalton's atomic theory (1808) also came too late to have much effect on the general climate of opinion in Shelley's time.

The prehistory of the Earth and its inhabitants provoked much speculation in the eighteenth century. Controversy raged between exponents of the cataclysmic and uniformitarian theories. The former, including Buffon and Cuvier, believed the Earth had suffered a series of catastrophes, with disastrous earthquakes and volcanic eruptions; while the latter, notably Hutton in his *Theory of the Earth* (1795), emphasized the gradual deposit of strata under the sea. Cuvier thought the catastrophes explained why many species known in fossil form no longer existed, for he regarded species as fixed unalterably. In this view he was following the great Linnaeus, who had brought order into biology by his comprehensive classification of plants and animals. The idea of fixed species was challenged between 1800 and 1810 by Lamarck, and also, ten years earlier, by Erasmus Darwin, whose theory of evolution closely foreshadows that of his grandson Charles.

This selective and all-too-rapid sketch of the scientific background can conveniently end with Erasmus Darwin, for he figures prominently in the next section, where Shelley's particular scientific interests are discussed.

3

The scientific training Shelley received at school was limited and unsystematic. At both Syon House and Eton, science was treated as an extra and taught by a visiting lecturer. Fortunately at both schools the lecturer was Adam Walker, a remarkable man who completely captivated Shelley. Walker kept the boys awake by seasoning his factual instruction with bold speculation, and he soon tickled Shelley's palate with his 'fairy tales of science'. Walker was no charlatan, however, and no mere purveyor of science-fiction : it would be fairer to call him an inspired amateur, a term which could be applied to most of the scientists of that time. Walker's usual lecture-course was published in 1799 as *A System of Familiar Philosophy*, a book with over 500 quarto pages and hundreds of illustrations. The main subjects treated in the *Familiar Philosophy* are astronomy, electricity (*i.e.* electrostatics), mechanics, hydrostatics, chemistry, the atmosphere, light and magnetism. The first four of these were well established and Walker shows a sound knowledge, enlivened by a flair for entertaining experiments ; in the other subjects, where theory was tentative, he speculated freely. It is not worth detailing his often eccentric ideas, apart from one which he continually emphasized : he believed that 'fire, light, heat, caloric, phlogiston, and electricity' were, if not identical, merely 'modifications of one and the same principle'.[3] This unifying hypothesis was the chief bee in his bonnet, and it no doubt buzzed merrily when he was lecturing to schoolboys. The hypothesis certainly appealed to Shelley, who made good use of it in *Prometheus Unbound*. Such abstract notions were, however, of less interest to him as a schoolboy than Walker's practical demonstrations. Shelley seized on two subjects in particular, electricity and chemistry, as the most promising for noisy and spectacular experiments which were not without the spice of danger or the charm of uncertainty. On the whole his experiments seem to have been fairly successful, presumably because he had Walker's lectures, and sometimes Dr. Lind's advice, to guide him. Curiosity at Nature's marvels and the desire to control them — the spurs to much scientific endeavour — were probably the main motives behind Shelley's experiments, though the sparks and explosions may also betray a modicum of subconscious protest against authority.

At Oxford Shelley was unlucky. He intended to continue his experimental work, and on arrival turned his rooms into a laboratory. But he had no encouragement at all either from the University, where scientific studies were then at their nadir,[4] or from his one real friend, Hogg, who was contemptuous of science, and also afraid of it, especially after he found himself pouring tea into a cup already half-full of concentrated acid. Hogg did his best, chiefly by sarcasm, to eradicate his friend's scientific bias. Hogg's picture of a Shelley obsessed by science may be overdrawn, for his *Life of Shelley* is notorious for its distortions; but so fierce a science-hater as Hogg would never have bothered to generate such a scientific smoke-screen if there had been no fire at all. Writing twenty years later, Hogg recalled how their first meeting ended with Shelley dashing off to a lecture on mineralogy, only to return crestfallen with the remark that the lecturer talked about 'stones! stones, stones, stones! nothing but stones, and so drily'.[5] This setback did not prevent him telling Hogg how science could transform the world by providing new sources of power and new means of transport, and by fertilizing barren regions, which could then be peopled with ex-slaves. Once launched on speculations like these Shelley would speak of science and liberty triumphing together, and enabling Man to tame both Nature and tyrants. Hogg, who was above such childish fancies, details some of Shelley's speculations to show how ridiculous they were. But events have overtaken Hogg, and the distorting-glass of his wording cannot hide a core of true prophecy in Shelley's visions: 'It is easy, even in our present state of ignorance, to reduce our ordinary food to carbon, or to lime; a moderate advancement in chemical science will speedily enable us, we may hope, to create, with equal facility, food from substances that appear at present to be as ill-adapted to sustain us. What is the cause of the remarkable fertility of some lands, and of the hopeless sterility of others? . . . The real difference is probably very slight; by chemical agency the philosopher may work a total change, and may transmute an unfruitful region into a land of exuberant plenty. . . . What a mighty instrument would electricity be in the hands of him who knew how to wield it, in what manner to direct its omnipotent energies. . . . The art of navigating the air is in its first and most helpless infancy; the aerial mariner still swims on bladders, and has not mounted even the rude raft. . . . The balloon . . . will enable us to traverse vast tracts with ease and rapidity, and to explore unknown countries without difficulty.' [6] Even if he had tried, Hogg could not have remembered this accurately after so many years. It is not likely, for example, that Shelley would have confined his remarks on air travel to lighter-than-air craft, for he probably knew of Cayley's famous essay on 'Aerial Navigation' in *Nicholson's Journal* for 1809–10, which contained the first genuine formulation of the principles of heavier-than-air flight.[7]

When Hogg visited Shelley's rooms he found them littered with scientific instruments, odd pieces of clothing and books, 'as if the young chemist, in order to analyse the mystery of creation, had endeavoured first to reconstruct the primaeval chaos. . . . He then proceeded, with much eagerness and enthusiasm, to show me the various instruments, especially the electrical apparatus; turning round the handle very rapidly, so that the fierce, crackling sparks flew forth; and presently standing upon the stool with glass feet, he begged me to work the machine until he was filled with the fluid, so that his long, wild locks bristled and stood on end. Afterwards he charged a powerful battery of several jars; labouring with vast energy, and discoursing with increasing vehemence of the marvellous powers of electricity, of thunder and lightning; describing an electrical kite that he had made at home, and projecting another and an enormous one, or rather a combination of many kites, that would draw down from the sky an immense volume of electricity, the whole ammunition of a mighty thunderstorm; and this being directed to some point would there produce the most stupendous results.' [8] Yet Hogg remained sceptical: 'His chemical operations seemed to an unskilful observer to promise nothing but disasters. His hands, his clothes, his books, and his furniture were stained and corroded by mineral acids. More than one hole in the carpet could elucidate the ultimate phenomenon of combustion; especially a formidable aperture in the middle of the room, where the floor also had been burnt by the spontaneous ignition caused by mixing ether with some other fluid in a crucible; and the honourable wound was speedily enlarged by rents, for the philosopher, as he hastily crossed the room in pursuit of truth, was frequently caught in it by the foot.' [8]

Shelley's experiments were inevitably slapdash, for at Oxford he was thrown prematurely on his own undeveloped scientific resources, deprived even of the intermittent help he had received at Eton from Walker and from Dr. Lind. Without a strong inner impetus he would never have persevered at all in the face of opposition from almost every quarter — from Hogg, from his family, from his College scout. That impetus was dissipated in a series of blind alleys because he never found a pattern of progress which was both congenial and fruitful. He had no chance to subject himself to the discipline of detailed practice, which is the surest way of lodging general principles in the mind, and his distaste for mathematics limited his grasp of the maturer sciences, which tend to formulate their theories mathematically.

The somewhat comic experiments described by Hogg were supplemented by a good deal of serious scientific reading (which Hogg fails to mention), and if we judge by the effect on his poems the author who meant most to Shelley was Erasmus Darwin. Darwin's main contributions to science were in biology, but, like Adam Walker, he was not afraid of speculation in other subjects. Darwin expounded his theories in the prose treatise *Zoonomia* and in the didactic poems *The Botanic Garden* and *The Temple of Nature*, published between 1789 and 1803. Darwin's poems served almost as a guide to existing knowledge, and he argued the merits of controversial theories in his many lengthy Notes. He could fit cold facts and scientific jargon into the straitjacket of the standard couplet so skilfully that the verse-form was sugar to the pill, not a hindrance to the sense, as it would have been in lesser hands. Consequently his poems were best-sellers, and he himself became famous as a savant : Coleridge once called him 'the first *literary* character in Europe and the most original-minded man'.[9]

Darwin is now remembered chiefly for making one of the most important of the steps which have brought the theory of evolution from its crude beginnings in ancient Greece [10] to its present form. In *Zoonomia* Darwin points out that some animals have changed in physique to perform special tasks, *e.g.* race-horses and load-carrying horses, and the many breeds of dog ; that others have become adapted to the climate, *e.g.* hares and partridges which in snowy countries turn white in the winter ; and that most warm-blooded animals are anatomically similar. Darwin concludes that all were 'produced from a similar living filament. In some this filament in its advance to maturity has acquired hands and fingers, with a fine sense of touch, as in mankind. In others it has acquired claws or talons . . . in others, toes with an intervening web, or membrane. . . .'[11] Darwin goes on to discuss rivalry between males for a mate and puts in a nutshell 'survival of the fittest' : 'The final cause of this contest amongst the males seems to be that the strongest and most active animal should propagate the species, which should thence become improved'.[12] These extracts show that if Erasmus had found more evidence to support his speculations he, instead of his grandson Charles, might now be the foremost name in the theory of evolution. Erasmus can cram a whole theory into one of his stiff couplets, as when he summarizes evolution through fish to amphibia and higher animals :

> Cold gills aquatic form respiring lungs
> And sounds aerial flow from slimy tongues.[13]

He then suggests that the human child may pass through rather similar stages in the womb, a hypothesis later elevated into the respected theory of recapitulation, now looked on as only partly true.[14] Shelley absorbed these ideas on evolution and the drier textbook botany of the poems, but he was excited more by Darwin's speculations outside the realms of biology, for example the theory that electricity is at the root of many atmospheric phenomena. And we may be sure he was impressed when he first read prophecies like these :

> Soon shall thy arm, unconquer'd steam ! afar
> Drag the slow barge, or drive the rapid car ;
> Or on wide-waving wings expanded bear
> The flying-chariot through the fields of air.
> Fair crews triumphant, leaning from above,
> Shall wave their fluttering kerchiefs as they move ;
> Or warrior-bands alarm the gaping crowd,
> And armies shrink beneath the shadowy cloud.[15]

Darwin was fascinated by aerial phenomena, and the Nymphs, Gnomes and Sylphs who crowd the pages of his poems take wing at the slightest provocation. Though Shelley rejected Darwin's stilted mannerisms, it was Darwin who showed him how to describe clouds, winds and storms scientifically in verse : *The Cloud* and the *Ode to the West Wind* owe more to Darwin than to Wordsworth.

Shelley's scientific experiments and reading continued after he left Oxford, though he lost or sold much of his apparatus during his continual travels. At Keswick in November 1811 he burnt hydrogen in the garden at night, as a demonstration for Harriet and Eliza; but the landlord asked him to leave because of 'odd things seen at night near your dwelling'. In the same year he read Darwin's *Botanic Garden* and in 1812 he bought Davy's *Elements of Chemical Philosophy*. His last known letter to his mother, in 1812, was to ask for his galvanic machine and solar microscope (later sold for £5), and in 1813 he wrote, 'I am determined not to relax until I have attained considerable proficiency in the physical sciences'. After 1811 he was at his best in astronomy, a subject which does not repel the amateur with too thorny a jargon. The first fruits of Shelley's astronomical studies appeared in the Notes to *Queen Mab* (which served as a shop-window for all his knowledge) and the final product, to be seen in *Prometheus Unbound* and subsequent poems, was the regular use of an increased proportion of astronomical words and images. His knowledge of astronomy was not entirely unpractical: he could, for example, pick out the constellations in the sky, though he rarely refers to them by name in his poems.[16]

In his later years the chief sign of his interest in science is the style of his Nature poems. But there are other signs too — his analytical descriptions, in letters to Peacock, of country he passed through, and his eager participation in Henry Reveley's steamboat project, which he generously and unwisely helped to finance.

4

A. N. Whitehead wrote in one of his best books, *Science and the Modern World*: 'Shelley's attitude to science was at the opposite pole to that of Wordsworth. He loved it, and is never tired of expressing in poetry the thoughts which it suggests. It symbolizes to him joy, and peace, and illumination. What the hills were to the youth of Wordsworth, a chemical laboratory was to Shelley. It is unfortunate that Shelley's literary critics have, in this respect, so little of Shelley in their own mentality. They tend to treat as a casual oddity of Shelley's nature what was, in fact, part of the main structure of his mind, permeating his poetry through and through. If Shelley had been born a hundred years later, the twentieth century would have seen a Newton among chemists.' [17]

Does our review of Shelley's scientific activities support the claim that he was a potential 'Newton among chemists'? However much one respects Whitehead's judgement, it is difficult to avoid answering with a qualified 'No'. Even before the days of teamwork, temperament was almost as important as intellect to the scientist, and Shelley would never have been patient enough to explore apparently unprofitable paths — often the prelude to discovery. Beyond this impatience, which sometimes also mars his poems, lay a second obstacle, his rebellious nature. To suit him a discipline had to be morally and aesthetically attractive. Would he ever have accepted the iron discipline of science: impersonal, amoral and aesthetically neutral? Perhaps, if he had seen that the results achieved within its limits can be elegant, and had believed that scientists are improved morally by the knowledge that they cannot cheat Nature; or perhaps not. All this is speculation. What is certain is that if Shelley had turned his hand to science in earnest his achievements would have been limited more by his temperament than his intellect.

Writers who figure in the history of science, like Bacon and Goethe, are rare; but Shelley's gift of expressing in his verse a scientific outlook which 'permeates it through and through' is even rarer. It is difficult to define this special scientific flavour. Probably its most important component is persistent analysis of Nature : being eager to delve beneath the surface of appearance, instead of seeing things whole like Keats and Shakespeare; searching out the causal chain between one facet of Nature and another, and linking those facets imaginatively or metaphorically to interpret the scene described. It is in his command of this last technique that Shelley scores. Erasmus Darwin, for example, is assiduous in seeking causal links between one fact and another, but he records his speculations straightforwardly, unimaginatively, in the scientific jargon of his day. Jargon perishes, and even a masterpiece of science is rarely read in its original form. (Newton's *Principia*, translated out of Latin, is now difficult reading even for the specialist mathematician, because Newton's style, terminology and technique are unfamiliar.) Shelley often cheats Time, at some cost in obscurity, by avoiding jargon and using scientific theory as the basis for an imaginative jump. Though the theory may have proved in part erroneous, its modern version often enables us to see the logic of the jump; we take a different path to the same end-point. For example, Shelley accepts Walker's theory that fire, heat, light, caloric,

phlogiston and electricity are as one. But Shelley discards
the outmoded technical terms caloric and phlogiston, so that
his version of the idea can be treated as true — in the sense
that heat, light and electricity may all be radiated as electromagnetic waves — whereas Walker's can't, because the very
terms he uses give him away. Any poet who wants to try
this style must decide for himself how much to blunt the
razor-edge precision of a 'fact' of contemporary science.
If he is too precise, or, worst of all, flirts with the jargon
of a rapidly developing science, he will become dated, and
eventually unreadable. It is another illustration of the
platitude that science and poetry do not readily mix : the
brew must be stirred with a very cunning hand if a palatable
product is to emerge.

The few writers who have taken an equal interest in
science and poetry seem to accept that no other major
English poet can seriously challenge Shelley in this hybrid
form. Whether this valuation, or the present chapter, is
justified can be judged from the examples in the next two
chapters. Shelley's nearest rivals are probably Tennyson
and Coleridge, whose *Ancient Mariner* has many tacit references to scientific theory and practice : even the myth of
the star within the nether tip of the crescent moon was based
on Herschel's observations of points of light on the dark
part of the surface, really 'bright spots' on the moon shining
by earthlight.[8] Wordsworth, on the other hand, as Whitehead says, had little real interest in science. He was intuitive not analytical in his approach to Nature. He
respected scientific achievement, it is true, and indeed he
used to provide the motto for the premier British scientific
journal,

> To the solid ground
> Of Nature trusts the mind that builds for aye.

But he disliked scientific method : 'we murder to dissect'
was almost a maxim with him.[19]

Two main conclusions can now be drawn. First,
Shelley's attitude to science emphasizes again the surprisingly modern climate of thought in which he chose to live.

We have already seen how he anticipated the trends of reform in politics and in social convention, and the drift away from organized religion. To these three we may now add a belief in the possibilities of science which would have seemed out of proportion until modern times. Whatever our own opinion of the twentieth century may be, we can hardly doubt that Shelley would have been very much at home in it.

The second conclusion refers to the 'scientific style' we shall meet in the next few chapters. Though too much of this style would be intolerable, a mastery of it, combined with sparing use, must add to a poet's stature.

NOTES TO VIII: A NEWTON AMONG CHEMISTS?

1. Laplace's claim sums up the eighteenth-century view, though it was made in 1814, in the *Essai Philosophique sur les Probabilités*.

2. See Sherwood Taylor, *Short History of Science* (1939), pp. 161–2.

3. Walker, *Familiar Philosophy*, preface, p. xi. For more details of Walker's speculations, see P. H. Butter, *Shelley's Idols of the Cave*, pp. 140–57.

4. See W. E. Dick, 'Science at Oxford', *Discovery*, Sept. 1954.

5. Hogg, i. 49. Chapter III of Hogg's *Life of Shelley* was reprinted from his 'Shelley Papers' in the *New Monthly Magazine* of 1832.

6. Hogg, i. 50–2.

7. Cayley's essay was reprinted by the Royal Aeronautical Society in 1910.

8. Hogg, i. 55–8.

9. Coleridge, *Letters* (ed. E. L. Griggs) i. 305. For further details of Darwin, see D. King-Hele, *Erasmus Darwin*.

10. See B. Farrington, *Greek Science*, i. 79. For the history of the word *evolution*, see C. Singer, *Short History of Scientific Ideas* (1959), pp. 500–503.

11. *Zoonomia* (1794) i. 506.

12. *Zoonomia* i. 507.

13. *Temple of Nature*, i. 333–4.

14. See, *e.g.*, J. Huxley, *Evolution in Action* (1953), pp. 21–3.

15. *Economy of Vegetation*, i. 289–96. For more details of Darwin's influence on Shelley, see C. Grabo, *A Newton among Poets*, and D. King-Hele, *The Essential Writings of Erasmus Darwin*, pp. 172–5.

16. See Hogg, i. 267–8. Arcturus and Orion figure in *Prince Athanase*, ll. 195–7. Jupiter and Venus appear in letters, e.g. *Letters* ii. 25, 30. See also A. J. Meadows, *The High Firmament* (1969), pp. 167–170.

17. A. N. Whitehead, *Science and the Modern World*, p. 104.

18. These bright spots were first observed, through Herschel's telescope, by Dr. Lind's wife on 4 May 1783. See *Keats–Shelley Memorial Bulletin*, XVIII (1967), p. 3.

19. For Wordsworth's attitude to science, see H. Dingle, *Science and Literary Criticism* (1949), pp. 129–32.

IX

PROMETHEUS UNBOUND

I say unto you which hear, Love your enemies,
do good to them which hate you.
St. Luke

1

Prometheus Unbound, a 'lyrical drama in four acts', is the greatest, though not the most perfect, of Shelley's poems, difficult to grasp in all its detail, yet clear enough in its broad aims. We are given a preview of Man's escape from the restraints now stifling him, and a forecast of the principles which he will have accepted before he attains the maximum of happiness and freedom open to him. Prometheus represents the mind of Man, and his liberation is symbolic of Man's.

The writing of *Prometheus Unbound* was done in three short spells. Act I was written in September and October 1818 at Este, near Venice; Acts II and III in March and April 1819 at Rome among the ruins of the Baths of Caracalla, under a 'bright blue sky'; and Act IV in November and December 1819 at Florence. The subject had been in Shelley's mind for over a year before he began to write — an unusually long incubation period for him — and he had considered Tasso and Job, as well as Prometheus, for his hero.

One of his reasons for picking the legend of Prometheus was the disagreement between the classical versions of it, which left him free to choose between them. According to Hesiod, Prometheus brought calamity on mankind when he angered the gods by stealing fire from heaven, and the innocent golden age came to an end. Shelley accepted this view in 1813 when, as a vegetarian, he eyed with distaste the inventor of cooking. But he never took kindly to the

idea of a primaeval golden age, and by 1819 he preferred
Aeschylus's version of the legend, as implied in the *Prometheus
Bound*. There Prometheus appears as Man's benefactor, who
brought fire, number, writing, medicine and the arts as
gifts from heaven to the hitherto ignorant, beast-like mortals.
This impudence infuriated Zeus, chief of the gods and no
friend to men. So Zeus had him chained to a rock in the
Caucasus. There Prometheus remains at the end of
Aeschylus's play, nursing a secret known to him alone : that
if Zeus should marry Thetis, he would beget a son more
powerful than himself — a prophecy Zeus would have found
horribly plausible, since he had ousted his own father
Cronos. Unless he reveals this secret, Prometheus is doomed
to remain shackled in the icy mountains for thirty thousand
years, his entrails being devoured daily by an eagle (or, in
some versions, a vulture). The *Prometheus Bound* was the
second part of a trilogy, and Aeschylus completed the story
in the third part, *Prometheus Unbound*, now lost, where
Prometheus was reconciled with Zeus.

Shelley creates a new myth from the skeleton of the old.
In his version Prometheus remains in torment until the time
is ripe for Demogorgon, the destined son of Zeus and Thetis,
to overthrow his father. After the downfall of Jupiter
(Shelley uses the Roman names for Zeus and the other
gods), Prometheus is formally unbound by Hercules. Shelley
chose a story with familiar names in it so that his readers
might feel at home among the *dramatis personae* and pass with
less effort in identification to the powers they represent —
probably a better plan than bringing on personifications
like Faith and Evil, or reviving obscure names, as Blake too
often did. The drama thus unfolds on two levels : ostensibly
it records a reshuffling of power among the Olympians ; at
the deeper level each character represents some trait in Man,
preferably a trait associated with that character in legend.
Thus the fact that Prometheus suffers avoidable pain implies
that Man is cruelly restricted by unnecessary chains ; while
Jupiter's fall is more impressive because, to minds conditioned by Greek myth, his name spells irresistible power.

2

Act I of *Prometheus Unbound* is modelled on the *Prometheus Bound* of Aeschylus.[1] Prometheus is chained throughout, in a remote part of the Caucasus. In this no-man's-land between heaven and earth he is permanently 'at home' to any gods or daemons who care to call on him, and their visits provide the framework for the action. The purpose of Act I is to expose Prometheus to temptation: his reactions show whether he is ripe for liberation. It turns out that he is (though this is not stated until Act II), so that Act I serves to define, obliquely not explicitly, the qualities of mind which, in Shelley's view, go with true freedom.

Prometheus is discovered bound to the wall of a ravine of icy rocks, still enduring the torments he has suffered for 'three thousand years of sleep-unsheltered hours' because he will not reveal his secret. His anguish is brought out forcibly in images alive with 'the pain of cutting, of tearing, of splitting . . . reinforced by cold':[2]

> The crawling glaciers pierce me with the spears
> Of their moon-freezing crystals, the bright chains
> Eat with their burning cold into my bones. . . .
>
> 208. 31-3

Though he can see no end to his affliction, Prometheus welcomes the passing of the hours because some day, one of those 'wingless, crawling hours' will preside over Jupiter's fall. 'Hours' figure prominently in *Prometheus Unbound*. Each Hour 'owns' the time it labels, and even exerts some control over the pattern of the events; thus the Hour of Jupiter's fall is almost his executioner.

In the long opening speech Prometheus defines his attitude to his oppressor Jupiter. At first, resenting his punishment, he had loathed the name of Jupiter and railed against him furiously. Now Prometheus pities him because he rules as an absolute tyrant, unloved by his subjects and doomed to fall. Prometheus ends his soliloquy by asking to be reminded of the frenzied curse he once pronounced against Jupiter. He is answered evasively, first by Voices

from the elements and then by The Earth herself, his
mother, who explains that she can repeat the curse only in
the language of the dead, which he fails to understand; she
dares not speak the language of the living

> lest Heaven's fell King
> Should hear, and link me to some wheel of pain
> More torturing than the one whereon I roll.

211. 140-2

She then recalls the disasters which followed Prometheus's
well-meant aid to Man:

> Then, see those million worlds which burn and roll
> Around us : their inhabitants beheld
> My spherèd light wane in wide Heaven. . . .
> . . . in the corn, and vines, and meadow-grass,
> Teemed ineradicable poisonous weeds
> Draining their growth, for my wan breast was dry
> With grief; and the thin air, my breath, was stained
> With the contagion of a mother's hate
> Breathed on her child's destroyer.

211. 163-5, 174-9

These quotations give us a foretaste of Act IV, with its
blend of exact science and vividly human metaphor. Shelley
sees the Earth as a living organism subject to pain and disease
which she passes on to Man, the unresented parasite on her
surface. This idea may derive from Adam Walker, who
used to tell his audiences that 'dead and inanimate as our
mother earth appears', she is 'fraught with veins and arteries
like the animal body'.[3] Pursuing this theme, Shelley hits
on an arresting and precise image, *the thin air, my breath*,
which is again curiously like Walker's definition: 'The
atmosphere is a thin fluid . . . principally made up of
heterogeneous matter exhaled from the earth'.[4] Shelley
also makes the different parts of his picture scientifically
consistent. The blight he describes leads to desert conditions
with few clouds (*my wan breast was dry*), and since clouds
reflect light well their removal would indeed make the earth's
spherèd light wane. Finally — and here we enter the realm of
speculation — Shelley's guess of a *million* inhabited worlds
is not without support from modern astronomers.[5]

The Earth, in her maternal wisdom, next offers to explain the mysteries of life :

> For know there are two worlds of life and death :
> One that which thou beholdest; but the other
> Is underneath the grave, where do inhabit
> The shadows of all forms that think and live
> Till death unite them and they part no more.
>
> 212. 195-9

Prometheus summons a ghost from this shadowy world to repeat the curse on Jupiter. But on hearing the curse again, he wants to unsay it, regretting he was once so vindictive: 'I wish no living thing to suffer pain'. His willingness to forgive is a necessary prelude to liberation, though The Earth misinterprets it as a sign of weakness.

That ends what might be called the first section of Act I, though Shelley gives no divisions. Prometheus's soliloquy, The Earth's autobiography, and the recitation of the curse sum up events to date, and set the stage for what follows.

In the second section (lines 311-657) Prometheus faces and survives temptation. He is watched by Ione and Panthea, two daughters of Ocean, who comment on the action, like a Greek chorus. Ione asks the questions, and Panthea (literally *all-seeing*) knows the answers. Thus on the symbolic plane, where Prometheus represents the mind of Man, Ione is Hope and Panthea informed Faith. As Ione and Panthea wait, 'Jove's world-wandering herald, Mercury' approaches over the mountains, bringing an ultimatum from Jupiter. Prometheus must either surrender his secret at once — and if he does he will live among the gods 'lapped in voluptuous joy' — or be handed over to the Furies, who have already arrived and lurk near gnashing their teeth. Prometheus rejects the bribe: he will not abandon the down-trodden race of men; he intends to answer evil with good, because kindness is 'keen reproach' to such as Jupiter; and he is content to await the destined Hour, comforted by the thought that it is always getting nearer. The well-meaning Mercury warns him that he may have a very long time to wait; but Prometheus is

unshaken, and Mercury, obeying a signal from Jove, speeds
away —

> See where the child of Heaven with wingèd feet
> Runs down the slanted sunlight of the dawn.
>
> 217. 437-8

So, with sandals twinkling, Mercury fades from sight, leaving the impression that he is a conscientious courier too
humane for his messages, with the divided loyalty of any
good-natured state servant employed by a brutal dictator.
Mercury's dictator, Jupiter, is not just another caricature of
an anthropomorphic God, but rather the guiding power
behind evil institutions, the essence of orthodoxy and reaction,
the enemy of Man's aspirations.

As soon as Mercury has gone the Furies, 'blackening the
birth of day with countless wings', begin their work.
Prometheus falters for a moment when he sees them, but
pain has been his lot for so many years that he can endure
their physical tortures nonchalantly :

> Yet am I king over myself, and rule
> The torturing and conflicting throngs within,
> As Jove rules you when Hell grows mutinous.
>
> 219. 492-4

The Furies, baulked, break into a snarling incantation in
one of the galloping metres Shelley handled so easily. Next,
changing their tactics, they cut Prometheus to the heart,
first by showing him the evils men have yet to suffer, and
then by presenting a picture of Christ, as a reminder that

> those who do endure
> Deep wrongs for man, and scorn, and chains, but heap
> Thousandfold torment on themselves and him.
>
> 221. 594-6

One of the Furies drives home the moral by predicting how
the forces for good on earth will run to waste by acting at
cross-purposes. A country's rulers either cling to custom
and are conditioned by hypocrisy, if born in the ruling
classes, or, if they are men of humble origin who have
wormed their way into power, delude themselves into

thinking that a system which lets them climb cannot be too
bad. In either case the governing classes

> dare not devise good for man's estate,
> And yet they know not that they do not dare.
> The good want power, but to weep barren tears.
> The powerful goodness want : worse need for them.
> The wise want love ; and those who love want wisdom ;
> And all best things are thus confused to ill.
> Many are strong and rich, and would be just,
> But live among their suffering fellow-men
> As if none felt : they know not what they do.
>
> 222. 623-33

Shelley was well aware, as these lines show, of the problems
which would remain even after reform had, on paper, been
effected. He ends his analysis neatly by quoting Christ's
words from the Cross, which apply more strongly to-day as
governments writhe in the grip of forces they can neither
control nor even comprehend.

Prometheus survives the Furies' onslaught, but his confidence is sapped ; it is time to relieve the tension, and the
rest of Act I is devoted to prophetic lyrics sung in turn by a
troop of spirits rather like those in Act I of Byron's *Manfred*.
Each spirit seems to represent some admirable human
quality, and together they prophesy Prometheus's liberation
by implying that he has developed, or is about to develop,
these virtues. The first four of these six lyrics bring news
of men on earth who are combating evil. The first spirit,
of heroism, speaks of those who are fighting for freedom.
The second spirit, of altruism, refers to the survivor of a
shipwreck

> who gave an enemy
> His plank, then plunged aside to die.
>
> 224: 721-2

The third spirit, of wisdom, describes a sage who had once
made a stir in the world. The fourth lyric is devoted to the
Poet, who

> will watch from dawn to gloom
> The lake-reflected sun illume
> The yellow bees in the ivy-bloom,

Nor heed nor see what things they be;
But from these create he can
Forms more real than living man,
Nurslings of immortality!

224. 743-9

The last two spirits have as their theme Love, with its
'shadows' Pain and Ruin. The sixth spirit's song is modelled
on a Homeric image elaborated by Agathon in the *Symposium*,[6] and much improved by Shelley :

Ah, sister ! Desolation is a delicate thing :
It walks not on the earth, it floats not on the air,
But treads with lulling footstep, and fans with silent wing
The tender hopes which in their hearts the best and
gentlest bear ;
Who, soothed to false repose by the fanning plumes above
And the music-stirring motion of its soft and busy feet,
Dream visions of aëreal joy, and call the monster, Love,
And wake, and find the shadow Pain, as he whom now
we greet.

225. 772-9

These songs comfort Prometheus, but the mention of
Love only saddens him by awaking memories of his own
beloved, Asia, who lives among the fertile valleys of the
'Indian Caucasus'. In the ancient myth Asia, a daughter
of Ocean, is unimportant. Love is the main theme of
Prometheus Unbound, however, and it is by his love for Asia
that Prometheus shows he is completely fit to be freed, that
he has positive virtues as well as the stoic qualities which
have enabled him to survive torture and temptation. Asia
herself, who appears in person in Act II, is poles apart,
temperamentally, from the confident, Amazonian Cythna.
Asia is submissive, diffident, eager to learn and quite
passive until roused by an intuition of Prometheus's release,
which comes when he thinks of her at the end of Act I.

In Act II Asia and her sister Panthea travel together
to Demogorgon's cave in the hope of finding out when
Prometheus is to be released. The Act begins with Asia
alone in her lovely vale at the crack of dawn, waiting for
Panthea, who is coming from Prometheus's rock. As soon

as she arrives the sisters discuss their dreams, which hint at Prometheus's release. Panthea in her dream felt as if she were a drop of dew vaporizing under the warmth of Prometheus's sun-like beams and being somehow absorbed into him. This confused sense of well-being gave way to clarity as she condensed again and focused his light, *i.e.* heard his words. This remarkable image, sustained through nineteen lines (71-89), is the first of many sublimations of sexual feeling into scientific form; the dispersals of morning mist in Act II often carry oblique sexual references. It might be expected that the metaphor of sun dispersing mist would imply the destruction of what the mist represents. But Shelley goes one step deeper scientifically by concentrating on the molecules of the droplets, which are activated by the sun and dance the more vigorously in his beams when the mist has vaporized.

This scientific vein continues when Asia and Panthea break off their discussion to follow Echoes which are beckoning them. They are led into a forest studded with rocks and caverns, and cheered on the way by choruses of spirits, who seem quite at home with the rhyme-scheme abbbacbddcbeefgffhhggii. These spirits live in strange places:

> The bubbles, which the enchantment of the sun
> Sucks from the pale faint water-flowers that pave
> The oozy bottom of clear lakes and pools,
> Are the pavilions where such dwell and float. . . .
> And when these burst, and the thin fiery air,
> The which they breathed within those lucent domes,
> Ascends to flow like meteors through the night,
> They ride on them, and rein their headlong speed,
> And bow their burning crests, and glide in fire
> Under the waters of the earth again.
>
> 233. 71-4, 77-82

To us there seems no connexion whatever between meteors from outer space and bubbles from decaying vegetation. But in Shelley's day it was not accepted that shooting-stars came from outside the earth: lightning, the aurora, shooting-stars and other aerial phenomena were all called 'meteors', whence the name meteorology. And, as P. H. Butter has pointed out, a complete gloss to Shelley's lines can be found in Adam Walker's *Familiar Philosophy*: 'In muddy ponds . . . bubbles of inflammable air will rise from the mud'. This gas either 'ignites in the character of Will-o'-th'-Wisp' or 'ascends to the upper regions, often forming meteors, falling stars'.[7]

This fanciful interlude ends as Asia and Panthea come out of the forest and climb to the top of the volcano where Demogorgon lives,

> Whence the oracular vapour is hurled up
> Which lonely men drink wandering in their youth,
> And call truth, virtue, love, genius, or joy,
> That maddening wine of life, whose dregs they drain
> To deep intoxication.

234. 4-8

The scenery is worthy of the deity who owns it. Around her Asia sees an expanse of billowy mist 'rolling on under the curdling winds', making an island of their vantage point and masking the country beneath. She hears the 'sun-awakened avalanche'

>   whose mass,
> Thrice sifted by the storm, had gathered there
> Flake after flake, in heaven-defying minds
> As thought by thought is piled, till some great truth
> Is loosened, and the nations echo round,
> Shaken to their roots, as do the mountains now.

234. 37-42

Whitehead has pointed out that the comparison will bear pressing: 'The final burst of sunshine which awakens the avalanche is not necessarily beyond comparison in magnitude with the other powers of nature which have presided over its slow formation. The same is true in science. The genius who has the good fortune to produce the final idea which transforms a whole region of thought, does not necessarily excel all his predecessors who have worked at the preliminary formation of ideas.'[8]

Asia and Panthea find themselves enveloped in the mist

and summoned in 'one of the most perfect Platonic lyrics in English poetry',[9] to descend 'to the deep':

> Through the shade of sleep,
> Through the cloudy strife
> Of Death and of Life;
> Through the veil and the bar
> Of things which seem and are,
> Even to the steps of the remotest throne,
> Down! Down! . . .
>
> 235. 56-62

At the base of the volcanic chimney they meet Demogorgon himself, 'a mighty darkness filling the seat of power' and exuding rays of gloom. Demogorgon is the most powerful figure in the drama. He is never properly visible to the other characters, even Jupiter, because he exists in a plane beyond their ken. He is the supreme executive power, yet he can act only when the states of mind of the participants warrant it. He is an Immanent Will, quiescent until activated by advances in the mind of Man. He stands ready to act as a catalyst in precipitating the great change when, and only when, Man has accepted the ideals of universal love and forgiveness. In Act I Prometheus, Man's representative, endured temptation and purged his mind of hate, envy and revenge. Before he is fit to be freed he must show love, too, and this he does in Act II, through Asia, who can be stirred to action only by the power of his love. Her journey to the underworld is thus the cue for his release: the entry of Ocean's daughters into Demogorgon's volcano has appropriately explosive results.[10]

The 'dread name' of Demogorgon, despite its Hellenic ring, is not to be found in the classical dictionaries. Demogorgon is mentioned by some late classical writers, *e.g.* Lucan, by Boccaccio in *Genealogia Deorum*, by Spenser in *The Faerie Queene* and by Milton in *Paradise Lost*. He receives a long note in Peacock's *Rhododaphne* and figures frequently in the letters of Hogg, Shelley and Peacock during 1817. The subterranean hide-out Shelley describes seems to be modelled on Spenser's:

Downe in the bottome of the deepe Abysse,
Where Demogorgon, in dull darknesse pent
Farre from the view of gods and heavens bliss,
The hideous Chaos keepes. . . .[11]

Asia and Panthea, undaunted by Demogorgon's amorph-
ous appearance, proceed to question him, and his enigmatic
replies make this scene the most difficult in the whole poem.
When Asia asks him who made the living world and all that
it contains, good and evil, he answers 'God', but refuses to
define his terms. This provokes Asia to give her own account
of the evolution of the world, which is in effect the version
of the Prometheus legend used by Aeschylus. Demogorgon
does not contradict Asia, but he cannot or will not reveal
more. In a reply rather less curt than usual he confesses that

a voice
Is wanting, the deep truth is imageless ;
For what would it avail to bid thee gaze
On the revolving world ? What to bid speak
Fate, Time, Occasion, Chance, and Change ? To these
All things are subject but eternal Love.

238. 115-20

Finally Asia asks when the destined hour of liberation will come, and at once she sees a procession of 'cars
drawn by rainbow-wingèd steeds' and driven by wild-eyed
charioteers. These are the immortal Hours hurrying to do
their stint of duty on earth. One of them, grim-faced,
stops to tell Asia that he is the Hour destined to preside
over Jupiter's downfall, now imminent. In modern idiom
he might be called Zero Hour or H-Hour. The next of the
Hours, that is Hour H-plus-one, is a young spirit 'with the
dove-like eyes of hope', who rides in 'an ivory shell inlaid
with crimson fire'. Asia is invited to go up in this vehicle,
which has a unique form of traction, as the Hour explains :

My coursers are fed with the lightning,
They drink of the whirlwind's stream,
And when the red morning is bright'ning
They bathe in the fresh sunbeam ;
They have strength for their swiftness I deem. . . .

Ere the cloud piled on Atlas can dwindle
We encircle the earth and the moon :
We shall rest from long labours at noon.

239. 163-7, 171-3

These lines are part of a lyric which can be treated as obscure background music for Asia's journey. But a more precise interpretation is possible, as Carl Grabo has shown. Shelley seems to have in mind the contemporary theory which held that atmospheric electricity was drawn up from the earth by the morning sun, became quiescent at noon and returned to earth at nightfall, in keeping with Adam Walker's speculation that electricity is 'a child of the sun'.[12] The lines quoted may thus, in modern idiom, be paraphrased as follows. 'My power unit operates by taking energy from electricity in the atmosphere. At dawn, when this electricity is sucked out by the sun, my air intake sweeps up the ions and stores the energy. This stored energy, together with more picked up as we travel, enables us to cover hundreds of thousands of miles during the morning. But at noon we have to rest because the air is no longer active and our stored energy must not be squandered.' This explanation, which is confirmed by a reference in Act III, adds nothing to the development of the drama ; but it does serve to warn us that behind an obscurity in *Prometheus Unbound* there usually lies not a riot of verbiage but an esoteric idea formulated in precise detail, and on this occasion an idea which may prove practical in space travel.

The spirit's car takes Asia and Panthea to a cloud-capped peak, and there Asia is transfigured. Her Platonic essence appears to Panthea, shining through the veil of her mortality. A voice in the air, really Prometheus himself, praises her radiance in what is perhaps the most highly-charged of all Shelley's lyrics, 'Life of Life'. The dazzling imagery depends on identifying love with light and fire :

Life of Life ! thy lips enkindle
  With their love the breath between them ;
And thy smiles before they dwindle
  Make the cold air fire ; then screen them

> In those looks, where whoso gazes
> Faints, entangled in their mazes. . . .
>
> 241. 48-53

The song certainly raises the emotional temperature : never
has love been celebrated with more fiery fervour. But the
intoxicating metre cannot mask some unpleasing technical
oddities. For example, the same vowel is repeated too
often, the first line, as read, *Life 'f Life thy lips inkindle,* being
all *i*; and then, with typical virtuosity, comes a twisted
echo in the last 1½ lines, *gazes 'n faints, their mazes entangled,*
with *a* instead of *i*.

Asia replies quietly to this fiery praise, beginning with a
vivid complex of sense images :

> My soul is an enchanted boat,
> Which, like a sleeping swan, doth float
> Upon the silver waves of thy sweet singing;
> And thine doth like an angel sit
> Beside the helm conducting it,
> Whilst all the winds with melody are ringing.
>
> 241. 72-7

The symbolism here is Neoplatonic : an individual life is
looked on as a river down which 'the soul moves as in a
boat to rejoin the sea of the infinite'.[13] Asia's soul is floating
down on the waves of sweet singing to a 'sea profound of
ever-spreading sound' akin to the timeless Platonic heaven
of pre-existence :

> Till through Elysian garden islets
> By thee, most beautiful of pilots,
> Where never mortal pinnace glided,
> The boat of my desire is guided. . . .
> We have passed Age's icy caves,
> And Manhood's dark and tossing waves,
> And Youth's smooth ocean, smiling to betray:
> Beyond the glassy gulfs we flee
> Of shadow-peopled Infancy,
> Through Death and Birth, to a diviner day.
>
> 242. 91-4, 98-103

As in *Alastor* and *The Revolt of Islam,* waves on the sea represent crises in the soul brought on by the storms of emotion.

Asia's song, which ends the second Act, is the emotional counterpart of her earlier philosophical quest, when with Panthea she bearded Demogorgon in his cave beyond 'the veil and the bar of things which seem and are'.[13]

The climax of the drama is now imminent. Act III opens in Heaven, where Jupiter sits confidently enthroned, with the lesser deities assembled. He introduces himself with a soliloquy, like Prometheus in Act I and Asia in Act II. Jupiter knows the destined Hour is near, but he quite mistakes its significance. For he believes Demogorgon will, like a dutiful child, stamp out the only troublesome 'spark' in the world, the soul of Man. After that Jupiter expects to reign omnipotent. The tension mounts as Demogorgon's chariot is heard thundering up Olympus, and Jupiter is confronted by Demogorgon's incarnation:

> *Jupiter* Awful shape, what art thou? Speak!
> *Demogorgon* Eternity. Demand no direr name.
> Descend, and follow me down the abyss.
> I am thy child, as thou wert Saturn's child;
> Mightier than thee: and we must dwell together
> Henceforth in darkness. Lift thy lightnings not.
> The tyranny of heaven none may retain,
> Or reassume, or hold, succeeding thee.
>
> 243. 51-8

For a moment Jupiter struggles. Then, finding his power ineffectual, he begs for mercy in the hope that Demogorgon is under the control of the tender-hearted Prometheus. But there is no escape for him, and he falls with Demogorgon. Despite his brief spell of authority Demogorgon is in no sense Jupiter's successor, as he himself emphasizes: 'the tyranny of Heaven *none* may retain'. Demogorgon's rôle is to observe Man's state of mind, as represented in Prometheus, and, when the time is ripe, to ensure that he has his reward.

After an interlude, which serves to confirm the change in the balance of power, Hercules formally unbinds Prometheus — strength serving wisdom and love. Hercules appears only because the legend demands it; after speaking 3½ lines he departs, never to be mentioned again. Prometheus

himself has so far only been able to display passive
virtues. Now he greets his long-lost Asia. By their mystic
union wisdom, gentleness, tolerance and forgiveness are
married to love and creative power, and Man is married to
Nature. Prometheus and Asia are to live in a cave, reminiscent of the Neoplatonic 'cave of mind', from which they
will contemplate the human world and catch its echoes and
shadows, among them

> the progeny immortal
> Of Painting, Sculpture, and rapt Poesy,
> And arts, though unimagined, yet to be.
> The wandering voices and the shadows these
> Of all that man becomes, the mediators
> Of that best worship Love, by him and us
> Given and returned.
>
> 247. 54-60

Before retiring to his cave, Prometheus turns to his
mother, Earth, asking her what changes she feels, and
Shelley returns to the vital empathic imagery of Act I:

> through my withered, old, and icy frame
> The warmth of an immortal youth shoots down
> Circling.
>
> 247. 88-90

Now she will always welcome Man when he returns to his
benign mother at death, and, as in *Queen Mab*, she will
bring forth plenty and provide pleasant weather. The
child-like Spirit of the Earth complements this picture
by describing the obvious changes on the planet: hard
features, angry looks and hollow smiles, the 'foul masks'
hiding the inmost spirit of good, have been torn aside, he
says, and all things have 'put their evil nature off'.

Little time has yet passed since Jupiter fell, and Hour
H-plus-one, the Hour with the ion-swallowing coursers, is
still in office. The Spirit of the Hour has been at work
spreading the good news over the world, and now returns
to present his picture of Man regenerated. The Spirit's
coursers have gone back to their birthplace — the sun,
which sucks up the atmospheric electricity they use as fuel,
and governs our measures of time. Deprived of her aerial

chariot the Spirit went wandering 'among the haunts and dwellings of mankind', and was at first disappointed to see no outward changes.

> But soon I looked,
> And behold, thrones were kingless, and men walked
> One with the other even as spirits do,
> None fawned, none trampled. . . .
> None wrought his lips in truth-entangling lines
> Which smiled the lie his tongue disdained to speak.
>
> 252. 130-3, 142-3

Women, too, were 'frank, beautiful and kind',

> Speaking the wisdom once they could not think,
> Looking emotions once they feared to feel,
> And changed to all which once they dared not be,
> Yet being now, made earth like heaven.
>
> 253. 157-60

All the symbols of authority, 'thrones, altars, judgement-seats, and prisons', stand vacant and unregarded now, while something akin to Godwinian anarchy reigns :

> The painted veil, by those who were, called life,
> Which mimicked, as with colours idly spread,
> All men believed or hoped, is torn aside ;
> The loathsome mask has fallen, the man remains —
> Sceptreless, free, uncircumscribed — but man :
> Equal, unclassed, tribeless, and nationless,
> Exempt from awe, worship, degree, the king
> Over himself ; just, gentle, wise : but man
> Passionless ? — no, yet free from guilt or pain,
> Which were, for his will made or suffered them ;
> Nor yet exempt, though ruling them like slaves,
> From chance, and death, and mutability,
> The clogs of that which else might oversoar
> The loftiest star of unascended heaven,
> Pinnacled dim in the intense inane.
>
> 253. 190-204

This final summary is not as clear as it might be, because the wording is careless and the punctuation is so arguable that I have altered it. The lines begin with the image of the veil, which for Shelley, as for many a Platonist before

N

him, denotes the wrappings of reality which swathe the inaccessible Platonic ideal.   It is unfair to complain about the string of negatives which follows : our language has no familiar wieldy words which are both appropriate and un-ambiguous : even if it had, the truism that happiness is best defined in negatives would justify the wording.   Shelley is careful to qualify his optimism by emphasizing that chance and death and mutability will persist.   He ends with a typical crescendo, which culminates in the striking final line. This may derive from Lucretius, with Shelley transcribing the Latin *inane* (empty space) used by Lucretius, just as in the *Ode to Liberty* he coins the phrase *daedal earth* from the *daedala tellus* of Lucretius.   Or it may derive from Erasmus Darwin's

> Hung with gold-tresses o'er the vast inane.[14]

3

Act IV of *Prometheus Unbound* is a sustained lyric praising the new world; Shelley does not refer overtly to Acts I-III, and adds nothing to the plot.   When he finished Act III in April 1819 he at first thought the poem was complete.   But he must soon have felt that a happy finale was needed to balance the grim Act I, for he made no attempt to prepare Acts I-III for publication during the seven months which passed before he began Act IV.

The 578 lines of Act IV comprise two series of choric songs or duets, separated by a quiet interval of Nature-analysis.   Ione and Panthea, who contribute this analysis, are the only characters of human form, and many of the choruses are sung by undefined troops of spirits.   Shelley thus jettisons two regular aids for compelling attention in drama — plot and character — and relies instead on metrical virtuosity, hypnotic rhythms and a sustained note of exulta-tion.   Many readers, dazzled by this *bravura*, are led on to the end too quickly, and emerge with the impression that this is verse which sounds fine but means nothing at all. Closer inspection shows, however, that at times Shelley is describing the mechanisms of Nature with a precision and wealth of detail unparalleled in English poetry.

In Act IV Ione and Panthea continue as commentators, and the choruses are sung for their benefit. First, they watch the spectres of bygone Hours bearing 'Time to his tomb in eternity', a sight which revives memories of the murky past:

> Once the hungry Hours were hounds
> Which chased the day like a bleeding deer,
> And it limped and stumbled with many wounds
> Through the nightly dells of the desert year.
>
> 256. 73-6

Now, in contrast,

> The pine boughs are singing
> Old songs with new gladness,

and time has become unimportant, because no dreaded tomorrows or sighed-for yesterdays mark its progress. Shelley was sure about this feature of his new world, for he had the timeless cosmos of Platonic ideas at the back of his mind, and he implies that time will only reassert itself if evil creeps in. Most readers probably accept his picture, but to some it will be distasteful. Timelessness either appeals or appals, according to temperament: it is not worth arguing about, just as it is not worth asking whether the opening and closing of a mussel implies endless boredom or ever-renewed bliss.

To confirm the rumour about the pine boughs, which might be wishful thinking, Shelley brings on a chorus of 'spirits of the human mind':

> We come from the mind
> Of human kind
> Which was late so dusk, and obscene, and blind. . . .
> And our singing shall build
> In the void's loose field
> A world for the Spirit of Wisdom to wield;
> We will take our plan
> From the new world of man,
> And our work shall be called the Promethean.
>
> 256. 93-5; 258. 153-8

Whenever the pace slackens an antiphonal chorus whips it up again :

> Then weave the web of the mystic measure;
> From the depths of the sky and the ends of the earth,
> Come, swift Spirits of might and of pleasure,
> Fill the dance and the music of mirth,
>   As the waves of a thousand streams rush by
>   To an ocean of splendour and harmony !

257. 129-34

Sheltered behind the urgent rhythms of lines like these, Shelley hints at his idea of unity in Nature by intertwining images belonging to different senses.[15]

After 180 lines in almost corybantic tempo the Spirits vanish, leaving Ione and Panthea to report quietly what they see next. Ione speaks first, about the new moon :

> I see a chariot like that thinnest boat,
> In which the Mother of the Months is borne
> By ebbing light into her western cave,
> When she upsprings from interlunar dreams;
> O'er which is curved an orblike canopy
> Of gentle darkness.

259. 206-11

The moon's chariot has for its wheels massive thunderclouds flecked with 'azure and gold' as they glint in the setting sun, like the sea beneath them. Driving the chariot is a white 'wingèd infant', the essence of mooniness :

> Its limbs gleam white, through the wind-flowing folds
> Of its white robe, woof of ethereal pearl.
> Its hair is white, the brightness of white light
> Scattered in strings; yet its two eyes are heavens
> Of liquid darkness, which the Deity
> Within seems pouring, as a storm is poured
> From jaggèd clouds, out of their arrowy lashes,
> Tempering the cold and radiant air around
> With fire that is not brightness.

259. 222-30

Here Shelley translates into human form the main features of the full moon's face. The obvious first impression of the moon as normally seen, its silver whiteness unrelieved by warmer colours, is driven home by the repetition of *white* and *bright*, relieved only by *dark*. The *wind-flowing folds* of its robe are immobile, like sculpture : they are the straggling, corrugated lunar mountain ranges. Its *eyes . . . of . . . darkness* are craters of the moon and the darkness is called *liquid* because Shelley is referring to craters in the dark patches of the surface, which were given the name 'seas' by Galileo (though Shelley knew they were dry, for he refers to 'solid oceans' in line 358). Bright lines radiate from some of the craters, forming ray-systems which have not yet been satisfactorily explained : these rays are, near the craters, their *arrowy lashes,* and further away they form *white hair . . . scattered in strings*. Shelley goes on to imagine the darkness of the *eyes* pouring itself out in radiation which tempers the cold air around Ione *with fire that is not brightness*. He is referring to infra-red rays, the 'dark heat rays' discovered by Herschel in 1800. It is fanciful to suggest that the whole of the moon's infra-red radiation is emitted from a small part of the surface, but when the rest of the imagery is so precise an imaginative touch does not come amiss.

Panthea, not to be outdone, describes an orb of complex structure, intended, it seems, to summarize in one figure the ultimate constituents of matter, the spirit and method of science, and a microcosm of the earth. The involved spheres described by Dante in the *Paradiso*, by Camões in the *Lusiads*, and by Milton in *Paradise Lost* [16] may have given Shelley the hint for this image ; but he develops it in far more detail than his predecessors. Panthea sees

A sphere, which is as many thousand spheres,	1
Solid as crystal, yet through all its mass	2
Flow, as through empty space, music and light :	3
Ten thousand orbs involving and involved,	4
Purple and azure, white, and green, and golden,	5
Sphere within sphere ; and every space between	6
Peopled with unimaginable shapes,	7
Such as ghosts dream dwell in the lampless deep,	8
Yet each inter-transpicuous, and they whirl	9
Over each other with a thousand motions,	10

Upon a thousand sightless axles spinning,   11
And with the force of self-destroying swiftness,   12
Intensely, slowly, solemnly roll on,
Kindling with mingled sounds, and many tones,
Intelligible words and music wild.
With mighty whirl the multitudinous orb
Grinds the bright brook into an azure mist
Of elemental subtlety, like light ;
And the wild odour of the forest flowers,
The music of the living grass and air,
The emerald light of leaf-entangled beams
Round its intense yet self-conflicting speed,
Seem kneaded into one aëreal mass
Which drowns the sense.

260. 238-61

Shelley was attracted by the notion that liveliness extended
to the smallest particles, and he therefore had an intuitive
'feel' for modern theories.   The result is that the elaborate
picture he paints in the lines above can be interpreted in
the modern idiom.   We may take the *many thousand spheres*
(line 1) or the *ten thousand orbs* (line 4) as individual atoms,
each consisting of a series of concentric electron shells (*sphere
within sphere*, line 6) with the outermost shells of neighbouring
atoms often interlinked (*involved*, line 4).   Stray electrons
(*unimaginable shapes*, line 7) drift through the *space between*
(line 6) the atoms.   On changing their energy-levels the
electrons give rise to a *flow* of radiation, the *music and light*
of line 3.   Whole atoms are constantly changing position
(*they whirl over each other*, lines 9-10), while at the same time
rotating (*upon a thousand sightless axles spinning*, line 11).
Looked at from outside the entire process can be recognized
as vibration (*the force of self-destroying swiftness*, line 12).   Of
course, Shelley did not foresee this interpretation ; nor is
the passage a good example of his scientific style.   For he is
deliberately vague, and it is only because of his correct
intuition of molecular movement that the lines are satisfying
to-day.   In his time there was little support for the idea
that heat was a form of motion, an idea suggested by Bacon,[17]
and put on a mathematical basis by Daniel Bernoulli in

1738. But Shelley enjoyed both heat and movement, and unconsciously linked the two. The kinetic theory of gases has confirmed his intuition that the molecular dance mounts to a frenzy as the temperature rises. Mixed up with these intuitions of modern theories, there is some fantasy and some propaganda in favour of his idea of unity in Nature. He tries to effect a marriage between odour, light and sound which *seem kneaded into one*, and here he may have been led on by Adam Walker, who was most impressed by the fact, pointed out by Newton, that the widths of spectrum occupied by each of the seven colours correspond exactly with the frequency-differences between the seven musical notes. This suggested the idea of 'luminous music', in which the colours corresponding to the notes would be thrown on a screen.[18]

Among the radiations issuing from the orb is a 'super X-ray' which reveals to Panthea the mysteries of the earth's interior. This radiation can penetrate time as well as space, and it exposes the 'melancholy ruins of cancelled cycles'. Taking his cue from *Endymion*,[19] Shelley brings on a museum-ful of fossilized relics and a rout of prehistoric monsters. He affirms his faith in evolution by referring pointedly to city-dwellers whose fossil remains are mortal but not human. Yet he ends perversely by making Panthea mention the cataclysmic theory

Ione's report on the moon and Panthea's on the history of the earth are followed by a gravitational love-song between the Earth and the Moon themselves. First, Shelley dons the mantle of a universal architect, as he nonchalantly guides the unwieldy masses in their orbits. It was in just such a mood that he wrote a letter encouraging Henry Reveley in his steamboat project: 'God sees his machine spinning round the sun and delights in its success, and has taken out patents to supply all the suns in space with the same manufacture. Your boat will be to the ocean of water what the earth is to the ocean of aether — a prosperous and swift voyager.'[20] Shelley's 'Earth' and 'Moon' are no machines, however: he thoroughly humanizes them. The Earth, the senior partner in the love-duet, is a masculine spirit representing the astronomical object Earth, yet like Mother Earth in Act I he responds to changes on his surface. His joy at Man's new freedom soon infects his satellite, the Moon. Shelley imagines her 'solid oceans' beginning to flow, while 'green stalks' and 'bright flowers' sprout from her sterile surface under the benign influence of a newly replenished atmosphere. The Earth, for his part, exults in Man's achievements. On earth now 'familiar acts are beautiful through love', and Man rules the material world as surely as the sun governs

> The unquiet republic of the maze
> Of planets, struggling fierce towards heaven's
> free wilderness.

263. 398-9

— a vivid picture of the apparent tug-of-war between gravitational attraction and 'centrifugal force'. Man has also mastered language, and has made great strides in science :

> The lightning is his slave; heaven's utmost deep
> Gives up her stars, and like a flock of sheep
> They pass before his eye, are numbered, and roll on!
> The tempest is his steed, he strides the air;
> And the abyss shouts from her depth laid bare,
> Heaven, hast thou secrets? Man unveils me; I have none.

264. 418-23

Of these four prophecies of Shelley's, three have been fulfilled, by the electric motor, by the progress of astrophysics and by the aeroplane; and the fourth has in part been fulfilled, too. For, though the secrets of the earth's interior are not yet *laid bare*, a good deal has been found out by measuring the rumbles of earthquake waves. This may have been what Shelley meant by *shouts* from *the abyss*; or it may be a coincidence that his wording fits modern techniques. If it is a verbal coincidence, a more curious one lurks behind, for certain surface earthquake waves are known to seismologists as 'Love waves'.[21] When Shelley distributed Universal Love through his new world, to guide Man among the waves of life (lines 409-11), he could scarcely have foreseen the career of Professor A. E. H. Love, after whom the earthquake waves are named.

After this résumé of their cues for joy, the Earth and the Moon begin the erotic myth in earnest:

> *The Earth.*   I spin beneath my pyramid of night,
> Which points into the heavens dreaming delight,
> Murmuring victorious joy in my enchanted sleep;
> As a youth lulled in love-dreams faintly sighing,
> Under the shadow of his beauty lying,
> Which round his rest a watch of light and warmth
> doth keep.
>
> 264. 444-9

The totally black shadow cast by the earth into sunlit space dwindles to a point at a distance of about 900,000 miles, and the earth thus forms the base of a slender cone of darkness. Shelley makes the most of this in the striking line, 'I spin beneath my pyramid of night'. In using *pyramid*, rather than *cone*, he may be harking back to a classical author who didn't know that the earth was a sphere, perhaps Pliny.[22] *His beauty* refers to the illuminated hemisphere of the earth, which is like a bright mantle *round* the sleeper at the earth's centre.

The cone of darkness plays its part in the Moon's reply. To Shelley light and dark were almost tangible, and so the Moon's most intimate contact with the Earth occurs at her eclipse:

> As in the soft and sweet eclipse,
> When soul meets soul on lovers' lips. . . .
> So when thy shadow falls on me.
>
> 265. 450-1, 453

The emotional tone does not prevent the Moon reporting carefully her own experience of gravitation:

> Thou art speeding round the sun
> Brightest world of many a one;
> Green and azure sphere which shinest
> With a light which is divinest
> Among all the lamps of Heaven
> To whom life and light is given;

I, thy crystal paramour
Borne beside thee by a power
Like the polar Paradise,
Magnet-like of lovers' eyes ;
I, a most enamoured maiden
Whose weak brain is overladen
With the pleasure of her love,
Maniac-like around thee move
Gazing, an insatiate bride,
On thy form from every side. . . .
Brother, wheresoe'er thou soarest
I must hurry, whirl and follow
Through the heavens wide and hollow,
Sheltered by the warm embrace
Of thy soul from hungry space,
Drinking from thy sense and sight
Beauty, majesty, and might,
As a lover or a chameleon
Grows like what it looks upon. . . .

265. 457-72, 476-84

Shelley stresses those features of the moon's motion which confirm his equation of love with gravitation. She always presents the same face to the earth ; so she is *gazing* on him lover-like. She looks at and revolves round him rather than the sun, although the sun's gravitational pull is more than twice as strong as his ; so she is faithful against odds, too, *wheresoe'er thou soarest I . . . follow.* Her face seems to wobble as she goes round — 'libration' is the technical term ; so she is indeed madly in love, *maniac-like* in her behaviour. (It may be objected that Shelley would not have been familiar with the moon's libration. But in his day basic astronomy of this kind was much more widely known than it is now, because it was among the few things that were known then. Adam Walker explains libration carefully.[23]) Shelley also exploits the phenomenon of earth-light — 'the old moon in the new moon's arms' — when he says the moon *grows like what it looks upon.* Not content with linking gravitation and love, Shelley hints that magnetism may play a part, too, when he refers to the attraction between the poles of magnets (*the polar Paradise, magnet-like*).

Shelley's concept of gravitational love spans the centuries in a strange way. For he may well have had the idea from the famous last line of Dante's *Paradiso*,

L' amor che muove il sole e l' altre stelle,

the words of a poet who died three hundred years before gravitation was formulated. Yet Shelley also links gravitation with electricity, magnetism, heat and light (in, *e.g.*, lines 376-7, 464-6, 437-43 and 322-3 respectively), and this brings him right up to date. Electricity, magnetism, heat and light were united by the electromagnetic theory of light, summarized mathematically in Maxwell's equations of 1873; gravitation still remains aloof, though Einstein spent his later years striving to bring it into an acceptable unified theory. Shelley generalizes his gravitational 'love' so well that we can take advantage of this extension in time when interpreting it: if we feel mediaeval, it can be the Aristotelian *primum mobile*; if we feel practical, we can think of it obeying Newton's inverse-square law; if we feel priggish, we can look on it as the tensor embodying the components of curvature of the four-dimensional space-time continuum.

As the Earth and Moon finish their duet Demogorgon reappears to sum up the poem's prophecy. He addresses himself to the widest possible audience, to the Earth, the Moon, Kings of suns and stars, Daemons and Gods; to 'ye happy Dead'; to the chemical elements, lead and the iodine in seaweed being singled out —

Ye elemental Genii, who have homes
From man's high mind even to the central stone
Of sullen lead; from heaven's star-fretted domes
To the dull weed some sea-worm battens on;

267. 539-42

to 'spirits whose homes are flesh', beasts and birds, worms and fish, leaves and buds, lightning and wind; and last, to Man, who was

once a despot and a slave;
A dupe and a deceiver; a decay;
A traveller from the cradle to the grave
Through the dim night of this immortal day.

267. 549-52

These invocations, to which undefined voices respond, point in a long-drawn crescendo towards Demogorgon's final summary:

This is the day, which down the void abysm
At the Earth-born's spell yawns for Heaven's despotism,
    And Conquest is dragged captive through the deep:
Love, from its awful throne of patient power
In the wise heart, from the last giddy hour
    Of dread endurance, from the slippery, steep,
And narrow verge of crag-like agony, springs
And folds over the world its healing wings.

Gentleness, Virtue, Wisdom, and Endurance,
These are the seals of that most firm assurance
    Which bars the pit over Destruction's strength;
And if, with infirm hand, Eternity,
Mother of many acts and hours, should free
    The serpent that would clasp her with his length,
These are the spells by which to reassume
An empire o'er the disentangled doom.

To suffer woes which Hope thinks infinite;
To forgive wrongs darker than death or night;
    To defy Power, which seems omnipotent;
To love, and bear; to hope till Hope creates
From its own wreck the thing it contemplates;
    Neither to change, nor falter, nor repent;
This like thy glory, Titan, is to be
Good, great and joyous, beautiful and free;
This is alone Life, Joy, Empire, and Victory.

267. 554-78

In the first of these three verses the syntax is strained because Shelley heightens the tension by inserting subsidiary clauses or phrases between subject and verb. This device usually increases the obscurity just as much as the tension, though it was used with notable success by Dylan Thomas, especially in his *Poem in October*. In the second of the three verses, which includes a reference to the tail-eating serpent symbolizing eternity, the δράκων οὐροβόρος,[24] Shelley suggests that the overthrown tyranny will revive if men degenerate in mind. He firmly believed that men will get the world they deserve; that true freedom cannot co-exist with hatred and revenge.

4

To gather the threads again after so many pages of detail it may be as well to recapitulate the myth embodied in *Prometheus Unbound*. Jupiter has chained Prometheus because he helped men to better themselves and would not yield up his secret — that the child of Jupiter and Thetis would overthrow his father. Prometheus defies the Furies sent to torture him, and shows he is wise, kindly and free from rancour. He thinks of Asia, his long-lost bride. She responds by visiting Demogorgon, the destined child of Jupiter, in his lair outside the physical world. Very soon after, Demogorgon ascends to Heaven, deposes Jupiter and retires to obscurity. Prometheus is unbound by Hercules and united to Asia.

This enigmatic sequence of events must be interpreted as myth rather than allegory. A detailed translation of the events into another medium, as in allegory, is not to be expected. It is rather the broad outlines which are of importance, some of the details being irrelevant. For example, the fact that Demogorgon is said to be Jupiter's son is not significant: it is merely a detail taken over from the Greek legend. The need to preselect the vital points makes it harder to interpret the myth. Shelley himself thought only five or six people would understand the poem,[25] and Mary warns us in her Note that 'it requires a mind as subtle and penetrating as his own to understand the mystic meanings scattered throughout the poem. They elude the ordinary reader by their abstraction and delicacy of distinction, but they are far from vague.' These warnings

need not deter us unduly, for now that so many scholars
have exercised their wits on the poem most of the subtleties
Mary mentions have been exposed, though it is only fair to
add that each new commentator seems to find more.

There is little doubt that Shelley's chief aim is to forecast
that Man can greatly improve his status, becoming almost
unrecognizably happier and wiser, if, and only if, he first
develops and encourages — genuinely, not with mere lip-
service — the Christian virtues of universal love and forgiveness. When Prometheus, Man's representative, shows he has
these qualities, Jupiter, the reactionary power, the 'everlasting No',[26] will topple from his throne. Then Prometheus will
wed Asia; so Man will combine wisdom, tolerance and
endurance with love and creative power, and live in harmony
with Nature.

Though it is generally agreed that this was Shelley's aim,
several variants have been suggested, and the most important
of them is the political interpretation. Shelley certainly
implies that political systems change when Jupiter falls
(though he always believed reform would be gradual, and
Jupiter's fall is sudden in the poem only because of the need
for a recognizable dramatic catastrophe). According to the
political interpretation, Jupiter's fall means reform's triumph,
Prometheus represents the enlightened thinkers of Shelley's
day, Mercury the supine drudges in the pay of the governing
classes (Jupiter), and the Furies the sycophants who grow
fat on the spoils of their master and let off steam by per-
secuting reformers. These identifications are not without a
grain of truth, but since Asia and Demogorgon are difficult
to fit in, the political variant is at best an illuminating side-
issue.[27]

Two other suggested variants, the Neoplatonic and the
scientific, are more helpful in clarifying symbols and obscurities than in translating the myth. Shelley's most
ambitious poem was not likely to have been written for the
greater glory of either Neoplatonism or science. Certainly
he was attracted by some of the Neoplatonists' symbols, but
he knew little of their arcana. Undoubtedly, too, Shelley

retained his early belief that scientific advance would go hand-in-hand with political and moral reform; and this faith declares itself fully in Act IV, which is, however, outside the myth.

If science matters so little in the interpretation, why, it may be asked, have I referred so often to the scientific undercurrents? There are three reasons: first, because the poem is most difficult where the undercurrents are strongest; second, because the usual commentaries tend to neglect the scientific allusions; and third, because of certain historical accidents in Shelley criticism. This third reason demands a little explanation. Between about 1925 and 1940 literary criticism was revivified by a potent injection of close analysis: the intention was to replace vague and often emotional generalizations by precise, logical analysis of detail. Unfortunately the pioneers of close criticism, though original, were not infallible, and they strangely misjudged Shelley. In retrospect it seems possible that they were angered by the inanities in some of his weaker lyrics and came to the better ones blinded by bias. Whatever the reason, some curious mistakes ensued,[28] and these are the historical accidents mentioned above. Since the pioneers had a high prestige in the 1930s their mistakes were ignored or forgotten, and their sniping was able to scar noticeably the façade of Shelley's reputation, and create an aroma of suspicion by implying that he didn't think clearly. Because this aroma still lingers on in some quarters, it is worth over-emphasizing that standards of scientific exactness which few other poets have even imagined are well within his range.

The philosophy behind the poem comes, as the variety of interpretation would suggest, not from one source but from several. The first which should be mentioned is Christianity. Shelley was an assiduous reader of the New Testament and in his vision of a world regenerated through universal brotherly love he is plainly following Christ's lead. So many of Christ's other doctrines appear that *Prometheus Unbound* can fairly be called one of the best poetic *exposés* of New Testament ethics. Shelley constantly commends passive resistance, forgiveness of wrongs and goodwill towards men ; and the veiled comparison between Christ and Prometheus in Act I confirms that he had Christian morality in mind.

The guiding light of Godwin suffers partial eclipse in *Prometheus Unbound*, because his ideas are often hardly relevant. Where they are relevant they are accepted readily enough : Shelley's 'new world of man' enjoys Godwinian anarchy ; he follows Godwin and Mary Wollstonecraft in advocating sexual equality ; on the subject of universal goodwill the Christian and Godwinian moralities overlap ; and, above all, Godwin buoyed Shelley's hope that human failings were eradicable. Without this hope *Prometheus Unbound* would never have been written. During his hide-and-seek with bailiffs and moneylenders in 1814, when he had lived like a vagrant, seeing human nature at its worst, he had been ready to despair : 'My imagination is confounded by the uniform prospect of the perfidy and wickedness and hardheartedness of mankind'.[29] Then to his rescue would come Godwin's arguments, backed possibly by Rousseau's and perhaps by Shakespeare's

> There is some soul of goodness in things evil,
> Would men observingly distil it out,

which he quoted in *Julian and Maddalo* and always tried to believe. He liked to imagine a shining core of good, 'the form that lives unchanged within', behind every shabby exterior, a thought-process similar to, though more decorous than, a biologist seeing in his mind's eye the beautiful viscera of an ugly man or a radiologist seeing the functional bone-structure. Shelley thus returns to Godwin for detail and for initial impetus ; but the poem's concepts transcend Godwinism.

For those concepts he turned, of course, to Plato. In *Prometheus Unbound* Shelley intertwines with remarkably little friction the ill-assorted strands of Platonism and Godwinism. The moral and political backgrounds are provided by Godwinism and Christianity, but Shelley is wearing heavily-tinted Platonic spectacles, through which he sees mundane objects, purged of their dross, as eternal Platonic forms. *Prometheus Unbound* is peopled with Platonic forms, which, for Shelley, are almost flesh and blood. Prometheus himself, it is true, deserves to be called a 'character' because of his struggle in Act I; but Asia is devoid of humanity, and represents an Idea, which has been called 'Creative Love', 'Nature' and everything between. Shelley often remoulds Platonic concepts to his own pattern. He was not a rigid adherent of any kind of Platonism — and here we must distinguish between (1) what Plato wrote, (2) what he was credited with and (3) the later, more systematic Neoplatonism. For Shelley, Platonism provided a treasure-chest of concepts, which he raided for his own ends. He applies to aesthetics the concept of ideal forms which Plato advanced as a theory of knowledge,[30] and he plays tricks with the Platonic theory of evil. The Platonist sees evil as a surface blemish which cannot extend to the eternal forms; Shelley transfers this notion to the real world to bring Plato into line with Godwin.

Shelley's interest in Plato had grown steadily as his devotion to practical reform waned. He made the transition not via the obvious link — from Godwin's utopia to Plato's, from *Political Justice* to *The Republic* — but via the shorter Socratic dialogues. He began re-reading these in earnest at Marlow late in 1817, when he was shifting to the realm of prophecy his hopes of reform in the world. Just then, too, he was feeling acutely the gaps in Godwin's earth-bound philosophy, and the theories of immortality, love and cosmology propounded in the *Phædo*, *Symposium* and *Timaeus* helped to fill those gaps. As a final, decisive factor, he had Peacock at his side that autumn, always ready to discuss and champion Plato. During 1818 Shelley read Plato systematically, and from then on many of his poems are imbued with Platonism. J. A. Notopoulos, in his exhaustive study of Shelley's Platonism, gives 53 quotations from *Prometheus Unbound*, comprising 280 lines, in which he finds traces of Platonism.[31]

Shelley's addiction to Plato throws light on his religious

o

opinions, which he tended to keep dark in his later years. Only out-and-out Platonists, for whom all European philosophy is in Whitehead's phrase a 'series of footnotes to Plato',[32] look upon Christianity and pantheism as mere branches on the tree of Platonism. It is more generally agreed, however, that the Christian doctrine of the immortality of the soul owes much to Plato. This suggests that Shelley may have accepted the Christian soul-concept until it parts company with Plato's by importing more detail. And we have already seen how insistently he advocated Christian morality. Yet he was vilified by the Christians of his day, because he accepted the label 'atheist', somewhat perversely if Trelawny reports him right: 'I used it to express my abhorrence of superstition; I took up the word, as a knight took up a gauntlet, in defiance of injustice'.[33] Were the Christians who detested him correct in seeing an unbridgeable gulf between him and Christianity? Or would he have become a Christian, as Browning [34] surmised? Even in *Prometheus Unbound*, the most Christian of his poems, a few strictures may be found, and on the very day he finished Act IV he wrote: 'Added days and years and hours add to my disapprobation of this odious superstition'.[35] Probably his chief stumbling-block was the doctrine of sin. Shelley always did what his conscience dictated. He was never diverted by practical obstacles or by what people thought. In him there was no uneasy gap between thought and act, as Mary recalled: 'Many men have his opinions. None fearlessly and conscientiously act on them, as he did. It is his act that marks him.'[36] Consequently he had scant respect for the Christian teaching on sin. It is chiefly because of the concept of sin that Christians have little hope of paradise on earth; instead they rely on reaching a utopia beyond the grave if they conquer sin. Godwin, on the other hand, seeing Man as a nobler animal, contemplates an earthly utopia, and in *Prometheus Unbound* Shelley shows he is still on Godwin's side by sketching a 'new world of *man*'. Two years later he was still firmly agnostic. In a revealing note to *Hellas* he says he finds 'inexplicable and incredible' the 'hypothesis of a Being resembling men in the moral attributes of His nature', who calls us out of non-existence and punishes us for indulging the propensities for sin which He planted in us. 'That there is a true solution of the riddle, and that in our present state that solution is unattainable by us, are propositions which may be regarded as equally certain.' Nor did he ever move nearer Christianity. In a letter written three months before he died he referred to 'the delusions of Christianity . . . no man of sense can think it true'.[37] And Trelawny quoted him as saying 'the delusions of Christianity are fatal to genius and originality: they limit thought'.[33]

Finding out what Shelley did not believe is much easier than deciding what he did believe. He wrote down no *credo* in his later years and his views have to be deduced from somewhat conflicting data. If Shelley's religion had to be defined in a single phrase, it might not be too wide of the mark to say 'a mixture of Platonism and pantheism'. For him, all Nature is the expression of a pervading, non-personal spirit of good, which he closely links with the One, the Platonic prototype. As he sees it, the soul is absorbed into the One Spirit after death. It has no individual existence like the Christian soul; instead it enjoys what might be called a state of posthumous Nirvana. This concept gave him an admirable framework for *Adonais*, enabling him to put Keats's death in perspective with a sureness which rivals Milton's in *Lycidas*. The One Spirit enters his poems most often when he treats it as the essence of natural objects. On these occasions his pantheism (if that is the right word) is more turbulent than Spinoza's calm certainty or the simpler Nature-faith of Wordsworth, who first led Shelley towards goddess Nature. Since the One Spirit hardly explains evil, Shelley sometimes lets dualism creep in. Then, for a time, he sees the world as a fight between good and evil, which he often equates with light and dark, following either the Manichaeans or Plato in the *Republic*. All attempts to sum up Shelley's views in a paragraph are doomed to failure; and this one is no exception.[38]

After spending so long on the background it is time to look at *Prometheus Unbound* as literature. Merely flicking over the pages reveals one notable feature, the variety of metre: 'thirty-six distinct verse-forms are to be found, besides the blank verse. . . . As a rule blank verse marks passages of transition or repressed feeling, while at every climax of passion the poetry rushes into lyrical form.' [39] The basic blank verse, which accounts for over half the poem, is varied in tone to differentiate between characters: thus, of the soliloquies which open Acts I, II and III, Prometheus's is craggy and harsh, Asia's mild and delicate, and Jupiter's magisterial. But it is the lyrics that are most admired. At first their urgent music seduces us into suspending our critical faculties. But if we don't like being seduced and are provoked into tearing the verses to shreds, we usually find they are rooted in a firm intellectual bedrock which, when exposed, often has a scientific or Platonic colour.

One of Shelley's stylistic mannerisms is over-use of compound adjectives. *Prometheus Unbound* sports 147 of these, distributed fairly evenly through the Acts: [40] they range from conventional to *outré*, from *all-conquering* and *panic-stricken* to *inter-transpicuous* and *tempest-wrinkled*. Compound adjectives result from too much thought rather than too little — there are, for example, fifteen in the sixty-seven lines of Keats's *Ode to Psyche* — and they are welcome as signs of the care Shelley was taking in *Prometheus Unbound*. The device of compounding, though condemned by Coleridge, has ancient sanction, from Demetrius; [41] and many poets, from Homer and Shakespeare downwards, have found it useful for compressing images. Shelley had good cause to use it. His poetry, like the music of Mozart or Chopin, often seems too frail to bear the burden of its fame, or stand up to a gale of scorn. Interlocking adjectives help to strengthen the airy verses, as a wire-mesh strengthens a balloon or a compressed-air bottle.

Another stylistic trick is the use of symbol at tense moments. The symbol-making begins with Shelley seeing mundane objects as the manifestations of eternal Platonic forms, just as the mathematician treats an object like a stretched string as a real-life version of his abstraction, a straight line. This ancient analogy of Platonist and mathematician can be carried further, to the private symbols, which, like x, y and z, bear little resemblance to the objects they represent. This further step was taken by the Neoplatonists, who developed a systematic symbol-language. Some of Shelley's symbols resemble the Neoplatonists', but it is difficult to say whether this is conscious imitation or, as Yeats suggested, an intuitive rediscovery of symbols which appeal to the collective unconscious of Man. Yeats, who was writing in 1900 before Jung, argued that at odd moments such symbols can convince us that 'our little memories are but part of some great memory that renews the world and men's thoughts age after age'.[42] Not everyone will accept Yeats's mystical views, but no one can deny that he explains Shelley's symbols brilliantly. Yeats also points out that, as Shelley matured, more and more images which had once been spontaneous took on, albeit unconsciously, the definiteness of symbol. This crystallization of imagery into symbolism was beginning in *Alastor* and *The Revolt of Islam*, and Yeats's theory of the great memory is again relevant, because both these poems were, in a sense, maps of Shelley's unconscious.

The main symbols can quickly be summarized. Water represents existence; streams or rivers are paths for existence. Boats floating on streams, or sometimes on the sea, are thus souls journeying through life. The water is calm if things are going smoothly, and rough if the soul is vexed. Whirlpools signify perils: *e.g.* in *The Revolt of Islam*, 'the stream of life . . . doth on its whirlpools bear . . . our bark' (line 2590). Caves stand for minds which receive impressions from the external world, either as shadows or, if the cave has water in front, as images in the water. Towers represent introspective minds, engaged in scientific or artistic creation or in philosophic thought. *Veil* usually refers to the veil between life and death, between the impermanent and the ideal. The statements above are

dogmatic, but only for the sake of brevity : different interpretations sometimes apply ; and often the words are
innocent of symbolic nuance. This is to be expected, for
Shelley is not producing a neat set of artificial equations.
He is merely resorting to the same imagery, perhaps unconsciously, perhaps half-consciously, when faced with ideas
and emotions which defy direct expression. For a justifica-
tion of his method we can call on Yeats again : 'It is only
by ancient symbols, by symbols that have numberless
meanings besides the one or two the writer lays an emphasis
upon, or the half-score he knows of, that any highly subjective art can escape from the barrenness and shallowness
of a too-conscious arrangement into the abundance and
depth of nature'.[43] Though Shelley gave no such clear-cut
explanation he would no doubt have applauded Yeats, for
he expressed rather similar views in the *Defence of Poetry*.

Though the origin of Shelley's symbols may be in doubt,
the literary antecedents of *Prometheus Unbound* are not, and
one of the foremost of them is, appropriately enough,
Homer. Shelley learnt his mannerism of compound adjectives from Homer, and his gods have the Homeric habit
of being equally at home in heaven and on earth. Shelley's
partiality for *wingless,* as the opposite of *wingèd*, is a result
of long familiarity with Homer's *wingèd words* — the ἔπεα
πτερόεντα which every schoolboy knows (or used to) being
almost a term of banter between Shelley, Hogg and Peacock.[44] Shelley also uses again the eagle-*versus*-snake
imagery, which derives from the *Iliad*.[45]

A more obvious Greek model is Aeschylus. We have
already seen how Shelley based his myth on *Prometheus
Bound*. In Act I the topography and over a dozen phrases
come straight from *Prometheus Bound*; and in describing the
Furies Shelley could hardly fail to take note of the *Eumenides*.
Aeschylus contributes little to the plot, however, and in Acts
II-IV he is almost forgotten. There are echoes from other
Greek writers, besides Aeschylus, Homer and Plato ; but
Shelley's wide reading among the Greeks and his debt to
them have probably been aired enough in these pages.[46]

From the Greeks we jump the centuries to Spenser, whose influence has not entirely waned, though it is far less potent than in *The Revolt of Islam*. Because *Prometheus Unbound* is a myth, not an allegory, there are none of those arbitrary interventions which are so infuriating in the *Faerie Queene*; and Shelley has outgrown the richly descriptive Spenserian verse of *The Revolt of Islam*. He cannot be said to forsake Spenser entirely, however, since the complete *dramatis personae* of *Prometheus Unbound* is to be found in the *Faerie Queene*.⁴⁷

Shelley ranged far and wide over space, time and creed in his borrowings. We have already jumped from the pagan Greeks to Spenser, the champion of the Protestant faith; now we jump again, to a Catholic priest in Spain, Calderón. Shelley had begun reading Calderón in Spanish during the summer of 1819, and his influence, which showed itself at once in *The Cenci*, grew steadily. In Act IV of *Prometheus Unbound* some phrases in the love-song of the Earth and Moon seem to be echoes from Calderón's *El Mágico Prodigioso* — from the third of the scenes later translated by Shelley, that of Justina's temptation.

After Calderón comes his contemporary Milton, for Shelley invites a comparison between *Prometheus Unbound* and *Paradise Lost* when he argues in his preface that Prometheus is more satisfactory as a hero than Satan, who can never fully win our approval. The chief similarity between *Prometheus Unbound* and *Paradise Lost* is the ambitious theme. In both, the poet, god-like, controls the doings of angels or demigods in a world of his own making; in neither is humour or the common touch essential. But the two poems are very different in technique. Milton's masterly, Latinized, blank-verse paragraphs are poles apart from Shelley's fresh, eager, kaleidoscopic verses. Milton delights in sonorous proper names, which he, like Dickens and Gilbert, chose unerringly, and he often buttresses the background scenery with geographical names. But these geographical metaphors tend to keep his immortals earthbound, whereas Shelley's soar easily to the empyrean.

In his preface, Shelley says no poet can avoid reflecting the current literary climate, and apologizes for any imitation in *Prometheus Unbound*. In fact, he borrowed little from any contemporary, except possibly Goethe. Shelley knew *Faust*, Part I, which was published in 1808, and he is using a weapon from Goethe's armoury when he enlivens *Prometheus Unbound* with frequent changes of metre. Some of his scenes, for example Asia's visit to Demogorgon, are reminiscent of *Faust*, Part II, but since Goethe did not publish any of this until 1827 the resemblances must be fortuitous. Apart from these few parallels with Goethe, Shelley was little influenced by German writers. He did not share Coleridge's enthusiasm for German philosophy, and it is only by chance that his interest in science is more characteristic of the German romantics than the English.

5

In *Prometheus Unbound* Shelley succeeds in working his moral, political and philosophical ideals into a well-knit poetic theme. He also successfully fuses the two sides of his nature, the rational and the emotional, which had inspired *Queen Mab* and *Alastor* respectively. *Prometheus Unbound* is free from the touches of hysteria, the extremism, the inconsistencies and the bias which marred his previous long poems, and although some faults remain, Shelley is not wholly to blame for them. The poem could be clearer, for example, but the obscurity is not wilful : it is the result of a struggle to communicate ideas which are beyond the resources of language. And, as a second example, the poem is rather feeble as a drama, but not because Shelley digresses : structurally the poem is one of his best, and he never strays far from the theme in Acts I-III. Then, in the detached Act IV, the events of Acts I-III are celebrated chorally. Though Act IV adds nothing to the plot, no one would wish to see it omitted, because it is unique in English poetry for its intimate blend of exact science and dazzling verse, its sustained animation and exultation, and its pervading philosophy of unity in Nature. It is creative myth of a high order, a reminder that Shelley was 'the most spontaneous of myth-makers and the most scientifically-minded poet of the age'.[48]

It would be churlish to find fault with the spirit which animates the poem. Shelley looks forward to a happier world based on Christian charity between men : cynics may scoff, but can they offer anything better ?

Prometheus Unbound may not make its fullest appeal until the world is more settled. But even in this troubled century it has had its champions. In the words of Sir Maurice Bowra, 'His triumph is that . . . through the enchantment which his poetry sets on us we are able to explore regions of which he is the discoverer and almost the only denizen, and to know in his company the delights of a condition in which the old quarrel of poetry and philosophy is healed and the pallid abstractions of analytical thought take on the glow and the glory of visible things'.[49] *Prometheus Unbound* was 'for many years a sort of gospel' to Gilbert Murray, who knew nearly all of it by heart.[50] W. B. Yeats, on re-reading it, remarked that 'it seems to me to have an even more certain place than I had thought among the sacred books of the world'.[51] And Sir Herbert Read has called it 'the greatest expression ever given to humanity's desire for intellectual light and spiritual liberty'.[52]

NOTES TO IX: *PROMETHEUS UNBOUND*

1. For details, see V. Scudder's edition of *Prometheus Unbound* (1892), pp. 121–44.
2. R. H. Fogle, *The Imagery of Keats and Shelley*, p. 71.
3. A. Walker, *Familiar Philosophy*, p. 306.
4. A. Walker, *Familiar Philosophy*, p. 203.
5. See, *e.g.*, P. Moore, *The Sky at Night*, Volume Two (1968), pp. 86–94.
6. *Iliad*, XIX. 91–3, quoted in Plato, *Symposium*, 195.
7. A. Walker, *Familiar Philosophy*, pp. 231–2. P. H. Butter, *Shelley's Idols of the Cave*, p. 150.
8. A. N. Whitehead, *Introduction to Mathematics* (1911), pp. 217–18.
9. J. A. Notopoulos, *The Platonism of Shelley*, p. 247.

10. See G. M. Matthews in *Shelley: Modern Judgements* (ed. R. B. Woodings), pp. 178–89.

11. See *New Shelley Letters*, Nos. 52, 53, 58; and Spenser, *Faerie Queene*, IV. ii, 47. See also *F.Q.*, I. v. 22.

12. A. Walker, *Familiar Philosophy*, p. 323. The 'morning, noon and night' theory is propounded in Beccaria's *Treatise on Atmospheric Electricity*, English translation, 1776. See C. Grabo, *A Newton Among Poets*. For the real causes of ionization in the atmosphere, see B. Schonland, *Atmospheric Electricity* (1953).

13. See C. Grabo, *Prometheus Unbound*, pp. 89–92.

14. Lucretius, *De Rerum Natura*, I. 7, 228; *Ode to Liberty*, l. 18 (and *Hymn of Pan*, l. 26), E. Darwin, *Economy of Vegetation*, i. 98.

15. See R. H. Fogle, *Imagery of Keats and Shelley*, pp. 137–8.

16. *Paradiso*, XXXIII; *Lusiads*, pp. 233–4, in Penguin translation; *Paradise Lost*, V. 618–27.

17. Bacon, *Novum Organum* (New York, 1902), pp. 121–59.

18. See A. Walker, *Familiar Philosophy*, p. 406, and E. Darwin, *Loves of the Plants*, interlude III.

19. Lines 289–91 echo *Endymion*, III. 123–4. Lines 270–318 resemble *Endymion*, III. 119–36, Southey's *Curse of Kehama*, XVI, and *Richard III*, I. iv. 24–33.

20. *Letters* ii. 158.

21. For details, see H. Jeffreys, *The Earth* (5th ed., 1970), p. 40.

22. See Pliny, *Nat. Hist.*, Bk. II, cap. 7. Shelley refers to the 'cone' of night in *Epipsychidion* (l. 228) and *The Triumph of Life* (l. 23).

23. A. Walker, *Familiar Philosophy*, pp. 491–2.

24. See J. A. Notopoulos, *The Platonism of Shelley*, pp. 186–8.

25. *Letters* ii. 388.

26. J. W. Beach, *The Concept of Nature in 19th-century English Poetry*, p. 241.

27. See C. Baker, *Shelley's Major Poetry*, pp. 283–6.

28. Those guilty of the mistakes include T. S. Eliot, W. Empson, R. Graves and F. R. Leavis. Some of these mistakes are mentioned on pp. 61, 109, 216, 228–9, 242, 346.

29. *Letters* i. 408.

30. Plotinus goes halfway towards Shelley's concept.

31. J. A. Notopoulos, *The Platonism of Shelley*, pp. 232–62.

32. A. N. Whitehead, *Process and Reality* (1929), p. 53.

33. Trelawny, *Recollections*, p. 190.

34. Browning, *Essay on Shelley*, p. 150.

35. See *Prometheus Unbound*, I. 594–6, 603–15, and *Letters*, ii. 166.

36. Mary Shelley, *Letters*, ii. 13. For Shelley's attitude to sin, see E. Barnard, *Shelley's Religion*, pp. 146–56.

37. *Letters* ii. 412.

38. For Shelley's religious views, see E. Barnard, *Shelley's Religion*, and J. Thomson, *Biographical and Critical Studies*, pp. 283–8. See also E. R. Wasserman, *Shelley's Prometheus Unbound*.

39. V. Scudder's edition of *Prometheus Unbound* (1892), pages l and liv.

40. There are 43 in Act I (833 lines), 42 in Act II (687 lines), 36 in Act III (512 lines) and 26 in Act IV (578 lines).

41. Demetrius, *On Style* (Everyman edition, p. 223). Coleridge, *Biographia Literaria*, chap. I.

42. W. B. Yeats, *Ideas of Good and Evil*, p 113.

43. W. B. Yeats, *Ideas of Good and Evil*, pp. 127–8.

44. See *New Shelley Letters*, p. 97. *Wingless* occurs in *Prometheus Unbound*, I. 48; I. 500; II. i. 16.

45. See p. 87.

46. For classical influences on Shelley, see J. A. K. Thomson, *Classical Background of English Literature*, pp. 230–3, or N. Rogers, *Shelley at Work, passim*.

47. Apollo, *Faerie Queene*, III. iv. 41; Asia, III. ix. 39; Demogorgon, IV. ii. 47; Furies, II. xii. 41; Hercules, II. vii. 54; Ione, IV. xi. 50; Jupiter (Jove), III. i. 57; Mercury, II. xii. 41; Ocean, IV. xi. 18; Panthea, II. x. 73; Prometheus, II. x. 70.

48. D. Bush, *Science and English Poetry*, p. 111.

49. C. M. Bowra, *The Romantic Imagination*, p. 125.

50. *The Listener*, vol. 42, p. 272 (18 Aug. 1949); and vol. 45, p. 13 (5 Jan. 1956.)

51. W. B. Yeats, *Ideas of Good and Evil*, p. 91.

52. H. Read, *The True Voice of Feeling*, p. 271.

X

BLITHE SPIRIT

And walks with angel-step upon the winds.

ERASMUS DARWIN, *Loves of the Plants*

1

BETWEEN March and December 1819 Shelley wrote most of *Prometheus Unbound* and *A Philosophical View of Reform*, the whole of *The Cenci*, *The Mask of Anarchy* and *Peter Bell the Third* and several of his most famous lyrics, including the *Ode to the West Wind* — some 6000 lines of verse in all. After the usual hibernation, the lyric impulse took command again in the spring, and the unity among the lyrics written between September 1819 and July 1820 makes it natural to group them together in this chapter.

Before entering the imaginative world of the lyrics we must see how Shelley and Mary have been faring in the real world since we left them four chapters ago. They had moved to Florence in October 1819 and their son was born there in November. The Florentine art galleries delighted Shelley, but its cold and wet winter did not. So in January 1820 the Shelleys moved down nearer the coast, to Pisa. There they renewed acquaintance with some friends they first met the previous autumn, Mr. Tighe and Lady Mountcashell, who lived under assumed names, 'Mr. and Mrs. Mason', to be respectable. All the Shelleys' close friends abroad had previous connexions with either Mary's family or Shelley's, and the Masons were no exception. For Mary Wollstonecraft had acted as governess to the family of Lord Kingsborough in 1787–8, and had been idolized by his eldest daughter, the future Mrs. Mason (who may have named herself after the virtuous lady in Mary's *Original*

Stories from Real Life). Shelley liked these new friends, especially Mrs. Mason, who was cultivated yet practical, a Lady yet a Liberal. While the Shelleys were in Pisa from January to June 1820, scarcely a day passed without their meeting the Masons.

2

In the autumn of 1820 *Prometheus Unbound, with other poems* was published in London : the *other poems* alone would have been enough to make the book famous, for they included the *Ode to the West Wind, The Cloud*, the *Skylark, The Sensitive Plant* and the *Ode to Liberty*. The first three of these stand together, an abiding monument to Shelley's passion for the sky : 'I take great delight in watching the changes of the atmosphere'.[1] In all three the metre is unusual, yet not unbecoming. In all three the tone is subjective, yet not undisciplined : for if we lump the three together we find a tough core of exact science — chiefly aerodynamics, astronomy, botany, hydrodynamics and meteorology — which can withstand and even benefit from a leavening of personality.

The earliest of the three lyrics of the sky is the *Ode to the West Wind*, 'conceived and chiefly written', Shelley tells us, in the Cascine, 'a wood that skirts the Arno, near Florence'. The rustle of crisp dead leaves swept along in the west wind is often remarkably loud in the Cascine, and this unending leaf-race dominates the first lines of the poem. The ode is in five 14-line stanzas, and the rhyme-scheme is the exacting *terza rima* :

> O wild West Wind, thou breath of Autumn's being,
> Thou, from whose unseen presence the leaves dead
> Are driven, like ghosts from an enchanter fleeing,
>
> Yellow, and black, and pale, and hectic red,
> Pestilence-stricken multitudes : O thou,
> Who chariotest to their dark wintry bed
>
> The wingèd seeds, where they lie cold and low,
> Each like a corpse within its grave, until
> Thine azure sister of the Spring shall blow

Her clarion o'er the dreaming earth, and fill
(Driving sweet buds like flocks to feed in air)
With living hues and odours plain and hill :

Wild Spirit, which art moving everywhere ;
Destroyer and preserver ; hear, oh, hear !

577. 1-14

That opening, *O wild West Wind*, is a famous example of alliteration, and there is more to follow. Because of this, and because Swinburne, who often exploited Shelley's verbal tricks, overworks alliteration, Shelley is sometimes condemned for 'indulging' in alliteration. But in fact Shelley is restrained and skilful with alliteration and assonance. Blatant Swinburnian alliteration is reserved for comic effect — *polygamic Potter*, for instance, in *Peter Bell the Third*, or 'He burned the hoofs and horns and head and hair' in the *Hymn to Mercury*. In the *Ode to the West Wind*, 'thou breath of Autumn's being', at the end of the first line, is more than mere alliteration: it establishes the wind as the agent of seasonal change, and brings in a human metaphor to account for its presence. This latter technique recurs in line 3, where Shelley injects life into a dull litter of dead leaves flying in the wind by making them 'ghosts from an enchanter fleeing'. Dead leaves resemble ghosts more than may at first appear. Both are the remains of living organisms ; both are unpredictable in their detailed movements ; dead leaves weigh very little and the same presumably applies to ghosts (except those unlucky enough to be in chains). The parallel might seem to fail on the score of colour : the leaves are of many colours — Shelley attributes this, logically enough, to disease — whereas ghosts are, according to popular superstition, colourless. But superstition is fallible, and a lightning mental census of ghosts leaves the impression that the best specimens are coloured : Banquo's ghost had gory locks and the Ghost of Christmas Present must surely have had a ruddy face. After this human, or superhuman, explanation of the leaves' activity comes a pseudo-scientific one : the winged seeds are *charioted* by the wind. A moving

chariot subjects its occupants to an upward force nearly
equal to their weight, and much smaller forward or side-
ways forces; and a steady wind can do just that to a winged
seed or a leaf. To an aerodynamicist, for whom the winged
seed differs only in degree, not in kind, from a jet airliner —
one of the chariot's modern descendants — the metaphor
seems natural. The winged seeds bring us to the central
theme of the first stanza, the balance of death and rebirth in
vegetation: the sombre lines 2–8 balance the hopeful lines
9–12; *living* in line 12 answers *dead* in line 2, and the Spirit
is both *destroyer* and *preserver*; Autumn 'breathes' the west
wind and Spring blows her clarion (birdsong) to wake the
dreaming seeds in their *wintry bed*. The urgency is well sustained
too: in line 11 Spring is seen *driving* the sap up the trees,
forcing out millions of buds to feed on the carbon dioxide of
the air.

The second stanza begins with a fine cloudscape, composed of two quite different types of cloud, fractostratus
and cirrus:

> Thou on whose stream, mid the steep sky's commotion,
> Loose clouds like earth's decaying leaves are shed,
> Shook from the tangled boughs of Heaven and Ocean,
>
> Angels of rain and lightning : there are spread
> On the blue surface of thine aëry surge,
> Like the bright hair uplifted from the head
>
> Of some fierce Maenad, even from the dim verge
> Of the horizon to the zenith's height,
> The locks of the approaching storm. . . .
>
> 578. 15-23

As Shelley sees it, about two-thirds of the sky is blue and
about one-third, from nearly overhead to as far as the eye
can see in the west, is covered by a high filmy layer of
white, streaky mare's-tail or plume cirrus, which, as its
name implies, looks like dozens of horses' tails or plumed
helmets streaming in the wind. Low in the west are jagged
detached clouds, scud or fractostratus, grey and watery,
approaching fast in the rising wind. It is a familiar scene

on the south coast of England, warning of a watery end
to a fine summer's day.   In the first $3\frac{2}{3}$ lines of Shelley's
stanza, the *loose clouds, shed* like *earth's decaying leaves* into the
airstream, are the fractostratus clouds, harbingers of rain.
The *tangled boughs* from which these leaf-like clouds are shaken
are those regions of air whose slightly adverse pressures,
temperatures and humidities make them the destined birthplace for clouds[2]. These parcels of air, turbulent, ever-
changing in shape like wind-blown boughs, contain a mixture
of water vapour from *Ocean* and air from *Heaven*. The
subsequent 5 lines describe the mare's-tail cirrus, the
bright hair spread as if on the *blue surface* of the sky, and
streaming like the hair of a girl running into a strong
wind.   The cirrus stretches from the *horizon*, which is *dim*
because obscured by the scud, to the *zenith*.   The simile of
the Maenads probably appears because Shelley had recently
seen Maenad figures in the Uffizi Gallery at Florence : the
simile is apt, for Maenads had the odd habit of rushing
around with hair streaming.   Since the word 'cirrus',
coined by Shelley's contemporary Luke Howard, means 'a
lock of hair', the emphasis on hair is justified.   And, as
spreading cirrus often heralds a depression, Shelley neatly
links his imagery with the weather outlook in the final
locks of the approaching storm, a phrase which is used as a
caption to a photograph of plume cirrus in Grant's *Cloud
and Weather Atlas*.[3] These lines seemed worth detailed analysis
because literary critics unversed in cloud physics have not
appreciated the richness of Shelley's image. F. R. Leavis,
for example, completely misinterpreted the lines because he
failed to distinguish between the fractostratus and cirrus
clouds.[4] And presumably he has not erred alone.

The third stanza shows how the sea responds to the onset
of the west wind. First, Shelley imagines the 'blue
Mediterranean' having his summer snooze

> Beside a pumice isle in Baiae's bay,

where he can see

> old palaces and towers
> Quivering within the wave's intenser day,

as Shelley himself did when he sailed the Bay of Baiae during his stay at Naples. He refers in a letter to 'the ruins of its antique grandeur standing like rocks in the transparent sea under our boat. . . . The sea . . . was so translucent that you could see the hollow caverns clothed with the glaucous sea-moss, and the leaves and branches of those delicate weeds that pave the unequal bottom of the water.' The coming of the West Wind disturbs the sea's calm and has a message, too, for the underwater growths:

> The sea-blooms and the oozy woods which wear
> The sapless foliage of the ocean, know
> Thy voice, and suddenly grow gray with fear,
> And tremble and despoil themselves.
>
> 578. 39-42

As Shelley explains in a note, 'the vegetation at the bottom of the sea, of rivers, and of lakes, sympathizes with that of the land in the change of seasons, and is consequently influenced by the winds which announce it'.

The first three stanzas, all addressed to the Wind and ending with the request 'Oh, hear!', describe the effect of the wind on land, sky and sea, through leaves, clouds and waves. In stanza 4 these three facets of the wind's power are linked in an intensely personal way:

> If I were a dead leaf thou mightest bear;
> If I were a swift cloud to fly with thee;
> A wave to pant beneath thy power. . . .
>
> 578. 43-5

But he is not, and he is left, earthbound, chained by 'a heavy weight of hours', to brood over his sorrows and indulge in a self-abasing prayer to the wind.

But in stanza 5 he recovers his poise. The tone is still sad, but dynamic images crowd in to propel the poem to a satisfying finale:

> Drive my dead thoughts over the universe
> Like withered leaves to quicken a new birth! . . .
> Be through my lips to unawakened earth
> The trumpet of a prophecy! O, Wind,
> If Winter comes, can Spring be far behind?
>
> 579. 63-4; 68-70

The verse technique and structure of the *Ode to the West Wind* could scarcely be improved : it is the most fully orchestrated of Shelley's poems, and consequently the most difficult to read aloud. The ever-fluctuating tempo and the artfully random pauses in the long lines reflect the lawless surging of the wind and its uneasy silences. This device is not overworked : the wonder is that Shelley could use it all when grappling with the problems of the *terza rima* and operating within a rigid structural framework. In conformity with this framework, which seems to be in the style of Calderón, the first three stanzas are designed to show the wind's power in three spheres of Nature, ready for the prayer to the Wind, as pseudo-god, in the fourth stanza. The keynote of the first three stanzas is balance. Their settings, land, sky and sea, give equal emphasis to the three states of matter, solid, gaseous and liquid. Each of the four seasons has its appointed place, and there is a full range of colours — red, yellow, blue, grey and black explicitly, white and green implicitly. Turmoil is balanced against calm, life against death, detail against generalization, cold against warmth, plain against hill, and so on. The fourth stanza neatly links the themes of the first three, but the note of self-pity sounds too loudly for our anti-sentimental ears. Still, it would be unfair to condemn Shelley because he failed to foresee our distaste for what was in his day called 'true feeling'. Indeed the blame for Shelley's worst line —

> I fall upon the thorns of life! I bleed! —

might be visited on Erasmus Darwin, who once wrote

> I faint! I fall! ah me! . . .
> I freeze! I freeze![5]

And Shelley did have good cause to be depressed: he had lost his children Clara and William within a year, and was now anxiously awaiting what he referred to obliquely in the poem, and directly in a letter, as the *new birth*.[6] After this defeatist fourth stanza, the fifth shows a new vigour, with a nicely ironic question to round off a nearly faultless poem.

3

If we stop to admire the view, we expect to see half land and half sky, and if we are Britons in our native haunts the sky is likely to be clouded. A rational visitor from another planet, knowing this and knowing we had words like hill, road, tree, bush, grass and leaf for one half of the scene, might ask what the corresponding cloud-words were. And we should have to admit we had none. The English-man's interest in the weather is proverbial, and his ancestors, who were exposed to it more, were presumably just as interested : yet they never bothered to name the clouds. Some people think cloudscapes are just as fascinating as landscapes or buildings. But not the word-makers : they classified one half of their surroundings and ignored the other. The system of Latin names for clouds now used by meteorologists originated as late as 1803. Latin is a poor substitute for the vernacular, however. If an Englishman greeted his neighbour with a bold 'Good morning, fine altocumulus castellatus to-day', the ice which had taken years to break would quickly re-form. The lack of homely cloud-words reflects a general indifference, and it is scarcely surprising that clouds were for so long a blind spot in artistic perception. Until the time of the Romantics, most painters tried to include as little sky as possible in their pictures, and any clouds which did creep in were usually either vague or over-stylized and physically impossible. Some of the Dutch painters, Van Ruisdael and Van de Velde especially, did begin to give the sky a fair share of the canvas, but it was not until after Luke Howard had classified cloud forms that real progress was made. Howard's *Essay on Clouds* appeared in a journal in 1803, but it was apparently little known until reprinted in his book *The Climate of London* (1818–20). Several poets and painters, some stimu-lated by Howard's work, became interested in clouds at this time. Many of Constable's cloud studies belong to the years 1821–2, and Turner's preoccupation with clouds and vapours began about the same time. In 1820 Goethe wrote his article on *The Shape of Clouds according to Howard*, which ends with the four poems called *Stratus, Cumulus, Cirrus* and *Nimbus*. And in the same year Shelley wrote his most famous lyrics of the sky, in particular *The Cloud*, thereby doing as much as anyone to open up this new vista of artistic perception.[7]

The Cloud is original not only in its subject but also in its technique. Shelley performs adroitly a trick which, though overplayed since, had rarely been tried before — the trick of writing as if he was the cloud instead of merely describing it.[8] He also manages to keep up an unceasing flow of imaginative invention : each verse of the poem creates a little world of its own. The poem is not confined to one type of cloud. It is a survey of all types, though with a bias towards cumulus and cumulonimbus, the forms with most individuality. Shelley follows this protean cloud's fortunes through every phase of its life-cycle, through rough and smooth, night and day, summer and winter. Thus he fuses together a creative myth, a scientific monograph and a gay, picaresque tale of cloud-adventure.

In the first twenty lines we see the Cloud in all its moods. Gentle, bringing 'fresh showers for the thirsting flowers' or shade for the leaves. Ferocious,

> I wield the flail of the lashing hail,
>   And whiten the green plains under,
> And then again I dissolve it in rain,
>   And laugh as I pass in thunder.
>
>   600. 9-12

Or indifferent,

> I sift the snow on the mountains below,
>   And their great pines groan aghast ;
> And all the night 'tis my pillow white,
>   While I sleep in the arms of the blast.
>
>   600. 13-16

The eight lines quoted are enough to show the poem's controversial features, and some of its merits, too. The chief complaints have been aimed at the metre, which is said to lapse into sing-song, and at the allegedly careless handling of personal pronouns and possessive adjectives. A verse-

form with such insistent quickfire rhymes and end-stopped
lines certainly creates many problems. Shelley cannot hope
to hide weak rhymes, yet he must not let the sense become
slave to the sound. He aggravates his troubles by insisting
on scientific accuracy and using words of childish simplicity :
of the 60 words in the lines quoted, 50 are one-syllable and
10 two-syllable. He sets out along a perilous tightwire,
which most poets would keep clear of, and despite a few
lurches he arrives at the end triumphant. How is it done?
First, there are the frequent changes in metre. Basically the
poem is a mixture of iambs and anapaests, but intruders are
welcomed, and Shelley shuffles his feet into almost every
possible permutation. For example, the first fifteen of the
alternate short lines have thirteen different scansions. The
result could be chaotic ; but it is not, because the rhyme
pattern keeps things in order. The lengths of the verses are
also varied, to match the varied grouping in bands of altocumulus, and the continual adventure of the rhyming
reflects the cloud's precarious life. The floating pronouns
are part of the adventure, but they might have been tethered
more firmly. In the section quoted, *it* in line 11 refers
to *hail* in line 9, and *'tis* in line 15 refers to *snow* in line 13.
Although no confusion arises here, the connexions with the
nouns could be more obvious. Knowing the pitfalls of the
rhyme, we might continue this detailed criticism by scrutiniz-
ing the lines quoted for redundant or misplaced words.
There is one misfit, *again* in line 11, which would more
naturally read 'And then I dissolve it again in rain'. After
this fault-finding it is only fair to mention a few of the
merits of these lines. A hailstorm's recurrent bursts of fury,
seemingly motiveless, are explained at once by 'I wield the
flail of the lashing hail', and the Cloud is humanized again,
just as happily, in 'I laugh as I pass in thunder'. Even
better are the last two lines quoted, in which the human
metaphor is exceptionally precise : 'all the night' the snow
on the mountain peak is 'my pillow white, While I sleep in
the arms of the blast'. The cloud is capping the peak, remaining stationary and fixed in shape, though the particles

composing it are constantly changing because of the strong winds raging round.[9]

In the second verse Shelley implies that clouds are controlled by atmospheric electricity, which in his day was thought far more important than it really is. He may have had the idea from Adam Walker, who states that 'Water rises through the air, flying on the wings of electricity. . . .'[10] Wherever the idea came from, it is the one piece of science in *The Cloud* which needs correcting. Shelley leads up to the topic plausibly, via towering anvil thunderclouds:

> Sublime on the towers of my skiey bowers,
> Lightning my pilot sits. . . .
> Over earth and ocean, with gentle motion,
> This pilot is guiding me.

This picture is not without a grain of truth, for electricity, though scarcely a *pilot*, does play an important part in the development of cumulonimbus clouds.

The third and fourth verses follow the Cloud through a day and a night, beginning at dawn:

> The sanguine Sunrise, with his meteor eyes,
> And his burning plumes outspread,
> Leaps on the back of my sailing rack,
> When the morning star shines dead.

601. 31-4

The intangible cloud is anchored to firm, homely images: it is strong enough to bear the weight of the sunlight which leaps on its back (in contrast to, say, a comet's tail, which quails before the radiation pressure of sunlight). The cloud begins to bear its load of light a few minutes after sunrise, when *the morning star shines dead*. For all the stars, Venus included, seem to fade as the sun's diffused light fills the sky: they are dead to the world. But Venus can be seen with the naked eye well after dawn, if we look in the right place.[11] The other stars, too, are shining as brightly as ever, and we should see them if we flew high enough to escape most of the glare of light scattered from the atmosphere. In short they *shine dead*.

From morning Shelley moves quickly to sunset, noting

that the wind often drops then, especially on the coast. After dusk the full moon rises, and takes the place of honour :

> That orbèd maiden with white fire laden,
> Whom mortals call the Moon,
> Glides glimmering o'er my fleece-like floor,
> By the midnight breezes strewn ;
> And wherever the beat of her unseen feet,
> Which only the angels hear,
> May have broken the woof of my tent's thin roof,
> The stars peep behind her and peer.
>
> 601. 45-52

Again the intangible is made concrete. We can almost hear the photons pattering down when the moonlight is called *the beat of her unseen feet*. This is followed by an elaborate visual image :

> I widen the rent in my wind-built tent,
> Till the calm rivers, lakes, and seas,
> Like strips of the sky fallen through me on high,
> Are each paved with the moon and thesè.
>
> 601. 55-8

— *these* being the stars. Shelley is thinking of an extensive cloud-sheet, probably altocumulus, which has gaps in its outlying parts. The moon and stars will shine through these gaps, and their light will be reflected if it falls on calm water, so that an observer near the centre of the cloud may see images in the water of areas of sky similar in shape to the gaps in the cloud. This picture is presented in the simplest of words: only three out of thirty-four — *widen*, *rivers* and *fallen* — are of more than one syllable. The only fault is the clumsy *these* in the last line.

The Cloud begins the fifth verse as cirrostratus, which produces haloes —

> I bind the Sun's throne with a burning zone,
> And the Moon's with a girdle of pearl

— and ends as showery cumulonimbus, decorating the sky with rainbows as it passes :

> The sphere-fire above its soft colours wove,
> While the moist Earth was laughing below.

Sphere-fire says more about the sun than any other two-syllable word can. *The moist Earth* is *laughing* because we most often notice rainbows as the sun emerges after a shower, when plants and birds seem to enjoy life more, and the raindrops on grass and leaves glint in the sunlight. Though Shelley may not have been aware of all the processes which go to form a rainbow, his verb *wove* can hardly be bettered. Nor can his adjective *soft*, for the colours in a rainbow overlap, unlike those in the sharp spectrum of a slit of light formed by a prism. The rainbow is an old battleground in the war between art and science. The artist's view was put at Haydon's 'immortal dinner' when Lamb and Keats apparently agreed to condemn Newton for analysing away the poetry of the rainbow.[12] But when a budding scientist first learns how a simple model can explain the exact position and colour-sequence of the primary rainbow, and predict secondary and rarer bows, his new insight into Nature's mechanism adds to his delight in the rainbow's beauty. In *The Cloud* Shelley tries to blend the two approaches.

In the last and best verse Shelley sums up the Cloud's life-cycle :

I am the daughter of Earth and Water,
　　And the nursling of the Sky ;
I pass through the pores of the ocean and shores ;
　　I change, but I cannot die.
For after the rain when with never a stain
　　The pavilion of Heaven is bare,
And the winds and sunbeams with their convex gleams
　　Build up the blue dome of air,
I silently laugh at my own cenotaph,
　　And out of the caverns of rain,
Like a child from the womb, like a ghost from the tomb,
　　I arise and unbuild it again.

602. 73-84

Even a captious critic can find few faults here. Being captious, he will be suspicious of the fluent first line. But *daughter of Earth and Water* really does cover every cloud-birth: Earth and Water are the parents if a dust particle acts as nucleus for the cloud droplets, or if the water molecules evaporated from land; and, even if oceanic water vapour condenses on a salt particle, the salt was originally washed off the land. The captious critic might also think *with never a stain* too negative, and (if creative) might propose *cleared of all stain* instead. A third objection is to the last line, where *it* refers not to the nearest noun, but to *dome* four lines before. This objection is difficult to sustain because the two are firmly linked by their verbs — *build up the blue dome* and *unbuild it.*

A more generous critic might point to two remarkable images. The first sums up the undying circulation of the particles which compose the cloud :

> I pass through the pores of the ocean and shores ;
> I change, but I cannot die.

The 'sweat' of the ocean is the chief raw material for the cloud, and the pores of the shores are the rivers and rivulets which return the cloud's remains to the sea. (*Pores* is used by Erasmus Darwin in 'each nice pore of ocean, earth, and air'[13].) During its life-cycle the cloud material may assume any of the three states of matter: as vapour, a liquid droplet or an ice particle. *I change* thus covers changes of state as well as of shape, size and colour. The second notable image is the *sunbeams with their convex gleams*. The earth's atmosphere bends a ray of sunlight into a curve concave downwards, or convex to an observer in a cloud looking down. Few poets, probably, have been aware of this, and fewer still would think of putting it in a poem. Yet atmospheric refraction is by no means negligible : it gives us nearly ten minutes extra daylight every day. When we watch the sun resting on the horizon at sunset, we only see it by courtesy of the atmosphere. Remove the atmosphere, and the sun would disappear below the horizon. Adam Walker was particularly interested in atmospheric refraction and the fullest table in his *Familiar Philosophy* is devoted to it.[14]

In *The Cloud* Shelley heightens our appreciation of inorganic natural processes by investing them with personality.

The tone of the poem, detached and scientific, shows he is not deluded by his own make-believe. The blend of science and human imagery recalls Act IV of *Prometheus Unbound*, but the intensity of the latter has dissolved into geniality : the verb *laugh* occurs four times in *The Cloud*. The playful metaphors often hide Shelley's firm grasp of the physics. For example, in line 8 he says that the earth *dances about the sun*. So indeed it does, performing, more faithfully than any ballerina, gyrations more complex than any human choreographer could devise. Shelley was doing his best to bridge the gap between science and the humanities. His attempt is more valuable to-day because the gap is wider and because *The Cloud* has in the last fifty years become a regular anthology-piece. Unfortunately the non-scientist usually reads it without noticing the scientific discipline being observed ; while the scientist rarely reads it at all.

Shelley wrote *The Cloud* because he enjoyed watching the sky and wanted to record what he saw. We need not seek ulterior motives, for there is nothing freakish about his interest, which he shared with the greatest English painters of his day, Turner and Constable. To find a parallel for *The Cloud* we have only to look at one of Constable's cloud-scapes. Like Shelley, he gives us clouds in all their moods, but with a preference for cumulus. Shelley's affinity with Turner is even closer. Both were great colourists. Both revelled in mists, storms, heavy seas and angry clouds, and Turner had himself strapped to the mast of a ship to savour the full fury of a storm. It is a pity that neither of them ever flew just below cloud-base on a day of heavy squalls and gale, for this reveals a scene which might have enriched their foul-weather studies. As it is, however, Shelley is the greatest English weather-poet : it is no accident that he provides more chapter-mottoes than any other poet for a standard work like G. Manley's *Climate and the British Scene*. And to illustrate his poems, what better than paintings by Turner, whose preoccupation with the play of light on atmospheric vapours, with 'light as modified by objects',[15] came to dominate his artistic life ?

The Cloud is one of Shelley's purest lyrics. It is like a clear mountain stream, quite unsullied by the muddy residues of his own troubles. We may, if we wish, equate the cloud's brief life with Man's, and suggest that the cloud's revival after death offers consolation for Man; but Shelley could scarcely have intended us to draw this moral, because he remains emotionally aloof throughout the poem, and the continual scientific detail applies to clouds, not men. Philosophical, doctrinal and personal overtones, if they exist at all, are decidedly muted. We are given a scientific monograph, enriched by imaginative invention, warmed by human metaphor and made more piquant by the ever-present death-sentence hanging over the cloud.

4

Probably the most famous, and certainly the most hackneyed, of Shelley's poems is the ode *To a Skylark*. In it he compares the bird's easy movements and fluent song with Man's clumsy attempts at each, and deduces, tongue in cheek, that the bird has superhuman talents. The theme is thus a conceit, not an eternal truth; but Shelley contrives the fiction so persuasively that we gladly suspend disbelief. The origin of the poem is described in Mary's Note: 'It was on a beautiful summer evening, while wandering among the lanes whose myrtle-hedges were the bowers of the fire-flies, that we heard the carolling of the skylark. . . .' That evening walk, near Leghorn in June 1820, provided the material for stanzas 1-6. In the splendid first stanza, risky half-rhymes fall neatly into place:

> Hail to thee, blithe Spirit!
>> Bird thou never wert,
> That from Heaven, or near it,
>> Pourest thy full heart
> In profuse strains of unpremeditated art.

The last two lines are an inspired variation on Thomson's
> Poured forth his unpremeditated strain.[16]

In the early stanzas we are often reminded of the *West Wind* and *The Cloud*. The *Skylark*'s metre, like theirs, is chosen to suit its subject. The four short lines match the quick wing-beats of the lark's hectic climb, and the long final Alexandrine represents its easier descent. A skylark is more substantial than a wind or a cloud, and Shelley reverses the technique of *The Cloud* by seeking airy similes. Thus in the first three stanzas he calls the lark a *blithe Spirit*, a *cloud of fire* and an *unbodied joy*. The *cloud of fire* could be a real cloud aglow in the setting sun, or the fire-flies mentioned by Mary.

To a Skylark is very easy to read, apart from stanzas 4 and 5, which are a little obscure, and at the same time rich in undertones :

> The pale purple even
>   Melts around thy flight ;
> Like a star of Heaven
>   In the broad daylight,
> Thou art unseen, but yet I hear thy shrill delight,
>
> Keen as are the arrows
>   Of that silver sphere,
> Whose intense lamp narrows
>   In the white dawn clear
> Until we hardly see — we feel that it is there.

602. 16-25

(*Keen* stands for *which is as keen*, a legitimate abbreviation, but one which adds nothing to the clarity.) Shelley watches the lark rise until he loses it in the evening sky, just as he would lose sight of the morning star if he watched it long enough at dawn. He knows the skylark is there : he can hear it. He knows Venus is still there, too, in daylight ; as surely as he would if she were shooting arrows at him — the arrows of her son Cupid, which are as sharp as the lark's notes are clear. Some further subtleties have been under-lined by William Empson : [17] calling the star a *sphere* links the skylark's song with the music of the spheres ; the sphere *narrowing* hints at the eyes narrowing in an 'ecstasy of Romantic appreciation' ; the arrows correspond to the bird's separate notes or the star's separate twinkles. It is worth mentioning such details because the *sphere* is often misread

as the moon, the arrows being the huntress Diana's.   This
reading cannot be accepted, partly because of these details,
partly because *intense* applies better to Venus than to the
moon, and partly because the moon can easily be seen by
day, so that *we hardly see* would be inappropriate.   These
stanzas also show Shelley's skill in exploiting inter-sense
imagery, as Glenn O'Malley has noted in his interesting
book.[18] The singing lark, a dark pinpoint almost invisible
high in the glaring sky, is equated with Venus, the bright
pinpoint lost in the 'noise' of the bright sky, yet with her
arrows of light reaching us just as surely as the lark's song.

His initial impetus propels Shelley through six stanzas
of the poem.   Then he pauses to look for the secret of the lark's
apparent joy.

> What thou art we know not;
>   What is most like thee?
> From rainbow clouds there flow not
>   Drops so bright to see
> As from thy presence showers a rain of melody. . . .
> 602. 31-5

We are given another taste of inter-sense imagery here and
in some of the answers to the question: the first answer,
'a Poet hidden in the light of thought', echoes the 'bright
Reason's ray' of *Queen Mab*.   Shelley saw thought as a
glorious illumination breaking our all-too-common mental
torpor. He goes on to praise the lark in stanza after stanza,
contrasting its carefree life with our worries about past or
future. The lark has no reviewers, slanderers or creditors
to trouble him, and we heed his song. Shelley would gladly
change places:

> Teach me half the gladness
>   That thy brain must know,
> Such harmonious madness
>   From my lips would flow
> The world should listen then — as I am listening now.
> 603. 101-5

The *Skylark*, like *The Cloud*, is a fine invention. It is
not so 'unattached', not so pure a lyric as its predecessor;

for whenever Shelley exaggerates the lark's good luck he is obliquely emphasizing Man's troubles, and in particular his own. But since the spotlight is on the lark, not Man, the poem leaves a happy impression and has given the skylark a fame denied to the sparrow, thrush or seagull. The exaggeration of the lark's virtues is acceptable in the poem, but does become open to objection at second hand, as in Hardy's musings over 'Shelley's Skylark' —

> Somewhere afield here something lies
> In Earth's oblivious eyeless trust
> That moved a poet to prophecies —
> A pinch of unseen, unguarded dust :
>
> The dust of the lark that Shelley heard,
> And made immortal through times to be ; —
> Though it only lived like another bird,
> And knew not its immortality.

Such sentiment outraged the debunkers of the 1920s, and they reacted by dragging the skylark down into the mud, as in Huxley's *Point Counterpoint*. To-day the mud-slinging seems sterile: we understand the objection, of course, but we also think we can see beyond it.

Shelley took more care than usual over the *Skylark*, and Neville Rogers [19] has traced its successive revisions, as revealed in the Bodleian notebooks. The last three lines of the first stanza quoted on page 229, for example, began as

> From the . . . star flow not
>   Clear . . . to see
>   The silver
> As from thy presence showers rich melody.

The first two lines became

> From the clouds there flow not
> Beams so sweet to see,

and then

> From the rainbow flow not
> Drops so bright to see,

before Shelley wrote his final draft —

From rainbow clouds there flow not
 Drops so bright to see
As from thy presence showers a rain of melody.

The final version is enriched by the oblique references to birdsong's liquid sound, and the fact that the brightest drops fall from clouds which are capable of giving rise to rainbows.

5

The longest of the 'other poems' published with *Prometheus Unbound* was *The Sensitive Plant*. Its theme—growth and decay in Nature—reminds us of the *West Wind* and *The Cloud*, but the scenic background has narrowed from the wide sky to a controlled sample of Nature, a flower garden. Shelley traces the fortunes of the garden, and particularly of one mimosa in it, through a year from spring to winter. It is a tale of degeneration, for the owner of the garden dies in the summer, leaving the weeds to do their worst. Most of the poem is description, simple, direct and detailed, as the opening lines suggest :

A Sensitive Plant in a garden grew,
And the young winds fed it with silver dew,
And it opened its fan-like leaves to the light,
And closed them beneath the kisses of Night. . . .
589. 1-4

These are not the only lines which begin with the childlike *And* : there are 59 more in the remaining 307 lines. This overdose of *and* gives the poem a most innocent tone, as well as being a convenient way of avoiding stress on the first syllable of a line.

In Part I we see the garden at its best, in spring and early summer. After introducing the Sensitive Plant, in the lines already quoted, Shelley catalogues the other flowers in the garden, mentioning sixteen plants by name in the first sixty lines. He endows most of them with human feelings and backs up his fiction by mixing sense-images, as if to imply that flowers may have as many senses as humans :

And the hyacinth purple, and white, and blue,
Which flung from its bells a sweet peal anew
Of music so delicate, soft, and intense,
It was felt like an odour within the sense.

589. 25-8

The Sensitive Plant sports no gaudy flower to impress the world. But, as its name proclaims, it has 'that within which passeth show', a capacity for deeper feeling than its flashy neighbours can guess at.

Part II is devoted to the Lady who looks after the garden — Milton's Eve, thinly disguised. This guardian-angel, possessed of every gentle virtue, lives alone, lavishing on the garden the powers of her 'lovely mind'. The flowers rejoice when they hear her coming ; and well they may, for she props them up when they droop and waters them when they are thirsty. She takes away noxious insects in a basket, but spares 'many an antenatal tomb, Where butterflies dream of the life to come'. Then in high summer, she dies.

In Part III we see Hamlet's

unweeded garden
That grows to seed ; things rank and gross in nature
Possess it merely.

I. ii. 135-7

After the wind and rain of autumn, 'broken stalks' lie 'bent and tangled across the walks'. The balance of power has shifted, and it is the turn of

thistles, and nettles, and darnels rank,
And the dock, and henbane, and hemlock dank. .. . . .
And plants at whose names the verse feels loath. . . . .

594. 54-5, 58

By the time spring comes again, the Sensitive Plant is a leafless wreck, strangled by rough and hardy growths.

Shelley draws no moral from his sad tale. He rounds it off non-committally by stating a Platonic philosophy he always found attractive : that our 'real' world is only the shadow of true reality —

in this life
Of error, ignorance, and strife,
Where nothing is, but all things seem,
And we the shadows of the dream,

It is a modest creed, and yet
Pleasant if one considers it,
To own that death itself must be,
Like all the rest, a mockery. . . .

596. 122-9

The weakest feature of the poem is its metre. Shelley
no doubt chose anapaests because *of a sensitive plant* is a
double anapaest, but his struggle to avoid accenting the
first syllable of a line sometimes leads him into false stresses
elsewhere, and when the metre does run smoothly it is apt
to be monotonous. In the concluding lines he 'subsides into
iambics with relief'.[20]

It is a misguided criticism to complain that Shelley, by
writing about a Sensitive Plant, is shirking life's problems.
He chooses to narrow his aim, to trace analytically and in
minute detail the progress of the natural cycle in a flower-
garden. Wordsworth never came near this in all his vast
output of Nature-poetry: he would rather view 'ten
thousand . . . at a glance', than ask 'where they go in the
winter'. Indeed *The Sensitive Plant* owes more to Erasmus
Darwin than to Wordsworth, especially in its personifications.
For in Darwin's *Loves of the Plants* the pistils and stamens of
flowers are treated as virgins and their lovers, and if Part I
of Shelley's poem seems rather precious Darwin's poem is
ten times more so. Shelley does correct the preciosity, too,
with the savagery of Part III and the gentle philosophy of the
Conclusion; and he is utterly unsentimental in handling
death and decay.

But *The Sensitive Plant* is also far more than illuminating
Nature-poetry, as Earl Wasserman has shown in his subtle
analysis.[21] The poem is, he says, a linguistic triumph because
a language that implies the reality of the external world is
shaped by the throwaway style into a medium expressing instead the mental existence of that world with respect to man.

After the subtleties of Wasserman it is rather a come-
down to have to mention the naïve theory that the Lady, the
goddess of the flowers, personifies Love or Intellectual
Beauty, with Shelley himself in the rôle of the Sensitive

Q

Plant. Shelley has suffered much from interpreters, who
have at one time or another alleged that the Poet in *Alastor*,
Laon, Lionel, Prince Athanase, Beatrice Cenci, Prometheus,
the West Wind, the Cloud, the Skylark and the Sensitive
Plant are all merely Shelley in disguise. Though there may
be a few grains of truth in these identifications, it would be
ludicrous to accept them all. Identifying Shelley with the
Sensitive Plant seems one of the least plausible of the interpretations : yet it appealed to the Victorians, and led to
their curious picture of a mimosa-Shelley unfit for the bustle
of a workaday world. This picture, which now seems
absurd, lingered long after being discredited because it was
immortalized, as a fly in amber, in Arnold's misleading
dictum about the 'beautiful and ineffectual angel'.[22]

6

The other lyrics of 1819–20 are varied in subject and quality.
Many of them, like the four discussed already, deal with
some facet of Nature ; several revivify Greek myths, lovingly,
in a few brief stanzas ; some are sentimental album-pieces.

The weakest poems, those in the last category, come
first chronologically, since most of them were written for
Sophia Stacey, a visitor who broke the Shelleys' quiet routine
at Florence in the last two months of 1819. There was
nothing very remarkable about Miss Stacey, who was a
ward of Shelley's uncle, Robert Parker, except that she
could sing well. A good singer never failed to enslave
Shelley's Muse, and when Miss Stacey politely asked him
for songs to fit some tune she liked he was pleased to oblige.
This was the origin of such poems as the *Indian Serenade* (I
arise from dreams of thee . . .), *To Sophia* (Thou art fair
and few are fairer . . .), *To ——* (I fear thy kisses . . .)
and possibly *Love's Philosophy*. Most of these are little more
than metrical exercises : *To Sophia*, for example, has double
rhyme throughout. Shelley himself did not think any of
them worth publishing among the 'other poems' with
Prometheus Unbound. He would be dismayed to know how
many modern readers obtain their chief impression of his

poetry from trifles like these, which somehow find their way
into most anthologies. One of Jane Austen's young ladies
— or Sophia Stacey, who fits that description well — would
have been delighted to receive such poems as *billets-doux*, but
it is surprising that modern anthologists are so easily pleased.
Their chief darling, the *Indian Serenade*, was to the tune of the
aria 'Ah perdona' from Mozart's *La clemenza di Tito*, and
a recently discovered manuscript shows the poem is a mere
imitation.[23] The *Indian Serenade* was set to music again in
1837, the first of the forty lyrics by Shelley which suffered
this fate before 1886,[24] followed by heaven knows how many
since. Deprived of its musical setting, the *Indian Serenade* is
feeble; it is mechanical in metre, empty of matter, and
sentimental in tone. *To* ——, equally trifling, has at least
the merit of being neatly rounded:

> I fear thy kisses, gentle maiden,
>   Thou needest not fear mine;
> My spirit is too deeply laden
>   Ever to burthen thine.
>
> I fear thy mien, thy tones, thy motion,
>   Thou needest not fear mine;
> Innocent is the heart's devotion
>   With which I worship thine.
>
> 610. 1-8

Love's Philosophy is slightly more substantial, a feather-
weight rather than a flyweight. It is based on an Anacreontic drinking-song, which Shelley probably knew in the
original Greek as well as in the free translations by Cowley
and Moore.[25] Shelley's version is much freer than theirs,
and he changes the subject from drinking to love:

> The fountains mingle with the river
>   And the rivers with the Ocean,
> The winds of Heaven mix for ever
>   With a sweet emotion;
> Nothing in the world is single;
>   All things by a law divine
> In one spirit meet and mingle.
>   Why not I with thine? . . .
>
> 583. 1-8

After this 'Sophia Stacery' it is a relief to turn to the stronger lyrics of 1820, and especially to that grim and sinewy fragment *A Vision of the Sea*, which washes preciosity overboard before you can say 'conger eel'. It is in anapaests and begins at a cracking pace :

'Tis the terror of tempest. The rags of the sail
Are flickering in ribbons within the fierce gale :
From the stark night of vapours the dim rain is driven. . . .

596. 1-3

The pitiful rags of sail flutter from the mast of a doomed ship which is driving before the wind on this supremely dirty night, enveloped in rain, encircled by waterspouts and pursued by lightning. Each slide down into the false calm of a wave-trough promises to be its last, and eventually, dismasted, it breaks its back :

The chinks suck destruction. The heavy dead hulk
On the living sea rolls an inanimate bulk.

597. 31-2

The seamen aboard, stricken by disease or disaster, have all perished. The only survivors are a woman with her child at the helm, and two tigers, in the hold. At dawn the wind falls, the sea subsides into a 'long glassy heave' and the two tigers escape. Tiger number one fights with a sea-snake, while a shark, 'the fin-wingèd tomb of the victor', lurks near by. Tiger number two stalks towards the highest point of the sinking ship, where the woman still clings to her child. Suddenly, from nowhere, a boat comes speeding along, with a crew of twelve keen oarsmen and three sure marksmen. The latter dispose of tiger number two. There the fragment ends, leaving the woman and child unrescued and no next week's instalment to follow.

A Vision of the Sea is ludicrously melodramatic, its syntax is strained, its imagery riotous, its metre 'uncouthly handled and clotted with consonants'.[26] If poetry 'takes its origin from emotion recollected in tranquillity',[27] the *Vision of the Sea*, where emotion seems to pour white-hot from mind to paper, can scarcely be called a poem. Rather it is a Gothic nightmare-fantasy, a welling-up of the unconscious, belong-

ing to a *genre* which is rare nowadays because modern poets,
conditioned by psychoanalysis, are shy of parading their
neuroses weakly disguised as 'dreams' or 'visions'.

The *Vision of the Sea* is also a belated reminder of Shelley's
admiration for seamen and their way of life. At Lynmouth
in 1812 he was convinced of the 'engaging and frank
generosity of seafaring men', while he wrote off the land-
lubbers as 'rapacious, mean, cruel and cowardly'. He
seems to have thought that anyone who could stand up to
the sea could do the same to tyrants —

> Who that could rule the elements and spurn
> Their fiercest rage would bow before a slave
> Decked in the fleetingness of Earthly power ? [28]

Vestiges of this attitude remained in later years, though he
may have changed his mind at the last, if, as is possible, his
boat was rammed by a Leghorn fishing-smack.

In complete contrast to the *Vision of the Sea* are two re-
creations of Greek myth, the *Hymn of Pan* and *Arethusa*.
The first is in three 12-line stanzas, each ending with the
delicate refrain 'my sweet pipings'. Only in the last
stanza are we told about Pan's pursuit of Syrinx, which
explains why he plays so passionately, and allows a most
effective metrical change :

> I sang of the dancing stars,
>   I sang of the daedal Earth,
> And of Heaven — and the giant wars,
>   And Love, and Death, and Birth, —
>   And then I changed my pipings,
> Singing how down the vale of Maenalus
>   I pursued a maiden and clasped a reed.
> Gods and men, we are all deluded thus !
>   It breaks in our bosom and then we bleed. . . .
>   614. 25-33

The poem on Arethusa is a delightful string of twinkling
verses :

> Arethusa arose
> From her couch of snows
> In the Acroceraunian mountains, —

> From cloud and from crag,
>   With many a jag,
> Shepherding her bright fountains.
>   She leapt down the rocks,
>   With her rainbow locks
> Streaming among the streams. . . .
>
> 611. 1-9

Here we have the expert technician, fitting in awkward words like Acroceraunian without visible effort. The metre is the same as *The Cloud*'s, as is obvious when the lines are rearranged :

> At sunrise they leap from their cradles steep
>   In the cave of the shelving hill ;
> At noontide they flow through the woods below
>   And the meadows of asphodel. . . .
>
> 612. 79-84

Another poem very like *The Cloud* in spirit is the *Hymn of Apollo*. Stationing himself in the sun, Shelley traces its action on earth during a summer day, and tempers the facts with some speculation. He is right when he guesses that

> the pure stars in their eternal bowers
>   Are cinctured with my power,

since most stars obtain their energy, like the sun, by transmuting hydrogen into helium. He extends this idea in the next couplet :

> Whatever lamps on Earth or Heaven may shine
> Are portions of one power, which is mine.
>
> 613. 23-4

It was a claim that could fairly be made, because the lamps of Heaven generate light in the same way as the sun, while Man's energy-sources — coal, oil, etc. — utilize stored-up energy supplied by the sun. Only recently, with atomic power, have we tapped non-solar sources of energy ; and when the fusion reactor succeeds we shall have learnt to use the sun's own fuel.

In the last of these lyrics we return from astronomical speculation to descriptive botany, for in *The Question* we are presented with another posy of flowers. In *The Sensitive*

Plant and *The Question* Shelley names thirty-six plants or flowers. Perhaps he was taking his cue from the flower-scene in *The Winter's Tale*, from the lines beginning

>   daffodils
> That come before the swallow dares, and take
> The winds of March with beauty.
>
>   IV. iv. 118-20

Though flower-poetry is suspect as pretty-pretty to-day, Shelley's verses are so fluent and unassuming that criticism would be almost a lapse in taste :

> I dreamed that, as I wandered by the way,
>   Bare Winter suddenly was changed to Spring. . . .
> And in the warm hedge grew lush eglantine,
>   Green cowbind and the moonlight-coloured may,
> And cherry-blossoms, and white cups, whose wine
>   Was the bright dew, yet drained not by the day ;
> And wild roses, and ivy serpentine. . . .
> And nearer to the river's trembling edge
>   There grew broad flag-flowers, purple pranked with white,
> And starry river buds among the sedge,
>   And floating water-lilies, broad and bright. . . .
>
>   614. 1-2, 17-21, 25-8

Nature-poems like *The Question* reveal Shelley's obvious delight in detail, in the delicate tracery of flowers, leaves, foam, frost and clouds. Yet he could hardly have enjoyed these details if, as the reports of his friends suggest, he was short-sighted and never wore spectacles. His stoop, mentioned by many of those who met him, probably arose because he liked to read while standing or out walking. He is then said to be 'peering', a tendentious word which leads to 'peering near-sightedly'. Medwin describes him as 'bent, owing to near-sightedness and his being forced to lean over his books with his eyes almost touching them'.[29] Yet as a marksman Shelley could rival Byron, who prided himself on his skill : they used to fire with pistols at a half-crown fourteen yards away, and on one day Shelley hit it three times ;[30] and he wrote in a letter, 'I find the very blades of grass and the boughs of distant trees present themselves

to me with microscopical distinctness'.[31]   On the basis of
this evidence we can only conclude that he had one myopic
eye, and one normal or slightly long-sighted.

7

Most readers judge Shelley by his lyrics, and blithely ignore
his longer poems. Are they very wrong to do this? And
do the lyrics they meet most often in anthologies give a
distorted picture of Shelley?

Of these two questions the first is the more difficult,
because different people would give very different answers.
If we could ask Shelley, he might say that it was as silly as
judging Shakespeare by his songs, Blake by 'Little lamb . . .',
Keats by *Meg Merrilies* or Eliot by *Macavity*. For he greatly
undervalued his lyrics : his references to them in letters are
few and disparaging. It would be like asking Sir Arthur
Sullivan if he minded being known merely as half Gilbert-&-
Sullivan. If, on the other hand, we asked the chimerical
'average reader', he would give a diametrically opposite
answer, saying that he enjoyed the lyrics, but found the
longer poems difficult. Most of the non-average readers —
the radicals and anarchists, Platonists and atheists, vegetarians and scientists, and those who have some sympathy
with one or more of these isms — would insist on the importance of one or more of the longer poems. A few of the
non-average readers, those who detest all the isms and are
thoroughly put off, would say there was little to choose, both
being deplorable. The different attitudes of these groups
are not easily reconciled, and if we want an answer it can
only be a timid and obvious one : reading just the lyrics
gives a seriously incomplete picture ; whether it is a false
one will depend on which lyrics are read.

That raises the second question, 'Do the poems most
often chosen by anthologists give a distorted picture?' The
answer is, unfortunately, 'yes'. To see why, we have to
go back to 1861, when Palgrave's *Golden Treasury* was published. Shelley was given a generous share of space in the

Golden Treasury: indeed, if we except Shakespeare and Wordsworth, he has nearly twice as many entries as any other poet. Palgrave's selection was admirable in its way and for its time. But his anthology was of 'songs and lyrics' so that he tended to choose the most song-like poems; and he, like most Victorians, enjoyed verses which we now call grossly sentimental. Thus, although he included some of the best poems, he also seems to have had a special talent for choosing those now regarded as the weakest. All this would be of historical interest only, but for the fact that Palgrave's selection has become definitive. Granger's *Index to Poetry*, which gives lists of the anthologies where any particular poem may be found, shows that the *Ode to the West Wind* is the lyric of Shelley's chosen most often (77 anthologies), closely followed by the *Skylark* (76). After that come *Ozymandias* (70), *To Night* (62), *The Cloud* (60), 'Music, when soft voices die' (58), the *Indian Serenade* (55), 'One word is too often profaned' (47), 'When the lamp is shattered' (47) and 'O world! O life! O time!' (34). Nine out of these first ten appear in the *Golden Treasury*: the only one to have made good without a 'Palgrave certificate' is *The Cloud*. Palgrave's taste may, or may not, have been impeccable. What is certain is that most subsequent anthologists have been decidedly unenterprising. Shelley himself would probably have approved of about half the anthologists' favourites. Of the ten poems listed above, only four, *Ozymandias*, the *West Wind*, *The Cloud* and the *Skylark*, were published in his lifetime, and these four are certainly stronger than the other six.

It is a sad critical blunder to lump all Shelley's lyrics together. Some he took trouble over; others were provoked by a trivial stimulus, never revised, and never even given a title. He wrote the 672 lines of *The Witch of Atlas* in a three-day interval between other poems (14-16 August 1820), an *average* output (if he worked proper Trade Union hours) of twenty-eight lines an hour. Presumably he wrote more trivial poems even faster — almost at shorthand speed perhaps — and critics invite ridicule when they analyse at length

an album-piece dashed off in five minutes. Shelley made
it harder for us to distinguish between album-piece and
masterpiece by giving both the smooth metrical clothing
he seemed to manufacture so easily. If we want to know
which is which, we have to undress them again. Most
anthologists, perhaps out of modesty, perhaps out of sloth,
shrink from this task. The surface finish seems to be enough
for them, and because 'they have failed to excise a few
patently sentimental poems from the canon, Shelley has been
needlessly slandered.

For it seems to have been these weaker poems which
provoked the attacks on Shelley in the 1930s. Under the
scrutiny of close criticism the weaknesses were plainly
visible. It was then hastily assumed that all Shelley's
poems were superficial, and that there was no need to be
more than superficial in criticizing them. Some of the
mistakes made by one of the most militant of the critics,
F. R. Leavis, have been noticed in earlier chapters; and it
is only fair to mention, too, the errors of a critic more
influential still, T. S. Eliot, who was incensed by Shelley's
ideas, especially his religious scepticism, rather than by the
weak-kneed lyrics. Eliot, in one of the strangest of his
literary utterances, so far misled himself as to call Shelley
'sometimes almost a blackguard',[32] and then accused him
of muddled thinking. To prove the accusation he blatantly
misquoted Shelley : in three extracts he cited, fifteen lines
in all, there were several confusing mis-punctuations and
five wrong words, one of which made nonsense of the
syntax.[33] Professor Barnard has remarked that 'such reckless
misquotation . . . renders worthless the critic's verdict',[34]
and Sir Herbert Read has roundly stated that 'Mr. Eliot's
objection to Shelley's poetry is irrelevant prejudice'.[35]
There is no need to say more, because Eliot later completely
reversed his verdict,[36] and even quoted nine lines from
Prometheus Unbound at the climax of *The Cocktail Party*.

Apart from these eruptions in the 'thirties, Shelley's
lyrics have remained in favour with the critics. The
Victorians, though they looked askance at his 'ideas',

approved of his lyrics. Palgrave reflected their liking.
Swinburne magnified it when he claimed that Shelley's
'depths and heights of inner and outer music are as divine
as nature's, and not sooner exhaustible. He was alone the
perfect singing-god. . . .' [37] Critics more recent and more
reticent than Swinburne have written in a similar vein. For
two examples, we may take first a respected historian of
literature, Louis Cazamian, who called Shelley 'above all a
lyric poet, the greatest that England or perhaps modern
Europe has produced',[38] and second, Charles Morgan, who
wrote : 'His instrument was unique. There is no poet, not
even Shakespeare in his lyrics, who has Shelley's effect of
birdsong pouring and pouring out. His lyrics are not
written ; they burst from the hedgerow, the sunshine, the
air ; they give to the hearer that lift of the heart, that sense
of penetrating rapture, which Nature gives, and love, but
contrivance never.' [39]

It was in these apparently spontaneous poems that Shelley
was making his chief innovation, and that a modest one, in
poetic technique. He extended the range of verse-forms and
injected personality into poems of Nature. In his hands,
the technique is fresh and lively, and he revels in it. Later,
in other hands, the technique became more polished and
less vigorous. Tennyson, with his fine ear, set the example
of restraint, and the later Victorians followed him, with the
flagrant exception of Swinburne, who let personality overflow. Bridges, the early Yeats and De La Mare brought
the technique to the *cul-de-sac* of perfection ; Yeats's later
breakaway from it marked the beginning of a new technique-
cycle.

Having mentioned both extremes of the see-saw of
critical opinion on Shelley's lyrics, it would be as well to
end by trying to estimate the average. The more sentimental lyrics we do not like to-day, for we are shy of sentiment. Shelley probably didn't like them either : none of
them were published in his lifetime. In these sentimental
poems and in a few others, too, we may regret his careless-
ness, for we have been conditioned by close criticism, and

don't like to see a word out of place. In these poems imperfect syntax, homeless pronouns and makeweight adjectives remind us that Shelley rarely spent long enough revising. He would have done better to have reserved his best technique for subjects worthy of it; not to have written the worse half of his poems, and to have used the energy saved to revise the better half. But that was not his way. If it had been, he would have been more of a journeyman and less of a genius. These weaknesses — too much sentiment and too little care — mar only a few of his poems. In the majority he is completely unsentimental and reasonably careful. In the best he combines a firm intellectual grasp with astonishing fluency of technique : the *West Wind*, *The Cloud* and the *Skylark* are unsurpassed and almost unchallenged, the supreme lyrics of the sky.

NOTES TO X: BLITHE SPIRIT

1. *Letters* ii. 20 and 25.

2. The imagery of the boughs probably arose because Shelley was so impressed by the waterspouts he saw out at sea from Leghorn in the summer of 1819. They looked like tree-trunks, and he refers to 'the black trunks of the waterspouts' in *A Vision of the Sea*. The clouds near the waterspout would then be seen as being shaken off the boughs of the waterspout tree. See Henning Krabbe, *Shelleys Poesi* (Copenhagen, 1953), pp. 276–7.

3. H. D. Grant, *Cloud and Weather Atlas* (New York, 1944), p. 44. Plate I in Ludlam and Scorer's *Further Outlook* (1954) shows a cloudscape like Shelley's, except that the low clouds are fractocumulus not fractostratus. See also Ludlam and Scorer's *Cloud Study* (1957), p. 61.

4. F. R. Leavis, *Revaluation*, p. 205.

5. E. Darwin, *Loves of the Plants* iv. 263, 265.

6. For the genesis of the poem, see N. Rogers, *Shelley at Work*, pp. 211–29, particularly (for the *new birth*), p. 217.

7. For background to this paragraph, see J. Ruskin, *Modern Painters*; K. Badt, *John Constable's Clouds* (Routledge, 1950); W. J. Humphreys, *Fogs and Clouds* (Baltimore, 1926.)

8. See E. Blunden, *Shelley*, pp. 229–30. It is possible, but not likely, that Shelley had the idea from the chorus in *The Clouds* of Aristophanes.

9. For details of this banner cloud, see J. S. Collis, *The Moving Waters* (1955), p. 28. For photographs, see Grant, *Cloud and Weather Atlas*, pp. 90–1.

10. A. Walker, *Familiar Philosophy*, p. 358.

11. See A. Walker, *Familiar Philosophy*, p. 518. The idea that stars can be seen by day from the bottom of a mine (*e.g.* Walker, p. 468) is unfounded, however. See *Discovery*, vol. 18, p. 96, March 1957.

12. See Haydon, *Autobiography and Journals*, p. 317.

13. *Economy of Vegetation*, i. 85. See also Walker, *Familiar Philosophy*, p. 306.

14. A. Walker, *Familiar Philosophy*, p. 526. In latitude 51° the increase in length of day is 7·4 minutes at equinox and 9·6 minutes at solstice.

15. Hardy's phrase. See E. Hardy, *Thomas Hardy* (1954), p. 218.

16. J. Thomson, *The Castle of Indolence* I. LXVIII.

17. W. Empson, *Seven Types of Ambiguity*, pp. 156–9.

18. G. O'Malley, *Shelley and Synesthesia.*

19. N. Rogers, *Shelley at Work*, pp. 207–10.

20. A Clutton-Brock, *Shelley, the Man and the Poet*, p. 226. See also R. Bridges, *Milton's Prosody* (O.U.P., 1921), pp. 96–9.

21. E. R. Wasserman, *The Subtler Language*, pp. 251–284.

22. M. Arnold, *Essays in Criticism*, second series, Byron.

23. See G. M. Matthews, *Shelley, selected poems*, p. 30.

24. See J. P. Anderson's Bibliography in W. Sharp's *Life of Shelley*, pp. xix–xx.

25. Cowley's Anacreontic is in the *Oxford Book of English Verse;* Moore's is in his *Odes to Anacreon* (1800), 21.

26. A. Quiller-Couch, *Studies in Literature II*, Shelley II.

27. Wordsworth, Preface to *Lyrical Ballads*.

28. Quotations from *The Voyage* (1812), in *Esdaile Poems* (ed. N. Rogers), pp. 56–7.

29. T. Medwin, *Revised Life of Shelley*, p. 233.

30. See E. E. Williams, *Journal*, p. 118; also Trelawny, *Recollections*, p. 176.

31. *Letters* i. 572.

32. T. S. Eliot, *The Use of Poetry and the Use of Criticism*, p. 89.

33. The quotations are on pp. 25, 90 and 92 of *The Use of Poetry and the Use of Criticism*. The wrong words are: mankind; then . . . that; dross or. *Then* makes nonsense of the syntax.

34. E. Barnard, *Shelley's Religion*, p. 6.

35. H. Read, *In Defence of Shelley*, p. 70.

36. See preface to L. Vivante's *English Poetry* (1950).

37. Swinburne, *Essays and Studies*, p. 215.

38. E. Legouis and L. Cazamian, *History of English Literature* (1948 edition), p. 1058.

39. C. Morgan, *Sunday Times*, 18 Jan. 1948.

XI

DAYDREAMS AND
NIGHTMARES

Content thee with a visionary rhyme.
Witch of Atlas

1

THE summer of 1820 was quite a happy one for Shelley,
as the lyrics of the last chapter would suggest. The baby
Clara had died in his first Italian summer; the 3-year-old
William in the second; now the third summer had come,
and Percy Florence, despite his parents' fears, continued to
thrive. Like his unfortunate brother and sister, however,
he was at first denied the advantages of a settled home.
For when the Gisbornes left on a visit to England in May
1820 (with the manuscript of *Prometheus Unbound* among their
luggage), they offered their house at Leghorn to the Shelleys.
The saving in rent was not to be despised, and the Shelleys
moved there from Pisa, but only for seven weeks. The
summer heat proved rather trying in Leghorn, which
Mrs. Gisborne called 'the Wapping of Italy',[1] and early in
August the Shelleys moved again, to the Baths of San
Giuliano, a summer resort four miles from Pisa near the
foot of the hills. At the end of August Clare returned alone
to Leghorn, after six years in their household. One source
of domestic friction thereby ended, for Mary and Clare had
found 'something to fight about every day'; [2] but another,
Godwin and his debts, was as active as ever. Godwin was
still abusively demanding money, although Shelley had now
given him nearly £5000, raised at ruinous rates of interest,
and because of these and other old debts was in financial
straits himself when he should have been well off.

The Shelleys' stay at the Baths of San Giuliano ended abruptly in late October when the river Serchio overflowed. Their house was flooded and they escaped by boat from an upstairs window. After this adventure they returned to Pisa, and, since its mild winter climate suited them, made it their home for the next eighteen months.

Between March and August 1820 Shelley wrote most of the lyrics discussed in the last chapter and six longer poems as well. Of these six, the two shortest, the lofty odes *to Liberty* and *to Naples*, stand apart : for in all the others he relaxes, treating unpretentious themes gaily and affably. The four light-hearted poems are the *Letter to Maria Gisborne*, with its versified small-talk; the frisky, whimsical and sportive *Hymn to Mercury* and *Witch of Atlas*; and the boisterous *Swellfoot the Tyrant*.

2

Though Shelley's hopes of political reform in Europe had flagged, actual rebellions against tyrannic rulers could re-awaken his former ardours and hatreds. He wore a ring with the motto *Il buon tempo verrà* (the good time will come), and his pen was ever at the service of insurgents. The years 1820 and 1821 were marked by a series of revolts in southern Europe, the first being in Spain. The Bourbon Ferdinand VII had been restored to the Spanish throne in 1814, after the Napoleonic wars. He revoked the liberal constitution drawn up by the Cortes in 1812, restored the Inquisition and ruled despotically. Discontent flared into revolution early in 1820, and Ferdinand was forced to accept a liberal government, which lasted till 1823. When Shelley first heard of the revolt he talked of visiting Spain in person, like some left-wing poet of the 1930s. In fact, he merely followed the newspaper reports and sublimated his enthusiasm into a poem, the *Ode to Liberty* —

> My soul spurned the chains of its dismay,
> And in the rapid plumes of song
> Clothed itself, sublime and strong. . . .

604. 5-7

This formal ode is a history of the idea of Liberty, as Shelley sees it. We are often reminded of the Fairy's lecture in *Queen Mab*, for the poem is alleged to be spoken by an equally convenient mouthpiece, an oracular 'voice out of the deep'. In the primaeval non-liberal era, we are told, all was chaos. This was followed by tyranny, and it was not until the golden age of Greece that the dormant seeds of liberty germinated. Side by side with liberty, the arts arose, and provided a lasting monument in Athens, which

> Gleamed with its crest of columns, on the will
> Of man, as on a mount of diamond, set ;
> For thou wert, and thine all-creative skill
> Peopled, with forms that mock the eternal dead
> In marble immortality, that hill
> Which was thine earliest throne and latest oracle.
>
> 605. 70-5

The torch of liberty passed from Greece to Rome, there to be snuffed out by materialism. Man had dared to resign his hard-won rights, and Liberty was left to mourn in 'utmost islets inaccessible'. Shelley then illustrates the revival of Liberty in Europe, with references to Alfred, to Renaissance Italy, Luther, Milton and the French Revolution. After that he chides the European nations of his day, with the honourable exception of Spain, for condoning tyranny. He even starts to arraign kings and priests, as if he had put back the clock to *Queen Mab* :

> Oh, that the free would stamp the impious name
> Of KING into the dust. . . .
> Oh, that the wise from their bright minds would kindle
> Such lamps within the dome of this dim world,
> That the pale name of PRIEST might shrink and dwindle
> Into the hell from which it first was hurled. . . .
>
> 608. 211-12, 226-9

After this diatribe the oracular voice dies away, and the tension gradually slackens in the *diminuendo* of the last stanza :

Then, as a wild swan, when sublimely winging
  Its path athwart the thunder-smoke of dawn,
Sinks headlong through the aëreal golden light
    On the heavy-sounding plain,
    When the bolt has pierced its brain ;
As summer clouds dissolve, unburthened of their rain ;
  As a far taper fades with fading night,
    As a brief insect dies with dying day, —
  My song, its pinions disarrayed of might,
    Drooped ; o'er it closed the echoes far away
Of the great voice which did its flight sustain,
    As waves which lately paved his watery way
  Hiss round a drowner's head in their tempestuous play.

                                        610. 273-85

As a clarion-call to fight for freedom, there is nothing
in English poetry to equal the *Ode to Liberty* : if we are really
one of the freedom-loving peoples, we ought to be carried
away with enthusiasm, following in the wake of John Stuart
Mill, who used to weep when reading the poem to his friends.
But if we want to be stuffily objective we can point out that
the greatest poetry avoids open propaganda, while the *Ode
to Liberty* is flagrantly propagandist, like *Queen Mab* and *The
Revolt of Islam*. And if we have slipped too far down into the
groove of conventionality we may not like to see kings
thwacked and priests baited. The poem is, then, a fine
piece of propaganda, an anthem for passionate freedom-
lovers ; but those who are more bashful in wooing freedom
may find it too biased.

The *Ode to Liberty* is Shelley's most ambitious and successful Pindaric ode. Its nearest relations in English are
Gray's *Progress of Poesy* and Coleridge's *Ode on the Departing
Year*. Shelley adopts the required rhetorical tone, and he
proceeds patiently, nineteen times, through the daunting
labyrinth of the rhyme-scheme ababcdddcecedee. It was
fortunate that he liked to accept the challenge of difficult
traditional verse-forms. Otherwise his metrical gifts might
have been squandered in tentative experiment. In the *Ode
to Liberty* he is more successful than either Gray or Coleridge
in avoiding the great danger of the formal ode — that the

R

language may become as stilted as the rhyme-scheme.
Shelley uses only a minimum of eighteenth-century abstractions, like Pity and Hope, and he enlivens the poem with
startling images, like

> . . . every Aeolian isle
> From Pithecusa to Pelorus
> Howls, and leaps, and glares in chorus.

He shows he is not going to let the verse-form cramp him
when he twice carries through a clause from one stanza to
the next, a liberty which Gray would never have counten-
anced, even in an ode to Liberty. Yet, despite Shelley's
efforts to revivify and liberalize it, the formal-rhetorical ode
seems to have an obstinately un-English streak, which he
cannot wholly eradicate.

The second liberal revolt to excite his interest broke out
at Naples in July 1820. The Neapolitan rebels proclaimed
Constitutional Government in the approved style, but the
king, after outwardly agreeing, called for help from the
Austrians. Their subsequent invasion met little resistance,
and a despotic régime was restored in March 1821. Shelley
celebrates the rising in the highly abstract *Ode to Naples*.
He begins by sketching, delicately, his own impressions of
the city and its surroundings. Then he declares bluntly,
'prophesyings . . . seize me'. His seizure takes the form
of an elaborate sequence of Epodes, Strophes and Anti-
strophes; and this time he falls heavily into the traps of
the formal ode. The grand manner overcomes him. His
words are solemn, formal and abstract. He keeps up an
ardent tone only with the aid of a rash of exclamation marks.
In the 126 lines of the ode proper there are over 40 capital-
letter abstract nouns (Hope, Truth, Fraud, Wrong, etc.)
and 34 exclamation marks. This style leaves us cold to-day,
because we distrust anything pompous. Our distrust may
be neurotic; but even when judged by its own standards
the *Ode to Naples* has little to commend it. Vital metaphors
are wanting, the theme seems forced, and the method
hackneyed—the *all hail* technique, for example, provides
incongruous echoes of the witches in *Macbeth*.

These odes were Shelley's only contribution to the liberal
risings. Byron, on the other hand, was deeply entangled in
the conspiracies of the *Carbonari* in the Romagna, and his
rooms at Ravenna were being used as an ammunition
dump. Though Shelley was by far the keener reformer in
theory, he gave no practical aid, largely because he did
not mix much with Italians, unlike Byron, who had soon
made friends with the natives, especially those of the opposite
sex.

3

Early in July 1820 Shelley sent a long letter in verse to
Mr. and Mrs. Gisborne, who were then in London. Mrs.
Gisborne's son, Henry Reveley, was an ambitious engineer
with a scheme for building a steamboat to ply between
Marseilles and Leghorn. Shelley was always eager to help
in the advance of applied science, and he had partially
financed the project, probably to the tune of £400. Progress
was disappointingly slow, and Shelley called the steamboat
'a sort of Asymptote which seems ever to approach and
never to arrive'.³ He was not destined to add to his laurels
by becoming the entrepreneur of the first paddle-steamer in
the Mediterranean, for the project was abandoned later in
1820. This fiasco was to lead to some coolness between the
Shelleys and the Gisbornes : losing one's money is not the
happiest way of learning the hard lesson that the path from
the idea to the engineered article is crowded with pitfalls.
But the future cast no shadows, and we find Shelley happily
writing the *Letter to Maria Gisborne* in Henry Reveley's study-
workshop, sitting amidst 'great screws and cones, and
wheels and groovèd blocks', mathematical textbooks, odd
hooks and 'a most inexplicable thing with lead in the
middle'.

> Whoever should behold me now, I wist,
> Would think I were a mighty mechanist,
> Bent with sublime Archimedean art
> To breathe a soul into the iron heart
> Of some machine portentous.

363. 15-19

In fact, his machine-making is frivolous : he merely indulges
in his favourite pastime of sailing model boats, by floating
a 'hollow screw with cogs' in a make-believe pond — a
walnut bowl full of quicksilver.

Shelley reminds Mrs. Gisborne of their talks together
and their reading, particularly of Calderón. For Mrs.
Gisborne had taught him Spanish, just as in 1814 Mrs. Boinville and Cornelia Turner had introduced him to Italian
and later in 1820 Mrs. Mason, was to read Greek with him.
Shelley laughed at the similar pattern of these three friendships : 'You will think it my fate either to find or to imagine
some lady of 45, very unprejudiced and philosophical . . .
in every town that I inhabit'.4

Probably the most interesting items in the poem are the
vignettes of friends in London. Shelley's respect for Godwin's
former powers is unabated :

> You will see
> That which was Godwin, — greater none than he
> Though fallen — and fallen on evil times — to stand
> Among the spirits of our age and land,
> Before the dread tribunal of *to come*
> The foremost.
>
> 367. 196-201

Leigh Hunt, too, he praises generously; he points to the
virtues of Hogg, 'a pearl within an oyster-shell, one of the
richest of the deep'; and he gives a keen analysis of Peacock's art :

> his fine wit
> Makes such a wound, the knife is lost in it;
> A strain too learnèd for a shallow age,
> Too wise for selfish bigots; let his page,
> Which charms the chosen spirits of the time,
> Fold itself up for the serener clime
> Of years to come, and find its recompense
> In that just expectation.
>
> 368. 240-7

In this poem and elsewhere Shelley gave Horace Smith un-
stinted praise. Hunt reported him as saying: 'Is it not
odd that the only truly generous person I ever knew, who

had money to be generous with, should be a stockbroker?
And he writes poetry too . . . and yet knows how to make
money, and does make it, and is still generous.' [5]   Smith
deserved this praise, for during 1821 he involved himself
in a long-drawn-out struggle to thwart a lawyers' plot for
robbing Shelley.   These sketches of Shelley's own friends
are acute and genial; but the most brilliant of his pen-
portraits is reserved for an old friend of Mrs. Gisborne,
Coleridge.   Into seven lines he distils a whole essay in
psychological criticism :

> You will see Coleridge — he who sits obscure
> In the exceeding lustre and the pure
> Intense irradiation of a mind,
> Which, with its own internal lightning blind,
> Flags wearily through darkness and despair —
> A cloud-encircled meteor of the air,
> A hooded eagle among blinking owls.
>
> 368. 202-8

After these pictures of London friends, Shelley turns to
the city itself and particularly its seamier side :

> a shabby stand
> Of Hackney coaches — a brick house or wall
> Fencing some lonely court, white with the scrawl
> Of our unhappy politics.
>
> 369. 265-8

This realistic vein persists to the end of the poem.   Shelley
looks forward to Mrs. Gisborne's return in lines which,
from one so abstemious, can safely be called gluttonous :

> we'll have tea and toast ;
> Custards for supper, and an endless host
> Of syllabubs and jellies and mince-pies,
> And other such lady-like luxuries, —
> Feasting on which we will philosophize !
>
> 370. 303-7

The *Letter to Maria Gisborne* stands, with Pope's *Epistle to
Dr. Arbuthnot,* as one of the few successful English verse-
letters.   The verse, unlike Pope's, is far from perfect technically.   But this is compensated by the urbane tone and genial

humour. The *Letter* is most acceptable in an age shy of pretensions; it is civilized without being affected; 'affectionate without being mawkish';[6] humorous without being malicious.

The tradition that 'Shelley had no humour' dies hard, and plenty of nails for its coffin are supplied by the *Letter*. Private, impromptu and unrevised, it reflects the tone of his conversation. In his serious poems he suppressed this natural humour. It clashed with his concept of the dedicated poet. Humorous touches, he felt, would pave the way to compromising his beliefs: the shock of seeing Southey and Wordsworth compromised had left its mark. Also, humour might give the reviewers another opening for ridicule. It was only when he relaxed, forgetting reviewers and compromise, or when he was sure of his audience, that he lapsed into humour. It is a far cry from the sustained tension of *Prometheus Unbound* to 'tea and toast', 'custards for supper', or this nonsense about Mary (whose pet-names were Pecksie, the Maie and the Dormouse):

> On her hind paws the Dormouse stood
> In a wild and mingled mood
> Of Maieishness and Pecksietude.[7]

4

In mid-July Shelley finished translating one of the most delightful of the so-called Homeric Hymns, the *Hymn to Mercury*. His impish humour continues in this poem, and embellishes an already attractive plot. Mercury (Hermes), the 'not quite legitimate' baby son of Jove and Maia, discovers a tortoise outside his cave when he is only a few hours old. Hermes promptly kills it and fashions from its shell the first lyre:

> And through the tortoise's hard stony skin
> At proper distances small holes he made,
> And fastened the cut stems of reeds within. . . .
> . . . and stretched o'er all
> Symphonious cords of sheep-gut rhythmical.

681. 57-9, 62-3

Having tuned his instrument the baby god is 'seized with a sudden fancy for fresh meat', and he gleefully dances off to the Pierian mountains, where Apollo's oxen are grazing. Hermes drives fifty choice heifers away to the far-off river Alpheus, slaughters two, roasts them and carefully removes the traces—

> And when he saw that everything was clear,
> He quenched the coal, and trampled the black dust,
> And in the stream his bloody sandals tossed.
>
> 685. 179-81

Then he creeps back to his cradle, secure in his baby innocence. The powerful Apollo is furious at losing his heifers, and he is soon on the track of Hermes, who resorts to crafty evasion when accused :

> 'An ox-stealer should be both tall and strong,
>   And I am but a little new-born thing,
> Who, yet at least, can think of nothing wrong.'
>
> 689. 350-2

Apollo is not satisfied with his story and hales him before all-seeing Jove, who tells the child to lead the way to the pastures where he has left Apollo's cattle. *En route* Hermes turns humiliation to triumph by so charming Apollo with his lyre and childish arts that Apollo quite forgives him.

The *Hymn to Mercury* is the best of Shelley's verse-translations. Homer, or whoever the author was, had devised what used to be called a rattling good yarn. It is indeed one of the first detective-stories,[8] since much is made of the breaking of Hermes's alibi and his reversing the footprints of the oxen to mislead Apollo. Shelley faithfully transmits the Homeric relish in the physical details of the heifer-sacrifice and the lyre-making, subjects well off his usual beat. The beguiling story sets off the prime virtues of the translation, the carefree tone and artfully offhand versification. This is Shelley's first attempt at *ottava rima*, the instrument which best suited Byron's daring rhymes and flashing wit. In Shelley's hands it is made to play quite another tune — a prolonged scherzo. Never was his style happier than in this civilized translation of a primitive legend.

It was perhaps the *Hymn to Mercury* which inspired

Matthew Arnold's perverse comment that Shelley's translations were better than his original poems.[9] Shelley himself
deprecated translation : 'it were as wise to cast a violet into
a crucible that you might discover the formal principles of
its colour and odour, as seek to transfuse from one language
into another the creations of a poet'.[10]   He translated only
when at a loss for original ideas. As a result, the dates of his
translations are scattered more or less at random through
his writing career, and this is as convenient a moment as
any to take a quick look at them.

Shelley's translations occupy more than two hundred
pages in his collected works, and cover six languages —
Greek, Latin, French, German, Italian and Spanish. His
translations from the Greek are the most numerous. They
include two of Plato's dialogues — the *Symposium*, discussed
in Chapter V, and the *Ion*, the dialogue on poetic inspiration
— and some half-dozen 'epigrams of Plato', among them the
disturbing *Circumstance* :

> A man who was about to hang himself,
>   Finding a purse, then threw away his rope ;
> The owner, coming to reclaim his pelf,
>   The halter found, and used it. So is Hope
> Changed for Despair — one laid upon the shelf,
>   We take the other. . . .
>
> 721. 1-6

Other verse-translations from the Greek include several
Homeric hymns besides the *Hymn to Mercury*, and a lively
version of the short play in which Euripides dramatized
the story of Polyphemus and Odysseus, *The Cyclops*. His
translations from the Latin are few and fragmentary :
Spinoza, Pliny and Virgil are the authors represented.
Shelley found the Romans far less attractive than the
Greeks, so the dearth of translations from them is no surprise.
He was also lukewarm in his admiration of French literature
(excluding Rousseau), and his only known translation from
French is of the *Marseillaise*. Shelley knew Latin and French
well but he was not very familiar with German.[11] He liked
Goethe's *Faust*, however, and translated over 500 lines from

it, including the Walpurgis-night scene. We might expect him to have translated more from Italian, since he admired Dante and Petrarch and was often living in the provinces of Italy most closely associated with them. But there are only about 150 lines from Dante and a few other oddments. It is a different story when we come to Spain. Shelley was an enthusiast for Calderón and translated over 650 lines from *El Mágico Prodigioso*. In this play, a young pagan scholar, Cyprian, tries to win the love of a Christian girl, Justina, by making a compact with the devil; but her faith is strong and she defies the devil; Cyprian, in despair, is converted; finally he and Justina are martyred together. *El Mágico Prodigioso* is one of the finest of Calderón's plays and Shelley seems to have been specially attracted by its Faustian theme.

These translations are of a high standard, and they have been uniformly praised, even by Matthew Arnold as we have seen. In translations, where Shelley's own ideas are suppressed, his skill as a verse-technician emerges unobscured and that is why critics who don't like his ideas do like his translations. Only four of his longer translations are complete, and two of these, the *Ion* and *The Cyclops*, appear in Everyman's Library. The many incomplete ones are still publicized from time to time, when reviewers of new translations quote them to expose weaknesses in those they are reviewing. Most of Shelley's verse-translations were from authors whom he probably regarded as the greatest poets or poet-dramatists of five nations — Homer, Virgil, Goethe, Dante and Calderón. Of all the authors he translated Shelley was attracted most by Plato, Dante and Calderón. He was not at all dismayed that Dante and Calderón usually wrote for the greater glory of the Catholic Church. He could now tolerate dogmatic orthodoxy, which a few years before repelled him. Shelley held Calderón in the highest esteem, referring to him as 'a kind of Shakespeare', and Coleridge apparently had a similar opinion, though nowadays it would be thought eccentric to rank Calderón above Lope de Vega.[12]

5

The Witch of Atlas, a carefree extravaganza, written at the rate of over 200 lines a day in August 1820, resembles the *Hymn to Mercury* in its theme and in its playful *ottava rima*. Shelley's capricious Witch is a female version of Hermes. She has no human frailties and can roam wherever her skittish fancy leads her.   Shelley's use (or misuse) of the word *witch* is one of his habitual idiosyncrasies : his witches are pleasant enchantresses, *e.g.* the 'quaint witch Memory' and 'the witch Poesy'.[13]   He begins the poem by introducing the Witch's mother, one of the Atlantides, whose beauty captivated the Sun and made him change her into a vapour, then a cloud, then a meteor, and finally into

> one of those mysterious stars
> Which hide themselves between the Earth and Mars.

The daughters of Atlas gave their names to the stars of the Pleiades and Hyades groups, and Shelley is modernizing this legend to account for the minor planets or asteroids, the first of which had been discovered on 1 January 1801 by the Italian astronomer Piazzi — though asteroids with orbits partly inside that of Mars were not known in Shelley's day. The poem is full of such inventions, and the Witch herself is often lost amid the distractions.

The Witch lives in a cave among the Atlas mountains. She is so gentle, lovely and powerful that beasts of every kind, from the 'sly serpent' to the 'brinded lioness', as well as men, come to be cured of their vicious habits.

> The magic circle of her voice and eyes
> All savage natures did imparadise.
>
> 373. 103-4

The gods come, too, marvelling at her powers.   In the deepest recesses of her hideout this 'wizard lady' stores amazing treasures — sounds, visions, odours, drugs, spells and substances unknown on earth.   Among her more solid chattels is

> the fairest and the lightest boat
> Which ever upon mortal stream did float.
>
> 378. 295-6

For this boat she moulds, deftlier than any Frankenstein, a living pilot, a hermaphrodite with the graces of both sexes and the defects of neither. This pilot takes her wherever she pleases, for the boat can sail in air as well as water.

> She would often climb
> The steepest ladder of the crudded rack
> Up to some beakèd cape of cloud sublime,
> And like Arion on the dolphin's back
> Ride singing through the shoreless air ; — oft-time
> Following the serpent lightning's winding track,
> She ran upon the platforms of the wind,
> And laughed to hear the fire-balls roar behind.

383. 481-8

Sometimes she comes down and watches mortals as they sleep. She can see the naked beauty of their souls, and send them apt dreams, to solve their problems or warn them of their faults. At other times the Witch plays pranks on the gods : the story of these is

> A tale more fit for the weird winter nights
> Than for these garish summer days, when we
> Scarcely believe much more than we can see.

388. 670-2

As Mary remarked in her Note, *The Witch of Atlas* is 'peculiarly characteristic' of Shelley's tastes, 'wildly fanciful, full of brilliant imagery' ; in it he discarded 'human interest and passion, to revel in the fantastic ideas that his imagination suggested'. This want of human interest and the weak plot are the main defects of the poem. Shelley endows the Witch with unlimited power and then lets her travel aimlessly, dispensing nebulous gifts and playing practical jokes. Such behaviour may be amusing in a baby-god like Hermes who can be chastised by his elders ; in the Witch it seems merely irresponsible. Shelley's reply to this criticism is in the prefatory stanzas, where he admits the poem is absurd and asks 'why not ?'

> though no mice are caught by a young kitten,
> May it not leap and play as grown cats do,
> Till its claws come ?

371. 5-7

Much can be said for the poem if we accept that it is a kittenish frolic. With the *Hymn to Mercury* and the *Letter to Maria Gisborne*, the *Witch* rebuts the charge that Shelley is 'too serious'. The playful tone is again controlled skilfully; the versification is fluent; the imagery is bold and varied.

This bold imagery and easy technique show up well in stanza 16, where Shelley explains how the Witch stored odours. She kept them, he tells us, in 'a floating net' which

> a love-sick Fairy
> Had woven from dew-beams while the moon yet slept.

The odours, trying to escape, would beat their wings against the net, like

> bats at the wired window of a dairy.

The build-up of the image follows a familiar pattern. To begin with, the fanciful idea : odours in a cage. Then the first elaboration : the cage woven by a fairy with a thread lighter than gossamer. Next the piling-up of detail to turn fancy into fantasy : the fairy love-sick and the thread 'dew-beams while the moon yet slept'. In Shelley's time the moon was thought to influence dewfall, and this accounts for the phrase 'the dew-mingled rain of the calm moonbeams' in *Prometheus Unbound*. In fact, dew is usually heaviest on nights when the moon can be seen because clouds are absent, not because the moon is present. For Shelley, therefore, dew-beams are non-existent when the moon is away ; for us they are completely non-existent. Finally, just before it flies off to the empyrean of absurdity, Shelley anchors his fancy with the arresting homely simile of the bats at the dairy window. The pattern is complete.

The allusions to scientific theories and ancient myths in the poem do not justify esoteric interpretation, for the tone is bantering throughout, and Shelley warns off would-be interpreters :

> If you unveil my Witch, no priest nor primate
> Can shrive you of that sin. . . .

372. 46-7

Interpreters have been busy nevertheless. The foremost of them, Carl Grabo, gave in his book *The Meaning of the Witch of Atlas* an impressive list of qualities personified by the Witch, and showed how Shelley had woven Greek and Egyptian myths, scientific half-truths and Neoplatonic symbols into the fabric of the poem. Shelley does, it is true, make use of Greek and Egyptian myths; occasionally, too, there is a whiff of scientific speculation, and the discovery of jet streams in the stratosphere has fully justified his reference to

> streams of upper air
> Which whirl the earth in its diurnal round;

and he does sometimes resort to Neoplatonic imagery, as when he refers to 'the liquid surface of man's life' and laments that we sail so clumsily upon it:

> We, the weak mariners of that wide lake
> Where'er its shores extend or billows roll,
>   Our course unpiloted and starless make
> O'er its wild surface to an unknown goal.
>
> 385. 546-9

But Shelley never integrates these allusions; he flits from one myth to another. The poem may, as Harold Bloom claims, be 'the supreme example of mythmaking poetry in English'. But it is not so easy to accept Professor Grabo's conclusion that the Witch, daughter of Apollo and a sea nymph, is meant to represent: first, the goddess of love and electricity (the equation of *Prometheus Unbound* being maintained); second, Isis, goddess of the Moon and fertility, controlling the weather through atmospheric electricity; and third, the creative spirit of intellectual beauty.[14] That such a theory has been seriously proposed does show that even in this fanciful poem dashed off so quickly, there is a rich intellectual background. And, as might be expected, there are also a few specific literary borrowings. Virgil mentions a priestess living among the Atlas mountains in Book 4 of the *Aeneid*, which Shelley had recently read. The playful form of speech may derive from Niccolò Forteguerri's *Ricciardetto*, an epic in *ottava rima*, which Shelley and Mary had been reading aloud in July.

The Witch's boat is suspiciously like the 'wondrous boat' in Canto XV of Tasso's *Gerusalemme liberata*.

To explain the hermaphrodites in the poem — the pilot, and the Witch herself, who is once likened to

> a sexless bee
> Tasting all blossoms and confined to none —

we must go back to pre-literary sources. The sex of gods is a curious feature of primitive religions, and one which sometimes lets us see into the minds of the worshippers. The early god-makers often chose the hermaphrodite because it made plain to the meanest mind that gods differed from men, and also because it symbolized a wholeness mortals were always striving for and could never attain. Many of the myths explaining the origin of the sexes depend on figures openly or latently androgynous, *e.g.* Aristophanes's cartwheelers in Plato's *Symposium* or Adam before he lost his rib. Shelley had the same basic motives as the myth-makers and an added incentive provided by his own Age. For at the end of the eighteenth century, scientists were greatly interested in hermaphrodites. They figure in Erasmus Darwin's evolutionary theory and appear quite frequently in the *Philosophical Transactions* of the Royal Society: for example a long paper by Sir Everard Home in 1799 is devoted to a hermaphrodite dog. So hermaphrodites were there ready for Shelley to use as symbols for completeness and a superhuman range of experience.

6

In the summer of 1820 all England was agog over the most undignified exposure in the history of her royalty, the 'Queen's Trial'. In 1795 the outspoken and unladylike Princess Caroline had come to England to marry the Prince of Wales (as he then was), only to part from him a year later. From then on Caroline had been a continual embarrassment to the government. Since 1814 she had been touring the Continent with an odd and vulgar retinue, and her behaviour was the scandal of Europe. The Delicate Investigation of 1806 had left her name only slightly tarnished. The Milan Commission of 1818, after examining thirty-one Italian witnesses, concluded she was guilty of adultery. When the Prince became King in 1820, he and his Tory ministers offered Caroline no place in the Coronation ceremonies. She, rash as ever, returned to England in June to claim her rights. The government replied by accusing her of infidelity, an action they had shirked while George III was alive. They thus rallied the Whigs to her side and, by seeming to persecute her, made her the idol of the people. The Whigs needed little encouragement, for when the Regency began in 1810 they had expected the Prince to call them to office, and on being disillusioned a substantial minority led by Whitbread expressed their pique by allying themselves with Princess Caroline. So when the crisis came in 1820, a strong Whig faction, then led by Brougham, was ready to defend the Queen.

The Queen's Trial occupied the House of Lords for three months, from August to November. Their lordships heard evidence from the lowest types of foreign servants, who were ready to blacken anyone's name and delighted the country's gossips by divulging 'one scandalous indecorum after another'.[15] Brougham's speeches in defence of the Queen were masterly, and when the Lords approved the third reading by a majority of only nine, Lord Liverpool withdrew the Bill. The London mob celebrated this satisfactory end to their free entertainment in the traditional way, by 'smashing the windows of those who refused to join in the illuminations'.[16] And the rest of the country did not lag far behind. Dr. Gideon Mantell's journal records typical scenes in Shelley's home county :

Nov. 11, 1820. I was awoke at five o'clock this morning by the ringing of the Church bells, the tolling of Old Gabriel, and the rejoicings of the people in the streets, in consequence of the bill against the Queen having been thrown out in the House of Lords. All business is at stand, every one is rejoicing : the poorer classes decorated themselves with laurels, every huxter's horse or mule had branches stuck in their harness : the genteel folks wore red roses. This evening the band has been parading the streets.   The Town [Lewes] is to be illuminated on Monday evening.[17]

The end of the Queen's persecution was also the end of her popularity —

> Most gracious Queen, we thee implore
> To go away and sin no more ;
> But if that effort be too great,
> To go away at any rate !

Caroline was always slow to take a hint, and with a last melodramatic gesture she drove to Westminster Hall for the Coronation ceremonies in July 1821. She was kept out by force and died a fortnight later, perhaps of a broken heart but more probably of an overdose of a purgative.

In his rumbustious, Aristophanic satire *Swellfoot the Tyrant*, which purports to be 'a tragedy . . . translated from the original Doric', Shelley mixes classical legends with the cant of the scurrilous pamphlets and cartoons being read so avidly in England. Shelley was one day disturbed by the grunting of pigs in a near-by market while he was reading aloud to Mrs. Mason. Encouraged by the precedent of Aristophanes's *Frogs* he decided to have a chorus of pigs, who were to represent the common people. This is rather an insult to those 'heirs of glory, heroes of unwritten story', as they were called in *The Mask of Anarchy*, but the Lords and Ladies suffer even worse indignities from Shelley's broad humour.[18]

The 'tragedy' is set, logically enough, in Thebes, where Swellfoot and his vile ministers rule their brutish subjects. Shelley's portrait of Swellfoot follows the cartoon-figure of George IV, which is faintly offensive to the refined taste of the twentieth century :

> These graceful limbs are clothed in proud array
> Of gold and purple, and this kingly paunch
> Swells like a sail before a favouring breeze,
> And these most sacred nether promontories
> Lie satisfied with layers of fat. . . .
>
> 390. 2-6

Food is Swellfoot's obsession : how is he to keep up the supply of good bacon for his feasts when his pig-people are starving? His chief ministers, Mammon (who has some of Lord Liverpool's traits) and Purganax (a caricature of Castlereagh), are worried about something graver, the following oracle:

> 'Boeotia, choose reform or civil war!
> When through the streets, instead of hare with dogs,
> A Consort Queen shall hunt a King with Hogs,
> Riding on the Ionian Minotaur.'
>
> 393. 113-16

Swellfoot's Queen is called Iona after Io, the unfortunate priestess who was turned into a cow and pursued all over Europe by a gadfly. Iona is also plagued by a Gadfly, representing the Milan Commission of 1818, and the Gadfly is supported by a Rat and a Leech (Sir John Leach had been responsible for setting up the Commission). Iona, tired of being stung by the Gadfly, upsets Swellfoot by appearing in Thebes. Neither the military prowess of Laoctonos (Wellington) nor the persuasive rhetoric of Dakry (Eldon) can prevent the swine acclaiming her their champion. Purganax proposes a trial by ordeal to test the Queen's innocence. The supernatural liquor in a Green Bag is to be poured over her. (The charges against the Queen were presented to Parliament in a green bag.) The Queen agrees to the test, then seizes the Bag and flings its contents over Swellfoot and his Court. They change into a rabble of filthy and ugly animals. The watching pigs eat the loaves meant for Swellfoot's guests and immediately become bulls. The Queen mounts the Ionian minotaur, John Bull, and gallops out to hunt her enemies.

A bald summary hardly does justice to the plot, which is heavy with symbolism, full of intricate detail and alive with long-forgotten ripples of political controversy. Shelley uses Peacock's technique of translating names with studied pedantry. He had first tried this in *Peter Bell the Third*, when he called Wordsworth *Verbovale*. Here we have *Swellfoot*, which is an apt name for a gouty monarch, as well as being the literal translation of *Oedipus*. And the parallel is maintained with the oracle, which corresponds

s

to the riddle of the Sphinx in Sophocles.   Then there is
Dakry, or *weeper*, for Eldon, who was famous for timely
weeping.   Finally, with verbal casuistry worthy of an
Elizabethan, Shelley translates *Ionian Minotaur* into 'plain
Theban' as *John Bull*.   In his use of animals Shelley antici-
pates George Orwell's *Animal Farm*.   By making the wants
of the people simpler, the machinations of their rulers
become plainer.   Swellfoot's aim is to live and eat well,
and he can't let all his pig-people die off because he needs
their labour and bacon.   Purganax gives pigs ribbons round
their legs, and their sows 'tawdry lace and bits of lustre
glass', to ensure they will vote for him.   The pigs bring
Shelley to terra firma and almost justify his entry in the marriage register at Edinburgh, 'farmer, Sussex'.   He handles
hog-wash and the various organs of pigs with surprising
ease.   It is another world indeed from *The Witch of Atlas*.

The broad humour of *Swellfoot*, its gusto, and its well-knit
plot deserve a worthier theme.   Shelley knew the Queen
was but a tawdry champion of liberty: 'How can the
English endure the mountains of cant which are cast upon
them about this vulgar cook-maid they call a Queen?'[19]
His poem was written hurriedly and published anonymously
(with *Oedipus Tyrannus* as the first title) probably in December,
when the Queen's trial was over.   Only seven copies had
been sold when Horace Smith, who had arranged for its
publication, was visited by a 'burly Alderman' representing
the Society for the Suppression of Vice, which at this time
was exceptionally active.[20]   To save the publisher from a
libel action Smith had to destroy the remaining copies.

7

In July and August 1820, as if taking his Muse for a summer
holiday, Shelley added a distinctive new chapter to his
works.   The *Letter to Maria Gisborne*, the *Hymn to Mercury*,
the *Witch of Atlas* and *Swellfoot* are all alive with varied
humour.   Not everyone will like all four : some will find the
Witch too fanciful, or the *Letter* too prosaic ; for others *Swellfoot* will be too pungent, too near Rowlandson.   By explor-

ing these various facets of humour, Shelley was arming
himself with a new weapon — sly fun, which often peeps out
in his later poems. The bantering tone of his talk was at
last filtering into his poems, warning us again not to judge
him only by stridently-titled pamphlets, dream-lyrics and
grandiose schemes for reform.

August 1820 marks the end of the outburst of vigorous
poetry which began in the spring of 1819 with Acts II and
III of *Prometheus Unbound* and *The Cenci*. The poems of the
next six months, mostly short lyrics with Time as a theme,
are few and sad. The first is the cheerless dirge *Autumn* :

> The warm sun is failing, the bleak wind is wailing,
> The bare boughs are sighing, the pale flowers are dying,
> > And the Year
> On the earth her death-bed, in a shroud of leaves dead,
> > Is lying.
> Come, Months, come away,
> From November to May,
> In your saddest array. . . .
>
> 620. 1-8

There are two short pieces about the moon, which Shelley,
like Coleridge, found particularly attractive. One piece,
that beginning 'And like a dying lady . . .', has some confused echoes from Sidney's sonnet 'With how sad steps . . .'
The other is clear, sober and faintly cynical :

> Art thou pale for weariness
> Of climbing heaven and gazing on the earth,
> > Wandering companionless
> Among the stars that have a different birth, —
> And ever changing, like a joyless eye
> That finds no object worth its constancy ?
>
> 621. 1-6

Another dirge ushers in the New Year, and the grim *Time*
marks the climax of this sombre season :

> Unfathomable Sea ! whose waves are years,
> > Ocean of Time, whose waters of deep woe
> Are brackish with the salt of human tears !
> > Thou shoreless flood, which in thy ebb and flow
> Claspest the limits of mortality,

> And sick of prey, yet howling on for more,
> Vomitest thy wrecks on its inhospitable shore ;
> Treacherous in calm, and terrible in storm,
> Who shall put forth on thee,
> Unfathomable Sea ?
>
> 637

Shelley's favourite Neoplatonic image of the soul voyaging across the sea of life-and-time is here expressed boldly and epigrammatically, with an added nuance to explain how the salt got into the sea. The shores of this sea are the *limits of mortality* which the boat of the soul is launched from, and wrecked on. The adjective *shoreless* is thus confusing, to say the least, and the fascinating finality of the poem cannot wholly mask this inconsistency.

There are no such inconsistencies in the carefully wrought poem *To Night*, and the tone is not quite so grim. But there is no sign of the resilience and gaiety of the previous summer's lyrics :

> Swiftly walk over the western wave,
> Spirit of Night !
> Out of the misty eastern cave,
> Where, all the long and lone daylight,
> Thou wovest dreams of joy and fear,
> Which make thee terrible and dear, —
> Swift be thy flight ! . . .
>
> 636. 1-7

The poem is something of a *tour de force*, for Shelley was naturally a creature of the day, and his lover's welcome to Night is not spontaneous. The personifications, Day, Night, Death and Sleep, might have been insipid; but they are not, because the imagery, which is narrowly erotic to match the lover's welcome, keeps the atmosphere tense. *To Night*, like *Time*, is circular in form: the action ends where it began. This form was not a favourite with Shelley. He preferred the rocket lyric — a soaring climb under full power followed by a free, relaxed descent. As Tennyson put it, not very happily, he 'seems to go up, and burst'.[21]

These sombre lyrics were written at a time when Shelley's outer life appears to have been reasonably happy, so they reflect his life, if at all, in its worst moments. When not at work on a long poem, Shelley wrote only if the spirit moved him. Time passed unnoticed when he was content; it was in the brief spells of depression or illness that the short poems were usually written. This is a reminder that in the winter of 1820–1 as usual, he was often troubled by pains in his side. Sometimes 'he would roll on the floor in agony' [22] and remarks in his letters, like 'I am pretty ill, I thank you, just now',[23] show that he had the invalid's preoccupation with health. Tiresome though it may seem now, his ill health can't be explained away in terms of Romantic death-wishes. It was a real hardship to him, and we who live in an age when continual pain is much rarer should not underrate its effect. Certainly it would account for the tone of some of the gloomy lyrics.

NOTES TO XI: DAYDREAMS AND NIGHTMARES

1. Mrs. Gisborne, *Journal*, p. 52.
2. Clare's *Journal*, 4 July 1820.
3. *Letters* ii. 179.
4. *Letters* ii 180.
5. Leigh Hunt, *Autobiography*, p. 196.
6. D. Davie, *Purity of Diction*, p. 141.
7. *New Shelley Letters*, p. 86.
8. See C. Seltman, *The Twelve Olympians* (1952), p. 68.
9. M. Arnold, *Essays in Criticism,* second series, Byron.
10. *Defence of Poetry* (ed. Brett-Smith), p. 29. See also *Letters* ii. 153.
11. See N. Rogers, *Shelley at Work*, pp. 77–8.
12. For Calderón's influence on Shelley, see S. de Madariaga, *Shelley and Calderón*; N. Rogers, *Shelley at Work*; and J. M. Cohen, *History of Western Literature* (1956), pp. 159–63 and 356. For Shelley's quoted opinion of Calderón, see *Letters* ii. 115. For comment on Shelley's translations from Dante and Calderón, see Todhunter, *Study of Shelley*, pp. 208–19, Brand, *Italy and the English Romantics*, p. 62, and J. Raben, in *Shelley, Modern Judgements*, p. 196.
13. *Letter to Maria Gisborne*, l. 132: *Mont Blanc*, l. 44
14. See H. Bloom, *Shelley's Mythmaking*, pp. 165–204 and C. Grabo, *The Meaning of the Witch of Atlas*, pp. 106–7.
15. A. Bryant, *The Age of Elegance*, p. 393.
16. R. Fulford, *George the Fourth* (1949), p. 213.
17. Quoted in *Sussex Bedside Anthology* (Bognor, 1950), p. 459.
18. S. Reiter, *Shelley's Poetry*, pp. 252–65, has a good commentary.
19. *Letters* ii. 207.
20. See A. E. Beavan, *James and Horace Smith*, p. 176, and N. St. John-Stevas, *Obscenity and the Law* (1956), p. 35.
21. See Everyman edition of the *Golden Treasury*, p. ix.
22. Medwin, *Revised Life of Shelley*, p. 269.
23. *Letters* ii. 301.

XII

EPIPSYCHIDION

'Ανδρός γε θνητοῦ παῖς ἔμμεναι, ἀλλὰ θεοῖο.
οὐδὲ ἐῴκει

[She] seemed not to be the child of a mortal man,
but of a god.

Iliad

1

THE winter of 1820–1 brought pleasures as well as pain :
Epipsychidion was the outcome of an exciting new friendship.
At the end of November, Shelley, Mary and Clare had been
introduced to a beautiful 19-year-old Italian girl, Teresa
Viviani. Teresa, or Emilia as the Shelleys came to call her,
was a budding poetess, and her new friends duly admired
her fluent verses and eloquent *Essay on Love*. Her father
was a State dignitary — governor of Pisa and head of one
of the four provinces of the Grand Duchy of Tuscany —
but this did not prevent him being mean with money. For
three years he had 'imprisoned' Emilia in a convent school,
and there she was to remain until he could find a husband
who would take her without a dowry.

A Gothic novelist could hardly have devised a situation
more likely to excite the Shelleys' interest. As if to show
that life copied art, here was a beautiful heiress imprisoned
by a tyrannic father who was probably just about to choose
her a repulsive husband. In fact, she was suffering little
worse a fate than many Italian girls of high birth who had
no suitors ; but Shelley did not see it in that light, and Mary,
as became the daughter of Mary Wollstonecraft, was most
indignant at the callous wording of Italian marriage contracts. These contracts were, in practice, very elastic, and
Byron, a fully-fledged *Cavaliere Servente*, ruefully compared Italy with Turkey : 'here the *polygamy* is all on the
female side'.[1] Emilia's plight was enticing enough to the

Shelleys : add her talents and she was irresistible. At first they thought she was a near-genius, and Mary even compared her with the foremost Renaissance authors. Emilia naturally did her best to live up to this valuation and, like Harriet Westbrook, she knew how to draw Shelley by harping on her 'imprisonment'. The Shelleys were, for her, the one bright spot in a drab world, and she was ready to praise them with Latin extravagance and candour. In one letter she said of Shelley, 'he has a human exterior, but the interior is all divine'.[2]

Shelley returned the compliment in *Epipsychidion*, the most exalted of love-songs, where he hailed Emilia as a 'Seraph of Heaven, too gentle to be human' :

> in the fields of Immortality
> My spirit should at first have worshipped thine,
> A divine presence in a place divine.

414. 133-5

Emilia was near enough to tantalize and just remote enough to avoid disillusioning him until the poem was finished. She little knew she was winning herself renown as the 'onlie begetter' of this the most fervent of his poems in praise of an idealized *anima*. Shelley hardly ever saw Emilia alone, and Mary must have known almost all that passed between them.[3] Though a little piqued, she referred nonchalantly to 'Shelley's Italian Platonics'.[4] Shelley fretted because he could do so little to help Emilia. *Epipsychidion*, though flattering, was hardly practical aid. So he drew up an obviously hopeless petition to the Grand Duchess of Tuscany pleading for Emilia's release. Before *Epipsychidion* went to the printers', however, he came to a more sober estimate of her talents, and little more than a year later we find him writing : 'The *Epipsychidion* I cannot look at ; the person whom it celebrates was a cloud instead of a Juno ; and poor Ixion starts from the centaur that was the offspring of his own embrace'.[5] What a falling-off was here ! Emilia demeaned herself in the Shelleys' eyes when she meekly accepted the husband chosen by her father, and asked for a large loan to help a friend of hers. Mary found a nursery rhyme to sum the matter up :

> As I was going down Cranbourne lane,
> Cranbourne lane was dirty,
> And there I met a pretty maid,
> Who dropped to me a curtsey ;
> I gave her cakes, I gave her wine,
> I gave her sugar-candy,
> But oh! the naughty little girl,
> She asked me for some brandy.[4]

So it is not surprising that when Shelley sent *Epipsychidion* to be published, anonymously, he said it was 'in a certain sense . . . a production of a portion of me already dead ; and in this sense the advertisement is no fiction'.[6] According to the advertisement, 'the writer . . . died at Florence, as he was preparing for a voyage to one of the wildest of the Sporades'. The poem is addressed openly to 'The Noble and Unfortunate Lady, Emilia V——', and prefaced with a translation from the first *canzone* of Dante's *Convito*, which warns us of its obscurities :

> My Song, I fear that thou wilt find but few
> Who fitly shall conceive thy reasoning,
> Of such hard matter dost thou entertain. . . .
>
> 411. 1-3

2

Epipsychidion falls into three parts, loosely linked. In the first, lines 1-245, Shelley introduces the seraph-Emilia as a 'poor captive bird' fluttering vainly behind 'unfeeling bars', and then he soars into an ionosphere of sparkling flattery :

> I never thought before my death to see
> Youth's vision thus made perfect. Emily,
> I love thee ; though the world by no thin name
> Will hide that love from its unvalued shame. . . .
> . . . Art thou not void of guile,
> A lovely soul formed to be blessed and bless ?
> A well of sealed and secret happiness,
> Whose waters like blithe light and music are,
> Vanquishing dissonance and gloom ? A Star
> Which moves not in the moving heavens, alone ?

A Smile amid dark frowns ? . . .
A Metaphor of Spring and Youth and Morning ;
A Vision like incarnate April, warning,
With smiles and tears, Frost the Anatomy
Into his summer grave.

413. 41-4, 56-62, 120-3

There are nearly 150 lines in this vein, but it is no use
quoting more, because extracts do not register the sustained
pressure, which saves the dangerously piled-up comparisons
from collapsing into bathos. The comparisons become more
abstruse, and the symbols prevalent later in the poem are
foreshadowed, when Emilia is called 'a Splendour leaving
the third sphere pilotless'. This refers to the Ptolemaic
cosmology, or the Dantean, which is explained fully in the
Convito:7 the *third sphere* is that of the planet Venus — the
terzo ciel in the first line of the *canzone* whose last lines preface *Epipsychidion*. But before bringing in the astronomical
symbols, Shelley interpolates forty lines in a conversational
tone, relics of the first draft for the poem, which was half-
humorous, in the manner of the *Letter to Maria Gisborne*.

Shelley could hardly have completed a poem like
Epipsychidion without airing his views on the marriage laws.
Though theoretically he still favoured the free love of *Political
Justice*, he would probably, like Godwin, have admitted that
human nature was too imperfect for abolition of marriage ties
to be a desirable reform. Caught in this equivocal attitude,
he took refuge in a good-humoured protest against convention :

I never was attached to that great sect,
Whose doctrine is, that each one should select
Out of the crowd a mistress or a friend,
And all the rest, though fair and wise, commend
To cold oblivion, though it is in the code
Of modern morals, and the beaten road
Which those poor slaves with weary footsteps tread,
Who travel to their home among the dead
By the broad highway of the world, and so
With one chained friend, perhaps a jealous foe,
The dreariest and the longest journey go.

415. 149-59

Next come some lines which 'gravelled' T. S. Eliot.[8]
Certainly they are open to possible misreading :

> True love in this differs from gold and clay,
> That to divide is not to take away.
> Love is like understanding, that grows bright,
> Gazing on many truths; 'tis like thy light,
> Imagination. . . .

415. 160-4

For Shelley *true love* means ideal love, 'Platonic love', or,
to dilute it further, intellectual companionship : the comparisons with *understanding* and *imagination* make this plain.
But it is not at all plain at a first reading, because *true
love* has acquired a different meaning, rooted in the age of
chivalry and nourished by the long tradition of English
and Scottish ballads and love-songs. We can hardly accept
Shelley's amended meaning when there are so many
familiar quotations like

> My true love hath my heart and I have his. . . .
> The course of true love never did run smooth. . . .

or even

> But me and my true love will never meet again
> On the bonnie, bonnie banks o' Loch Lomon'.

Shelley had, as he foresaw (in line 44), stumbled over the
nuances of the word *love*. Many readers who are irritated
by these lines about 'true love' without really knowing why
probably half-suspect him of trying to discredit the chivalric
convention and the love-ballad tradition, especially perhaps
since Emilia, like a troubadour's lady, is inaccessible.
Though they may be persuaded they are wrong, they may
still wonder why Shelley chose to emphasize the divisibility
of ideal love. Perhaps it was because he wanted to convince
himself that he was not guilty of slighting Mary. Or
perhaps he was merely echoing Virgil's discourse on love in
Dante's *Purgatorio*.[9]

Shelley goes on to describe the goddess he fancies he
sees in Emilia :

> There was a Being whom my spirit oft
> Met on its visioned wanderings, far aloft,

In the clear golden prime of my youth's dawn,
Upon the fairy isles of sunny lawn,
Amid the enchanted mountains. . . .
Then, from the caverns of my dreamy youth
I sprang, as one sandalled with plumes of fire.
                                    416. 190-4, 217-18

When the Being had gone he despairingly

   questioned every tongueless wind that flew
   Over my tower of mourning, if it knew
   Whither 'twas fled, this soul out of my soul.
                                    417. 236-8

These lines lead on naturally to the second part of the
poem, Shelley's search for the lost spirit, and their last
words give the clue to the meaning of the word 'Epipsychidion'. In the Ptolemaic cosmology the earth was fixed
and the planets moved on epicycles or 'wheels upon
wheels'. Shelley builds up his title with the astronomical
analogy in mind, adds the Greek affectionate diminutive
-idion, and replaces *cycle* by *psyche*, so that Epi-psych-idion
means 'a little soul upon a soul', a Platonic inner soul.
Finally, allowing for the oblique reference to the *Epithalamion* convention, we may translate 'Epipsychidion' as
'a song of praise about the little soul within the soul'.
Shelley's changeless little soul is akin to the spirit he called
Intellectual Beauty, glimpses of which are reward enough
for dull years of waiting.

3

In the second part of the poem, his search for the lost
psychidion, he meets many symbolic figures, and conjecture runs rife in interpreting them. He begins with a
direct allusion to the parable of the cave in Plato's *Republic*,
where imprisoned mortals see only shadows cast on the
inner wall by idols moving past the entrance:

   In many mortal forms I rashly sought
   The shadow of that idol of my thought.
                                    417. 267-8

Then he describes the symbolic 'shadows' in turn: one
whose voice was venomed melody and whose touch was

'electric poison'; one who 'was true — oh! why not true to me?'; the cold chaste Moon, the Queen of Heaven's bright isles; the Tempest and the Planet; the authentic vision of the Sun, 'dissolving the dull cold in the frore air'; and finally the Comet, beautiful and fierce.

This string of obscure figures is usually treated as a list of Shelley's lady-loves. The 'true' one is then Harriet Grove, the Moon is Mary, the Sun is Emilia and the Comet Clare. The lady of electric poison and the Tempest-Planet remain unidentified. Shelley seems to encourage this interpretation, for he equates the Sun with Emilia, and Mary in her journal seems to admit she herself was the Moon.[10] She may have been wrong, however, for *Epipsychidion* was probably a forbidden subject. Mary usually made fair copies of Shelley's manuscripts to send to the printers'; *Epipsychidion* was copied by Shelley himself. In her 1839 edition of his works there is no Note on the poem, which is probably one of those 'other verses' Mary confessed she would 'like to obliterate for ever'.[11]

Though there is certainly a strong vein of autobiography here, it would be silly to suppose this interpretation is the 'hard matter' Shelley refers to in the prefatory verses, which was to be understood only by the 'esoteric few'.[6] The symbols cry out for a more intellectual explanation; and the cry can be answered by one of the naïver theories of Plato, whose appearance in a poem so full of ideals need cause no surprise.

Carlos Baker [12] has shown how Plato's threefold division of the soul throws light on *Epipsychidion*. In the *Republic*, the *Timaeus* and the *Phaedrus* the soul is alleged to be divided into (1) an immortal spirit, which controls the other two parts, (2) a higher mortal or rational soul and (3) a desiring part, which guides the appetites.[13] These three components were supposed to reside in brain, heart and belly respectively. Plato's immortal soul corresponds to Shelley's epipsychidion, sun-symbol and idea of the imagination. Plato's higher mortal soul can be equated with Shelley's moon-symbol and concept of reason. Plato's appetitive soul corresponds to Shelley's Comet and idea of unruly emotion or desire.

This explanation may at first sound like a scholar's artifact. But Shelley himself hints at it twice in the *Defence of Poetry*, written just after *Epipsychidion*. In the published *Defence* he refers to 'the three forms into which Plato had distributed the faculties of mind', and the following sentence in a cancelled early draft of the *Defence* might almost be a definition of 'The cold chaste Moon, the Queen of Heaven's bright isles' : 'He would extinguish Imagination which is the Sun of life and grope his way by the cold and uncertain and borrowed light of that Moon which he calls Reason . . . the Queen of his pale Heaven'.[14] Thus the 'Platonic explanation' is not utterly far-fetched, and it helps to clarify some of the obscurities. It is difficult to accept unreservedly because Shelley often implies his symbols are persons.

To add to the confusion he sometimes treats the symbols literally, as the astronomical objects, not the things they represent. Many lines can therefore be read in three different ways. Take, for example, Shelley's description of the Comet,

> Who drew the heart of this frail Universe
> Towards thine own ; till, wrecked in that convulsion,
> Alternating attraction and repulsion,
> Thine went astray and that was rent in twain ;
> Oh, float into our azure heaven again !

419. 369-73

On the first interpretation, the biographical, this means that Clare was attracted to Shelley, and sometimes repulsed by him. Frustrated, she threw herself at Byron, with the result that Shelley's heart was now torn between the conflicting interests of Clare and Byron. Finally, Shelley asks Clare, who was away in Florence, to join his household again. On the second interpretation, the Platonic, Shelley is regretting that the wild horse of emotion has in the past led him astray, and hoping it will return permanently to its yoke and obey its charioteer, the immortal soul — to use Plato's own metaphor.[15] On the third interpretation, the astronomical, 'this frail Universe' is, as implied in line 345, the earth, and the Comet is a small planet which once approached and collided with the earth. The planet was smashed to pieces in the collision and partially re-formed as a comet (a theory not discredited in Shelley's day), while the moon was torn out of the earth, which was thus *rent in twain* — a phrase which may derive from Erasmus Darwin's account of the moon's origin : 'earth's huge sphere exploding burst in twain'.[16] The *alternating attraction and repulsion* could refer either to the initial attraction between the earth and the embryo comet, followed by the apparent repulsion when they recede from each. other, or to the fact that a comet's head moves round the sun under gravitational attraction, while its tail points away from the sun, because its minute particles are repelled by the pressure of sunlight, as Adam Walker guessed, correctly.[17]

These astronomical comparisons should not be taken too far, for they are only a side-issue ; nor should they be underestimated. From the title downwards, the poem is riddled with astronomical allusions. For example, when Shelley describes the Moon as

> That wandering shrine of soft yet icy flame
> Which ever is transformed, yet still the same,
> And warms not but illumines,

he is thinking primarily of the astronomical object, not of Mary or Reason. Again, when he refers to the Sun and Moon as *twin spheres of light* (line 345), he is not suggesting that Mary and Emilia, or Imagination and Reason, are twins. The adjective *twin* is pertinent because the mean angular diameters of the sun and moon, as seen from the earth, differ by less than three per cent, and his phraseology is more careful than might be thought. How easy it would have been, and how illegitimate scientifically, to call Emilia (Sun) and himself (Earth) *twin spheres*, for in line 45 he had exclaimed, 'Would we two had been twins of the same mother !' Shelley confirms he has the astronomical spheres in mind when he says they

> Awaken all [Earth's] fruits and flowers, and dart
> Magnetic might into its central heart ;

And lift its billows and its mists, and guide
By everlasting laws, each wind and tide
To its fit cloud, and its appointed cave.

419. 347-51

To summarize this difficult second section of the poem,
it might not be too gross an oversimplification to say that
the symbols began as autobiography, had a Platonic theory
grafted into them, and finally took on a life of their own as
astronomical objects. Occasionally these three explanations blend harmoniously; more often they clash, to the
confusion of the reader. Needless obscurity can never be
admired, and though the lengthy explanations may seem to
create an aroma of profundity, this is by far the weakest
part of the poem.

4

In the third part of the poem, beginning at line 388, Shelley
abruptly changes his drift and whisks Emilia off to a dream-
island. He is surer of himself in this pure romantic wish-
fulfilment, and there are no longer so many rhetorical
questions and exclamations. He is content to work up the
suspense with plain statement, and the only question or
exclamation between lines 388 and 573 occurs in the
introduction :

A ship is floating in the harbour now,
A wind is hovering o'er the mountain's brow;
There is a path on the sea's azure floor,
No keel has ever ploughed that path before;
The halcyons brood around the foamless isles ;
The treacherous Ocean has forsworn its wiles ;
The merry mariners are bold and free :
Say, my heart's sister, wilt thou sail with me ?
Our bark is as an albatross, whose nest
Is a far Eden of the purple East ;
And we between her wings will sit, while Night,
And Day, and Storm, and Calm, pursue their flight,
Our ministers, along the boundless Sea,
Treading each other's heels, unheededly.

420. 408-21

They will sail to a dream-island in the Aegean, a 'favoured place' with thick woods, clear rivulets and air heavy with the scent of flowers. The blue sea kisses its 'sifted sands and caverns hoar'; no storms or diseases ever mar its beauty. The pastoral people, few and innocent, breathe the last spirit of the age of gold. Shelley and Emilia will go to a solitary house on the mountain-side, with a view over the woods to the sea.

> I have sent books and music there, and all
> Those instruments with which high Spirits call
> The future from its cradle, and the past
> Out of its grave, and make the present last
> In thoughts and joys which sleep, but cannot die,
> Folded within their own eternity.
> Our simple life wants little, and true taste
> Hires not the pale drudge Luxury, to waste
> The scene it would adorn.

422. 519-27

'We two' will be 'the living soul of this Elysian isle', and 'under the roof of blue Ionian weather' will wander over its meadows, up its mountains and along its pebbly shores. 'We shall be one spirit within two frames',

> the wells
> Which boil under our being's inmost cells,
> The fountains of our deepest life, shall be
> Confused in Passion's golden purity,
> As mountain-springs under the morning sun.

423. 568-72

After a few lines more the poem ends, rather suddenly.

This section needs no analysis. It is intelligible on whatever level we choose to read it, whether, like Carlos Baker, we treat the physical details as metaphors to express communion of souls, or, like Edward Bostetter, we take them literally[12].

5

Because of *Epipsychidion* Shelley is notorious for idealizing the women he admired. He certainly had a tendency to idealize, but the facts scarcely support the common assumption that the pattern of all his friendships with women was fervent idealization quickly followed by disillusion, as with Emilia. It was three years before Harriet disappointed all his hopes; his love of Mary may have been fading rather than growing in his last year, yet love it remained; he liked Sophia Stacey well enough to write poems for her, without ever seeing her as a goddess incarnate; Jane Williams, who inspired the finest lyrics of the last year, he disliked at first. On the few occasions when Shelley did fancy he saw his ideal in mortal shape he knew he would be disillusioned. *Alastor* was a sermon against idealizing, and in letters he wrote: 'I think one is always in love with something or other; the error — and I confess it is not easy for spirits cased in flesh and blood to avoid it — consists in seeking in a mortal image the likeness of what is perhaps eternal. . . .⁵ Some of us have in a prior existence been in love with an Antigone, and that makes us find no full content in any mortal tie.' ¹⁸ The *modus operandi* of the idealization he laid bare, too, in the *Discourse on the Manners of the Ancients*, in a passage which serves almost as a definition of Jung's *anima*:

This object [the inspirer of sentimental love] or its archetype for ever exists in the mind, which selects among those who resemble it that which most resembles it; and instinctively fills up the interstices of the imperfect image, in the same manner as the imagination moulds and completes the shapes in clouds, or in the fire, into the resemblances of whatever form, animal, building, etc., happens to be present to it.¹⁹

Emilia was a lay-figure similar enough to the archetype to spur Shelley to fill in the gaps. He knew it was an illusion but he was glad to find himself taken in by it, just as a cynic may be glad to recover his childish sense of wonder. If he could work up enthusiasm for his ideal he never hesitated to write about it, and on this occasion the result was memorable.

For in the first part of *Epipsychidion* Shelley gives new life to the old theme of the poet extravagantly praising his beloved. This theme, deriving from the troubadours,

T

widened by Dante in the *Vita nuova* and *Paradiso* and by
Petrarch in his sonnets, was brought into English by Wyatt
and Surrey, and exploited thoroughly by their successors.
Lyrics and sonnets in praise of Julia, Celia, Stella, etc. ;
Spenser's *Epithalamion* ; Crashaw's religious-erotic poems
to Saint Teresa ; all these suggest themselves as possible
ancestors of *Epipsychidion*. But the sustained aspiration of
Shelley's stream of metaphors bears little resemblance to the
ups and downs of a sonnet sequence, to Spenser's catalogue
of his bride's charms or to Crashaw's ambiguous images.
Only in the mysteries of the second part of *Epipsychidion*,
where he was copying one of the weaker features of Shakespeare's sonnets, does Shelley owe much to an English model.
He is indebted more to Plato, Dante and Boccaccio. To
Plato he turned for the ideal love defined in the *Symposium*
and the trinity of the soul described in the *Republic*. Dante,
besides contributing so powerfully to the love-poem tradition,
showed how to use the Ptolemaic astronomy, in the *Convito*,
and provided a specific model for Shelley, in the *Vita Nuova*.
The link with Boccaccio comes through his poem *Teseida*,
which *Epipsychidion* often resembles in detail, with numerous
verbal echoes.[20] In spirit, however, Shelley's poem is closer
to the *Vita Nuova*, since both are idealized histories of the
poet's own life and feelings. Both also show how society's
constraints on love inspire love-poems by forcing poets to
sublimate their yearnings. If Italian customs had been
freer Shelley would have known Emilia better, and would
have been disillusioned before writing his poem.

The third part of *Epipsychidion* is the most original, for
Shelley integrates various traditions and goes beyond all of
them, making a permanent addition to the stock of romantic
fictions. The theme of young lovers in a paradisal isle is
now so hackneyed, after a century of being overwritten and
nearly half a century of being overfilmed, that Shelley's feat
is apt to be overlooked. Islands have been found convenient for isolating a group of characters in fiction from
the *Odyssey* onwards. Isles of love and bowers of bliss, with
luscious vegetation sheltering luscious nymphs, have been

common from Camões and Tasso onwards. The 'golden age', so dear to the eighteenth century, is responsible for the pastoral natives amid smiling scenery, like the figures in a Claude landscape; and the Romantic Nature-cult is there to back it up. Shelley unites these various traditions, and utilizes the trend towards equality and intellectual communion between men and women, which accounts for the 'books and music'. At the same time, taking a hint perhaps from Erasmus Darwin,[21] he exploits all the physical trappings of the isle which can be invested with an erotic tinge — the wind, the sea, the isle's natural beauty, its fountains, lakes and rivulets, the sun dispersing the dew. 'The blue heavens bend with lightest winds, to touch their paramour', the mountains. The 'pebble-paven shore' trembles and sparkles 'under the quick, faint kisses of the sea'. The sun clears the sea-mists, and exposes one by one the isle's charms, till with the removal of the last veil the isle's beauty 'like a naked bride . . . blushes and trembles at its own excess'. The island was for Shelley a persistent escape-image. In a letter to Mary later that year he wrote :

My greatest content would be utterly to desert all human society. I would retire with you and our child to a solitary island in the sea, would build a boat, and shut upon my retreat the floodgates of the world.[22]

Thus he may not have been conscious of drawing together these traditions and natural aids. Certainly his blending is the more effective because it seems as fresh and unselfconscious as the isle itself.

The fluent verse, too, helps in persuading us to accept the fiction. So smooth is the flow that it is something of a shock when we first notice he is using iambic pentameters arranged in rhyming couplets, the metre which served Pope so well. This verse-form is too inflexible to allow Shelley full scope, and *Epipsychidion*, despite its many felicities, is not, technically, one of his best efforts. In technique it is most like *Julian and Maddalo*, having the same metre, and often the same urbane tone; a similar structural rift and at one point similar phrases; similar mysteries and doubts whether real life underlies them.

Emilia broke winter's numbing grip on Shelley. Usually he wrote nothing but a few lyrics between the end of October and the beginning of March. The two exceptions to this rather surprising rule are Act IV of *Prometheus Unbound*, written in November and December 1819 while Shelley was living at Florence, and *Epipsychidion*, written in January and February 1821, when, incidentally, the weather was exceptionally clement.[23]

The drama of Shelley and Emilia, despite its high passion, had a farcical finale. Emilia's father found two suitors for her, and the one whom she rejected, Danielli, was frantic in his despair. Emilia asked Shelley to try to calm him. So, with the ink hardly dry on one of the most fervent of love-songs, Shelley obeyed his charmer's request to smooth the path for her own *mariage de convenance* — and laughed at himself for doing so: 'It seems that I am worthy of taking my degree of M.A. in the art of Love, for I have contrived to calm the despairing swain, much to the satisfaction of poor Emilia. . . .'[24]

NOTES TO XII: *EPIPSYCHIDION*

1. Byron, letter to Hobhouse, 3 Oct. 1819. See I. Origo, *The Last Attachment*, pp. 132–4, for an example of Italian marriage rules.

2. Quoted in White, ii. 251.

3. Shelley's letter to Byron of 14 Sept. 1821 may seem to contradict this: 'Pray do not mention anything of what I told you; as the whole truth is not known and Mary might be very much annoyed at it'. But he means Mary would be annoyed if it were publicized.

4. Quoted in White, ii. 324–5.

5. *Letters* ii. 434.

6. *Letters* ii. 262.

7. Dante, *Convito* (or *Convivio* as it is now known), second Treatise, Chs. III–IV.

8. T. S. Eliot, *The Use of Poetry and the Use of Criticism*, p. 92.

9. Dante, *Purgatorio*, XV. 46–75.

10. Mary's *Journal*, 5 Oct. 1822. For the 'biographical explanation', see White, ii. 261–7.

11. Mary's *Journal*, 12 Feb. 1839.

12. C. Baker, *Shelley's Major Poetry*, pp. 233–8; E. Bostetter, in *Shelley, Modern Judgements*, p. 241.

13. Plato, *Republic*, 437–42.
14. Quotations from *Defence of Poetry* (ed. Brett-Smith), pp. 42 and 109.
15. Plato, *Phaedrus*, 253–4.
16. E. Darwin, *The Economy of Vegetation*, ii. 76.
17. A. Walker, *Familiar Philosophy*, p. 395. ·We now know that a comet's tail is also strongly influenced by the streams of charged particles issuing from the sun, the solar wind as it is called.
18. *Letters* ii. 364.
19. *Jul* vii. 228.
20. See H. Huscher, *Keats–Shelley Memorial Bulletin*, XIV, p. 30.
21. E. Darwin, *Loves of the Plants*, iv. 221–44.
22. *Letters* ii. 339.
23. See Mary's *Journal*, 8 Mar. 1821. The fragmentary *Prince Athanase* (? Dec. 1817) may be another exception to the rule. The date of *Queen Mab* is uncertain.
24. *Letters* ii. 292.

XIII

DEFENDING POETRY

οὐκ ἀνθρώπινά ἐστι τὰ καλὰ ταῦτα ποιήματα οὐδὲ ἀνθρώπων,
ἀλλὰ θεῖα καὶ θεῶν.

These transcendent poems are not human as the work
of men, but divine as coming from God.

PLATO, *Ion*

1

As soon as he had finished *Epipsychidion* Shelley set about
replying to Peacock's half-serious attack on poetry, *The
Four Ages of Poetry*, which had appeared in Ollier's *Literary
Miscellany* of 1820. In this witty essay Peacock argues that
poetry goes through four phases, or ages, and that once
these are past it is obsolete. In the first of the four ages,
the iron age, he says, 'rude bards celebrate in rough numbers
the exploits of ruder chiefs'. The bards can lisp in numbers
without much trouble since the language is only half-
formed, and they act as amateur historians, theologians,
moralists and legislators. In the second age, the golden,
poetry attains perfection. It is undisturbed by its nascent
rivals — history, science and philosophy — and is cultivated by the greatest intellects of the day. In the third or
silver age, having to contend with these rivals and a rigid
language, poetry emerges polished, fastidious and superficial.
The fourth age, of brass, rejects the polish of the silver age
and goes back to the barbaric age of iron, while professing
to recover the age of gold. Poetry has then become a
triviality, unworthy to stand beside the useful arts and
sciences. Homer represents the golden age of classical
poetry, and Virgil the silver ; the brass age is that of Rome's
decline. Coming to English poetry, Peacock apparently
consigns Chaucer to the iron age ; Shakespeare represents

the golden age; Dryden and Pope the silver; the age of
brass began with Wordsworth's village legends picked up
'from old women and sextons'. Peacock concludes: 'a
poet is a semi-barbarian in a civilized community . . .
poetry was the mental rattle that awakened the attention of
intellect in the infancy of civil society' (16, 18).[1]

Shelley's reply, *A Defence of Poetry*, was to have been in
three parts. The first part, the only one written, discusses
general principles. The second and third parts would have
invoked these principles to defend contemporary poetry
against its critics. Shelley sent the *Defence* to Ollier in
March, a month after *Epipsychidion*, for inclusion in the
next issue of the *Literary Miscellany*. But there was no next
issue; so the *Defence* was earmarked for the Byron-Hunt
magazine *The Liberal*. In the original version Shelley made
seven references to Peacock's essay, and these were deleted
by John Hunt in 1823 when he was preparing the *Defence*
for printing. But *The Liberal* also became defunct before the
Defence could appear in it. When Mary Shelley finally
published the essay in 1840, she retained Hunt's cut version.
On balance his cuts are welcome. They hide the essay's
controversial origin without seriously weakening its bite.
Occasionally, however, Shelley's choice of topics seems a
trifle odd, and this is because he defends most tenaciously
where Peacock's attack is keenest, and not always at the
weakest points. Peacock's plausible half-truths had a pro-
voking air of finality, and Shelley rose to the bait. The
Defence is as dogmatic in tone as Peacock's attack, though in
his letters to Peacock Shelley treated the matter jokingly.

Shelley's views on poetry derive from Plato, or rather
one of Plato's two divergent theories. In the *Republic* poets
and painters are disparaged because they imitate life and so
are one step further from the divine ideal which life itself
imitates. But in the dialogues on poetic inspiration, particularly the *Ion*, which Shelley was reading when Peacock's
essay reached him and translated during 1821, and the
Phaedrus, which he read in 1820, Plato suggests poets are
possessed by a divine madness and in their moments of

inspiration are the gods' interpreters. Shelley takes over this latter argument. He contends that poets alone pierce the barrier of reality to display the underlying eternal archetypes ; that 'a poem is the very image of life expressed in its eternal truth'.

One other model ought to be mentioned, Sir Philip Sidney's *Apology for Poetry* (or *Defence of Poesy*), which Shelley read just before writing his own essay. Sidney's most important argument, which Shelley accepts, is that poetry can be the best moral teacher. Appealing via the emotions and short-circuiting the logical chain, it insinuates truths which moral philosophers may preach to empty air till doomsday.

2

Shelley begins the *Defence of Poetry* by saying what he means by 'poetry' and how he thinks it makes its appeal. He first distinguishes between reason, which analyses and enumerates things known, and imagination, through which mind acts on known things to effect a new synthesis. Poetry may be defined, he says, as 'the expression of the imagination'. This generalized definition is apt, because he deals with poetry 'in the most universal sense', often including all the arts within his ambit. The poet, he says, uses vitally metaphorical language, which 'marks the before unapprehended relations of things and perpetuates their apprehension'. The poet penetrates the façade of custom to participate in the eternal, the infinite and the one, and by revealing this underlying indestructible order he acts indirectly as legislator and prophet : he has never resigned the functions Peacock granted him only in the iron age. Though poets often use 'measured language' to create harmonious sound-recurrences, verse-forms undergo continual innovation. Shelley agrees with Sidney that while verse is the 'fittest raiment' for poetry it is not essential, as the poetical prose of Plato shows. Shelley, like Wordsworth, emphasizes that poetry and pleasure always go together :

A poet is a nightingale, who sits in darkness and sings to cheer
its own solitude with sweet sounds; his auditors are as men
entranced by the melody of an unseen musician, who feel that
they are moved and softened, yet know not whence or why.

(31)

— an encomium fit to set beside Sidney's 'tale which
holdeth children from play and old men from the chimney
corner'.[2] As well as giving immediate pleasure, poetry does
good unobtrusively, not by dinning moral precepts in men's
ears, but by investing familiar objects with a divine aura
and by enlarging the mind:

The great instrument of moral good is the imagination . . .
poetry enlarges the circumference of the imagination . . . poetry
strengthens the faculty which is the organ of the moral nature
of man, in the same manner as exercise strengthens a limb.

(33)

This is an important claim, which can go far to justify the
arts against puritan objections, and also shows why Shelley
thought moral teaching could not be effected by the poet
obtruding his own views of right and wrong.

Shelley next embarks on a selective history of European
poetry and drama from Homer to the seventeenth century,
and this takes up over a third of the essay. He begins with
drama. The Athenian drama, he says, united language,
action, music, painting, dancing and religion, in a way
never since rivalled: it was perfect of its kind, because each
of its constituent arts had reached perfection. But the
blending of comedy with tragedy added a new dimension to
drama, and *King Lear* is to be rated above the *Agamemnon*
and *Oedipus Tyrannus*. (Of the Shakespearean tragedies,
Shelley liked best those with primitive settings: *Macbeth*
was another of his favourites; *Hamlet* had too many courtly
conceits for his liking.) Next, Shelley contends that when
social life decays, so does drama, and the poetry in it becomes
mere imitation. In such periods — Shelley singles out the
Restoration — wit displaces humour; malice displaces
sympathy; and there is a recrudescence of obscenity,
'which is ever blasphemy against the divine beauty in life'.

Turning from drama to poetry, Shelley finds little to praise in the Roman poets and artists, who, apart from Lucretius and Virgil, imitated Greek models instead of facing the problems of their own time. 'The true poetry of Rome lived in its institutions.' Christianity was not to blame for poetry's decline in the first thousand years of the Christian era, he says. On the contrary, the poetry of Christ's doctrine held within it the germ of the poetry and wisdom of antiquity, and, surviving the dark ages, eventually flowered in the partial emancipation of slaves and women, which in turn gave poetry a fresh impetus by inspiring the romances of chivalry and the poems of sexual love. Dante's poetry he sees as the bridge thrown over the stream of time, uniting the modern and ancient world.

Dante was the first awakener of entranced Europe; he created a language, in itself music and persuasion, out of a chaos of inharmonious barbarisms.

(48)

Shelley admired most the *Paradiso*, 'a perpetual hymn of everlasting love'. Dante wore Homer's mantle; he was the second great epic poet. Milton was the third, and the fact that all three used outmoded cosmologies need not deter us :

A great poem is a fountain for ever overflowing with the waters of wisdom and delight; and after one person and one age has exhausted all its divine effluence which their peculiar relations enable them to share, another and yet another succeeds, and new relations are ever developed, the source of an unforeseen and an unconceived delight.

(48-9)

Shelley abandons his critical history at this point, before really beginning on English poetry, and proceeds to refute Peacock's argument that poets should yield the crown to reasoners. The exertions of inventors, he says, are most valuable in their own sphere, in reducing the wants of our animal natures. Inventors and political economists should, however, beware that their ideas 'do not tend, as they have in modern England, to exasperate at once the extremes of luxury and want'. We have more scientific knowledge than we can deal with. Our need is 'the poetry of life', which alone can co-ordinate the ever-growing strands of knowledge. 'Man, having enslaved the elements, remains himself a slave' — a paradox which has grown sharper with the years.

The final and most famous part of the essay is a vigorous panegyric. Shelley begins by claiming that poetry comprehends all science, and that all science must be referred to it. He means, presumably, that imaginative effort is needed before applying reason, even in science; or as Wordsworth put it, 'poetry . . . is the impassioned expression which is in the countenance of all science'.[3] Poetry, asserts Shelley, brings 'light and fire from those eternal regions where the owl-winged faculty of calculation dare not ever soar'. The light and fire pass from the eternal regions to the poet in his moments of inspiration, which Shelley describes from his own experience. These moments are 'as it were the inter-penetration of a diviner nature through our own; but its footsteps are like those of a wind over the sea, which the coming calm erases, and whose traces remain only, as on the wrinkled sand which paves it' (54-5). No poet, he tells us, can say 'I will compose poetry'.

For the mind in creation is as a fading coal, which some invisible influence, like an inconstant wind, awakens to transitory brightness; this power arises from within, like the colour of a flower which fades and changes as it is developed, and the conscious portions of our nature are unprophetic either of its approach or its departure.

(53)

Shelley interprets the toil and delay recommended by critics as 'no more than a careful observation of inspired moments', a secondary process linking the inspirations. He then apologizes for vagaries of behaviour in some poets of his own day: because poets are unusually sensitive to pain and pleasure, he says, they may avoid the one and pursue the other with abnormal ardour. These vagaries are too much noticed and should not obscure the fact that 'in spite of the low-thoughted envy which would

undervalue contemporary merit . . . our own will be a
memorable age in intellectual achievements'. The *Defence*
ends with passionate rhetoric. Some sentences from the last
paragraph, and an earlier one, epitomize the argument and
the style :

Poetry . . . makes immortal all that is best and most beautiful
in the world . . . arrests the vanishing apparitions which haunt
the interlunations of life . . . redeems from decay the visitations
of the divinity in man. . . .

(55)

Poets are the hierophants of an unapprehended inspiration ; the
mirrors of the gigantic shadows which futurity casts upon the
present ; the words which express what they understand not ;
the trumpets which sing to battle and feel not what they inspire ;
the influence which is moved not, but moves. Poets are the
unacknowledged legislators of the world.

(59)

3

After a first reading of the *Defence of Poetry*, when the details
have faded from memory, the impression which remains is
that Shelley has struck to the root and avoided entangle-
ment in side-issues. If the background of ideas which he
outlines is accepted, poetry and indeed all the arts seem to
fit naturally into the scheme of things. His inspirational
view of poetry derives from Plato, but it could hardly have
been in better accord with the poetic climate of his own
day. For Wordsworth, Coleridge, Keats and Shelley, poetry
was in a sense a religion : they were as mystics waiting for the
godhead to speak. When this afflatus failed Coleridge wrote
no more poetry and Wordsworth wrote no more good
poetry. Shelley and Keats did not live to see the day when
they would have to ask, in earnest, 'whither is fled the
visionary gleam ? ' The inspirational theory is also consistent
with Shelley's outlook on life. He was apt to look on the
world as a vale of tears lit by rare flashes of divine fire,
which are preserved, if at all, in inspired poetry. And in
the *Defence* he even assents to Tasso's claim : *Non merita*

nome di creatore, se non Iddio ed il Poeta (Only God and the poet deserve the name of creator).[4]

'Inspiration' is a red rag to those who like everything explained. In deference to the cautious modern taste we have to call a poet a craftsman, not a deity's go-between. Most poets who have written on the subject seem to agree with Shelley, however,[5] and, now that Freudian jargon provides an escape-route, even the harder-boiled critics usually admit that poetry wells up from the unconscious, to be observed, criticized and edited by the conscious mind. Shelley's stress on inspiration does not mean he fancied he could do without reason. He was so used to thinking 'long and deep' that he took it as axiomatic. As he once said to Medwin, 'the source of poetry is native and involuntary, but requires severe labour in its development'.[6] In the *Defence* he chose to emphasize the source rather than the development. This reluctance to descend from the heights and discuss the detailed technique of poetry was one of his vestigial aristocratic traits. The 'severe labour' of knocking the inspiration into acceptable poetic form seemed to him a backstairs job. Arguing about it in public would be as much a breach of etiquette as discussing how to peel potatoes at a State banquet. Neither in his letters nor in the *Defence* does he quote a single line of poetry for critical purposes. There would probably have been more discussion of detail in the unwritten second and third parts of his essay; but generality is the keynote in the part he did write.

In the *Defence* Shelley never mentions the poetic theories of Wordsworth and Coleridge. Though this omission is partly explained by the generality of his essay, it still seems surprising, for Wordsworth's prefaces had been hotly debated in the previous twenty years and Coleridge's *Biographia Literaria* had been out for only four years. Shelley knew both well, and twice in the *Defence* he almost paraphrased Wordsworth. But he stood far enough away from the shift in taste marked by the *Lyrical Ballads* to be able to accept their fruitful innovations and ignore their aberrations. He thus escaped the unsettling effects of a rebellion in style, and avoided expending his energy on crude pioneer work in a new idiom. He was born at a lucky time : new techniques were available but had not been fully exploited.

Shelley's critical history of poetry is generally in accord with modern views, and when some casual judgement seems a little off the mark, the point is usually debatable. When, for example, he rates the *Paradiso* above the *Inferno*, we can find him so unlikely a brace of supporters as Carlyle and T. S. Eliot.[7] Shelley enlivens his critical history with many sweeping generalizations, as stimulating and arguable as Toynbee's. One of Shelley's favourite ideas, that poetry flourishes most at times of political and social awakening, does, for all its flaws and exceptions, link seemingly remote areas of experience and help us to see life whole. This idea also encouraged him in his hopes of reform, for he recognized that he was living in a great age of poetry. It would have been instructive to see how he rated his contemporaries, in the second and third parts of the *Defence*. What is known of his views suggests that his literary judgement might have passed even this test. He admired Scott's and Peacock's novels. Wordsworth and Byron were for him great poets, though both had written badly at times. He disapproved of the popular favourites Campbell, Rogers and Barry Cornwall, and of the too-luscious poetry of Hunt and the early Keats, but he praised Hunt's prose and Keats's later work.[8]

Shelley's own practice was usually, but not always, consistent with the theories of poetry in the *Defence*. He had violated the theories by obtruding his own views of right and wrong in *Queen Mab* and *The Revolt of Islam*. Nor was he always convinced of poetry's supremacy. Two years before, he wrote : 'I consider poetry very subordinate to moral and political science, and if I were well, certainly I should aspire to the latter ; for I can conceive a great work, embodying the discoveries of all ages, and harmonizing the contending creeds by which mankind have been ruled'.[9] This sick-room fantasy expressed his secret doubts whether poetry could flourish until the world mended its wicked ways, and whether poetry's unacknowledged legislation could really speed the mending.

It is hardly necessary to-day to do more than mention that Shelley saw the evils of the Industrial Revolution and the perils attending the march of science. That science has outrun our ability to use it logically, that 'man having enslaved the elements remains himself a slave', is now a truism so tedious that the very sight of it is apt to provoke a yawn and a helpless shrug. What is obvious now was not so plain then, but Shelley, despite his eagerness to advance applied science, recognized the dangers.

The *Defence of Poetry* is Shelley's best prose work, and its place as a classic statement on the subject is probably secure. It has had few detractors and many admirers. One of the keenest of the admirers is G. Wilson Knight, who was prepared to 'hazard the thought that this short essay is the most important original prose document in our language'.[10] If that is too much to swallow we may turn to W. B. Yeats, who called it 'the profoundest essay on the foundation of poetry in English',[11] and Sir Herbert Read, who echoed him with 'the profoundest treatment of the subject in the English language'.[12]

NOTES TO XIII: DEFENDING POETRY

1. Numbers in brackets after quotations from the *Defence of Poetry* and the *Four Ages* refer to the page numbers in *Peacock's Four Ages of Poetry, Shelley's Defence of Poetry, etc.*, ed. H. F. B. Brett-Smith, 2nd edition, Oxford, 1923.

2. Sidney, *Apology*, ed. H. A. Neecham (Ginn, London, n.d.), p. 25.

3. Wordsworth, Preface to *Lyrical Ballads*.

4. Neither the wording nor the authorship of this remark is certain.

5. See, *e.g.*, Keats, *Letters*, p. 108; A. E. Housman, *The Name and Nature of Poetry* (1933) R. Graves, *The Crowning Privilege* (Cassell, 1955), p. 82. See also J. Press, *The Fire and the Fountain* (1955), Ch. 1.

6. T. Medwin, *Revised Life of Shelley*, p. 347.

7. Carlyle, *On Heroes and Hero-worship*, and T. S. Eliot, *Essay on Dante* in *Selected Essays, 1917–1932* (Faber, 1932).

8. For Shelley's opinions, see Medwin, *Revised Life of Shelley, passim*, and White, ii. 233–4.

9. *Letters* ii. 71.

10. G. Wilson Knight, *Christ and Nietzsche*, p. 27.

11. W. B. Yeats, *Ideas of Good and Evil*, p. 93.

12. H. Read, *True Voice of Feeling*, pp. 226–7. For further discussion of the *Defence*, see A. C. Bradley, *Shelley's View of Poetry*.

XIV

ADONAIS

Where youth grows pale, and spectre-thin, and dies.

KEATS, *Ode to a Nightingale*

1

JOHN KEATS died at Rome, aged 25, on 23 February 1821. When his fatal tuberculosis finally declared itself in the previous June the Gisbornes were in London, and they sent the news to Shelley, who promptly wrote to Keats inviting him to Pisa: 'This consumption is a disease particularly fond of people who write such good verses as you have done, and with the assistance of an English winter it can often indulge its selection. . . .' [1] Keats's reply was appreciative but non-committal. A month later, in September 1820, he left England with Joseph Severn, reaching Naples in October and Rome a few weeks after. There, in what is now the Keats-Shelley Memorial House in the Piazza di Spagna, Keats passed his last harrowing months, nursed devotedly by Severn. Shelley meanwhile, hearing Keats had arrived in Italy, apparently wrote to him again in February. The first news of his death reached Shelley in mid-April; but he did not know full details until mid-June, and by then he had finished his elegy *Adonais*, 'the image of my regret and honour for poor Keats'.[2] Few poets have had lives so unfortunate as Keats's. None has finer memorial verses than these fifty-five Spenserian stanzas.

From our vantage point in time we can see how much Keats and Shelley had in common: why then weren't they more friendly? Ever since their first meeting at Leigh Hunt's cottage in 1817, Shelley, who was three years older, had tried to befriend this 'rival who will far surpass me'.[3]

But Keats did not respond. There are several possible reasons. He may have been upset at the very start, for Shelley began badly by advising him not to publish, and this rankled with Keats, though Shelley later helped him find a publisher.[4] He may have reacted subconsciously against Shelley's aristocratic origin, as Haydon and Hunt suggested. He may have resented Shelley displacing him as the object of Hunt's admiration. And he certainly feared Shelley would try to act as director of studies: 'I refused to visit Shelley, that I might have my own unfettered scope',[5] he wrote in 1817.

In their attitudes to poetry they seem at first sight to be in agreement. Both set great store by imagination, which they saw as a beauty-seeking faculty. 'What the imagination seizes as Beauty must be truth',[6] Keats asserted; and, as the *Defence of Poetry* shows, Shelley would have agreed. Both joined the quest which occupied and restricted all the Romantic poets, the quest for beauty, especially in Nature. The voice of Nature, be it the sounding cataract, the murmuring of flies on summer eves or the deep autumnal tone of the west wind, haunted them like a passion. These shared interests created a bond which, stiffened by their shared unpopularity as poets, proved solid enough to start Shelley on *Adonais*.

Yet the gulf which separated them in life is also apparent in their attitudes to poetry. Shelley always has an eye for reform, and most of his long poems are vehicles for ideas; while Keats accepts life as it is, and is content with plain tales, free of politics, philosophy and religion. The division is sharpest in their first long poems, *Queen Mab* and *Endymion*. Keats loved poetry consistently, for its own sake. Shelley was more fickle: in the *Defence* as passionate as Keats; at other times wavering, as in the letter quoted three pages ago — 'I consider poetry very subordinate to moral and political science . . .' Keats's letters bristle with quotations from the English poets, especially himself; Shelley, in his letters after 1814, only once writes out a poem of his own, and quotes only seven other lines of English poetry. Keats

U

in his poems gives the impression of savouring every word, while Shelley often seems in a hurry. This difference extends to their imagery. Keats favours static, smooth, rounded, heavy images ; Shelley's are swift, jagged, piercing and light. Heat and cold are for Shelley warring extremes, for Keats complementary.[7] While Shelley revels in wild winds, storm clouds and rough seas, Keats basks in warm sunshine with no stir of air to dimple the sea. In savouring Nature, Keats is more sensuous, simpler and more passive than Shelley, who usually analyses, generalizes and makes patterns out of the chaotic hail of sense-impressions. Shelley would never have said, 'O for a life of sensations rather than of thoughts'. In view of these differences in taste, Keats was wise to fight shy of Shelley, if living under his roof also meant living under his tutelage.

After touching on relations between Keats and Shelley, it is natural to mention Byron, too, for these three are the most compact trio among the major poets of the world. Their habits and social circles differed, but their life-lines through space-time clung together. All three were born within a space of forty miles and a span of seven years. All were in England early in 1816 and in Italy five years later. All died within twenty miles of Mediterranean shores between 1821 and 1824. Shelley was the only one of the three to appraise fairly the work of the other two. He saw the faults of *Endymion*, admired the 1820 volume,[8] though for *Hyperion* rather than the Odes, and called Keats a 'great genius'.[9] He was Byron's best contemporary critic. Had he 'ever written a formal *critique* of Byron's poetry, it would have left very little for succeeding generations to add'.[10] Curiously enough, each of the three seems to have pitied the other two, often a little condescendingly. Shelley wrote : 'Lord Byron had almost destroyed himself at Venice. . . . Poor fellow — he is now quite well', and 'I send you the elegy on poor Keats'. The compliment was returned, by Keats — 'Poor Shelley, I think he has his Quota of good qualities' — and by Byron — 'as to poor Shelley . . . he is . . . the least selfish and mildest of men'. Between Byron and Keats the condenscension was near contempt. Keats was reported as saying, 'How horrible an example of human nature is this man who has no pleasure left him but to gloat over and jeer at the most awful incidents of life'. And Byron was no less scathing about Keats : 'the *outstretched* poesy of this miserable Self-polluter of the human mind'.[11]

2

Byron and Shelley both thought the death of Keats was hastened by hostile criticism of his poetry ; and Shelley stated his own attitude to reviewers in the *Lines to a Reviewer* —

> Alas, good friend, what profit can you see
> In hating such a hateless thing as me ?
>
> 625. 1-2

So we need not be surprised at the growth of the legend that Shelley and Keats were persecuted by reviewers. Once established the legend thrived, because it fitted the sentimental picture evoked by their early deaths and the sensitivity they showed in their Nature-poems. Did the critics really deserve such blame ?

The first quarter of the nineteenth century was a great age for poetry-reviewing. A high standard was set by the *Edinburgh Review*, founded in 1802 by Sydney Smith, Jeffrey and Horner with Jeffrey as editor and Brougham as chief contributor.[12] To counter the *Edinburgh*'s Whig bias, the Tory *Quarterly Review* was started in 1809 at Scott's instigation. The editor, Gifford, ruthlessly altered articles he disagreed with. Scott and Southey were his worthiest contributors ; the others, such as Croker, usually toed the party line and damned everything from the opposite camp, which, unluckily for the *Quarterly*'s long-term reputation, the best poets belonged to. A third notable periodical, *Blackwood's Edinburgh Magazine*, unlike the two *Reviews*, was not wholly devoted to criticism and was issued monthly. From 1817 its editor was John Wilson ('Christopher North'), and J. G. Lockhart was a leading contributor. The *London Magazine*, founded in 1820, was a brilliant rival of

Blackwood's in its one year under the editorship of John Scott. There was also the weekly *Examiner*, edited by the Hunts, which from 1808 onwards provided an outlet for radical opinion.

The Reviews treated Keats and Shelley in oddly varied ways. The *Edinburgh* ignored Shelley entirely, and did not review Keats until August 1820, when he was already in his last illness. Then Jeffrey, in a generous review of *Endymion* and the 1820 volume, said he was 'exceedingly struck with the genius they display'.[13] The *Quarterly* ran true to form and attacked both Shelley and Keats, rather heavy-handedly. Shelley very much resented its review of *The Revolt of Islam*. But, apart from some vague slanders, this review was merely a defence-reflex from the custodian of convention :

. . . he has loosened the hold of our protecting laws, and sapped the principles of our venerable policy; he has invaded the purity and chilled the unsuspecting ardour of our fireside intimacies; he has slandered, ridiculed and blasphemed our holy religion. . . .[14]

The *Quarterly*'s reviewer of *Endymion*, Croker, though contemptuous of the poem, made no offensive remarks beyond calling Keats the 'simple neophyte' of Hunt. The most violent reviews came from *Blackwood's*, which in 1817 began a series of articles, probably by Lockhart, on 'The Cockney School of Poetry', defined as the followers of Hunt, 'a vulgar man perpetually labouring to be genteel'. The fourth article, on Keats, referred to the 'settled, imperturbable drivelling idiocy of *Endymion*', and gave Keats this advice : 'It is a better and a wiser thing to be a starved apothecary than a starved poet : so back to the shop, Mr. John, back to plaster, pills and ointment-boxes'.[15] Shelley, though a friend of Hunt, was not included in the 'Cockney' articles, perhaps because he was heir to a baronetcy. In January 1819 Lockhart reviewed *The Revolt of Islam*, and said Shelley 'had proved himself a great poet'.[16] And, in reviewing *Prometheus Unbound*, *Blackwood's* declared that Shelley 'was destined to leave a great name behind him', though the poem was called a 'pestiferous mixture of blasphemy, sedition and sensuality'.[17]   The other Reviews were, like the 'Big Three', divided over Shelley and Keats. Hunt in the *Examiner* consistently praised Shelley;[18]   the *Literary Gazette* thought the author's reward for *Prometheus Unbound* should be 'a cell, clean straw, bread and water, a strait waistcoat, and phlebotomy'; while the *Edinburgh Monthly Review* believed *The Cenci* showed 'he might easily and triumphantly overtop all that has been written during the last century for the English stage'.[19]   On the whole the extremists tend to cancel out, and it can hardly be said that the reviewers persecuted Shelley and Keats.[20]

Their tone may seem unduly pungent: but it was the fashion for these essay-reviews to be enlivened by spite, and readers expected it.   Southey, one of the few who avoided such fireworks, felt his uniqueness so keenly that he chose as his epitaph 'In an age of personalities he abstained from satire'.[21]   Southey would never have written anything half so uncivil as *Blackwood's* attack on Hunt:

The very concubine of so impure a wretch as Leigh Hunt would be to be pitied, but alas! for the wife of such a husband!   For him there is no charm in simple seduction; and he gloats over it only when accompanied with adultery and incest. . . .[22]

The Reviews did not have things all their own way, however.   Hazlitt told Gifford, editor of the *Quarterly*:

[You] sacrifice what little honesty and prostitute what little intellect you possess to any dirty job you are commissioned to execute.[23]

Shelley and Keats suffered sharper reviews because the literary atmosphere had previously been poisoned by too much of this figurative foul language.

In these circumstances Shelley and Keats were both a little naïve in expecting general acclaim.   Later their reward would have come, and they could have joined the ranks of the Great Victorians.   Keats was born in the same year as Carlyle, and Shelley, who was a fortnight older than Lord John Russell, would, if he had enjoyed his father's longevity, have outlived Dickens, Disraeli, Darwin, Kingsley,

Mill, the Brontes, Thackeray, Rossetti, Carlyle, Trollope and
George Eliot; he could have read Shaw's early novels, and
more than half Hardy's. By 1883 he might have become a
figure even more venerable than Tennyson. But expecting
veneration or public acclaim in 1820 was as unrealistic as
hoping to convert the bishops or the Irish. The reading
public, like the Sussex folk round Horsham, 'wouldn't be
druv', and were content to let his poems mildew on the
booksellers' shelves. Shelley craved for recognition, and
its absence quite disheartened him at times: 'I wonder why
I write verses, for nobody reads them. It is a kind of disorder,
for which the regular practitioners prescribe what is called a
torrent of abuse; but I fear that can hardly be considered a
specific.'[24] Certainly he would have had to wait a long time
for wholehearted praise, unless he had changed his opinions
or masked them. As it is, he stings critics to anger because
he always spoke his mind. In his own day the most searching attack came from Hazlitt, who lost many friends by
publicizing their weaknesses:

The author of *Prometheus Unbound* . . . has a fire in his eye, a
fever in his blood, a maggot in his brain, a hectic flutter in his
speech, which mark out the philosophic fanatic. . . . He is
clogged by no dull system of realities, no earth-bound feelings,
no rooted prejudices, by nothing that belongs to the mighty
trunk and hard husk of nature and habit, but is drawn up by
irresistible levity to the regions of mere speculation and fancy,
to the sphere of air and fire, where his delighted spirit floats in
'seas of pearl and clouds of amber'. There is no *caput mortuum*
of worn-out, thread-bare experience to serve as ballast to his
mind; it is all volatile intellectual salt of tartar, that refuses
to combine its evanescent, inflammable essence with any thing
solid or any thing lasting. Bubbles are to him the only
realities. . . .[25]

Even if the reviewers had been consistently spiteful to
Keats, the tradition that he was 'snuffed out by an article'
would still seem fantastic: literary disagreements provoke
only verbal duels to-day. Yet just one week before Keats
died, John Scott, editor of the *London Magazine*, was killed

in a duel after a quarrel over his articles criticizing *Black-wood's* for their 'Cockney School' series. By a further quirk of chance the *London Magazine*'s review of Keats's 1820 volume, probably by Scott, was one of the first to suggest Keats had been distressed by the criticism of *Endymion*. Much of the blame for turning the suggestion into tradition falls on Shelley and Byron. It suited Shelley to have Keats slain by reviewers in *Adonais*. He could then use the Adonis-myth and place Keats beside others who had met violent deaths — Lucan, Sidney, Chatterton. It was all very plausible, especially when Byron added his flashy verses,

> Who killed John Keats?
> 'I,' says the *Quarterly*,
> So savage and Tartarly;
> ''Twas one of my feats,'

and

> 'Tis strange the mind, that very fiery particle,
> Should let itself be snuffed out by an article.[26]

Shelley begins the preface to *Adonais* with a tribute to Keats: 'I consider the fragment of *Hyperion* as second to nothing that was ever produced by a writer of the same years'. Then he develops the legend about the reviewers. The most wounding attack on Keats was in *Blackwood's*, but Shelley mentions only the *Quarterly*'s reviewer, whom in the poem he calls a 'nameless worm' and a 'noteless blot on a remembered name'. In the preface he says:

The savage criticism on his *Endymion*, which appeared in the *Quarterly Review*, produced the most violent effect on his susceptible mind; the agitation thus originated ended in the rupture of a blood-vessel in the lungs; a rapid consumption ensued. . . . These wretched men know not what they do. They scatter their insults and their slanders without heed as to whether the poisoned shaft lights on a heart made callous by many blows or one like Keats's composed of more penetrable stuff.

This tirade was enough to end the equivocal wooing of Shelley by *Blackwood's*. Their reviewer of *Adonais*, George Croly, whose poem *Paris* Shelley had ridiculed in his preface, said he 'could prove from the present Elegy that it is possible to write two sentences of pure nonsense out of three'.[27]

3

Shelley embarks on the main theme of *Adonais* without preamble:

> I weep for Adonais — he is dead!
> O, weep for Adonais! though our tears
> Thaw not the frost which binds so dear a head!
> And thou, sad Hour, selected from all years
> To mourn our loss, rouse thy obscure compeers,
> And teach them thine own sorrow! Say: 'With me
> Died Adonais; till the Future dares
> Forget the Past, his fate and fame shall be
> An echo and a light unto eternity!'
>
> Where wert thou, mighty Mother, when he lay,
> When thy Son lay, pierced by the shaft which flies
> In darkness? Where was lorn Urania
> When Adonais died? . . .

432. 1-13

For his mythology, Shelley makes use of two Greek poems in the pastoral tradition of Theocritus. The first is the elegy for Adonis attributed to Bion, which he copies closely at times, particularly its opening: 'Woe, woe for Adonis, he hath perished, the beauteous Adonis, dead is the beauteous Adonis, the Loves join in the lament. . . .'[28] The second Greek poem is the elegy for Bion attributed to Moschus, in which Bion is alleged to have been cruelly poisoned by an unknown hand. (The little that is known about Bion and Moschus need not concern us, for it is now thought that they probably didn't write these two elegies.) Shelley makes plain in the second stanza how he is going to use the Adonis legend. As in the myth Venus mourns her son Adonis, slain by the boar, so Shelley's Urania mourns her son Adonais, killed by that wild beast the reviewer, whose shaft 'flies in darkness' because he is anonymous. There are two Uranias in classical mythology: Urania the Muse of

Astronomy, and Aphrodite Urania, goddess of heavenly love (as opposed to Aphrodite Pandemos, goddess of earthly love). Shelley's Urania is the second of these. By exalting her status and making Adonais her son, he robs the Venus-Adonis myth of its erotic element, which would have been out of place in an elegy. The change from Adonis to Adonais was an inspired piece of word-coining. The extra vowel creates a richer and more gracious flavour. The long-drawn final syllables add an elegiac undertone, and 'Adonis' seems curt and flat after 'Adonais'. The metrical problems too are eased by the extra stress — Ádonáis instead of Adónis. Shelley's attempt to fit the elegy for Bion into this Adonis-framework does lead to one glaring inconsistency: Adonais is 'pierced by a shaft' in stanza 2, but he 'drinks poison' in stanza 36. The manner of his death hardly matters, however, and the discrepancy between these versions is as irrelevant as the fact that neither applies to Keats. The framework of Greek myth is, even in the first stanza, reinforced by Shelley's own inventions. As in *Prometheus Unbound*, he personifies Hours, singling out from its commonplace fellows the Hour which presided over the death of Adonais. At the beginning of the second stanza there is a curious echo from *The Curse of Kehama*. Shelley's

Where wert thou, mighty Mother [*i.e.* Urania], when he lay,
When thy Son lay. . . .

has a similar trick of repetition and a similar proper name to Southey's

Where art thou, Son of Heaven, Ereenia, where
In this dread hour. . . .[29]

Stanzas 3-29 elaborate the myth and ideas introduced in the first two stanzas. Stanzas 3-6 continue the appeal to Urania. In stanzas 7-17 a bevy of remote abstractions grieve for Adonais — Dreams, Splendours, Glooms, veiled Destinies, twilight Phantasies,

All he had loved, and moulded into thought,
From shape, and hue, and odour, and sweet sound.

434. 118-19

The ritual of their obsequies derives largely from Bion and Moschus. Then in stanzas 18-21, Shelley expresses his own sorrow. At last, in stanzas 22-9, this lamentation stings Urania to action. Speeding from her secret Paradise over the hardened hearts and barbed tongues of men,

> which, to her aery tread
> Yielding not, wounded the invisible
> Palms of her tender feet where'er they fell,

she reaches the spot where Adonais lies. She too harps on the reviewers —

> Why didst thou leave the trodden paths of men
> Too soon, and with weak hands though mighty heart
> Dare the unpastured dragon in his den?
>
> 437. 236-8

Urania's excursion is modelled closely on the elegy for Adonis: 'Aphrodite . . . goes wandering . . . with feet unsandalled, and the thorns as she passes wound her. . . . Why wert thou thus overhardy to fight with beasts?' [30] Urania's lament is the climax of the invocations in the Greek pastoral style. As she finishes speaking, we are quietly brought back to real life.

In stanzas 30-5 contemporary poets, in the guise of mountain shepherds with 'garlands sere' and 'magic mantles rent', come to pay tribute to Adonais. Shelley chooses Byron and Moore as the first two mourners, crediting them with sentiments neither pretended to feel:

> The Pilgrim of Eternity, whose fame
> Over his living head like Heaven is bent,
> An early but enduring monument,
> Came, veiling all the lightnings of his song
> In sorrow; from her wilds Ierne sent
> The sweetest lyrist of her saddest wrong,
> And Love taught Grief to fall like music from his tongue.
>
> 438. 264-70

A genuine mourner, Leigh Hunt, 'gentlest of the wise', appears in stanza 35. Among the ruck of poets less famous than Byron or Moore is Shelley himself,

> one frail Form,
> A phantom among men ; companionless
> As the last cloud of an expiring storm
> Whose thunder is its knell ; he, as I guess,
> Had gazed on Nature's naked loveliness,
> Actaeon-like, and now he fled astray
> With feeble steps o'er the world's wilderness,
> And his own thoughts, along that rugged way,
> Pursued, like raging hounds, their father and their prey.
>
> 438. 271-9

Shelley here makes a striking image out of the legend of Actaeon, the huntsman who was turned into a stag and hunted by his own hounds because he watched Diana bathing. Four stanzas (31-4) are devoted to this self-analysis, and since Shelley admits that he 'in another's fate now wept his own', they are not free from self-pity. Yet the stanzas are memorable ones, with some fine images, and the real objection to them is that they shouldn't be there at all : a briefer mention of himself would have been more seemly.

To counterbalance his over-praise of the poet-mourners Shelley heaps invective on the suspected murderer, the reviewer, in stanzas 36-8. Then, finally abandoning the pastoral convention, he begins the last and best part of the poem.

The last seventeen stanzas are an exultant denial of death's victory, from a typically Shelleyan angle. We are told we should not mourn for Keats : he has been absorbed into the immutable One Spirit, the Platonic prototype which worldly forms stem from. Death draws aside the veil shielding men from this Spirit's light, a blinding radiance distantly related both to the 'celestial light' of Wordsworth's *Immortality* ode and to the 'something far more deeply interfused' of *Tintern Abbey*.

> He is not dead, he doth not sleep —
> He hath awakened from the dream of life.
> 'Tis we who, lost in stormy visions, keep
> With phantoms an unprofitable strife,
> And in mad trance strike with our spirit's knife
> Invulnerable nothings. . . .
>
> 440. 343-8

The spirit of Keats, who sought beauty so eagerly, has been fused with the One Spirit which injects the essence of beauty into all things by forcing stubborn material into approximations of the ideal forms, observed by us as 'Nature'.

> He is made one with Nature : there is heard
> His voice in all her music, from the moan
> Of thunder to the song of night's sweet bird ;
> He is a presence to be felt and known
> In darkness and in light, from herb and stone,
> Spreading itself where'er that Power may move
> Which has withdrawn his being to its own ;
> Which wields the world with never-wearied love,
> Sustains it from beneath, and kindles it above.
>
> 441. 370-8

In the next four stanzas Shelley makes use of the Greek quotation which serves as a motto for *Adonais*. This is one of the epigrams attributed to Plato,

> Ἀστὴρ πρὶν μὲν ἔλαμπες ἐνὶ ζωοῖσιν Ἑῷος·
> νῦν δὲ θανὼν λάμπεις Ἕσπερος ἐν φθιμένοις,

which he translated :

> To Stella.
> Thou wert the morning star among the living,
>   Ere thy fair light had fled ; —
> Now, having died, thou art as Hesperus, giving
>   New splendour to the dead.
>
> 720

By substituting the Latin for the Greek 'star' Shelley has turned the male *Aster* into *Stella*. Otherwise his rendering is faithful, though lengthy. This motto becomes relevant when Shelley likens the stars of the sky to the world's great poets, for whom death is 'a low mist which cannot blot the brightness it may veil'. The white radiance of the One Spirit, far beyond human ken, is best mirrored by the greatest poets, the brightest stars. The persistent exploitation of Shelley's imagery in the cinema world has at least proved its vitality. We accept it more readily too because it is so familiar. Shelley was doing the job of a publicity-agent, providing a build-up for a new poetry-star — a ludicrous yet logical comparison. The great poetry-stars of the past, especially the 'inheritors of unfulfilled renown', who met violent death while young, rise to meet Adonais as he approaches. These, Chatterton, Sidney, Lucan, 'and many more whose names on earth are dark', tell him that

> 'It was for thee yon kingless sphere has long
> Swung blind in unascended majesty,
> Silent alone amid an Heaven of Song.
> Assume thy wingèd throne, thou Vesper of our throng!'
>
> 442. 411-4

He is the Vesper because he is the latest, because the evening star is associated with Venus, and hence with Aphrodite Urania, and also perhaps because he is to be the brightest of their company.

Shelley next advises anyone who persists in mourning to visit Keats's grave in the beautiful Protestant Cemetery at Rome. Keats needs no reflected glory from the ages, empires, and religions which at Rome 'lie buried in the ravage they have wrought'. Rather Rome will be glad to have some share in his glory.

As the poem nears its end Shelley returns to wider issues, with a famous image:

> The One remains, the many change and pass;
> Heaven's light for ever shines, Earth's shadows fly;
> Life, like a dome of many-coloured glass,
> Stains the white radiance of Eternity,
> Until Death tramples it to fragments.
>
> 443. 460-4

This is more than 'the best epigrammatic expression of Platonism in English poetry'.[31] Were it rigidly Platonic the *stain* would be a tarnish; but for Shelley *stain* often means *enrich by colouring*, as it clearly does here, in view of the tacit comparison with stained glass. Like most all-appealing images, this one can be variously interpreted. Does

> Life, like a dome of many-coloured glass,
> Stains the white radiance of Eternity

mean that the climate of thought in our day is as light focused under a many-coloured dome made of glass panels representing living individuals? Most individuals transmit no white radiance at all: their panels would be black. Certain artists and thinkers succeed in transmitting components of the supernal light: their panels would be coloured. The more numerous the transmitters the brighter would be the general illumination; the more balanced the components, the whiter the light at the focus. This enticing explanation fails, however, because a death would merely remove one panel, not smash the dome to fragments. Alternatively, we may simply treat the dome as life, and the coloured glass as life's many facets. A third and richer reading is to think of an individual standing as if beneath a dome. The white radiance shines, like sunlight, on the outer surface of the dome. Those who are dull of soul never realize the light is there: the glass in their domes is a dirty grey. Those who are not so dull have some coloured glass in their domes, and each colour corresponds to some route for the light, *e.g.* poetry, science, music, the ecstasies of love, earthly or divine. The larger the area of any colour, the more intense the appreciation; the more colours, the broader the appreciation. Were there panels of every colour in the right proportions, the resulting rays could be grouped into white again, so that the whole radiance would have been appreciated, if only dimly. Death shatters the dome, and the full light blazes in; very rarely a panel may be removed during life to give a glimpse of the full light. Though the emphasis is on these last three lines, the first two, with their hint of Plato's cave —

> The One remains, the many change and pass;
> Heaven's light for ever shines, Earth's shadows fly —

serve an essential purpose by playing on our desire for security. Various technical tricks enhance their appeal: the repetition of the vowel *a* in the first line and *i* in the second; the play on *m-n* in the first line and on *f-sh-s* in the second — *for* ever *shines* . . . *shadows* *f*ly; and the absence of adjectives, which creates a sense of urgency and gives more force to *many-coloured* and *white* in the next lines.

The poem ends with satisfying *bravura*. Shelley, ensconced in his soul-boat, zooms out of sight on his way to join Adonais :

> The breath whose might I have invoked in song
> Descends on me ; my spirit's bark is driven
> Far from the shore, far from the trembling throng
> Whose sails were never to the tempest given ;
> The massy earth and spherèd skies are riven !
> I am borne darkly, fearfully, afar ;
> Whilst, burning through the inmost veil of Heaven,
> The soul of Adonais, like a star,
> Beacons from the abode where the Eternal are.

444. 487-95

Shelley here accurately foretells his own death a year later. But he is visiting Adonais only in fancy ; so it is a chance prophecy, arising because he liked to travel by boat, in fact as well as fancy.

4

Shelley was right in calling *Adonais* 'the least imperfect of my compositions'.² It is structurally the most coherent and technically the most polished of his longer poems. With a narrower scope than in *Prometheus Unbound* he succeeds more completely. *Adonais* is one of the few poems in which he achieves all his aims³². Keats's death gives him a fine chance to utilize his religion-philosophy of Platonism-pantheism. His picture of Adonais being absorbed into the One Spirit, which

> wields the world with never-wearied love,
> Sustains it from beneath, and kindles it above,

is acceptable to people of most religions, because it can be read as a generalized version of their own faith. This handy background philosophy is defined clearly yet without undue emphasis. There is none of the esoteric sludge which clogs the channels of communication in *Epipsychidion*, and only once or twice do we feel we are being asked to grieve too loud and too long. Shelley avoids this, the chief danger of elegy, by appealing to every mood : a passively receptive reader of *Adonais* passes through grief and pity, anger and contempt, hope and aspiration, to restrained exultation.

A similar chain of emotions is to be found in *Lycidas*, which has much in common with *Adonais*. Both Shelley and Milton follow Theocritus with their pastoral setting and their direct expressions of sorrow. Both relieve the tension of grief by denunciation of the living, though here Shelley has the advantage, since the attack on the reviewers is germane to his theme, whereas Milton's clergy-baiting is a digression. Shelley has a further tactical advantage because Keats, unlike Milton's friend Edward King, has since become famous.

It was lucky Shelley knew so little of the causes and manner of Keats's death. Sympathy for a fellow-victim of reviewers was a sharper spur than the pious wish to commemorate Keats, and without his mistaken belief in the lethality of the reviews Shelley might never have written *Adonais*. To call the poem sublimated self-pity would be most unfair, however. Shelley admitted self-pity was a spur, but he had forgotten it by the time he reached those last seventeen stanzas 'of unsurpassed poetical splendour'.[33] Only a few days after finishing those stanzas he heard the painful story of Keats's last months. Had he known it earlier, he wrote, 'I do not think . . . I could have composed my poem — the enthusiasm of the imagination would have been overpowered by sentiment.'[9] Even if the effect had not been quite as stultifying as this, the detached tone which contributes so much to the poem's success would no longer have been possible.

By following the Greek pastoral convention Shelley restricts his scope and stiffens the poem structurally. He is at his best when working within limits, because he violates the limits only when he has something really pressing to say, and his inventiveness is less likely to overleap all boundaries and dissipate itself in random spurts. The first half of the poem could perhaps be improved by cutting the ritual ; but its discipline is a salutary check, and its solemn atmosphere a fitting prelude to the exultation of the last seventeen stanzas.

Shelley's technical mastery of the Spenserian stanza was the result of his long practice in *The Revolt of Islam*. He gives the stanza a music Spenser never knew, and he curbs its aggressive rhymes by running one line into the next and varying the position of the mid-line *caesura*. The long last line of the Spenserian stanza tends to round off the thought expressed, and, although in other poems Shelley spreads his fancies over several stanzas, in *Adonais* he is surprisingly obedient to the rule of 'one main thought per stanza', so that nearly every stanza is comprehensible on its own. This discipline, too, is beneficial, except in a few places where the thought is not quite worth nine lines. These few weak spots are disguised by the lulling music of the verse. Alliteration and assonance have rarely been used so tactfully as in *Adonais*, in lines like

Death feeds on his mute voice, and laughs at our despair. . . .
A light of laughing flowers along the grass is spread. . . .
With sparkless ashes load an unlamented urn. . . .

Shelley often varies tone and pace by play upon consonants, ranging from the languor of

Most musical of mourners, weep anew. . . .

to the Spartan resolve of

Not all to that bright station dared to climb.

Often, too, a striking image springs out of the blue to end a stanza :

the intense atom glows
A moment, then is quenched in a most cold repose. . . .
Like pageantry of mist on an autumnal stream. . . .
A herd-abandoned deer struck by the hunter's dart.

Yet in reading the poem we hardly notice effects like these, so smoothly do they work towards the success of the whole.

A good tailpiece for this chapter is provided by the fragment Shelley wrote to complete Keats's self-chosen epitaph, 'Here lieth one whose name was writ on water' :

x

'Here lieth One whose name was writ on water.'
But, ere the breath that could erase it blew,
Death, in remorse for that fell slaughter,
Death, the immortalizing winter, flew
Athwart the stream, — and time's printless torrent grew
A scroll of crystal, blazoning the name
Of Adonais!

658. 1-7

NOTES TO XIV: *ADONAIS*

1. *Letters* ii. 220.
2. *Letters* ii. 355.
3. *Letters* ii. 240.
4. See Keats, *Letters*, p. 507. (Forman's edition)
5. Keats, *Letters*, p. 53.
6. Keats, *Letters*, p. 67.
7. See R. H. Fogle, *The Imagery of Keats and Shelley*.
8. See *Letters* ii. 239, 262.
9. *Letters* ii. 299.
    10. J. Wain, *Contemporary Reviews of Romantic Poetry*, p. 116.
    11. The sources of these six quotations are: *Letters* ii. 317; *Letters* ii. 366; Keats, *Letters*, p. 70; Byron, letter to Moore, 4 Mar. 1822; Keats, *Letters*, p. 521; Byron, letter to Murray, 4 Nov. 1820.
    12. See J. Clive, *Scotch Reviewers*, pp. 186–97.
    13. Wain, *Contemporary Reviews*, p. 199.
    14. Wain, *Contemporary Reviews*, p. 167.
    15. *Blackwood's*, August 1818, quoted in W. M. Rossetti's edition of *Adonais* (1903), pp. 37–8.
    16. Quoted in White, ii. 158. For authorship, see *Times Lit. Sup.*, 12 Aug. 1955.
    17. Wain, *Contemporary Reviews*, pp. 173–6.
    18. Hunt's reviews are reprinted in R. B. Johnson, *Shelley–Leigh Hunt*.
    19. White, ii. 191; and ii. 196.
    20. See N. I. White, *The Unextinguished Hearth* for details.
    21. See E. Dowden, *Southey*, p. 171.
    22. *Blackwood's*, Oct. 1818, quoted in P. P. Howe, *Hazlitt*, p. 264.
    23. See Keats, *Letters*, p. 306.
    24. *Letters* ii. 213.
    25. Hazlitt, *On Paradox and Commonsense*.
    26. *Don Juan*, XI. 60.
    27. Quoted in W. M. Rossetti, *Adonais*, p. 38. For authorship, see *Times Lit. Sup.*, 6 Oct. 1950.
    28. Lang's translation (Theocritus, Bion and Moschus, rendered into English prose by A. Lang. Macmillan, 1889), p. 171.
    29. Southey, *Kehama*, XIV. 97–8.
    30. Lang's translation, pp. 172, 174.
    31. J. A. Notopoulos, *The Platonism of Shelley*, p. 298.
    32. As shown in the profound analysis of *Adonais* by E. R. Wasserman, *The Subtler Language*, pp. 305–61.
    33. Sir H. Newbolt, in *Poems of Shelley*, Nelson Classics edition, p. xv.

XV

HELLAS

Fair Greece, sad relic of departed worth.
BYRON. *Childe Harold*

1

TOWARDS the end of 1820 a group of friends had begun to gather round Shelley at Pisa, and more arrived during 1821. For some months after the Shelleys came to Pisa in January 1820, Mr. and Mrs. Mason had been their only close friends. Then in October, Shelley's cousin, Tom Medwin, once his school-fellow at Syon House and his collaborator in *The Wandering Jew*, arrived from India on what proved a lengthy stay. At first Shelley was glad to have his cousin's company; but soon Medwin became an ardent disciple, and his admiration began to cloy. The next member of the group, whom the Shelleys met in November, was the Irishman John Taaffe, an aspiring poet and author of the first English commentary on Dante, which Shelley and Byron both praised highly. It was in November, too, that they first saw Emilia, and in December they were introduced to 'Prince' Alexander Mavrocordato, who was soon to lead the Greeks, or rather their most important faction, in the struggle for independence. He was a frequent visitor during the next six months. Mary liked his vivacious quirks and was flattered that he was willing to spend time teaching her Greek. Shelley respected Mavrocordato and often played chess with him, but couldn't bear his modern Greek accent. Mavrocordato was to leave for Greece in June 1821, but the next arrivals, Edward and Jane Williams, who came from Geneva in January 1821 at Medwin's instigation, became lifelong friends. Edward Williams, a year younger than

315

Shelley, was a Lieutenant on half-pay. He had served in
the Navy for a short time, and in the Army in India, where
he met Jane. She had been deserted by her husband, and
now passed as Edward's wife. In India Edward had been a
keen hunter : he was in at the death of twenty-six tigers,
according to Taaffe.[1] Now he indulged in the gentler
pursuits of amateur painting and writing. He took to
Shelley at once :

Shelley is certainly a man of most astonishing genius, in appearance extraordinarily young, of manners mild and amiable, but
withal full of life and fun. His wonderful command of language,
and the ease with which he speaks on what are generally considered abstruse subjects, are striking ; in short, his ordinary
conversation is akin to poetry, for he sees things in the most
singular and pleasing lights : if he wrote as he talked, he would
be popular enough.[2]

Though it was some time before Shelley became 'reconciled
to Jane', he liked Edward immediately and was glad to find
him a sailing enthusiast. Sailing in small boats had always
been Shelley's favourite passive pleasure, and he preferred
to lie back and let the boat drift. Rowing, or fiddling with
sails, spoilt the sense of luxury. Since drifting was a chancy
means of locomotion he had in the past often been thwarted ;
but now he had an ex-sailor to do the practical jobs. He
and Williams kept to inland waterways in 1821, for their
first boat was a mere skiff. Even so, Shelley, who couldn't
swim, had some narrow escapes. The Shelleys again spent
the summer at the Baths of San Giuliano outside Pisa, and
the skiff proved useful for visiting the Williamses, whose house
was some four miles away along the Arno–Serchio canal.

The Shelleys invited Byron to their summer retreat. But
he was no longer the mobile Childe Harold, and it was
Shelley who did the travelling, across the Apennines to
Ravenna, in August 1821. Byron had been in his phase of
reckless dissipation at Venice when they last met, three years
before, and Shelley was pleasantly surprised to find him
'greatly improved in every respect — in genius, in temper,
in moral views, in health, in happiness'.[3] It was over two

years since Byron had begun his liaison with Teresa Guiccioli, and she was now separated from her husband Count
Guiccioli by a Papal decree, which obliged her to live in
the house of her father, Count Gamba. About a month
before Shelley's visit, Count Gamba and his son Pietro had
been expelled from the Romagna by the Papal authorities,
who suspected them (rightly) of planning an armed revolt,
and Teresa had to go with them. Their banishment was
probably a roundabout way of making Byron leave Ravenna,
for he had grossly abused his 'diplomatic immunity' as a
foreign nobleman by acting as virtual leader of the local
Carbonari. So far, however, he had stayed put at Ravenna,
coolly continuing to live in the *palazzo* belonging to Teresa's
husband, which he used as a private arsenal. When Shelley
arrived, one of the first things Byron asked him to do was to
dissuade Teresa, who was at Florence, from a scheme for
going to Switzerland. Shelley wrote her a long letter — 'an
odd thing enough for an utter stranger to write on subjects
of the utmost delicacy to his friend's mistress' [3] — and
Teresa accepted the suggestion that she join Byron in Pisa.
She and her brother went there at once. Uprooting Byron
and moving him a hundred miles was not so easy : he had
enough of Oblomov in his nature to make it doubtful
whether he would ever stir from Ravenna, if left on his
own. Shelley, knowing this, encouraged him by renting a
palazzo for him at Pisa, and sending eight waggons to
Ravenna for his household goods and livestock. The latter
is said to have included ten horses, eight enormous dogs,
three monkeys, five cats, an eagle, a crow, a falcon, a goat,
a badger, five peacocks, two guinea hens and an Egyptian
crane — all, except the horses, free to roam about the house,
which often resounded 'with their unarbitrated quarrels'.[4]

Byron's *impedimenta*, closely followed by himself, eventually arrived at Pisa in November 1821, a few weeks after
the Shelleys returned to the city from their summer house.
Their new home at Pisa was a top-floor flat on the Lung'
Arno, and the Williamses occupied the floor below. Byron,
who had by now added four geese to his menagerie, was

installed in the near-by Palazzo Lanfranchi. The Shelleys quickly made friends with Teresa Guiccioli and her brother Pietro Gamba, and they saw a good deal of Medwin. Shelley also kept up his friendships with the Masons and with Taaffe. So at the end of 1821, for the first time in Italy, he was among a large group of friends.

And more were due to come. While Shelley was at Ravenna Byron had agreed that Leigh Hunt should be invited to Italy as editor of a periodical, to which Byron and perhaps Shelley could contribute. Hunt accepted the invitation promptly. In November 1821 he left London by sea, with all his large family. By the end of the year they were expected daily at Pisa; but their ship was driven back by storms in the western approaches of the Channel, and they had to spend the winter at Plymouth. The ground floor of Byron's *palazzo*, which had been made ready for them, was to stand empty until June 1822. Another of Shelley's close friends, Horace Smith, started out for Italy overland in July 1821. But he had to abandon his plans for joining Shelley after getting no further than Paris, because his wife became too ill to travel.

The one newcomer who did materialize was Trelawny, a friend of Medwin and Williams. No picture of the Pisan circle would be complete without him, for his striking qualities more than made up for his late arrival, in January 1822. Two months younger than Shelley, Trelawny came to Pisa primed with exaggerated stories about his romantic exploits in the Far East, where, so he said, he had defied death again and again as captain of a privateer; and his future exploits in Greece, in both love and war, were to be just as bizarre. He looked the part too, six feet tall, with dark eyes, a hook nose, a mass of curly black hair and a swarthy skin. Byron was a little upset to meet a caricature of a Byronic hero in the flesh, and did not much care for Trelawny. Shelley was fascinated by him: here was a man untamed by custom and convention, full of tall stories about his adventures, egotistical, flamboyant and untruthful perhaps, yet generous, lively and stimulating. As for

Trelawny, he found in Shelley the lodestar of his life. Later in 1822 he bought the tomb next to Shelley's at Rome, and ended a lifetime of devotion to his memory, which included offers of marriage to Mary and Clare, by joining him there nearly sixty years later.

At first, Shelley apparently enjoyed living among a group of friends. Byron was in the habit of riding out from the city to practise shooting with pistols, at a half-crown stuck in the top of a cane, and Shelley often joined his party. Zealous Papal spies observed them, and reported that 'at last Lord Byron and his company of assassins have given us a taste of the temper they have already shown elsewhere. . . .' 5 This interpretation of their actions was most nearly borne out in their affray with a none-too-sober Italian dragoon. As they returned one day from shooting (*sans* ammunition), this dragoon galloped furiously past, brushing Taaffe and startling the horses. Taaffe was indignant, so Byron set off in pursuit, followed by the others. Shelley, who had the fastest horse, reached the dragoon first, with Trelawny close behind. Words followed, then blows. Among those unhorsed in the scuffle was Shelley, who, though not the best of riders, this time had the excuse that he had been knocked senseless by a blow on the head from the hilt of the dragoon's sabre. Byron rode on to fetch weapons. Taaffe, the original trouble-maker, had not yet caught up : he had stopped to retrieve his hat, which had fallen off — conduct ignominious enough to earn him the nickname of False-Taaffe. Things looked more serious a few minutes later when one of Byron's servants badly wounded the dragoon. The upshot of this silly brawl was that the Gambas and two of Byron's servants, but not the culprit, were, in mid-1822, after much official shilly-shallying, expelled from Tuscany by order of Governor Viviani (Emilia's father), and, as intended, Byron followed them.6 As these stories suggest, we know more about Shelley's life at this period than at any other. Two of the Pisan group, Medwin and Trelawny, wrote books on the strength of their experiences in the winter of 1821–2 — Trelawny's, despite its chronic inaccuracy, being the acutest contemporary memoir of Shelley — while four others, Mary, Teresa, Taaffe and Williams, left some account of these months.

Shelley's entry into group activities may have been a deliberate experiment in living. On leaving Oxford he had dreamt of living in a Godwinian 'genuine society'. Once convinced that this hope was futile, perhaps after the Irish expedition of 1812, he seemed to regard a group of three as the ideal social unit. Now after eight years he had the chance to try a larger number — perhaps with an eye to playing Plato's philosopher-king on a small scale? It was his idea to form the group; and he bound it together,[7] for soon after his death its members were scattered all over Europe. He could scarcely have fitted into this group and held it together if, as the Victorians liked to think, he was a 'pure impulsive character',[8] as incapable as a child of being tactful. When thwarted by organizations he couldn't hope to influence, he was sometimes impulsive and violent. But if some thorny human problem had to be tackled, or if some disagreeable or delicate business had to be transacted, it was the 'tactless' Shelley who took charge.

The best example of his patience and tact is the quarrel between Byron and Clare, which engaged his talents as mediator for five years. When the baby Allegra was brought to Italy in 1818 Byron agreed to arrange for her education, provided neither he nor Allegra ever saw Clare again. Clare handed her over reluctantly, and from then on relentlessly demanded to be allowed to see her child. Shelley was her go-between, an office which was no sinecure. To Byron, Clare was 'a damned bitch'[9] with only her own importunity to blame for her troubles. To Clare, Byron was 'my damned brute'[10] — the *my* would have annoyed him more than the *damned brute*. Shelley remained friendly with both throughout their protracted quarrel, and also, in the words of Allegra's biographer, 'stands out . . . as the most disinterested, most devoted, wisest friend [Allegra] had'.[11] One of Shelley's reasons for visiting Ravenna in August 1821, was to see Allegra, then 4 years old. He found her

mischievous and happy in her convent school at Bagnacavallo. He suggested that she should be brought to a
school near Pisa when Byron moved there, and Byron gave
the impression that he agreed to this. In fact, Allegra
remained at Bagnacavallo, despite hysterical protests from
Clare. Her forebodings were justified, for Allegra was to
die there in 1822, during a typhus epidemic.

2

Shelley and Byron both had something to gain from their
friendship, because they corrected each other's excesses.
Shelley greatly admired much of Byron's poetry, and when
Byron was near by he seems to have felt it was not worth
writing anything himself in face of such competition. His
self-abasement reached rock-bottom in the fulsome *Sonnet
to Byron* :

> [I am afraid these verses will not please you, but]
> If I esteemed you less, Envy would kill
> Pleasure, and leave to Wonder and Despair
> The ministration of the thoughts that fill
> My mind, which, like a worm whose life may share
> A portion of the Unapproachable,
> Marks your creations rise as fast and fair
> As perfect worlds at the Creator's will,
> And bows itself before the godhead there.
> But such is my regard, that, nor your fame
> Cast on the present by the coming hour,
> Nor your well-won prosperity and power
> Move one regret for his unhonoured name
> Who dares these words, — the worm beneath the sod
> May lift itself in worship to the God.[12]

These lines may bear out Landor's dictum, 'Shelley whom
envy never touched',[13] but they are rather misleading in
other respects. For Shelley never fell under Byron's spell.
He did not like Byron's cynical pose, his pointless debauchery
at Venice and the dark romantic style which had won him
his fame. Byron's influence on Shelley's poems was therefore slight, but it was in the right direction. Shelley, when

left to his own bent, was inclined to build castles in the air, which Byron would humorously raze to the ground. Byron's comments probably made him write more colloquially: it was talk with Byron that inspired his first poem in conversational style, *Julian and Maddalo* ; and the success of Byron's poems in this vein, *Beppo* and *Don Juan*, probably encouraged Shelley to continue with it in the *Letter to Maria Gisborne* and some later poems.

Shelley's influence on Byron was rather greater, for Shelley was among the few critics Byron respected. While they were in Switzerland in 1816, Shelley's pleas for Wordsworth and Nature had an immediate effect on *Childe Harold*. And *Manfred*, composed soon after, might be called an attempt (not very successful) in the Shelleyan style. Wordsworth, Coleridge, Keats and Blake had hard words for Byron's poetry in general, and even admirers of *Childe Harold* were offended by *Don Juan*. Yet Shelley at once knew *Don Juan* was his masterpiece: 'every word has the stamp of immortality'.[3] Byron, though he thought well of Shelley as a poet,[14] was impressed most by his personality. Byron's judgements of his friends were nothing if not scathing: praise from him is a commodity rare and to be prized. He told Lady Blessington that Shelley 'was the most gentle, most amiable, and *least* worldly-minded person I ever met',[15] and in a letter he wrote: 'Shelley . . . is to my knowledge the *least* selfish and the mildest of men — a man who has made more sacrifices of his fortune and feelings for others than any I ever heard of'.[16] Shelley helped to correct Byron's weakness for lapsing into a life of small talk and bored dissipation: for Byron took more notice of Shelley than of the many other friends who appointed themselves keepers of his conscience.

3

In 1821 the war to free Greece from Turkish rule was about to start in earnest. During the six years which passed before the decisive battle, Navarino, many nations were drawn into the conflict, and British interest in the war was stimulated by the drama of Byron's death at Missolonghi in 1824. From the outset Russia sided with Greece, not from the purest of motives, as Shelley remarked :

Russia desires to possess, not to liberate Greece; and is contented to see the Turks, its natural enemies, and the Greeks, its intended slaves, enfeeble each other until one or both fall into its net.[17]

Shelley, like many other people, thought Britain would help the oppressor Turkey, and he explained why :

This is the age of the war of the oppressed against the oppressors, and every one of those ringleaders of the privileged gangs of murderers and swindlers, called Sovereigns, look to each other for aid against the common enemy, and suspend their mutual jealousies in the presence of a mightier fear.[17]

He did not foresee that Britain would choose to side with Russia, as the lesser of two evils : he hoped for a Greek victory, but didn't really expect it. Yet the slenderest hope excited him. Here was the country he revered most, whose golden age he thought 'undoubtedly . . . the most memorable in the history of the world',[18] rising against the oppressor : it was almost as if *The Revolt of Islam* were coming true. And, if this was not enough, he had met Mavrocordato, one of the leaders of the revolt and future Greek Prime Minister, almost daily at Pisa until he left for Greece in June. With this personal spark to inflame two of his most passionate interests, Greece and liberty, Shelley was unlikely to remain silent on the subject for long.

By the end of October 1821 he had finished the drama, 'if drama it must be called',[17] of *Hellas*, and he dedicated it to Mavrocordato. Shelley's aim in this poem, which he called 'a mere improvise' and 'a sort of lyrical, dramatic, nondescript piece of business',[19] was to weave songs of Greece's ancient glories into the fabric of current events — a fabric which failed to materialize, because the war had not really started and news of it was sporadic and garbled.

For the skeleton of his plot Shelley again turns to Aeschylus, this time to *The Persians*, which centres round news of the battle of Salamis, brought by a messenger to the stay-at-home Persians in Susa. The usual Aeschylean choruses punctuate the action. With an eye on this model, Shelley duly sets his scene in Constantinople: he finds good material for his choruses; and he outdoes Aeschylus by bringing on not one messenger but four. What baffles him is the problem of describing in detail battles as yet unfought: he is reduced to drawing 'indistinct' and visionary figures on 'the curtain of futurity'.[17]

The action of *Hellas*, if action it must be called, can be dismissed quickly. The proceedings begin with the Turkish sultan Mahmud asleep, oblivious of the subversive choruses being chanted by Greek slave women. Then Mahmud wakes from a troubled dream, and his servant Hassan tells him that if he wants it explained he should consult an old Jew, who knows the secrets of 'the Present, and the Past, and the To-come'. This is Ahasuerus, the Wandering Jew of *Queen Mab* resuscitated. Anyone wanting to question him in the sea-cavern where he lives

> Must sail alone at sunset, where the stream
> Of Ocean sleeps around those foamless isles,
> When the young moon is westering as now,
> And evening airs wander upon the wave.
>
> 456. 166-9

After arranging for an interview with this sage, Hassan gives Mahmud a detailed survey of the war against the Greeks, stop-press items being provided by four messengers, who bring progressively worse news. The fourth message is brought by a blood-brother of the Bleeding Sergeant in *Macbeth* and, when Mahmud interrupts, the air becomes thick with echoes from *Macbeth*:

> I'll hear no more! too long
> We gaze on danger through the mist of fear,
> And multiply upon our shattered hopes
> The images of ruin. Come what will!
> To-morrow and to-morrow are as lamps
> Set in our path to light us to the edge
> Through rough and smooth. . . .
>
> 467. 640-6

The parallels with *Macbeth* are :

> I'll see no more. . . . Strange images of death. . . .
> . . . Come what come may
> Time and the hour runs through the roughest day. . . .
> To-morrow and to-morrow. . . . ˙
> And all our yesterdays have lighted fools. . . .[20]

As in *The Cenci*, Shelley unconsciously slips into Shake-spearean pastiche when he has nothing definite to say.

After another chorus comes the meeting of Mahmud with Ahasuerus, who first delivers a strange prophetic discourse full of mixed echoes from Marlowe, *Richard II*, *The Tempest*, Plato, Calderón and Descartes (lines 772-85), and then hypnotizes the somewhat bewildered Mahmud so that he can relive his dream. In his trance Mahmud sees the phantom of Mahomet the Second, who predicts the end of the Empire he created :

> A later Empire nods in its decay :
> The autumn of a greener faith is come,
> And wolfish change, like winter, howls to strip
> The foliage in which Fame, the eagle, built
> Her aerie, while Dominion whelped below.
> The storm is in its branches, and the frost
> Is on its leaves, and the blank deep expects
> Oblivion on oblivion, spoil on spoil,
> Ruin on ruin.
>
> 472. 870-8

Shouts off-stage break Mahmud's trance and scare away the phantom. The shouting signals a Turkish victory; but Mahmud now knows victories are hollow,

> Weak lightning before darkness ! poor faint smile
> Of dying Islam !
>
> 473. 915-16

And there the 'action' ends.

The finest part of *Hellas* is not the 'action' but the four choruses which punctuate it. The first and third of these recall the great days of Greece, Freedom's earliest home —

> Greece and her foundations are
> Built below the tide of war,

> Based on the crystàlline sea
> Of thought and its eternity ;
> Her citizens, imperial spirits,
>   Rule the present from the past,
> On all this world of men inherits
>   Their seal is set.
>
> 468. 696-703

As Shelley said in his preface : 'We are all Greeks. Our laws, our literature, our religion, our arts have their root in Greece.' And the Greek ideal of personal freedom is still powerful to-day.

The second chorus is specifically Christian, with echoes of Milton's ode *On the morning of Christ's Nativity*. Shelley was taking seriously his unusual position as champion of a Christian country against a pagan. In a Note he adds a typical disclaimer : 'Let it not be supposed that I mean to dogmatize upon a subject concerning which all men are equally ignorant'. This second chorus opens in hypnotic rhythm :

> Worlds on worlds are rolling ever
>   From creation to decay,
> Like the bubbles on a river
>   Sparkling, bursting, borne away.
>   But they are still immortal
>   Who, through birth's orient portal
> And death's dark chasm hurrying to and fro,
>   Clothe their unceasing flight
>   In the brief dust and light
> Gathered around their chariots as they go.
>
> 457. 197-206

A first reading of these lines can leave the impression that they mean nothing at all, the imagery and sound-effects being more than enough to overflow the reader's perceptive channels. In the Note Shelley explains that he is contrasting 'the immortality of the living and thinking beings which inhabit the planets, and to use a common and inadequate phrase, *clothe themselves in matter*, with the transience of the noblest manifestations of the external world'. *Worlds* in the first line may be read either literally, as planets on which life rises and declines, or as empires or civilizations on earth.

These material things decay but, in the Christian view, the human soul is immortal, travelling as in a *chariot* through the *dust and light* of life from birth to death. Shelley says the soul hurries *to and fro* on this journey : is this an oblique reference to the Buddhist and Hindu reincarnation doctrines, implying that each soul makes many birth-death journeys? Or is *to and fro* merely padding, so that the sense is simply

> Who, *from* birth's orient portal
> *To* death's dark chasm hurrying?

To and fro may well be padding, for there are several weak adjectival words in the last six lines, which even at a quick reading seem far less gripping than the first four : *still, orient, dark, unceasing, brief*, add little to the sense.

These choruses lead up to the well-known finale expressing the spirit of the poem. Since the action ends with Greek defeat, the finale is introduced cautiously :

> If Greece must be
> A wreck, yet shall its fragments reassemble,
> And build themselves again impregnably
> In a diviner clime,
> To Amphionic music on some Cape sublime,
> Which frowns above the idle foam of Time.
>
> 475. 1002-7

The finale itself, in the metre of Byron's *Isles of Greece*, combines Shelley's hopes for Greece and Man's future.

> The world's great age begins anew,
> The golden years return,
> The earth doth like a snake renew
> Her winter weeds outworn. . . .

The bold prophecy about the world's great age is made more plausible by *winter weeds outworn* : there is, first, the lulling alliteration ; second, the hint that the prophecy is as inevitable as the march of the seasons ; and third, *weeds*, ostensibly *clothes*, has a strong scent of garden weeds, which like our present discontents can be got rid of. It was probably the tail-eating serpent, symbolizing eternity, which provoked Shelley to mention a snake renewing its skin. For the whole finale is dominated by Time, and Shelley exploits our liking for both old familiar faces (Orpheus, Ulysses, Calypso) and shining new objects: the new golden age will be *brighter, serener, fairer, sunnier, loftier* than the old.

> A brighter Hellas rears its mountains
> From waves serener far. . . .
> A loftier Argo cleaves the main,
> Fraught with a later prize;
> Another Orpheus sings again,
> And loves, and weeps, and dies.
> A new Ulysses leaves once more
> Calypso for his native shore. . . .
>
> 477. 1066-7, 1072-7

Shelley often ends lyrics by dropping to earth with a bump, but never more heavily than here:

> Oh, cease! must hate and death return?
> Cease! must men kill and die?
> Cease! drain not to its dregs the urn
> Of bitter prophecy.
> The world is weary of the past,
> Oh, might it die or rest at last!
>
> 478. 1096-1101

4

Hellas is an imperfect monument of Shelley's 'intense sympathy' for the Greek cause. Marks of hurry are written all over it. Very little happens and that little is enfeebled by being reported. This might not matter if, as in *Prometheus Unbound*, there was a unifying theme. But there isn't, and Shelley too often relies on the atmospheric imagery he handled so adeptly, or on mere enthusiasm, to carry the verse through patches where the material is woefully thin. Imagery and enthusiasm, stretched out for 1100 lines, become rather wearing, though they would guarantee a potent brew if the 1100 lines could be distilled and the livelier fractions, say 200 lines, separated out. The poem is too episodic to deserve the name of drama. It lacks dramatic tension and lacks too the chronicle-play's saving grace of factual interest. The only character worth the name is Mahmud, the gloomy Turk, who is at times as hesitant as

Hamlet and as eager for supernatural solicitings as Macbeth. The other figures are puppets. On the whole, the poem must be reckoned a failure, although at times it reveals Shelley at his best.

Perhaps its most surprising merit is the impartiality which somehow creeps in among its martial alarums. Shelley is clearly on the Greek side, yet he keeps the balance even by making the Turks kindly people. Mahmud could easily have been cast in the same mould as Count Cenci; instead, except in moments of anger, he is hesitant and dismayed at the slaughter going on. Shelley had come a long way from the dialectic of *Queen Mab* and the crippling bias of *The Revolt of Islam*. He also stayed neutral in the two longest poems he had still to write, *Charles the First* and *The Triumph of Life*. He had now said goodbye to his old propagandist habits.

In verse technique *Hellas* shows him at his best and worst. When he has nothing to say he can keep the verse ticking over with a pastiche made up of echoes from his own poems and Shakespeare. At other times, striking images crowd the page and beguiling rhythms sweep us through them. The tone and imagery are often reminiscent of *Prometheus Unbound* and the *Ode to Liberty*, but there are some unusual twists, for example:

> the cold pale Hour,
> Rich in reversion of impending death.
>
> 473. 902-3

Legal phrases like this are rare in Shelley's verse. It was *Political Justice* that first taught him to regard law with distaste, and life's lessons only hardened this attitude. For it was the law that deprived him of his children, and on the many occasions when he wanted to raise money for Godwin or others, he usually had to spend a lot of time arguing with lawyers and then pay them for the privilege afterwards. In a letter to Hogg, himself a lawyer, written in the same month as *Hellas*, he called law 'that disease inherited from generation to generation, that canker in the birthright of our nature. . .' So it is not surprising that legal jargon never filtered into his verse and that this isolated legal

Y

metaphor is formal and chilling. For warmer images we
turn to the final choruses. The rich stanzas of 'The world's
great age . . .' have entranced innumerable readers, including
Bertrand Russell, who quotes them when explaining how
'Shelley dominated my imagination and my affection for
many years'.[21] And in his last years, living at Penrhyndeudraeth with Shelley's house at Tan-Yr-Allt in view from
his window, Russell turned again to Shelley. At the very end
of his *Autobiography* he writes, 'My views on the future are
best expressed by Shelley', and quotes the final stanza of
Hellas (as given on p. 328).

Shelley's passion for Greece was in keeping with the
Spirit of the Age. Greek sculpture was thought impeccable
then — its 'very fragments are the despair of modern art',
as Shelley put it — a view which prevailed until the end of
the century, even as late as Berenson's *Florentine Painters*. In
the last fifty years this absolute standard has been discarded
and many artists have shown disdain for the civilized Greeks
by finding models in the most primitive art. · The belief that
Greek art was perfect helped Shelley towards his Platonism.
It was right that the nearest approach to the ideal human
form should be the work of Plato's contemporaries. Shelley
was not always uncritical of Greek sculpture, however : unlike Keats, he was not bowled over by the Elgin marbles.
As this suggests, his sympathy with Greece, though intense,
was limited. We can't imagine Shelley worshipping the
Greek gods, whereas Keats perhaps might have, for in some
ways he 'was a Greek'.[13] Shelley, being able to read Greek,
admired rather the intellect and insight of their thinkers
and tragedians.

If Shelley's sympathy with the ancient Greeks was incomplete, his knowledge of modern ones was almost non-
existent. He knew just one, Mavrocordato, and in default
of fuller experience he thought of the modern Greek as 'the
descendant of those glorious beings whom the imagination
almost refuses to figure to itself as belonging to our kind'.[17]
Trelawny tried to cure him of this illusion by introducing
him to the captain of a Greek merchantman, who was against

the Revolution because it was bad for trade. Shelley refused
to be disillusioned. If the modern Greeks were base, it was
because they suffered under tyranny. With freedom's return
their faded haloes would sprout again.

5

The spring, summer and early autumn of 1821 brought a
rich and varied harvest of short poems to set beside the
three longer ones, *Epipsychidion*, *Adonais* and *Hellas*. Even
these longer poems were unpremeditated: the first and
third were inspired by chance acquaintance, with Emilia
and Mavrocordato; the second by the accident of Keats's
death. They provide a good illustration of Robert Frost's
saying that 'poets . . . stick to nothing deliberately, but
let what will stick to them like burrs where they walk in
the fields.'. The shorter poems were even more unplanned
and diverse: sad and gay, quiet and vigorous, rub shoulders
somewhat disconcertingly. The gay poems confirm other
signs that this was probably Shelley's happiest summer. He
had no pressing worries, his health was fair, and he found
an agreeable companion in Williams, who steered him
towards an outdoor life. The sad poems are mostly
backward-looking, and they remind us that the memory of
Emilia, though fading, was still poignant.

Emilia may have been in Shelley's mind when he wrote
the poem Palgrave chose to round off the *Golden Treasury*:

> Music, when soft voices die,
> Vibrates in the memory —
> Odours, when sweet violets sicken,
> Live within the sense they quicken.
>
> Rose leaves, when the rose is dead,
> Are heaped for the belovèd's bed;
> And so thy thoughts, when thou art gone,
> Love itself shall slumber on.
>
> 639. 1-8

How have such innocent-looking verses become so famous?
The first stanza is finely balanced: *when sweet violets*

answers *when soft voices* like an echo, and the after-lives of
sound and odour are exactly parallel. There is also some
quiet play on consonants: all four lines have *v* and *n*;
every line except the second has *ic(k)*, *s* (twice) and *w*;
while *g*, *j*, *p* and *h* (except in *th*) are missing. By the end
of the first stanza we feel we know the scheme. *Soft* and
sweet lull us into expecting a comfortable adjective in alternate
lines, and the surprise of finding no adjectives at all in the
second stanza is like slumping back into a deep armchair and
finding it hard. As a result, the second stanza, despite its
obvious sentiment, seems mildly astringent. By the time
we near the end, the pattern seems to have settled down
again, and we might expect the last line to be 'In my mind
shall slumber on'. Instead the pattern is violated again,
by a grammatical inversion, which makes *thoughts* the object
of *slumber on*. This second slight shock of surprise is enough
to hold the attention till the end, and by then we see that
the second couplet has the same pattern as the first: Love
slumbers on thoughts, as the beloved slumbers on rose
leaves. Thus, although the poem is hardly profound, its
form is flawless and its wording careful: there are none of
the meretricious words which sometimes slip into Shelley's
more trivial poems. *Soft* and *sweet* are needed to establish
the mood, and the only other word suspiciously like a makeweight, *itself* in the last line, gives necessary extra force to
the fresh idea introduced.[22]

There is a similar play on the word *love* in another
famous little poem, the one which begins with

> One word is too often profaned
> For me to profane it. . . .

and ends with

> The desire of the moth for the star,
> Of the night for the morrow,
> The devotion to something afar
> From the sphere of our sorrow.

> 645. 1-2, 13-16

— lines too often dragged in to show how weakly moth-like
Shelley was. This poem is one of those anthologists' darlings

so damaging to Shelley's reputation. Continual reprinting in anthologies has quite mummified it, and boredom is the stock response on meeting it again. The poem has a glossy finish to ćeter scratchers, but the ill-mannered cur who does scratch finds little beneath the surface gloss. The poem is a conceit, like most seventeenth-century love-poems, and may provoke the tetchy rebuke, 'More matter with less art'.[23]

A third and a better poem in this wistful vein is the song to the Spirit of Delight, direct, humble and bitter-sweet:

> Rarely, rarely, comest thou,
>   Spirit of Delight!
> Wherefore hast thou left me now
>   Many a day and night? . . .
>
> > 640. 1-4

Knowing that rational bait won't catch the irrational Delight, Shelley has to dissemble:

> Let me set my mournful ditty
>   To a merry measure;
> Thou wilt never come for pity,
>   Thou wilt come for pleasure. . . .
>
> I love all that thou lovest,
>   Spirit of Delight!
> The fresh Earth in new leaves dressed,
>   And the starry night;
> Autumn evening, and the morn
> When the golden mists are born. . . .
>
> > 640. 19-22, 25-30

After the sweet and the bitter-sweet come two bitter poems, of real despair. The first, near-perfect apart from a clumsy third line, is the lament

> O world! O life! O time!
>   On whose last steps I climb,
>   Trembling at those which I have trod before;
>   When will return the glory of your prime?
>   No more — Oh, never more!
>
> Out of the day and night
>   A joy has taken flight;

> Fresh spring, and summer, and winter hoar,
> Move my faint heart with grief, but with delight
> No more — Oh, never more!
>
> 643. 1-10

The second is called *Ginevra*, the name of an unwilling bride who survives her wedding by only a few hours. In the 200-odd lines there is scarcely a cheerful word. The brides-maids wonder

> what can ever lure
> Maidens to leave the heaven serene and pure
> Of parents' smiles for life's great cheat; a thing
> Bitter to taste, sweet in imagining,
>
> 650. 34-7

while the bride comforts herself with the thought that

> The flowers upon my bridal chamber strewn
> Will serve unfaded for my bier,
>
> 651. 80-1

like the funeral baked meats in *Hamlet*. The story, which derives from an old Italian tale, and the bridegroom's name, Gherardi, combine to give *Ginevra* a Gothic flavour. But the Italian tale is not to blame for the poem's morbid tone : perhaps Shelley was brooding over Emilia's coming marriage to a man not of her own choosing.

Another poem about an unwilling bride, with an even stronger Gothic tang, is *The Fugitives*. This time the bride manages to escape with her lover in a small boat, leaving her father and bridegroom thwarted on shore. Though fired at by cannon, and facing a stormy open sea in a boat made for lakes, the lovers are, needless to say, undismayed. In writing the poem Shelley was no doubt fortified by the memory of his own rough Channel crossing with Mary after their elopement. Certainly the poem is vigorous and read-able; yet it is only a minor variation on the already well-worn theme of *Lord Ullin's Daughter* and 'Young Lochinvar'.

We are in another, and a realer, world when we pass from the fugitive lovers' boat to *The Boat on the Serchio*, which records the start of one of Shelley's days on the river. He was often out of doors in the summer of 1821, and the

poem's imagery, being local and immediate, reflects this.
The very crack of dawn is palpable :

> Like a flock of rooks at a farmer's gun
> Night's dreams and terrors, every one,
> Fled from the brains which are their prey
> From the lamp's death to the morning ray.

655. 26-9

The boat is still at its moorings :

> Our boat is asleep on Serchio's stream,
> Its sails are folded like thoughts in a dream,
> The helm sways idly, hither and thither ;
>   Dominic, the boatman, has brought the mast,
>   And the oars, and the sails ; but 'tis sleeping fast,
> Like a beast, unconscious of its tether.

654. 1-6

Its owners, Melchior (Williams) and Lionel (a name Shelley
liked to give himself), walk down from their secluded home
under 'the hill' which 'screens Lucca from the Pisan's
envious eye' — a translation of Dante's

> monte
> per che i Pisan veder Lucca non ponno.[24]

The Boat on the Serchio is mainly mere scraps of talk, ranging
between day-dreams and terse command. One of the
subjects touched on is Eton, its only mention in Shelley's
poetry. Williams had been at Eton in Shelley's time, and
probably had some happy memories to counter Shelley's
sad ones. In the poem it is apparently Lionel (Shelley)
who refers to 'bottles of warm tea'

> Such as we used, in summer after six,
> To cram in greatcoat pockets, and to mix
> Hard eggs and radishes and rolls at Eton,
> And, couched on stolen hay in those green harbours
> Farmers called gaps and we schoolboys called arbours,
> Would feast till half-past eight.[25]

81-6

The poem peters out inconsequentially with a close description of the Serchio, to remind us how much Shelley liked
rivers. The aesthetic appeal of river scenery and the

psychological appeal of the symbolic boat-on-a-river were reinforced by two practical points :

Rivers are not like roads, the work of the hands of man ; they imitate mind, which wanders at will over pathless deserts, and flows through nature's loveliest recesses, which are inaccessible to anything besides. They have the viler advantage also of affording a cheaper mode of conveyance.[26]

The Boat on the Serchio, though fragmentary and unpolished, gives the happiest picture of Shelley's life in the summer of 1821, and it is one of his few poems of unalloyed gaiety. As in *Julian and Maddalo* and the *Letter to Maria Gisborne*, he exercises his talent for turning conversation into informal verse, and this time the tone is heartier, to match the outdoor setting.

Shelley was, as a rule, glad to escape from the dirt and squalor of Italian cities to walk in the country or sail on a river. Pisa seems to have disgusted him less than other towns. He said that 'our roots were never struck so deeply as at Pisa',[27] and it was the one town to inspire a poem (discounting the stylized *Ode to Naples*). This poem, *Evening : Ponte al Mare, Pisa*, is tranquil, and assured in technique, though it echoes the Lechlade poem of 1815.

> The sun is set; the swallows are asleep;
> The bats are flitting fast in the gray air;
> The slow soft toads out of damp corners creep,
> And evening's breath, wandering here and there
> Over the quivering surface of the stream,
> Wakes not one ripple from its summer dream. . . .
>
> Within the surface of the fleeting river
> The wrinkled image of the city lay,
> Immovably unquiet, and forever
> It trembles, but it never fades away.
>
> 654. 1-6, 13-16

If Shelley worshipped any image it was this one, of reflexion in water, already used in the *Ode to Liberty* and *Witch of Atlas*, and deriving from Wordsworth's *Elegiac Stanzas on Peele Castle* —

Whene'er I looked, thy Image still was there;
It trembled, but it never passed away.

Exploiting the appeal of water-reflexions was one of the most successful of the landscape-gardeners' experiments in sensibility, and, thanks to the lakes at Field Place, where the images are startling in their clarity, Shelley's taste for reflexion was formed early. It was a taste he continued to cultivate, for he was rarely far from lake, river or sea, living in turn at Oxford, Keswick, Lynmouth, Tremadoc, Killarney, Windsor, Virginia Water, Geneva, Marlow, Venice, Naples. He wrote in a notebook in 1821 : 'Why is the reflection in that canal far more beautiful than the objects it reflects? The colours more vivid yet blended with more harmony; the openings from within into the soft and tender colours of the distant wood and the intersection of the mountain lines surpass and misrepresent truth.' [28] He liked reflexion in smooth water, but a ruffled surface was even better, for the object is purged of its grosser sensuous qualities and given a serener dream-like air. He was glad Pisa could impinge on his senses without advertising the stench of its back streets, just as to-day, when it is noise that most offends the senses, he might be glad to look at London's façade near Westminster from the south bank of the Thames. The reflexion, and the distance it implies, lend enchantment to the view and attenuate the roar of the Embankment traffic. For Shelley, a further attraction of a river is that its waters are *fleeting* : at successive instants the scene comes to the eye via different masses of water, which can impose their own stamp, their own wrinkles, on the image. And since at any moment a mere breeze may shatter it, the image has the same piquant uncertainty as a pleasant dream which may be shattered by waking. Reflexion, by destroying or diluting the qualities of sound, smell and touch, invites concentration on the purely visual, which can be artistically exploited, as the Impressionists showed. Shelley is one of their unsung forerunners, and his Impressionist view of Pisa could be a companion-piece to Monet's *Church at Vernon.*

Among the remaining poems of 1821 we can find Herrick's grace, in *Mutability* —

> The flower that smiles to-day
>   To-morrow dies;
> All that we wish to stay
>   Tempts and then flies.
> What is this world's delight?
> Lightning that mocks the night,
>   Brief even as bright.
>
> 640. 1-7;

resigned beauty, in the lines *To Edward Williams* —

> The crane o'er seas and forests seeks her home;
>   No bird so wild but has its quiet nest,
>   When it no more would roam;
> The sleepless billows on the ocean's breast
> Break like a bursting heart, and die in foam,
>   And thus at length find rest:
> Doubtless there is a place of peace
> Where *my* weak heart and all its throbs will cease.
>
> 645. 41-8;

and close argument, in the arid sonnet on *Political Greatness* with its references to 'herds whom tyranny makes tame. . . . History is but the shadow of their shame.' Shelley describes his *beau idéal* of political greatness at the end of the sonnet:

> Man who man would be,
> Must rule the empire of himself; in it
> Must be supreme, establishing his throne
> On vanquished will, quelling the anarchy
> Of hopes and fears, being himself alone.
>
> 642. 10-14

NOTES TO XV: *HELLAS*

1. See C. L. Cline, *Byron, Shelley and their Pisan Circle*, p. 28.
2. Quoted in Trelawny, *Recollections*, p. 168.
3. *Letters* ii. 322–3.
4. *Letters* ii. 330.
5. See I. Origo, *The Last Attachment*, p. 304.
6. For details of this brawl and its outcome, see Cline, *Pisan Circle*, pp. 91–154.
7. See *Letters* ii. 339, and Cline, *Pisan Circle*, p. 192.

8. W. Bagehot, *Literary Studies*, Everyman edition, i. 67.
9. Byron, letter to R. B. Hoppner, 10 Sept. 1820.
10. Clare's *Journal*, 1 May 1820.
11. I. Origo, *Allegra*, p. 79.
12. The version given by E. Blunden, *Shelley*, p. 191.
13. See Landor, *Imaginary Conversations, Southey and Landor*, ii.
14. See Trelawny, *Recollections*, p. 168, and Medwin, *Conversations of Lord Byron*, p. 364.
15. Lady Blessington, *Journal*, p. 66.
16. Byron, letter to T. Moore, 4 Mar. 1822. For detailed discussion of the friendship of Shelley and Byron, see J. Buxton, *Byron and Shelley*.
17. Shelley's preface to *Hellas*, Oxford edition, pp. 446–8.
18. *Jul* vii. 223.
19. *Letters* ii. 411.
20. *Macbeth*, iv. i. 118; i. iii. 97; i. iii. 146–7; v. v. 19, 22.
21. B. Russell, *Fact and Fiction*, p. 15; also *Autobiography*, Vol. III (1969), p. 172.
22. Curiously enough, the original manuscript, and Mary's transcript, had the second verse of the poem first. See I. Massey, *Posthumous Poems of Shelley*, pp. 93 and 257.
23. For an opposite view, see B. P. Kurtz, *Pursuit of Death*, p. 245.
24. Dante, *Inferno*, XXXIII. 30.
25. Lines 81–6 in the text as amended by Neville Rogers, *Times Lit. Sup.*, 10 Aug. 1951.
26. *Letters* i. 490.
27. *Letters* ii. 339.
28. N. Rogers, *Shelley at Work*, p. 149.

XVI

THE TRIUMPH OF LIFE

the tusked, ramshackling sea exults . . .
As I sail out to die.

D. THOMAS, *Poem on his birthday*

1

IN the first three months of 1822 the circle of friends at
Pisa was thriving; but the social round was now almost
routine and the search for diversions became more deliberate.
One of these diversions was amateur theatricals, and it was
planned to act *Othello*. Though this plan came to nothing
the interest in drama continued. Williams was writing a
play and Shelley was supposed to be at work on another,
which was to have drawn on Trelawny's piratical adventures.
Shelley's play, known as the *Unfinished Drama*, might well
be renamed the *Unstarted Drama*, for its two fragments of
filigree verse have no dramatic interest.

In contrast stands another fragmentary play, *Charles the
First*, which shows signs of being genuinely dramatic.
Shelley had begun it over two years before and he now returned to it. But the factual discipline irked him : he complained that *Charles the First* was 'a devil of a nut to crack',[1]
and he wrote, or sketched out, only five scenes. In the first
we see the Masque of the Inns of Court, graced by the
King's presence and punctuated by comments from the
onlookers. A few of the spectators are impressed by the bigwigs and the pageantry ; most are disgusted at the vanity —

When lawyers masque 'tis time for honest men
To strip the vizor from their purposes.

490. 76-7

In the second scene the revelry is over and Charles is
dispatching State business. After rather curt orders to his

officers of State — Strafford, Laud and the rest — he thinks
aloud about future policy, prompted by his clown Archy,
whose shafts are feathered with unShelleyan metaphors :

I saw a gross vapour hovering in a stinking ditch over the carcass
of a dead ass, some rotten rags, and broken dishes — the wrecks
of what once administered to the stuffing-out and ornament of a
worm of worms. His Grace of Canterbury expects to enter the
New Jerusalem some Palm Sunday in triumph on the ghost of
this ass.

502. 436-41

Scenes III to V, which are fragmentary, do little more than
confirm that his Grace of Canterbury, Laud, would have
been villain of the piece.

To-day it is an article of faith that drama cannot succeed unless its idiom is contemporary, and that imitating
Shakespeare is the shortest road to ruin. If so, *Charles the
First* was foredoomed to disaster, for Shelley modelled it on
the Shakespearean history-play and did not avoid some faint
echoes from *Hamlet*, *Lear*, *Macbeth* and *Richard II*. If we
could forget this article of faith, however, our verdict would
be less confident. The play might have had *The Cenci*'s
virtues without its faults, for the language is strong and
direct, and the characters are convincing, though Laud is
perhaps a little too black, too like Count Cenci. The clown
Archy, next-of-kin to Lear's Fool, is, with his paradoxes
and veiled policy-criticisms, a character outside Shelley's
usual range.

The only lines in *Charles the First* now widely known
come from Archy's song in the fifth scene, which has nothing
to do with the play :

> A widow bird sate mourning for her love
>   Upon a wintry bough ;
> The frozen wind crept on above,
>   The freezing stream below.
>
> There was no leaf upon the forest bare,
>   No flower upon the ground,
> And little motion in the air
>   Except the mill-wheel's sound.

507. 9-16

Though the first line now seems rather sentimental, there is nothing else to cavil at. The poem has the finality of tinkling glass, and it exacts from many a reader the passing tribute of a moment's silence before he resumes the normal tempo of life. Its wintry tone sets it apart from the spring-and-summer Romanticism of its time : the widow bird is more like Hardy's aged thrush than Wordsworth's linnet.

2

Shelley had not at first taken much notice of Jane Williams. Domesticated, unintellectual, with a baby to look after and another imminent, she did not seem likely to have much in common with him. But when he came to know her better, he found her more congenial. She could calm him when he was on edge, or rouse him when he was glum. Her trump card was hypnotism, or 'animal magnetism' as it was then called.[2] Shelley liked taking a dose of this medicine to banish the pressing torments of consciousness, and he left a record of one such session in a poem, *The Magnetic Lady to her Patient*. Shelley was charmed, too, by Jane's singing, to the tunes she played on a guitar he gave her. She was the last of the singers, like Clare and Sophia Stacey, for whom he wrote short lyrics ; the last and homeliest of the soul-mates, in the lineage of Elizabeth Hitchener, Cornelia Turner and Emilia Viviani ; and the last of Shelley's friends to be pursued by Hogg, who made up for failing to win Harriet or Mary by living with Jane for the last thirty-five years of his life.

The first of several poems addressed 'To Jane' is the eager *Invitation* :

> Best and brightest, come away !
> Fairer far than this fair Day,
> Which, like thee to those in sorrow,
> Comes to bid a sweet good-morrow
> To the rough Year just awake
> In its cradle on the brake. . . .

Away, away, from men and towns,
To the wild wood and the downs —
To the silent wilderness
Where the soul need not repress
Its music lest it should not find
An echo in another's mind. . . .

668. 1-6, 21-6

This seems to beg comparison with the last part of *Epi-psychidion*, where Emilia is invited to the paradisal isle. But the motive and the cue for passion were not likely to come from one so comfortable and familiar as Jane : the passionate imperatives of *Epipsychidion* would be out of place here. Instead, Shelley reverts to the tone of his conversational poems. Like them, *The Invitation* is happy, catching the spirit as well as the metre of *L'Allegro*. It is also gracious and civilized, the first poem in which Shelley treats a sexual theme in level tones. Love was the last subject to be integrated into his conversational style : now he was ready to use the style in a major poem. That was to come in *The Triumph of Life*.

Jane accepted the invitation, and Shelley looked back with pleasure in *The Recollection* :

We wandered to the Pine Forest
    That skirts the Ocean's foam,
The lightest wind was in its nest,
    The tempest in its home.
The whispering waves were half asleep,
    The clouds were gone to play,
And on the bosom of the deep
    The smile of Heaven lay ;
It seemed as if the hour were one
    Sent from beyond the skies,
Which scattered from above the sun
    A light of Paradise.

We paused amid the pines that stood
    The giants of the waste,
Tortured by storms to shapes as rude
    As serpents interlaced. . . .

669. 9-24

This is perhaps the most serene of all Shelley's poems. The windless weather is so fused with Jane's calming influence that we sometimes forget which is which. The gentle, rather monotonous beat of the metre and the careful pictures of Nature seem to imply that nothing will ever change, from now till eternity :

> We paused beside the pools that lie
> Under the forest bough, —
> Each seemed as 'twere a little sky
> Gulfed in a world below ;
> A firmament of purple light
> Which in the dark earth lay,
> More boundless than the depth of night,
> And purer than the day.
>
> 670. 53-60

The poem ends with a flash of self-analysis, and a tacit tribute to Jane's soothing power :

> Less oft is peace in Shelley's mind,
> Than calm in waters, seen.
>
> 670. 87-8

Shelley wrote several poems in this 'Pine Forest that skirts the Ocean's foam' near Pisa. Trelawny found him there one day, sitting beside a fallen tree and gazing into the dark mirror of one of the pools, with books and papers scattered round. Trelawny picked up a fragment :

It was a frightful scrawl; words smeared out with his finger, and one upon the other, over and over in tiers, and all run together in most 'admired disorder'; it might have been taken for a sketch of a marsh overgrown with bulrushes, and the blots for wild ducks; such a dashed-off daub as self-conceited artists mistake for a manifestation of genius. On my observing this to him he answered : 'When my brain gets heated with thought, it soon boils, and throws off images and words faster than I can skim them off. In the morning, when cooled down, out of the rude sketch as you justly call it, I shall attempt a drawing.' [3]

This brings to life the process of poetic creation Shelley described in the *Defence of Poetry*. At times like this a stream of ideas and images seethed from the subliminal into his mind. As Macaulay remarked, 'the words bard and inspiration, which seem so cold and affected when applied to other modern writers, have a perfect propriety when applied to him'.[4]

The poem Trelawny found him writing was *With a Guitar, to Jane*, a piece of make-believe to go with his gift to her. In this poem his friends and himself are rechristened as characters from *The Tempest*, a favourite play of his. Edward and Jane are Ferdinand and Miranda; Shelley is Ariel, and he would be amazed to know how often this innocent pseudonym has since been misused as a guide to his character. *With a Guitar*, like *The Recollection*, mixes the playful with the poignant:

> Ariel to Miranda: — Take
> This slave of Music, for the sake
> Of him who is the slave of thee,
> And teach it all the harmony
> In which thou canst, and only thou,
> Make the delighted spirit glow. . . .
>
> 672. 1-6

The honeyed melody of such poems as this misled Arnold, author of many fallacious pronouncements about Shelley, to suggest that his proper sphere was music, whereas the truth seems to be that Shelley, like Yeats and Lamb, had no real ear for music.[5]

Another poem which may (or may not) be linked with Jane begins with the well-worn lines

> When the lamp is shattered
> The light in the dust lies dead —
> When the cloud is scattered
> The rainbow's glory is shed. . . .
>
> 667. 1-4

This poem has been exhibited to the public eye in far too many anthologies, and, as if such over-exposure was not embarrassing enough for so shy an object, it has in recent years also become a battleground for rival schools of critics. It has emerged from the fray carnage-strewn, having lost for ever its original innocent demeanour. Some of the comments on the poem have been a little perverse, not

z

least those of F. R. Leavis, who did not like *shed* in line 4 :
'only in the vaguest and slackest state of mind . . . could
one so describe the fading of a rainbow'.[6] Yet the bow is
created by the internal reflexion of sunlight in waterdrops
shed by the cloud, so that its glory is literally *shed* with the
last drops of the shower.

The first three stanzas offer little, except their skilled
verse technique, to justify the poem's high anthology-status.
The fourth and last stanza is better, though not without
flaws :

> [Love's] passions will rock thee
>   As the storms rock the ravens on high ;
> Bright reason will mock thee,
>   Like the sun from a wintry sky.
> From thy nest every rafter
>   Will rot, and thine eagle home
> Leave thee naked to laughter,
>   When leaves fall and cold winds come.
>
> 668. 25-32

Reasoners mock a downcast lover as the falsely bright sun
mocks the frozen on a wintry day : Shelley often calls
reason and thought *bright*, so the image is unforced. The
nest, once 'cemented' by love, decays with love's departure,
and cannot keep out hostile sneers (*cold winds*). *Eagle home*
seems to be merely an elaboration of *nest*.

Shelley kept till the end his power to strike fierce sparks
of feeling from material supplied gratis by Nature. We can
see such coruscation in two of the shorter poems of 1822.
One, whose text needs revising, is the delicate miniature
beginning :

> There was a little lawny islet
> By anemone and violet,
>   Like mosaic, paven. . . .
>
> 675. 1-3

The other is the dirge :

> Rough wind, that moanest loud
>   Grief too sad for song ;
> Wild wind, when sullen cloud
>   Knells all the night long ;

Sad storm, whose tears are vain,
Bare woods, whose branches strain,
Deep caves and dreary main, —
Wail, for the world's wrong!

                                   673. 1-8.

This is a poem in which the sound strongly reinforces the sense. The long-drawn initial spondees, such as *wild wind* and *bare woods*, are alone enough to create a gloomy tone, while the main verb *wail* is more satisfying because it caps a series of long *a*'s — *vain, bare, strain, caves, main*.

3

As spring advanced, the Pisan circle began to show signs of fragmenting. The protracted official inquiry into the brawl with the dragoon had set everyone's nerves on edge, and Byron, who had most to lose, was very irritable. Shelley found that two subjects particularly upset him, and both had to be discussed. The first was Hunt and the second Clare. When Shelley invited Hunt to Italy to set up and edit a periodical, eventually called *The Liberal*, he well knew that its fate lay in Byron's hands. Though it was Byron who had first suggested the periodical, the Hunts' unlucky delay on their voyage gave him time to change his mind. His English friends told him he would throw away what remained of his literary reputation if he publicly allied himself with the 'Cockney' Hunt. Byron would now have liked to withdraw altogether, and Shelley found him difficult to humour. To make matters worse he was speaking of Clare more cruelly than Shelley could tolerate. For Hunt's sake he could not quarrel with Byron. The only course was to leave Pisa. The Shelleys and Williamses had planned to rent a house on the coast for the summer. The sooner the better it seemed. Only one house was to let, Casa Magni, near Lerici, remote, small and inconvenient: was it worth taking? The question was answered when they heard Allegra had died of typhus in her convent at Bagnacavallo. Clare happened to be staying with them at the time and Shelley would not let her be told until she was at a safe distance from Byron. So he hustled the party to Casa Magni, where they arrived on 1 May.

Despite its many defects, Casa Magni was superbly situated. Behind, to the north, was a steep hillside, thickly wooded. In front, washing the walls, and sometimes the ground floor, too, were the waters of the Bay of Lerici, one of the many bays within the almost landlocked Gulf of Spezia. The coast was rugged, wild and weirdly beautiful, noted for 'alternate flawless calms and shattering sudden storms'.[7] 'The natives were wilder than the place', wrote Mary in her note on the poems of 1822,

more like savages than any people I ever before lived among. Many a night they passed on the beach, singing, or rather howling ; the women dancing about among the waves that broke at their feet, the men leaning against the rocks and joining in their loud wild chorus. We could get no provisions nearer than Sarzana, at a distance of three miles and a half off, with the torrent of the Magra between ; and even there the supply was very deficient. Had we been wrecked on an island of the South Seas, we could scarcely have felt ourselves farther from civilization and comfort.

Shelley was delighted with the place, and on fine days he and Williams sailed around the Gulf of Spezia in their new yacht the *Don Juan* (or *Ariel*), 'a perfect plaything for the summer' as Williams called her.[8] The *Don Juan* was 24 feet long, with an 8-foot beam and a draught of 4 feet. 'She is a fine spanking boat and sails like the devil',[9] wrote Trelawny, the professional sailor ; a shade too lively indeed for the amateur captain Williams and the incompetent seaman Shelley.

When Hunt at last reached Leghorn, at the end of June, Shelley and Williams went to welcome him : the *Don Juan* covered the forty miles from Casa Magni in fine style. Once the greetings were over Shelley began the delicate task of sounding Byron, whose distaste for *The Liberal* grew suddenly stronger when he found that Hunt had an ailing wife and six unruly children. And, on the very day Shelley arrived, Byron heard that his plans for the summer were ruined, because the Gambas had been ordered to leave Tuscany. So at first Byron was unhelpful. Within a few days, however, under Shelley's persuasion, he promised his *Vision of Judgment* for the first number of *The Liberal*, a handsome offer ensuring it success.

After disposing of this and other business Shelley and Williams were anxious to be back at Casa Magni. It was hot and sultry as they set sail from Leghorn just after noon on Monday, 8 July 1822. Some two hours later, when ten miles out, a squall hid them from view. The *Don Juan* was not seen again until fished up from ten fathoms in September.

Shelley's body was washed ashore at Viareggio on 18 July, and was buried in the sand for nearly a month. Then, by the sea's edge under a blazing August sun, the remains were burnt. Trelawny organized the funeral rites; Byron and Hunt were also there.

In retrospect there seems to be a touch of the inevitable about Shelley's death : being drowned and cremated in Italy in summer — what fitter end for one so fond of water, warmth and blue Italian skies? At the time, however, his death, a month before his thirtieth birthday, made no more stir than his unread volumes of verse. In London, Castlereagh's suicide was the wonder of the hour. For, by a curious irony, the poet and the statesman, so opposed in their beliefs and at opposite ends of Europe, had their funerals only four days apart.

4

Shelley's last poem, *The Triumph of Life*, was written in the early summer of 1822, sometimes aboard that fatal and perfidious bark the *Don Juan*. Death stepped in at line 544, and although we cannot judge the poem as a whole from the fragment written, it is long enough to reveal some changes in technique. Here at last is the detachment we look for vainly in his early work. Had the theme proved worthy of the language and tone, *The Triumph of Life* would have surpassed most, if not all, of his previous poems. Unfortunately we cannot be sure what the theme was, since

the title is doubly ambiguous. *Triumph* may mean simply
procession, for the existing fragment describes a procession of
phantoms. More probably, *triumph* means *victory*. If so,
is it the victory of Man over Nature and the restraints now
stifling him, as in *Prometheus Unbound*? Or is it the victory
of Life over men, as analogy with Petrarch's *Trionfi* would
suggest? The settled melancholy of the existing fragment,
and references to Life the *conqueror*, might imply the gloomier
alternative. But it would be unwise to jump to conclusions: for Act I of *Prometheus Unbound* was just as grim,
and gave no sign of the happy ending; also, the title
'Triumph of Life' strikes a buoyant note, and the gloomier
interpretation would imply an irony quite foreign to the
poem's tone, which is placid and objective, with more of
sorrow than of sarcasm. On balance it seems more probable
that Shelley intended to show Man triumphing over his
present travails, and that the existing fragment does correspond to Act I of *Prometheus Unbound*.

The first 40 lines of *The Triumph of Life* paint a cheerful
picture of dawn over the Apennine foothills, rather like *The
Boat on the Serchio*. After this painless, if misleading, start,
Shelley proceeds at once to his sombre vision of the human
race:

> Methought I sate beside a public way
> Thick strewn with summer dust, and a great stream
> Of people there was hurrying to and fro,
> Numerous as gnats upon the evening gleam,
> All hastening onward; yet none seemed to know
> Whither he went, or whence he came, or why
> He made one of the multitude.

508. 43-9

In the midst of this nightmare rush-hour, setting the pace,
is a chariot emitting a cold glare — the chariot of worldly
life. Its deformed charioteer has four faces, all blindfolded:

> little profit brings
> Speed in the van and blindness in the rear.

Closely chained to the chariot are those who, given power
over their fellow-men, failed to do good, through weakness,

folly or evil intent : many a buried Caesar, many a bygone
bishop, many a crowned head — all but saints and those who
died before their early ideals faded,

> All but the sacred few who could not tame
> Their spirits to the conqueror's — but as soon
> As they had touched the world with living flame,
> Fled back like eagles to their native noon ;
> Or those who put aside the diadem
> Of earthly thrones or gems.
>
> 510. 128-33

In front, youths and maidens outspeed the chariot, dancing
in wild ecstasy. For a time they avoid the worldly taint.
Then 'the fiery band which held their natures snaps', and
they fall under the chariot exhausted. Toiling along behind
the chariot is a hopeless throng :

> Old men and women foully disarrayed
> Shake their grey hair in the insulting wind,
> Limp in the dance and strain with limbs decayed
> To reach the car of light which leaves them still
> Farther behind and deeper in the shade.
>
> 511. 165-9

This picture of the pageant of life, stinging in its finality,
embodies some of Shelley's firmest beliefs. The enigmatic
four-faced charioteer is probably intended to personify those
who, though given the talents to guide mankind aright, have
been seduced by the glittering prizes of worldly power and
have forgotten their ideals during their climb. To-day,
when the chariot is being urged ever faster, by drivers just
as blind, to who knows what end, this imagery has lost none
of its sting. The crowds swarming round the chariot, given
no lead, may find transient joy in the delights of young love,
but they worship only the Pandemian goddess and not the
principle of disinterested love, which might give them a
worthy aim and end their random drifting. When they
have tired of their youthful revelry they wallow behind the
chariot, trying to recapture past pleasures. They succeed
only in sinking ever deeper into the shifting sands of worldly
compromise.

Shelley next finds a guide to help him make sense of the chaotic procession:

> Struck to the heart by this sad pageantry,
> Half to myself I said, 'And what is this?
> Whose shape is that within the car? And why' —
> I would have added — 'is all here amiss?'
> But a voice answered — 'Life!'
>
> 511. 176-80

The voice comes from

> what I thought was an old root which grew
> To strange distortion out of the hill side.
>
> 511. 182-3

This root-like form proves to be the shade 'of what was once Rousseau', and, just as Virgil guides Dante in the *Inferno* and *Purgatorio*, so Rousseau picks out for Shelley the interesting figures in the procession. The difference is that Virgil and Dante travel far while inspecting the sinners in the nine circles of Hell and the seven cornices of Mount Purgatory, whereas Rousseau and Shelley stand still as the ghastly pageant passes. Shelley wisely avoids trying to rival Dante at mapping the next world.

Rousseau first points to the shade of Napoleon —

> I felt my cheek
> Alter, to see the great form pass away,
> Whose grasp had left the giant world so weak
> That every pigmy kicked it as it lay;
> And much I grieved to think how power and will
> In opposition rule our mortal day,
> And why God made irreconcilable
> Good and the means of good.
>
> 512. 224-31

Then the 'mighty phantoms of an elder day' appear:

> All that is mortal of great Plato there
> Expiates the joy and woe his master knew not;
> The star that ruled his doom was far too fair,
> And life, where long that flower of Heaven grew not,
> Conquered the heart by love, which gold, or pain,
> Or age, or sloth, or slavery could subdue not.
>
> 513. 254-9

Plato is debarred from the highest place because he condoned homosexual love — or so Shelley seems to imply by his elaborate pun on the word *Aster*, which is (1) the name of the youth addressed in the Platonic epigram prefixed to *Adonais*, (2) the Greek for 'star', the *star* of line 256, and (3) the *flower* of line 257. After Plato, standing out from the ruck of Roman emperors, pontiffs 'who rose like shadows between man and God', and others of less note, came Aristotle and Alexander,

> The tutor and his pupil, whom Dominion
> Followed as tame as vulture in a chain.
>
> 513. 261-2

Though Alexander's conquests did not long survive his death, Aristotle's ideas lived on,

> Throned in the thoughts of men, and still had kept
> The jealous keys of Truth's eternal doors,
> If Bacon's eagle spirit had not leapt
> Like lightning out of darkness.
>
> 513. 267-70

Tired of this gloomy flow of spectres Shelley questions his guide, who obligingly recalls his own life-story with more interpretation than in the *Confessions*. The story is long and detailed, but only the outline need concern us. When young, Rousseau knew the mystic communion with Nature felt by many Romantics after him, when the earth seemed alive with 'magic sounds' and bathed in a supernatural light. The climax came when 'a Shape all light' offered him a crystal glass, and

> as a shut lily stricken by the wand
> Of dewy morning's vital alchemy,

he rose to drink from it. But before the glass touched his lips he hesitated; and the vision faded into a colder light which, so he was to find, emanated from the chariot of worldly life. The 'Shape all light' cannot be accurately defined. It might be described as the essence of what is seen or felt by those who think they have had mystic communion with some higher power, but it may also be intended to represent merely the guiding light of those who have high ideals. The 'Shape all light' is thus akin to the 'awful loveliness' of the *Hymn to Intellectual Beauty*, the 'white radiance' of *Adonais* and the 'Being robed in such exceeding glory' of *Epipsychidion*. This brilliant shape is usually seen only for a moment, because it soon fades into the light of common day, like the morning star after dawn, unless kept constantly in view; and only the chosen few are capable of such constancy. Rousseau often glimpsed the light when he renounced city life and retired alone to the country. Yet he was continually being lured or forced back into the polluting stream of worldly life: he lacked the will to keep the shape always in view. It is not surprising that, for Shelley, the countrified *Julie* (or *Nouvelle Héloïse*) was the most appealing of Rousseau's books. His wish to be alone with Nature, so evident in the *Confessions* and *Julie*, was a seed which fell on fertile ground and grew into perhaps the brightest flower of the Romantic movement, cultivated most by Wordsworth. But of all the English Romantics it was Shelley who was most like Rousseau. He shared Rousseau's extreme sensibility, his cold-shouldering by the literary public, his consequent persecution-complex, and his likings for mountain, forest and lake, for drifting aimlessly in a small boat and for treating waves as symbols of troubles in life.[10]

Having finished his life-story, Rousseau explains how the phantoms arise. People are continually throwing off shadows of themselves, he says, and the chariot's 'creative ray' transforms these shadows into the phantoms Shelley has seen. Producing shadows is exhausting, and the parent forms, like Rousseau, soon fall by the wayside, 'those soonest from whose forms most shadows passed'. This is clear as far as it goes, but it leaves much unsaid. Shelley wants to hear more:

'Then what is life?' I cried.

But as Rousseau begins his reply, the manuscript of the poem ends.

5

The Triumph of Life, with its hints of Dante and Petrarch, is a reminder that English poetry owes more to Italy than to any other foreign country. The process began when

Chaucer borrowed from Boccaccio, and from then on Italian influence grew, reaching a climax in Elizabeth's reign. A dozen of Shakespeare's plays have scenes set in Italy; many of the finest effects in the *Faerie Queene* come straight from the epics of Tasso and Ariosto; Petrarch's sonnet form, brought in by Wyatt and Surrey, was accepted by a decisive majority of poets. This Italian infiltration could not be ignored by later poets, and, as they wrestled with their rough native tongue, they had to keep half an eye on standards set by a language which grace and fluency have moulded. In the eighteenth century there arose a new taste for things Italian in the visual arts: the Italian garden, the craze for Canaletto, Palladian architecture, the landscape-garden mimicking (via Claude) Italian scenes, the aristocratic habit of the Grand Tour. The result was a revival of interest in Italian arts and literature, which showed itself strongly in poetry. Most of the major English poets — namely Wordsworth, Byron, Shelley and Keats — were in Italy in 1820; Landor was there, too, Hunt and Rogers were soon to come and Moore had just left. This mass emigration marked the high summer of Italian influence; the Brownings provide an Indian summer; then winter came. In 1821 'the Italian language is indispensably necessary for all young ladies',[11] but by the end of the century German had displaced Italian as the Englishman's second European language. To-day, German is widely taught in schools, Italian rarely. Ariosto and Tasso, classics for so long, are now mere names to most readers, and Dante is the only Italian poet represented in Everyman's Library.

Though Shelley's familiarity with Italian had for some years helped to smooth the flow of his lyrics, *The Triumph of Life* is the only major poem in which the chief literary influences are Italian. In *Prometheus Unbound, Adonais* and *Hellas,* Aeschylus and Theocritus provided models; in *Epipsychidion* Dante is one of several to whom he is indebted; in *The Cenci* he chose an Italian subject but looked to the Elizabethan dramatists for his style. In *The Triumph of Life* Dante's ghost haunts the poem from start to finish, reminding us of T. S. Eliot's remark that Shelley was the only nineteenth-century poet capable of following Dante's footsteps.[12] Shelley first approached Italian literature in 1813, by way of Tasso and Ariosto. As the years wore on he turned more to Petrarch and most of all to Dante. The phantom procession in *The Triumph of Life*, like that in the *Mask of Anarchy*, derives from Petrarch's *Trionfi*,[13] and the title of Shelley's poem was probably suggested by the third of the *Trionfi*, the *Trionfo della Morte*. But *The Triumph of Life* is Dantean in its cosmic sweep, in presenting a picture of life after death, and in many details. The first of these details comes right at the start. Shelley's opening lines are:

> Swift as a spirit hastening to his task
> Of glory and of good, the Sun sprang forth
> Rejoicing in his splendour, and the mask
> Of darkness fell from the awakened Earth . . .
> > at the birth
> Of light, the Ocean's orison arose,
> To which the birds tempered their matin lay.
>
> 507. 1-4, 6-8

This passage is not unlike lines 37-43 of the *Inferno*,

> The hour was morning's prime, and on his way
> Aloft the sun ascended with those stars,
> That with him rose when Love divine first moved
> Those its fair works; so that with joyous hope
> All things conspired to fill me, the gay skin
> Of that swift animal, the matin dawn,
> And the sweet season.

— as they are rendered by Cary, whose translation Shelley knew well. A second obvious link is the parallel between the Shelley-Rousseau companionship in *The Triumph of Life* and the Dante-Virgil in the *Inferno* and *Purgatorio*. A third link is the naming of the famous people in the procession, a feature common to Dante's *Divina Commedia* and Petrarch's *Trionfi*. A fourth link, the *terza rima*, may be more apparent than real: Shelley may have been swayed more by the success of Byron's *Prophecy of Dante* (1821), which is in *terza rima*, than by Dante himself or Petrarch. Though Shelley does not make Dante take part in the phantom procession

in *The Triumph of Life*, he duly pays his meed of tribute later
in the poem :

> a wonder worthy of the rhyme
> Of him who from the lowest depths of hell,
> Through every paradise and through all glory,
> Love led serene, and who returned to tell
> In words of hate and awe the wondrous story.

518. 471-5

Shelley does not always agree with Dante. For example,
he stigmatizes those who are preoccupied with worldly life
and hanker after the dead-sea fruits of ambition, a group
Dante places quite high, in Ante-Purgatory. There is also
a difference in presentation, for Shelley's phantoms are
frighteningly aimless, more like Kafka's characters than
Dante's neatly sorted groups of saints and sinners. To
conclude this Dantean paragraph we may hazard the guess
that the existing section of *The Triumph of Life* corresponds
roughly to the *Inferno* — or perhaps the *Inferno* plus *Purgatorio*, for Shelley would presumably not have followed the
Catholics in their threefold division of the after-world. If
this guess is right, *The Triumph of Life* might have ended with
a new *Paradiso* in some empyrean remote from the domain
of the chariot of worldly life and peopled by the cast-off
shadows of men's better selves. If this was the plan, the
theme, mood and method would be as summarized by the
child-like Spirit of Earth in *Prometheus Unbound* :

> Those ugly human shapes and visages
> Of which I spoke as having wrought me pain,
> Passed floating through the air . . .
>   . . . and those
> From whom they passed seemed mild and lovely forms
> After some foul disguise had fallen.

250. 65-70

Apart from Dante and Petrarch, literary influences on
The Triumph of Life are hard to find. There is a dubious
echo from Byron's *Prophecy of Dante*. A phrase here and there
has a Wordsworthian ring. The only certain antecedent is
in the *Faerie Queene*. The chariot of worldly life, overrunning

men, derives from Lucifera's coach, drawn by six 'unequall beasts', under whose hooves

> all scattered lay
> Dead sculs and bones of men, whose life had gone astray.[14]

In handling words Shelley was never more skilful than in *The Triumph of Life*. First, there is the metre. *Terza rima* is difficult in English, which is short of rhymes, and no poet has mastered it better. After his first try in *Prince Athanase* he kept his hand in with *The Woodman and the Nightingale*, the *Ode to the West Wind* and some translations of Dante. In *The Triumph of Life*, unrevised though it is, the *terza rima* has a fascination comparable, 'in its endless and interlinked progression, with the trooping of the sea waves towards the land'.[15] For, like the waves, the rhymes seem inevitable yet random. The effect is enhanced by the language, realistic and carefully casual. This is a mature, easy, plain style, not unlike T. S. Eliot's in *Four Quartets*. In his last two poems, *Charles the First* and *The Triumph of Life*, where this new style emerges, Shelley 'touched ground in the actual world and with no unsure foot, as he never did before'.[16] Earthbound readers often complain he has too little solid, material imagery. They applaud his own judgement : 'you might as well go to a gin-shop for a leg of mutton, as expect anything human or earthly from me'.[17] Yet this is a self-cancelling statement, of the 'I never say "never"' category, and there is every sign that a blunter style would have become habitual, if death had not claimed him. The language is not always flat and realistic in *The Triumph of Life*, however ; sometimes it is leavened by what might be called purple patches in his old manner. Rousseau's life-story, for example, takes us halfway back to *Alastor*. And Shelley still uses the technique of impassioned observation, as in this vignette of 'the old moon in the new moon's arms' :

> Like the young moon
> When on the sunlit limits of the night
> Her white shell trembles amid crimson air,

And . . . [doth] . . . bear
The ghost of her dead mother, whose dim form
Bends in dark aether from her infant's chair.[18]

509. 79-85

Though the language is flatter in *The Triumph of Life*, Shelley's philosophy of life is unchanged, and *Prometheus Unbound* needs no amendment. In the existing fragment of *The Triumph of Life* the spotlight is on integrity, on knowing yourself — the γνῶθι σεαυτόν so dear to the Greeks. This quality is vital in *Prometheus Unbound*, too, but Prometheus has shown it before Act I begins. In *The Triumph of Life* Shelley seems to be more exacting in his definition of the individual good life, which he implies should be spent pursuing the *summum bonum*, that 'shape all light' which lures artists, scientists, mystics, thinkers and youthful idealists to toil in its service. In judging Rousseau and Plato, Shelley seems to demand unbroken allegiance to this ideal, rejecting the comfortable Christian compromise of forgiving lapses. Had this trend in his thought gone on, he might have become preoccupied with the theme of loyalty to the guiding light, much as Shakespeare was with loyalty to individuals or the State. Can we keep this light in constant view if we are immersed in the dirty stream of worldly life? *The Triumph of Life* seems to answer 'No': the mud soon gets in our eyes. Instead we should avoid the 'contagion of the world's slow stain' by retiring, before our youthful ideals have faded, to live humbly, unnoticed and unsullied, far from the busy hum of men, the life Rousseau yearned for and Wordsworth stood for. This would probably be Shelley's advice to to-day's harassed men-of-affairs, who waste their energies trying to run ever faster in the treadmill of worldly life.

In *The Triumph of Life* Shelley was beginning to acquire the Olympian detachment which gives Dante and Shakespeare so much of their strength. Previously his feelings overpowered him when he looked at the world. These strong reactions were useful when he confronted Nature, but disturbing when he confronted men and women. The detachment that came in his last year was accompanied by

disillusion, as we can see from these verses he wrote four days
before he died :

> The hours are flying
> And joys are dying
> And hope is sighing
> There is
> Far more to fear
> In the coming year
> Than desire can bear
> In this.[19]

His subsequent poems, if he had lived to write them, would
probably have been cooler and more realistic. Would they
also have outshone his earlier work? His technique was
growing surer as the years passed, and the rule that a poet
is at his best after the age of 30 might have applied as well
to him as to Shakespeare, Milton, Wordsworth, Byron,
Tennyson and indeed almost every major English poet who
lived to be over 30.

NOTES TO XVI: *THE TRIUMPH OF LIFE*

1. *Letters* ii. 373.
2. See Southey, *Letters from England*, pp. 304–15.
3. Trelawny, *Recollections*, p. 197.
4. Macaulay, *Essay on Bunyan*, written 1831.
5. See M. Arnold, *Essays in Criticism*, first series, Maurice de Guérin; and
W. M. Rossetti, *Memoir of Shelley*, p. 96.
6. F. R. Leavis, *Revaluation*, p. 218. For hostile analyses, see *Revaluation*,
pp. 216–21, and A. Tate, *Reason in Madness* (1941), p. 97. For friendly ones,
see Propst, *Shelley's Versification*, pp. 64–5, Fogle, *Imagery of Keats and Shelley*,
pp. 258–64, and Wilson, *Shelley's Later Poetry*, pp. 26–30.
7. Aldous Huxley, *Those Barren Leaves* (Penguin, 1951), p. 80.
8. E. E. Williams, *Journal*, p. 148.
9. See R. Glynn Grylls, *Trelawny*, p. 83.
10. See Rousseau, *Confessions*, pp. 594 and 596, in Penguin translation.
11. New Monthly Magazine. See Brand, *Italy and the English Romantics*, p. 37.
12. T. S. Eliot, *Essay on Dante* in *Selected Essays* (1932).
13. See I. Roe, *Shelley, the last Phase*, pp. 196–210, for Petrarch's influence.
14. *Faerie Queene*, I. iv. 18 and 36.
15. *Shelley Memorials*, p. 191.
16. Todhunter, *Notes on the 'Triumph of Life'*: Shelley Society Papers, Part I.
17. *Letters* ii. 363.
18. Here and elsewhere I have made use of new texts by G. M. Matthews,
Studia Neophil., vol. 32 (1960) and D. H. Reiman, *Shelley's Triumph of Life*.
19. N. Rogers, *Shelley at Work*, p. 288.

XVII

LOOKING BACK

ὁ βίος βραχύς, ἡ δὲ τέχνη μακρή.

The life so short, the craft so long to learn.

HIPPOCRATES, *Aphorisms*

1

SHELLEY'S death did not pass entirely unnoticed. The upholders of the *status quo*, who attacked him while he was alive with a venom which now seems almost comic, seized their chance to have a final fling. Typical of the obituary notices in the Tory papers was the *Courier's*: 'Shelley, the writer of some infidel poetry, has been drowned; *now* he knows whether there is a God or no'.[1] The *Gentleman's Magazine* belied its name by referring to 'this tyro of the Juan school, that pre-eminent academy of Infidels, Blasphemers, Seducers and Wantons'.[2] In contrast, the *Examiner* printed a panegyric:

> while Freedom still retains
> Amid the waters of Corruption's flood,
> An Ararat whereon to rest her foot, —
> Thy spirit still will be revered on earth,
> And commune with the minds of unborn men.[1]

And Beddoes produced another:

> Write it in gold — a Spirit of the sun
> An Intellect ablaze with heavenly thoughts,
> A Soul with all the dews of pathos shining,
> Odorous with love, and sweet to silent woe
> With the dark glories of concentrate song,
> Was sphered in mortal earth.[2]

Among those who usually stood aloof from party strife, Lamb and Southey are worth quoting, for their reactions show how easily false reports and differences of opinion can

361

warp the judgement.   The kind Elia wrote, 'Shelley the
great Atheist has gone down by water to eternal fire', and
suggested the epitaph:

> Full fathom five the Atheist lies,
> Of his bones are hell-dice made.

The generous Southey wrote : 'I knew that miserable man,
and am well acquainted with his dreadful history. . . .
Shelley was not . . . wicked by disposition . . . but he
adopted the Devil's own philosophy.'[3]

Once Shelley was safely dead, the pattern of his life
made it easy to create a Shelley legend, and his daughter-
in-law Lady (Jane) Shelley must take much of the blame
for sponsoring the 'official' late-Victorian view of Shelley
as a devitalized angelic butterfly flitting to and fro in
obedience to some fore-ordained divine scheme.   Lady
Shelley was probably unconscious of any distortion as she
remoulded his image closer to her heart's desire, for the
material at her disposal was tempting.   Four of Shelley's
closest friends, all of whom had seen much of the world and
its ways, and were usually sparing of their praise, had this
to say about him.   Horace Smith: 'I could almost fancy
that I had been listening to a spirit from some higher
sphere . . . [come] to teach us how we might accelerate
the advent of a new golden age.'   Byron: 'without
exception the *best* and least selfish man I ever knew.   I
never knew one who was not a beast in comparison.'
Trelawny (on Shelley's death): 'the dredful certainty that
I have lost all which made existence to me endurable, nay,
a pleasure'.   Hunt: 'he was like a spirit that had darted
out of its orb, and found itself in another world'.[4]   From
such sources as these flowed the sugary flood of tribute to
Shelley's character, 'the sole thing sweeter than his own
songs were'.[5]   But much more material was lying ready to
be exploited.   Was there not every sign that the angel knew
how he would die?   In *Alastor*

> A restless impulse urged him to embark
> And meet lone Death on the drear ocean's waste.

Ignoring Maddalo's blunt warning, 'If you can't swim beware of Providence', he hears the sea 'breathe o'er my dying brain its last monotony' in *Stanzas in Dejection* and ends the *Ode to Liberty* on the same note :

As waves which lately paved his watery way
Hiss round a drowner's head in their tempestuous play.

610. 284-5

As a clincher there is the end of *Adonais* :

my spirit's bark is driven
Far from the shore, far from the trembling throng
Whose sails were never to the tempest given ;
The massy earth and spheréd skies are riven !
I am borne darkly, fearfully, afar.

444. 488-92

Did he even know when he was to die ? In *Queen Mab* he refers to 'a man of virtue and talent who should die in his thirtieth year'. To carry the process to its logical end, had he not almost as many marks of divine favour as Christ ? Both died violently at roughly equal ages, and was not Leonardo's 'Head of Christ' thought a good likeness of Shelley ? [6] Lady Shelley did nothing to discourage this comparison. She collected relics of Shelley in her house at Boscombe and displayed them in a shrine, where all visitors had to doff their hats in respect ; and she commissioned the Shelley monument in the Priory Church at Christchurch, 'Mary with Dead Shelley', an imitation of Michelangelo's 'Madonna with Dead Christ' at St. Peter's, Rome. Lured by such baits as these, by acquiescent biographers, and by artists who drew imaginary girlish Shelley-figures, Victorian readers were soon caught. So the legend grew that Shelley was like an angelic child, feeble in body, pure in mind, divinely guided, tactless and completely unpractical.[7]

The legend has taken a long time to die, partly because, in the absence of any faithful contemporary portrait of Shelley, the spurious Victorian ones have been reproduced *ad nauseam*. Even so, the legend would by now have been forgotten had it not been boosted first by Francis Thompson's curious essay (1909) and then by André

Maurois's best-selling novelette *Ariel* (1924), the first Penguin book, which has probably been the most damaging blow to Shelley's reputation in this century.

To-day, we look back on the legend as an almost complete misrepresentation. Peacock, the most reliable of Shelley's early biographers, said enough to discredit the feeble-physique theory :

During his residence at Marlow we often walked to London, frequently in company with Mr. Hogg. It was our usual way of going there, when not pressed by time. We went by a very pleasant route over fields, lanes, woods, and heaths to Uxbridge, and by the main road from Uxbridge to London. The total distance was thirty-two miles to Tyburn turnpike. We usually stayed two nights, and walked back on the third day. I never saw Shelley tired with these walks. Delicate and fragile as he appeared, he had great muscular strength.[8]

After leaving England his health improved. In 1822 he still looked as young as ever, apart from greying hair, and Trelawny said he had few rivals in walking over rough ground. Barring accidents, he would probably have fallen in with the Shelley habit of longevity : his father lived to be 90 years old, his mother and grandfather Sir Bysshe both lived to 83.

Nor is there any evidence that Shelley was unpractical. His business letters reveal a hard-headed negotiator, the veteran of many jousts with lawyers and moneylenders; and his friends often burdened him with delicate negotiations, where tact was vital. Rather there is every sign that he could have 'succeeded' in worldly life had he wished.[9] He would not be deflected from doing what his conscience told him — 'I go on until I am stopped; and I never am stopped', as he once said — and this quality would not have passed unnoticed in a society where it is so rare. Shelley was never tempted to seek worldly success, partly because the way would have been too easy : the premier Duke (and boroughmonger) of England was almost begging for his services as an M.P. in 1811. If he had immersed himself in the stream of worldly life he would probably have had better grasp of men's motives, but would have lost his ability to see the world as others don't see it. This ability, one of the few grains of truth in the angelic-child legend, was stressed by Mary in a note on *Queen Mab* :

The usual motives that rule men, prospects of present or future advantage, the rank and fortune of those around, the taunts and censures, or the praise, of those who were hostile to him, had no influence whatever over his actions, and apparently none over his thoughts. It is difficult even to express the simplicity and directness of purpose that adorned him.

The growth of Shelley's fame as a poet was devious. Until 1840 he was generally ignored in literary circles, though he had a few keen admirers, among them Beddoes, Landor, Browning and the Cambridge 'Apostles' including Tennyson. Meanwhile details of his life were being publicized, chiefly in books about Byron. At the same time *Queen Mab* was being frequently reprinted and read by Chartists and other radicals. The first biography of Shelley, Medwin's, appeared in 1847. Then, between 1850 and 1890, Shelley became respectable as a poet. His lyrics were admired by almost all the critics, the Shelley cult flourished, and the Shelley Society was formed — though it did not last long, because that fine forger Thomas J. Wise installed himself as honorary secretary *and* auditor, and exhausted the Society's funds by printing too many luxurious facsimiles of first editions. The respectable ladies and gentlemen of the 1880s, who made up the majority of Shelley's readers and of the Shelley Society, were well content with what was for them a golden age of prosperity and peace, and they quietly ignored Shelley's subversive 'ideas'. The reaction against this bourgeois attitude stemmed, appropriately enough, from Karl Marx, who said that Shelley, had he lived, 'would always have been one of the advanced guard of socialism'.[10] His lead was followed by the Avelings and then in the 'nineties by Henry Salt and Bernard Shaw, who redressed the balance by emphasizing the unspeakable radical, agnostic and vegetarian ideas. Someone foolishly asked Shaw to speak at the highly respectable centenary

celebrations in 1892. He replied with an article, *Shami*
the Devil about Shelley, giving 'a faithful account of Shelley
real opinions, with every one of which I unreservedl
agree', and suggesting the proposed library at Horsham be
'decorated with a relief representing Shelley in a tall hat,
Bible in hand, leading his children on Sunday morning to
the church of his native parish'.[11]

It was on the incomplete, pre-Shavian assessment, as
implied in *The Golden Treasury* for example, that Shelley
was accepted as one of the half-dozen greatest English
poets by the end of the century. His status has since been
hotly challenged and defended, for Shelley still attracts
violently partisan criticism. There have been, and always
will be, some who find his ideas repulsive. There are the
exponents of close criticism, who like to maul his soft-
centred lyrics but damage their teeth on the harder ones.
On the other hand, there are the biographers, the scholars
who have explored single facets of his achievement, and the
compilers of anthologies like *The Spirit of Man* and the *London
Book of English Verse*, who have given Shelley the predominant
place in their selections.

2

Shelley's writings are not concentrated on any single topic.
Looking back, we see a number of themes, woven together
to create a unity which human contrivance cannot give and
chance so rarely does. Perhaps the most important theme
is appreciation of Nature : certainly it came first in time,
for the garden at Field Place was designed to catch the eye
and to show off each species of plant and tree, while the
lakes relieved the solidity of the scene with the fleeting
glories of reflexion. The countryside of West Sussex and
the water meadows of Eton completed Shelley's education in
tame-Nature landscape. The Gothic novels prepared him
for sublime scenery, which he was able to savour to the full,
again with lakes to help, at Keswick, and then at Lynmouth
where he first lived by the sea. Thus, partly by accidents

of geography, he sampled Nature's products widely. And, by the accident of time, he was able to sail out on the flood-tide of Romantic Nature-worship. *Tintern Abbey* appeared when he was 6 years old, the *Immortality* ode when he was 15. At first he was content to follow the path of communion-with-Nature laid down by Wordsworth, who would presumably have nodded in approval at the Poet in *Alastor* and at Shelley's mystic involvement with Nature in the *Euganean Hills*. It is in *Prometheus Unbound* that Shelley goes beyond Wordsworth's horizons, in two different directions : first, he vivifies inert bodies like the earth and the moon, and second, he translates natural objects to a symbolic plane. Thus, instead of worshipping, Shelley exploits Nature ; and he does so again in *Epipsychidion*, utilizing every natural object which can contribute to the erotic atmosphere. He goes even further beyond Wordsworth's range with his scientific style for Nature-poetry.

This leads to the second theme, which is closely entwined with the first — Shelley's interest in science. His appetite for science was aroused in his schooldays and well nourished by Adam Walker and Dr. Lind. Electricity and chemistry were the favourite subjects, perhaps because sparks and explosions pleased the rebel in him and came nearest to the mystery and violence of the Gothic tales. Oxford was a wet blanket to all this fiery science, and, after *Queen Mab*, science was repressed in his poetry for six years before emerging, fully armed like Athene from the head of Zeus, in his analytical Nature-poetry, in poems like the *West Wind*, *The Cloud* and Act IV of *Prometheus Unbound*. The scientific interests had earlier found a more practical outlet, in his firm belief that science could and should raise living standards ; and this belief was always a prop to his hopes of reform.

His interest in reform, the next theme, began violently. He rebelled, outwardly sometimes, in spirit always, against the rituals of Eton. Thus began a lifelong aversion to cruelty, tyranny, authority, institutional religion, custom and the formal shams of respectable society. With his nonconformist instincts alert, he read *Political Justice* and was easily convinced by Godwin's indictment of the existing order in government, law, religion, commerce and class-privilege. Godwin's picture of an earthly utopia pervaded by universal benevolence greatly impressed him too. These ideas, and the vegetable diet, were advocated with burning sincerity in *Queen Mab*. But experience brought disillusion, and though Shelley's zeal for liberty in the abstract did not flag, his proposals for reform grew cooler and more practical. Time has proved the worth of the suggestions he made in the *Philosophical View of Reform* for the gradual reform of Parliament and the redistribution of wealth. He keenly advocated the emancipation of women, and, because he was the first poet to accept as axiomatic the modern views on sexual equality, he was able to enrich the concept of romantic love by improving the status of the girl, to make the lovers equals. By this innovation, by his faculty for idealizing and by his exploitation of the background scenery, he genuinely re-animates love-poetry in *Epipsychidion*.

The idealizing in *Epipsychidion* is one outcome of the next theme, Shelley's Platonism. He liked to treat natural objects and human life as bad copies of a remote ideal. This gave him a sharper appreciation of natural forms and was the basis for a theory of art, the theory that artists and poets try to strip off the worldly clothing from objects and expose the underlying ideal prototype. Platonism appealed to Shelley most, however, because the guiding power behind the ideal forms served him in lieu of a religion. In his late teens he reacted sharply against Christianity, and after flirting with atheism he became and remained what would now be called agnostic. But his was not a blank agnosticism, for his religious impulses were strong and his views were coloured by other creeds : prompted by Christ's ethical teaching, he commended neighbourly love and forgiveness in *Prometheus Unbound* and passive resistance in the *Mask of Anarchy*; there was a tinge of Buddhism about his view of the ego as a thing to be transcended, '*self*, that burr

that will stick to one. I can't get it off yet.'[12] The deepest
colouring of all, Platonism, began quite early, for he tried
to define the 'unseen power' behind the ideal forms in
the *Hymn to Intellectual Beauty*. This guiding power emerges
later in various guises, and often with a strong element
of pantheism, as the 'Being robed in glory' of *Epipsychidion*,
the One Spirit pervading all Nature of *Adonais* and the
'shape all light' of *The Triumph of Life*. The influence
of Platonism was not confined to art and religion: it also
affected his attitude to reform. A rationale of reform
was provided for him in *Political Justice*. But Godwin was
too mundane to satisfy him fully, and once his interest in
Platonism was established, Godwin's earthly paradise re-
emerged, as if sublimated, in the Platonic ideal. So Shelley's
faith in reform shifted to a higher plane, a level much better
suited to poetry.

Shelley's Platonism is one sign of his deep interest in the
ancient Greeks. He revered the golden age of Athens
because it had nurtured democracy and personal freedom,
though he saw, too, the faults in the Athenian system. He
admired the wisdom of the Greek philosophers, the skill of
the sculptors and the insight of the tragedians. These
enthusiasms are implicit in many of his poems and explicit
in *Hellas*. The Greek scientific pioneers did not directly
influence him; but he had their spirit of inquiry into Nature.

Shelley's stay in Italy helped to strengthen several of
his interests. The *Carbonari* and the rising at Naples spurred
his hopes of reform. The Italian landscape deepened his
appreciation of Nature. Italy, the artistic heir of Greece,
awakened him to the visual arts. And he was much influenced by the Italian poets, notably Dante.

To sum up, we have these main themes: a passionate
devotion to Nature, in the best traditions of the Age, but
going beyond tradition; a keen interest in science, for its
own sake and for its power to better Man's lot; a radical
egalitarian approach to social and political questions,
qualified by a growing distaste for worldly affairs; an
agnostic approach in religion, flavoured by Platonism and

by whiffs of pantheism and Christian ethics; admiration
for ancient Greece. All these interests helped to strengthen
his faith that Man, though now in chains, can learn to live
freely, happily, at peace, in a classless society with no
tyrannic king or Church to bow to,

> Equal, unclassed, tribeless, and nationless,
> Exempt from awe, worship, degree, the king
> Over himself; just, gentle, wise.
>
> 253. 195-7

And he had skill enough to fit these ideas, and many more,
smoothly into his poetry, which is enriched and not im-
peded by the intellectual cargo it carries.

His skill in poetry was a gradual growth. Shelley
always toiled devotedly in the service of his ideas, but at
first he was more devoted than wise. Often he emerged
from his quixotic forays bruised in spirit, and his early poems
were so uncompromising that they offended almost everyone : he was victim of a poetic fire and a passion for reform
both blazing out of control. *Queen Mab* (1812-13) is a
scream of indignation against the existing order in law,
politics, religion and commerce. *Alastor* (1815) is a *cri de
cœur* for solitude amid Nature, the logical end of Wordsworth's teaching. In *The Revolt of Islam* (1817) the motifs
of the two previous poems are fused in strident but un-
convincing dialectic. Then comes the move to Italy : the
fire spurring him still burns but is now coming under control.
The conversation-pieces *Rosalind and Helen* and *Julian and
Maddalo* (both 1818) bring in touches of realism and a calmer
tone. The severe self-discipline of *The Cenci* (1819) proves
that he can handle a difficult subject and master an un-
congenial style. In *Prometheus Unbound* (1818-19) he ex-
pounds his faith that men can become securely happy, free
of tyranny and of hatreds, with science harnessed to raise
material standards. With this message recorded, he lets
fancy lead him for the next two years. He turns to politics,
in the *Mask of Anarchy* (1819) and *Swellfoot* (1820). He
lavishes his technique on fine lyrics of the sky (1819-20).
He develops a familiar, skittish vein in the *Letter to Maria*

Gisborne, the *Hymn to Mercury* and the *Witch of Atlas* (all 1820). He seizes a chance to express the very essence of romantic love, in *Epipsychidion* (1821), and states his poetic credo, in the *Defence of Poetry* (1821). He shows his mastery of the elegiac, and his sympathy for Keats, in *Adonais* (1821), the most carefully wrought of his longer poems. He does his best for the Greek cause in *Hellas* (1821). Then he begins restating his philosophy of life in *The Triumph of Life* (1822), cut short by death.

From these many poems several features of technique stand out. The first is that Shelley did not rebel against accepted forms; he spent no energy on heavy pioneering in poetry. He did innovate, however, in a minor way, most successfully perhaps in the irregular interweaving of iambs and anapaests, and in finding a metre to fit the subject of a poem. Many of his best poems, *e.g.* the *Skylark*, *The Cloud* and *West Wind*, are in verse-forms invented by him which he never used again; and in the ninety-one shorter lyrics studied by L. Propst there are fifty-six different rhyme-patterns.[13] His chief stylistic invention is his scientific Nature-poetry, seen at its best in *The Cloud* and Act IV of *Prometheus Unbound*.

If he was not a rebel in technique, why did the readers of his own day find his poetry so difficult? It was chiefly because he rarely bothered to provide the narrative background they relied on finding. Southey's *Thalaba* and *Kehama*, Coleridge's *Ancient Mariner*, Wordsworth's *Prelude* and *Excursion*, Scott's *Lady of the Lake*, Keats's *Eve of St. Agnes*, Byron's *Childe Harold* and *Don Juan* — we have only to reel off the titles to be convinced that each has a strong backbone of narrative. Shelley did his best to conform in his first three long poems, *Queen Mab*, *Alastor* and *The Revolt of Islam*, but in none of them is the narrative element a success: he did not enjoy devising credible position- and time-sequences. To-day, we scarcely notice this gap in his equipment, for television, films and radio have stolen the narrative-poet's audience, and the epic travel-poems once so popular lie unread. Southey, Scott, Campbell and Rogers have paid the price of writing for their public. Shelley was never tempted to write for his public : he had none. Shelley's work is alive and real for us to-day because his great skill as a writer of verse was combined with a firm grasp of ideas and astonishing vision in foreseeing the modern climate of thought. He suggested in the *Philosophical View of Reform* the very measures of reform in Parliament and taxation which have since been effected and which we now take for granted. He anticipated the swing away from institutional religion and the growth of religious toleration. His interest in science is typical of our time rather than of his, and he foresaw how science's power would grow, how it might benefit Man or enslave him. He constantly campaigned for equality between the sexes. Almost all this prosaic prophecy, as it might be called, has come true. To realize his longer-term poetic prophecy, the paradise on earth of *Prometheus Unbound*, Man must conquer first Nature and second his own passions. The first goal comes nearer every day as science wins new ground ; the second seems as far off as ever.

NOTES TO XVII: LOOKING BACK

1. See White, ii. 391–2.
2. See S. Norman, *Flight of the Skylark*, pp. 23–4.
3. For the quotations from Lamb and Southey, see Lamb, *Letters*, Everyman edition, ii. 50, and ii. 53; and J. Simmons, *Southey*, p. 167.
4. For these four quotations, see A. H. Beavan, *James and Horace Smith*, p. 175; Byron, letter to J. Murray, 3 Aug. 1822; Grylls, *Trelawny*, p. 93; and Hunt, *Autobiography*, p. 331.
5. Swinburne, *Cor Cordium*.
6. A version of Leonardo's portrait appeared in two books as if it was of Shelley. See White, ii. 523.
7. For more details of the Shelley cult see S. Norman, *Flight of the Skylark*, and *The Shelley Legend* (ed. R. M. Smith). An early protest against it was made by Thornton Hunt, *Shelley — by one who knew him* (1863).
8. Peacock, p. 345.
9. See R. Fulford, 'Bysshe Shelley, M.P.', *The Listener*, vol. 43, p. 21 (1950).
10. Aveling, *Shelley's Socialism*, p. 4.
11. Bernard Shaw, *Pen Portraits and Reviews*, pp. 236–46.
12. *Letters* ii. 109.
13. L. Propst, *Shelley's Versification*, p. 41.

MAP OF ITALY
Showing places associated with Shelley

BOOK LIST

THIS selected list is divided into six sections, with the following subjects:

(1) Shelley's life.
(2) Biography of Shelley's circle of friends.
(3) Notable editions of Shelley's writings.
(4) Shelley criticism — what is sometimes unkindly called the Shelley industry, i.e. books about his philosophical, social and political ideas, as well as his poetry.
(5) General literary criticism touching on Shelley.
(6) Relevant background literature — books that either fill in the historical background or influenced Shelley (excluding classics like the works of Plato, Dante or Shakespeare).

The correct choice of section was not always clear, because the six categories overlap: for example, many biographies of Shelley include extensive comment on his poems.

In making my selections I have tended to favour the more recent books published in Britain or the U.S.A.: only an essential few of the nineteenth-century biographies are included, for example, and articles in periodicals do not appear, unless afterwards published in book form. The place of publication is London, unless otherwise stated. I have added comments to identify outstanding books or clarify uninformative titles.

1. SHELLEY'S LIFE
Helen Rossetti ANGELI, *Shelley and his Friends in Italy.* 1911.
Ruth BAILEY, *Shelley.* Duckworth, 1934.
Edmund BLUNDEN, *Shelley, a Life Story.* Collins, 1946.
　　The best short biography, full of graceful touches.
John BUXTON, *Byron and Shelley.* Macmillan, 1968.
　　A detailed double biography.
K. N. CAMERON, *The Young Shelley.* Gollancz, 1951.
　　The fullest account of his early life and work.
K. N. CAMERON (ed.), *Shelley and his Circle 1773–1822.* Harvard U.P. (London, O.U.P.) vols. I and II, 1961. Vols. III and IV, 1970.
　　The papers in the Pforzheimer Library, finely printed and edited.
Olwen W. CAMPBELL, *Shelley and the Unromantics.* Methuen, 1924.
E. CARPENTER and G. BARNEFIELD, *The Psychology of the Poet Shelley.* Allen & Unwin, 1925.

Arthur CLUTTON-BROCK, *Shelley, the Man and the Poet*. Methuen, 1909.

Margaret CROMPTON, *Shelley's Dream Women*. Cassell, 1967.

Elma DANGERFIELD, *Mad Shelley: a play*. M. Joseph, 1936.

Edward DOWDEN, *The Life of Percy Bysshe Shelley*. 2 vols. 1886. (Abridged version, 1 vol., Routledge, 1951).
> A fine biography, the standard life of Shelley for over forty years.

Jean Overton FULLER, *Shelley, a biography*. Cape, 1968.

Carl GRABO, *Shelley's Eccentricities*. Univ. of New Mexico Press, Albuquerque, 1950.

Francis GRIBBLE, *The Romantic Life of Shelley and the sequel*. 1911.

T. J. HOGG, *The Life of Percy Bysshe Shelley* (2 vols., 1858) 2 vols. Dent, 1933.
> Amusing, though sometimes tedious; quite unreliable, yet indispensable on Shelley's early life.

A. M. D. HUGHES, *The Nascent Mind of Shelley*. O.U.P., 1947.
> Valuable account of his early life and thought.

Roger INGPEN, *Shelley in England*. Kegan Paul, 1917.

G. M. MATTHEWS, *Shelley*. Longman, 1970.
> Short (40 pages), but admirable as an introduction.

Thomas MEDWIN, *Revised 'Life of Shelley'*. O.U.P., 1913.
> The original edition (1847) was the first biography of Shelley.

Thomas Love PEACOCK, *Memoirs of Shelley* (1855–60). Dent, 1933.
> The most reliable early biography.

Walter Edwin PECK, *Shelley, his Life and Work*. 2 vols. New York, 1927.
> The standard biography in the 1930s.

Ernest RAYMOND, *Two Gentlemen of Rome*. Cassell, 1952.

Ivan ROE, *Shelley, the Last Phase*. Hutchinson, 1953.

W. M. ROSSETTI, *Memoir of Shelley*. 1870.

H. S. SALT, *Percy Bysshe Shelley, Poet and Pioneer*. 1896.
> Emphasizes Shelley's radical ideas.

W. SHARP, *Life of Shelley*. 1887.

Lady (Jane) SHELLEY, *Shelley Memorials*. 1859.

Mary SHELLEY, *Notes to the 1839 edition of Shelley's Poetical Works*.
> Often reprinted, e.g. in Hutchinson's Oxford edition of Shelley's poems, these notes are the nearest Mary came to a biography.

R. M. SMITH (and others), *The Shelley Legend*. Scribner, New York, 1945.

J. A. SYMONDS, *Shelley*. Macmillan, 1878.

Francis THOMPSON, *Shelley*. 1909.
> Worthless, but once widely read.

James THOMSON, *Shelley, a Poem: with other Writings relating to Shelley*. Chiswick Press, 1884.

E. J. TRELAWNY, *Recollections of the Last Days of Shelley and Byron* (1858). Dent, 1933.
> Shrewd and lively, but not always reliable.

J. L. ULLMAN, *Mad Shelley*. Princeton, 1933.

Newman Ivey WHITE, *Shelley*. 2 vols. New York, 1940. (London, Secker & Warburg, 1947).
The standard 'Life', detailed, accurate — and very readable.
N. I. WHITE, F. L. JONES and K. N. CAMERON, *An Examination of 'The Shelley Legend'*. Philadelphia, 1951.

2. BIOGRAPHY OF SHELLEY'S CIRCLE OF FRIENDS

W. J. BATE, *John Keats*. Harvard U.P., Cambridge, Mass., 1963.
A. H. BEAVAN, *James and Horace Smith*. Hurst & Blackett, 1899.
Edmund BLUNDEN, *Leigh Hunt*. Cobden-Sanderson, 1930.
Edmund BLUNDEN, *Charles Lamb and his Contemporaries*. C.U.P., 1933
Louise S. BOAS, *Harriet Shelley*. O.U.P., 1962.
Sympathetic to Harriet, but sometimes slanderous to Shelley.
H. N. BRAILSFORD, *Shelley, Godwin and their Circle*. O.U.P., 1913.
Still the best book on this subject.
Vera CACCIATORE, *Shelley and Byron in Pisa*. Turin, 1961.
Richard CHURCH, *Mary Shelley*. Howe, 1928.
Claire CLAIRMONT, *Journals* (ed. Marion K. Stocking). Harvard U.P., Cambridge, Mass., 1968.
C. L. CLINE, *Byron, Shelley and their Pisan Circle*. Murray, 1952.
Edward DOWDEN, *Southey*. Macmillan, 1884.
Maria GISBORNE, *Journal* (ed. F. L. Jones). Univ. of Oklahoma Pr., Norman, Okla., 1951.
Robert GITTINGS, *John Keats*. Heinemann, 1968.
Widely regarded as the finest biography of Keats.
Rosalie Glynn GRYLLS, *Mary Shelley, a biography*. O.U.P., 1938.
Rosalie Glynn GRYLLS, *Claire Clairmont*. Murray, 1939.
Rosalie Glynn GRYLLS, *Trelawny*. Constable, 1950.
Rosalie Glynn GRYLLS, *William Godwin and his World*. Odhams, 1953.
Dorothy HEWLETT, *A Life of John Keats*. 3rd ed., Hutchinson, 1970.
Dorothy HEWLETT (ed.), *Keats–Shelley Memorial Bulletins*, III–XXI, 1950–70.
These annual bulletins of the Keats–Shelley Memorial Association contain varied articles on the life and work of Keats, Shelley, Byron and their circle.
P. P. HOWE, *The Life of William Hazlitt* (1922). Penguin, 1949.
Leigh HUNT, *Autobiography* (1850). Cresset Press, 1949.
R. B. JOHNSON (ed.), *Shelley–Leigh Hunt: How Friendship made History*. Ingpen & Grant, 1928.
John KEATS, *Letters* (ed. M. Buxton Forman). O.U.P., 3rd ed., 1947
John KEATS, *Letters* (ed. H. E. Rollins). 2 vols. C.U.P., 1958.
The standard edition.
Keats–Shelley Journal, vols. I–XIX, New York, 1951–69.
Published annually by the Keats–Shelley Association of America. Contains varied articles and reviews on Keats, Shelley, Byron and their circle, and an immensely useful detailed annual bibliography.

E. J. Lovell, *Captain Medwin*. Macdonald, 1963.
E. C. McAleer, *The Sensitive Plant: a Life of Lady Mount Cashell*. Univ. of N. Carolina Pr., 1958.
Leslie Marchand, *Byron*. 3 vols. Murray, 1958.
 The standard life of Byron.
André Maurois, *Byron*. Cape, 1930.
Thomas Medwin, *Conversations of Lord Byron*. Colburn, 1824.
Howard Mills, *Peacock: his Circle and his Age*. C.U.P., 1969.
Elizabeth Nitchie, *Mary Shelley*. New Brunswick, N.J., 1953.
Iris Origo, *Allegra*. 1935 (Revised version in *A Measure of Love*, Cape, 1957).
Iris Origo, *The Last Attachment*. Cape and Murray, 1949.
C. Kegan Paul, *William Godwin: his Friends and Contemporaries*. 2 vols. King, 1876.
Elizabeth R. Pennell, *Mary Wollstonecraft Godwin*. W. H. Allen, 1885.
Peter Quennell, *Byron in Italy*. Collins, 1941.
Neville Rogers (compiler), *Keats, Shelley and Rome*. Johnson, 1949.
Winifred Scott, *Jefferson Hogg*. Cape, 1951.
Mary Shelley, *Letters* (ed. F. L. Jones). 2 vols. Univ. of Oklahoma Pr., Norman, Okla., 1944.
Mary Shelley, *Journal* (ed. F. L. Jones). Univ. of Oklahoma Pr., Norman, Okla., 1947.
 Brief daily records of the lives of Shelley and Mary on about 2000 days between 1814 and 1822.
Jack Simmons, *Southey*. Collins, 1945.
Muriel Spark, *Child of Light*. Tower Bridge Pub., 1951.
Carl van Doren, *The Life of Thomas Love Peacock*. Dent, 1911.
R. M. Wardle, *Mary Wollstonecraft*. Univ. of Kansas Pr., 1951.
Edward E. Williams, *Journal* (ed. F. L. Jones). Univ. of Oklahoma Pr., 1951.
G. Woodcock, *William Godwin*. Porcupine Press, 1946.

3. NOTABLE EDITIONS OF SHELLEY'S WRITINGS

The fullest single edition is *The Complete Works of Shelley*, edited by Roger Ingpen and W. E. Peck. Julian edition. 10 vols. London and New York, 1926–9. (Reprinted 1965: price £52).

A new Oxford edition of Shelley's poems, edited by Neville Rogers, is in preparation: Volume 1 will be published in 1972. Until the new edition is complete, the standard Oxford edition is

Percy Bysshe Shelley, *Poetical Works* (ed. Thomas Hutchinson). O.U.P., 1905. (Frequently reprinted). New reprint, corrected by G. M. Matthews, 1970.

 The definitive edition of Shelley's letters is

F. L. Jones (ed), *The Letters of Percy Bysshe Shelley*. 2 vols. O.U.P., 1964.

 The most complete editions of Shelley's prose are the Julian edition and

D. L. CLARK (ed.), *Shelley's Prose*. Univ. of New Mexico Pr., Albuquerque, 1954.
  A substantial selection appears in
Shelley: Selected Poetry, Prose and Letters (ed. A. S. B. GLOVER). Nonesuch Press, 1951.
  The important 'Philosophical View of Reform' is reprinted in
R. J. WHITE (ed.), *Political Tracts of Wordsworth, Coleridge and Shelley*. C.U.P., 1953.
  The early poems of the Esdaile notebook have appeared in two editions:
P. B. SHELLEY, *The Esdaile Notebook* (ed. K. N. Cameron). Faber, 1964.
P. B. SHELLEY, *The Esdaile Poems* (ed. N. Rogers). O.U.P., 1966.
  Many volumes of selections from Shelley are available, notably
A. M. D. HUGHES (ed.), *Shelley, Poetry and Prose*. O.U.P., 1931.
G. M. MATTHEWS (ed.), *Shelley: Selected Poems and Prose*. O.U.P., 1964.
Neville ROGERS (ed.), *Shelley: Selected Poetry*. Houghton Mifflin, Boston, 1968. (O.U.P., 1969).
  For more specialized texts or textual studies, see the book by Reiman cited in section 4, the volumes edited by K. N. Cameron listed in section 1, and the following:
A. M. D. HUGHES (ed.), *Shelley, Poems published in 1820*. O.U.P., 1910 (2nd ed., 1957).
Irving MASSEY, *Posthumous Poems of Shelley*. McGill-Queen's Univ. Pr., Montreal, 1969.
W. S. SCOTT (ed.), *New Shelley Letters*. Bodley Head, 1948.
C. H. TAYLOR, *The Early Collected Editions of Shelley's Poems*. Yale U.P., New Haven, 1958.
L. J. ZILLMAN (ed.), *Shelley's 'Prometheus Unbound': the Text and the Drafts*. Yale U.P., New Haven, 1968.

4. SHELLEY CRITICISM
Edward and Eleanor Marx AVELING, *Shelley's Socialism* (1888). Preger, Manchester, 1947.
Carlos BAKER, *Shelley's Major Poetry*. Princeton U.P., New Jersey (London, O.U.P.), 1948.
  Valuable detailed critique of the long poems.
E. BARNARD, *Shelley's Religion*. Minneapolis, 1936.
J. BARRELL, *Shelley and the Thought of his Time*. Yale U.P., New Haven (London, O.U.P.), 1947.
E. S. BATES, *A Study of Shelley's Drama 'The Cenci'*. New York, 1908.
H. BLOOM, *Shelley's Mythmaking*. Yale U.P., New Haven, 1958.
G. BORNSTEIN, *Yeats and Shelley*. Univ. of Chicago Pr., 1970.
A. C. BRADLEY, *Oxford Lectures on Poetry*. O.U.P., 1909.
  Includes the essay 'Shelley's View of Poetry'.
P. H. BUTTER, *Shelley's Idols of the Cave*. Univ. Pr., Edinburgh, 1954.
  Surveys Shelley's imagery.

E. Chesser, *Shelley and Zastrozzi*. Gregg, 1965.

P. Edgar, *A Study of Shelley*. Toronto, 1899.

F. S. Ellis, *A Lexical Concordance to the Poetical Works of P. B. Shelley*. Quaritch, 1892.
An excellent classified concordance.

O. Elton, *Shelley*. Arnold, 1924.

R. H. Fogle, *The Imagery of Keats and Shelley*. Univ. of N. Carolina Pr., Chapel Hill, N.C., 1949.

Carl Grabo, *A Newton among Poets*. Univ. of N. Carolina Pr., Chapel Hill, N.C., 1930.

Carl Grabo, *The Meaning of the Witch of Atlas*. Chapel Hill, N.C., 1935.

Carl Grabo, *Prometheus Unbound: an Interpretation*. Chapel Hill, N.C., 1935.

Carl Grabo, *The Magic Plant: the Growth of Shelley's Thought*. Chapel Hill, N.C., 1936.

D. B. Green and E. G. Wilson (eds), *Keats, Shelley, Byron, Hunt and their Circles, A Bibliography 1950–1962*. Univ. of Nebraska Pr., Lincoln, Neb., 1964.
Compiled from the annual bibliographies in the *Keats–Shelley Journal*.

H. L. Hoffman, *An Odyssey of the Soul: Shelley's Alastor*. Columbia U.P., New York, 1933.

Henning Krabbe, *Shelleys Poesi*. J. H. Schultz Forlag, Copenhagen, 1953. (In Danish).

B. P. Kurtz, *The Pursuit of Death*. O.U.P., 1933.

F. A. Lea, *Shelley and the Romantic Revolution*. Routledge, 1945.

Hélène Lemaître, *Shelley, Poète des Éléments*. Didier, Paris, 1962.

D. J. Macdonald, *The Radicalism of Shelley*. Washington, D.C., 1912.

Gerald McNiece, *Shelley and the Revolutionary Idea*. Harvard Univ. Pr., Cambridge, Mass., 1969.

W. J. McTaggart, *England in 1819: Church, State and Poverty*. Keats–Shelley Memorial Association, 1970.

Sylva Norman, *Flight of the Skylark*. Reinhardt, 1954.
Discusses the development of Shelley's reputation.

James A. Notopoulos, *The Platonism of Shelley*. Duke Univ. Pr., Durham, N.C. (London, C.U.P.), 1949.
The definitive treatment of the subject, with a critical edition of Shelley's translations from Plato.

Glenn O'Malley, *Shelley and Synesthesia*. Northwestern Univ. Pr., Evanston, Ill., 1964.

Louise Propst, *An Analytical Study of Shelley's Versification*. Univ. of Iowa, 1933.

C. E. Pulos, *The Deep Truth: a Study of Shelley's Scepticism*. Lincoln, Neb., 1954.

T. M. RAYSOR (ed.), *The English Romantic Poets, a Review of Research.*
M. L. A., New York, 1956.
Includes long review of the literature on Shelley, by Bennett Weaver.
Herbert READ, *The True Voice of Feeling.* Faber, 1953.
Includes revised version of the essay 'In Defence of Shelley' (1936).
D. H. REIMAN, *Shelley's 'The Triumph of Life': a critical study.* Univ. of
Illinois Pr., Urbana, Ill., 1965.
D. H. REIMAN, *Percy Bysshe Shelley.* Twayne, New York, 1969.
Seymour REITER, *A Study of Shelley's Poetry.* Univ. of New Mexico Pr.,
1967.
George M. RIDENOUR, *Shelley, a Collection of Critical Essays.* Prentice-Hall,
Englewood Cliffs, N.J., 1965.
Neville ROGERS, *Shelley at Work.* O.U.P., 1967 (first edition, 1956).
A valuable critical inquiry, based on the evidence of the Bodleian
notebooks.
Earl J. SCHULZE, *Shelley's Theory of Poetry.* Mouton, The Hague, 1966.
M. T. SOLVE, *Shelley, his Theory of Poetry.* Chicago, 1927.
Floyd STOVALL, *Desire and Restraint in Shelley.* Duke U. P., Durham, N.C.,
1931.
A. C. SWINBURNE, *Essays and Studies.* 1888.
Includes 'Notes on the text of Shelley' (1869).
John TODHUNTER, *A Study of Shelley.* K. Paul, 1880.
An excellent survey, despite its antiquity.
Earl R. WASSERMAN, *Shelley's 'Prometheus Unbound': a critical reading.*
Johns Hopkins Pr., Baltimore, 1965.
Bennett WEAVER, *Towards the Understanding of Shelley.* Univ. of Michigan
Pr., Ann Arbor, 1932.
Milton WILSON, *Shelley's Later Poetry.* Columbia U.P., New York, 1959.
R. B. WOODINGS (ed.), *Shelley: Modern Judgements.* Macmillan, 1968.
An anthology of literary essays on Shelley since 1940.
R. G. WOODMAN, *The Apocalyptic Vision in the Poetry of Shelley.* Univ. of
Toronto Pr., 1964.
W. B. YEATS, *Essays and Introductions.* Macmillan, 1961.
Includes the profound essay on 'The Philosophy of Shelley's
Poetry' (1900).

5. GENERAL LITERARY CRITICISM TOUCHING ON SHELLEY

M. H. ABRAMS, *The Mirror and the Lamp.* O.U.P., 1960.
Matthew ARNOLD, *Essays in Criticism* (second series). 1888.
Walter BAGEHOT, *Literary Studies.* Dent, 1911.
Includes essay on Shelley (1856).
J. W. BEACH, *The Concept of Nature in Nineteenth-century English Poetry.*
Macmillan, New York, 1936.
Bernard BLACKSTONE, *The Lost Travellers.* Longmans, 1962.
C. M. BOWRA, *The Romantic Imagination.* O.U.P., 1950.

A. C. BRADLEY, *A Miscellany*. Macmillan, 1929.
Douglas BUSH, *Science and English Poetry*. O.U.P., 1950.
Donald DAVIE, *Purity of Diction in English Verse*. Chatto & Windus, 1952.
Roland A. DUERKSEN, *Shelleyan Ideas in Victorian Literature*. Mouton, The Hague, 1966.
    Traces Shelley's influence on Browning, Disraeli, Hardy, Shaw, Years and others.
T. S. ELIOT, *The Use of Poetry and the Use of Criticism*. Faber, 1933.
William EMPSON, *Seven Types of Ambiguity* (1930). 2nd edition, 1947.
Graham HOUGH, *The Romantic Poets*. Hutchinson, 1953.
G. Wilson KNIGHT, *The Starlit Dome*. O.U.P., 1941.
Shiv. K. KUMAR (ed.), *British Romantic Poets, Recent Revaluations*. Univ. of London Pr., 1968.
    Despite the title, the three chapters on Shelley are all from the 1940s.
F. R. LEAVIS, *Revaluation*. Chatto & Windus, 1936.
C. S. LEWIS, *Rehabilitations*. O.U.P., 1939.
F. L. LUCAS, *The Decline and Fall of the Romantic Ideal*. C.U.P., 1936.
Desmond MACCARTHY, *Humanities*. MacGibbon & Kee, 1953.
Allardyce NICOLL, *A History of Early Nineteenth-century Drama, 1800–1850*. C.U.P., 1930.
John Cowper POWYS, *Visions and Revisions*. Macdonald, 1955.
Mario PRAZ, *The Romantic Agony*. O.U.P., 1933.
Arthur QUILLER-COUCH, *Studies in Literature* (second series). C.U.P., 1927.
J. A. K. THOMSON, *Classical Influences on English Poetry*. Allen & Unwin, 1951.
John WAIN (ed.), *Contemporary Reviews of Romantic Poetry*. Harrap, 1953.
Earl R. WASSERMAN, *The Subtler Language*. John Hopkins Pr., Baltimore, 1959.
    Includes fine analyses of *The Sensitive Plant* and *Adonais*.
Newman Ivey WHITE, *The Unextinguished Hearth* (1938). Octagon Books, New York (London, Frank Cass), 1966.
    Reprints all the reviews and reports of Shelley in his lifetime.

6. RELEVANT BACKGROUND LITERATURE

W. ALBERY, *Parliamentary History of the Ancient Borough of Horsham*. Longmans, 1927.
C. P. BRAND, *Italy and the English Romantics*. C.U.P., 1957.
C. BRINTON, *The Political Ideas of the English Romanticists*. O.U.P., 1926.
Arthur BRYANT, *The Age of Elegance*. Collins, 1950.
J. CLIVE, *Scotch Reviewers*. Faber, 1957.
Thomas CREEVEY, *The Creevey Papers* (ed. H. Maxwell). 2 vols. Murray, 1904.
F. O. DARVALL, *Popular Disturbances and Public Order in Regency England*. O.U.P., 1934.

Erasmus DARWIN, *The Botanic Garden.* 1791.

Erasmus DARWIN, *The Temple of Nature.* 1803.

T. G. EHRSAM, *Major Byron.* Murray, 1951.

Roger FULFORD, *The Trial of Queen Caroline.* Batsford, 1967.

William GODWIN, *An Enquiry Concerning Political Justice.* 1793. (Ed. and abridged by R. A. Preston, Knopf, New York, 1926, 2 vols.) (Ed. F. C. L. Priestley, Univ. of Toronto Pr. and O.U.P., 1946, 3 vols.) The book that had most influence on Shelley's life.

William GODWIN, *The Adventures of Caleb Williams* (1794). Cassell, 1966. Godwin's most famous novel, prophetic of the hounding of individuals by governments in the twentieth century.

F. HAWES, *Henry Brougham.* Cape, 1957.

Benjamin Robert HAYDON, *Autobiography and Journals* (1853). Macdonald, 1950.

W. HORSFIELD, *The History, Antiquities and Topography of the County of Sussex.* 2 vols. Baxter, Lewes, 1835.

Desmond KING-HELE, *Erasmus Darwin.* Macmillan, 1963.

Desmond KING-HELE, *The Essential Writings of Erasmus Darwin.* MacGibbon & Kee, 1968.

G. Wilson KNIGHT, *Christ and Nietzsche.* Staples Press, 1948.

S. A. LARRABEE, *English Bards and Grecian Marbles.* Columbia U.P., New York, 1943.

Ione LEIGH, *Castlereagh.* Collins, 1951.

A. O. LOVEJOY, *The Great Chain of Being.* Harvard U.P., Cambridge, Mass., 1936.

M. A. LOWER, *The Worthies of Sussex.* Bacon, Lewes, 1865.

E. V. LUCAS, *Highways and Byways in Sussex.* Macmillan, 1904.

W. H. MARSHALL, *Byron, Shelley, Hunt and 'The Liberal'.* Univ. of Pennsylvania Pr., Philadelphia, 1960.

André MAUROIS, *Ariel, a Shelley Romance.* Paris, 1924.

Alberto MORAVIA, *Beatrice Cenci.* Secker & Warburg, 1965.

Charles PETRIE, *Lord Liverpool and his Times.* Barrie, 1954.

D. READ, *Peterloo.* Manchester U.P., 1958.

Corrado RICCI, *Beatrice Cenci.* Owen, 1956.

M. ROBERTS, *The Whig Party, 1807–1812.* Macmillan, 1939.

H. Crabb ROBINSON, *On Books and their Writers.* (ed. E. J. Morley). 3 vols. Dent, 1938.

Bertrand RUSSELL, *Fact and Fiction.* Allen & Unwin, 1961. Includes 'The Importance of Shelley' (1957).

Bernard SHAW, *Pen Portraits and Reviews.* Constable, 1932. Contains the essay 'Shaming the Devil about Shelley' (1892).

Bernard SHAW, *Sixteen Self-Sketches.* Constable, 1949.

Lady (Frances) SHELLEY, *Diary* (ed. R. Edgcumbe). Murray, 1912.

Robert SOUTHEY, *Letters from England* (1807). Cresset Press, 1951.

G. M. TREVELYAN, *Lord Grey of the Reform Bill.* Longmans, 1929.

D. P. Varma, *The Gothic Flame*. Barker, 1957.

Adam Walker, *A System of Familiar Philosophy in Twelve Lectures*. London, 1799.
　　Walker's course of lectures at Eton, which so impressed Shelley, was probably very similar.

R. J. White, *Waterloo to Peterloo*. Heinemann, 1957.

A. N. Whitehead, *Science and the Modern World*. C.U.P., 1926.

INDEX

Shelley's writings are indexed under their titles or first lines. Books and poems by other authors are indexed under the authors' names. Figures in **bold type** indicate the leading references on a subject.